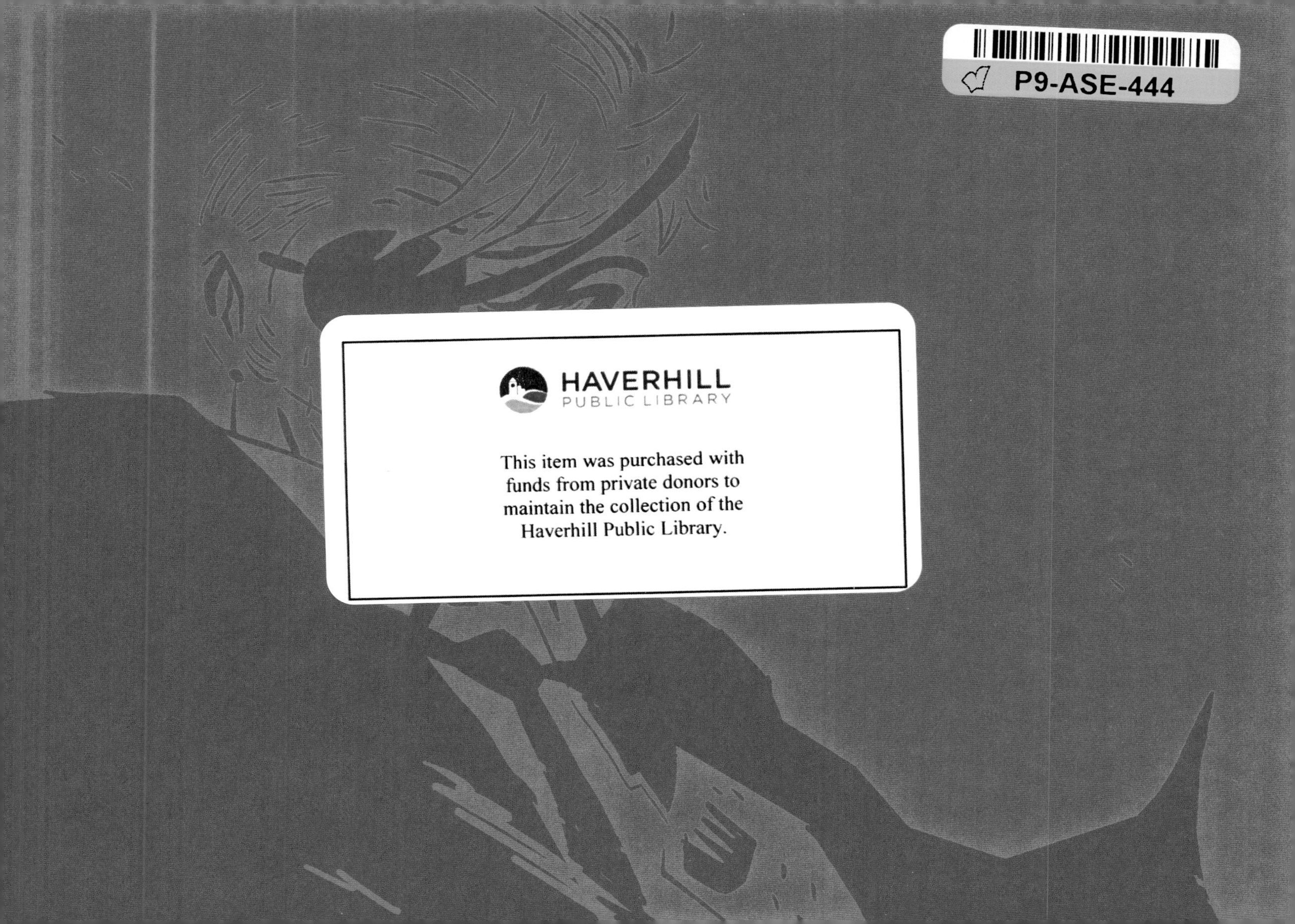

POLAR™

NO MERCY FOR SISTER MARIA

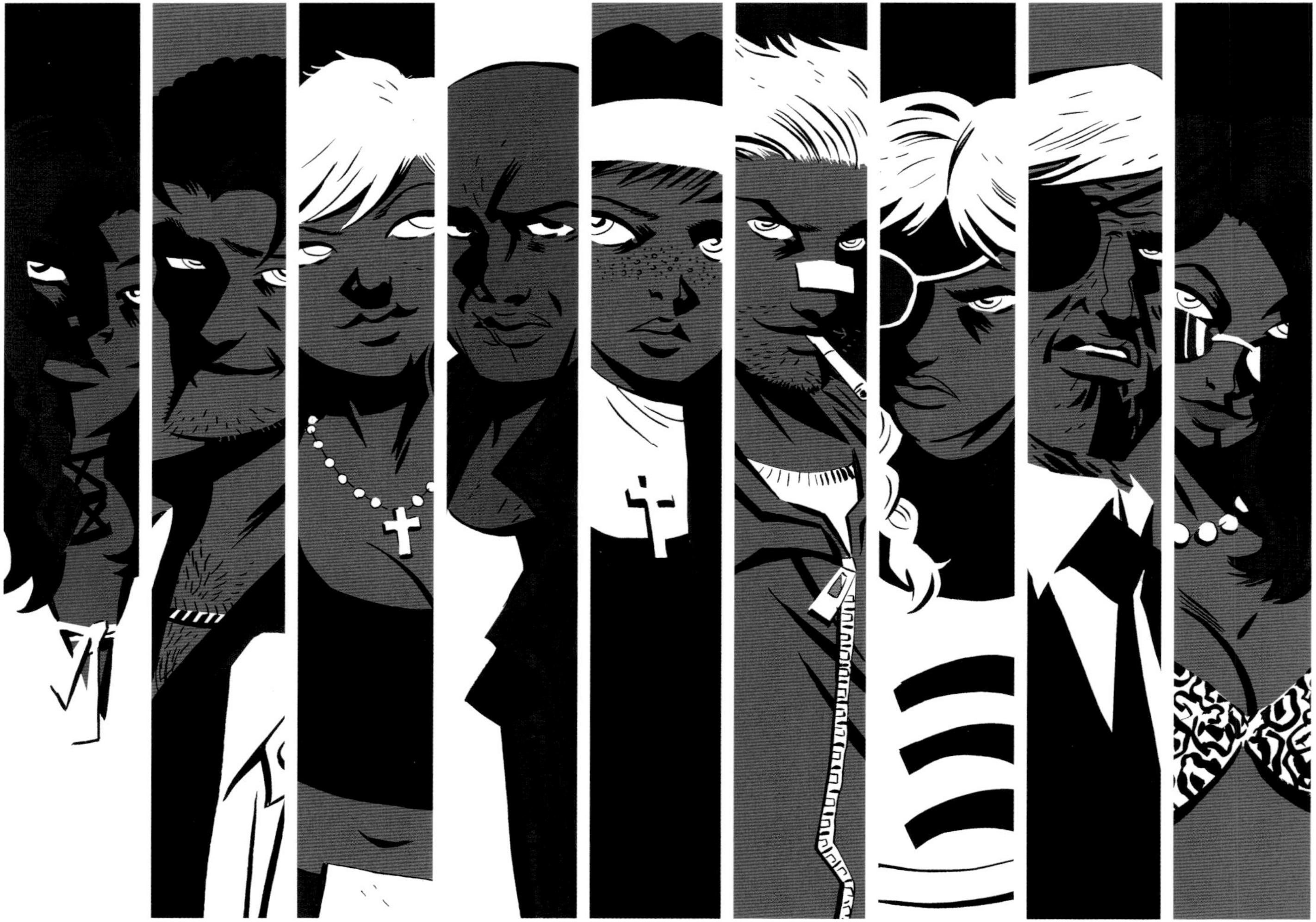

POLAR

NO MERCY FOR SISTER MARIA

VICTOR SANTOS

DARK HORSE BOOKS ®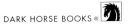

PRESIDENT & PUBLISHER
MIKE RICHARDSON

EDITOR
HANNAH MEANS-SHANNON

DESIGNER
JIMMY PRESLER

DIGITAL ART TECHNICIAN
CHRISTINA McKENZIE

SPECIAL THANKS TO
JIM GIBBONS and SPENCER CUSHING, for beginning this beloved project with me
HANNAH MEANS-SHANNON, for her inestimable help with the difficult end of this trilogy
PERE PÉREZ, for his martial arts choreographer cameo
RAÚL SASTRE, again, for his help with translation
JOHNNIE TO, SERGIO LEONE, JOHN WOO, SERGIO CORBUCCI, and MICHAEL MANN, for the code, the gunman, and the solitude

NEIL HANKERSON Executive Vice President • TOM WEDDLE Chief Financial Officer • RANDY STRADLEY Vice President of Publishing • MICHAEL MARTENS Vice President of Book Trade Sales • MATT PARKINSON Vice President of Marketing • DAVID SCROGGY Vice President of Product Development • DALE LaFOUNTAIN Vice President of Information Technology • CARA NIECE Vice President of Production and Scheduling • NICK McWHORTER Vice President of Media Licensing • KEN LIZZI General Counsel • DAVE MARSHALL Editor in Chief • DAVEY ESTRADA Editorial Director • SCOTT ALLIE Executive Senior Editor • CHRIS WARNER Senior Books Editor • CARY GRAZZINI Director of Print and Development • LIA RIBACCHI Art Director • MARK BERNARDI Director of Digital Publishing • MICHAEL GOMBOS Director of International Publishing and Licensing

Published by Dark Horse Books
A division of Dark Horse Comics, Inc.
10956 SE Main Street
Milwaukie, OR 97222

DarkHorse.com
PolarComic.com

International Licensing: (503) 905-2377
Comic Shop Locator Service: (888) 266-4226

Library of Congress Cataloging-in-Publication Data

Names: Santos, Victor, 1977- author, illustrator.
Title: Polar. Volume 3, No mercy for Sister Maria / Victor Santos.
Other titles: No mercy for Sister Maria
Description: First edition. | Milwaukie, OR : Dark Horse Books, 2016.
Identifiers: LCCN 2016011751 | ISBN 9781506700533 (hardback)
Subjects: LCSH: Comic books, strips, etc. | BISAC: COMICS & GRAPHIC NOVELS / Crime & Mystery.
Classification: LCC PN6777.S29 P67 2016 | DDC 741.5/946--dc23
LC record available at http://lccn.loc.gov/2016011751

First edition: August 2016
ISBN 978-1-50670-053-3

10 9 8 7 6 5 4 3 2 1
Printed in China

PART ONE

THE HUNTERS AND THE PREY

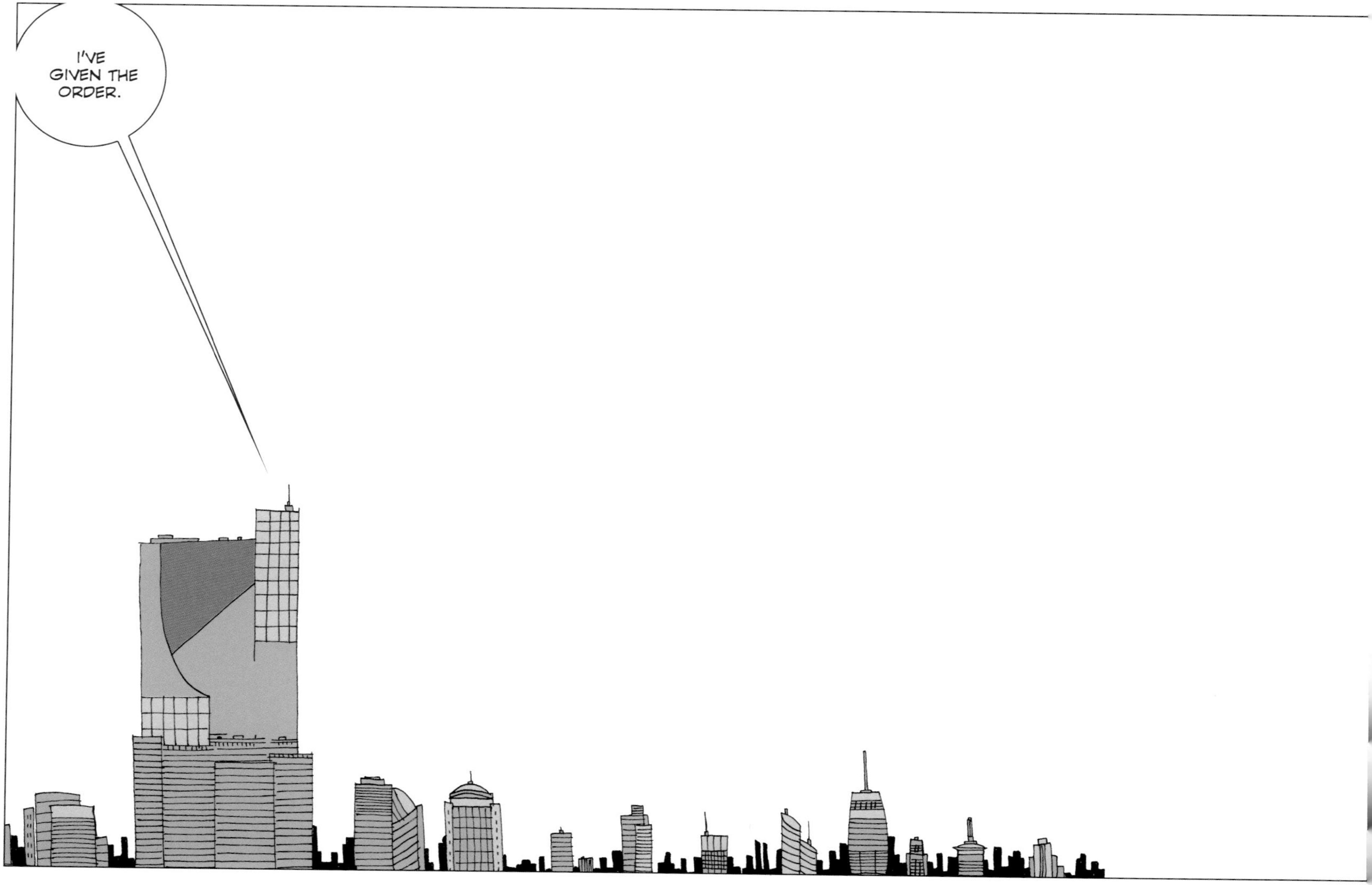
I'VE GIVEN THE ORDER.

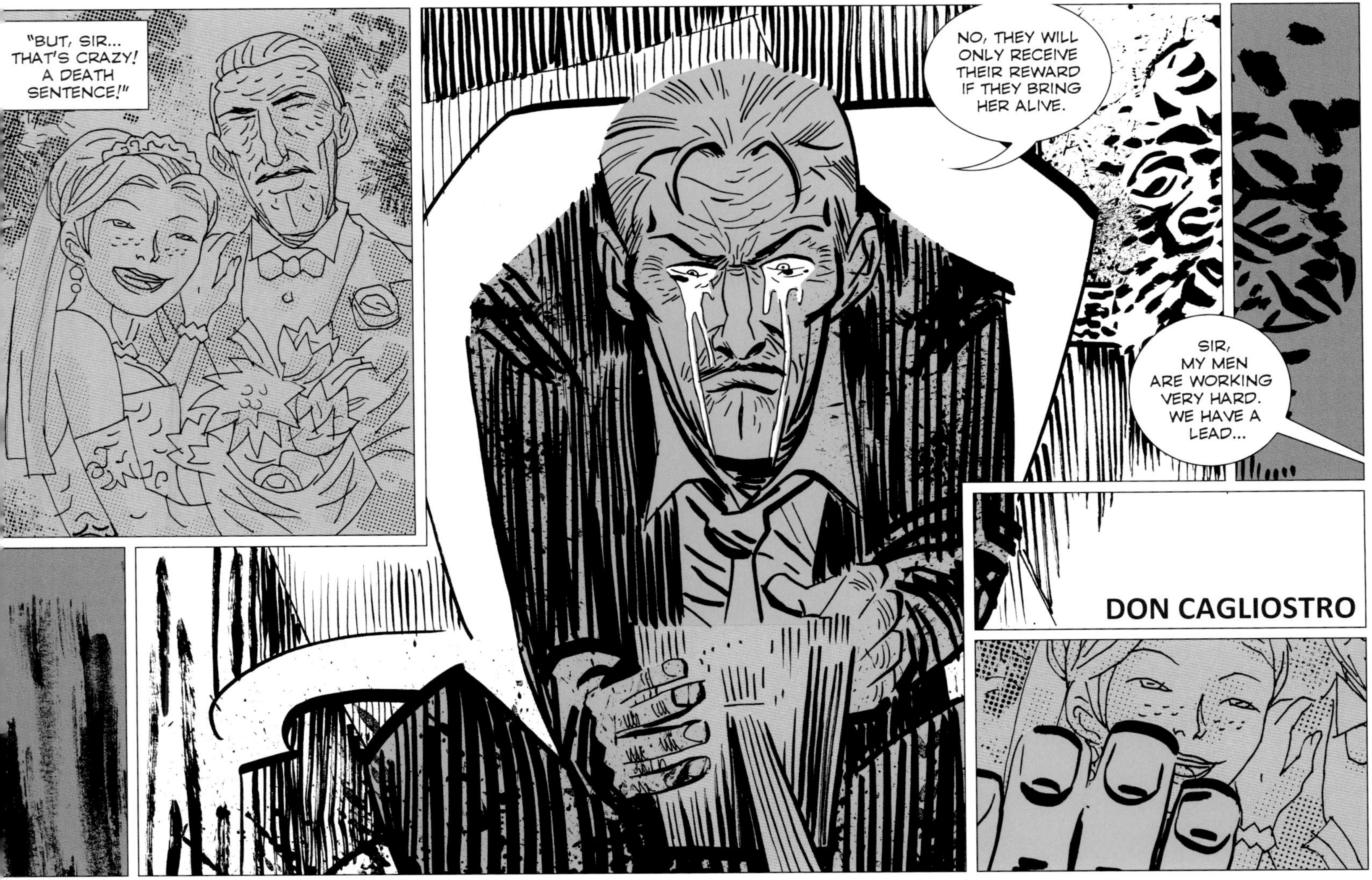
"BUT, SIR... THAT'S CRAZY! A DEATH SENTENCE!"
NO, THEY WILL ONLY RECEIVE THEIR REWARD IF THEY BRING HER ALIVE.
SIR, MY MEN ARE WORKING VERY HARD. WE HAVE A LEAD...
DON CAGLIOSTRO

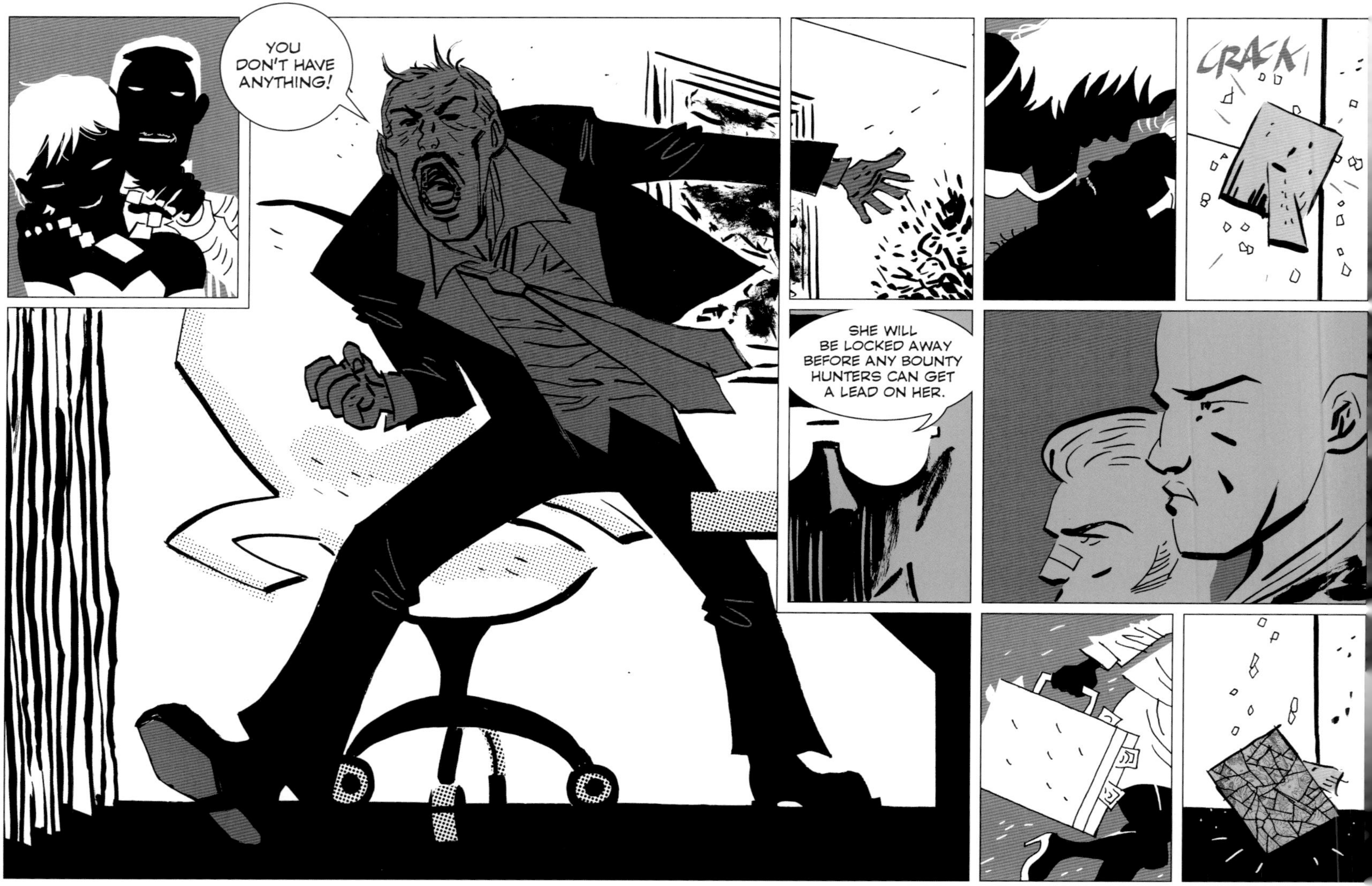
YOU DON'T HAVE ANYTHING!
CRACK
SHE WILL BE LOCKED AWAY BEFORE ANY BOUNTY HUNTERS CAN GET A LEAD ON HER.

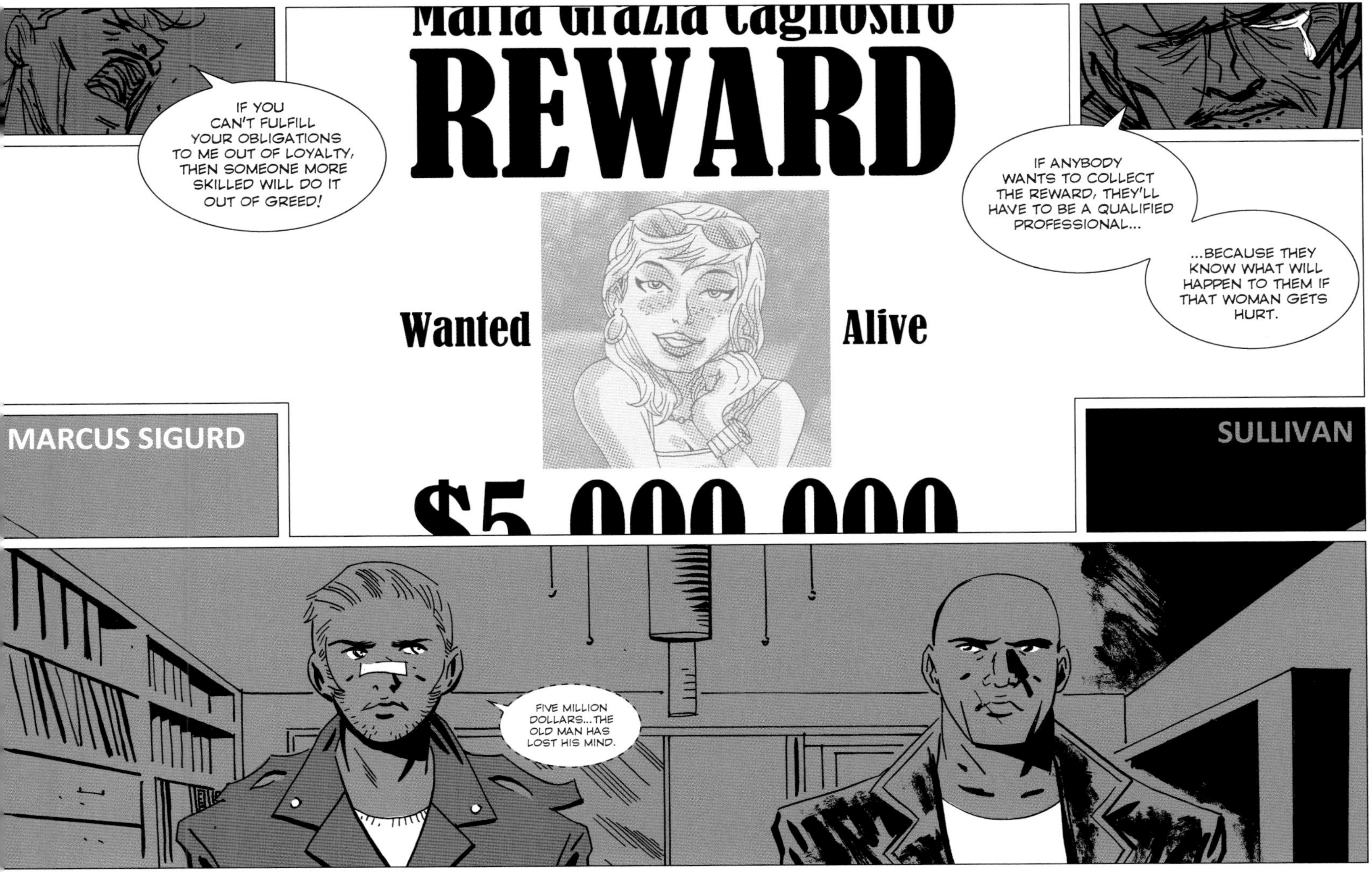
IF YOU CAN'T FULFILL YOUR OBLIGATIONS TO ME OUT OF LOYALTY, THEN SOMEONE MORE SKILLED WILL DO IT OUT OF GREED!
Maria Grazia Cagliostro
REWARD
Wanted
Alive
$5 000 000
IF ANYBODY WANTS TO COLLECT THE REWARD, THEY'LL HAVE TO BE A QUALIFIED PROFESSIONAL...
...BECAUSE THEY KNOW WHAT WILL HAPPEN TO THEM IF THAT WOMAN GETS HURT.
MARCUS SIGURD
SULLIVAN
FIVE MILLION DOLLARS...THE OLD MAN HAS LOST HIS MIND.

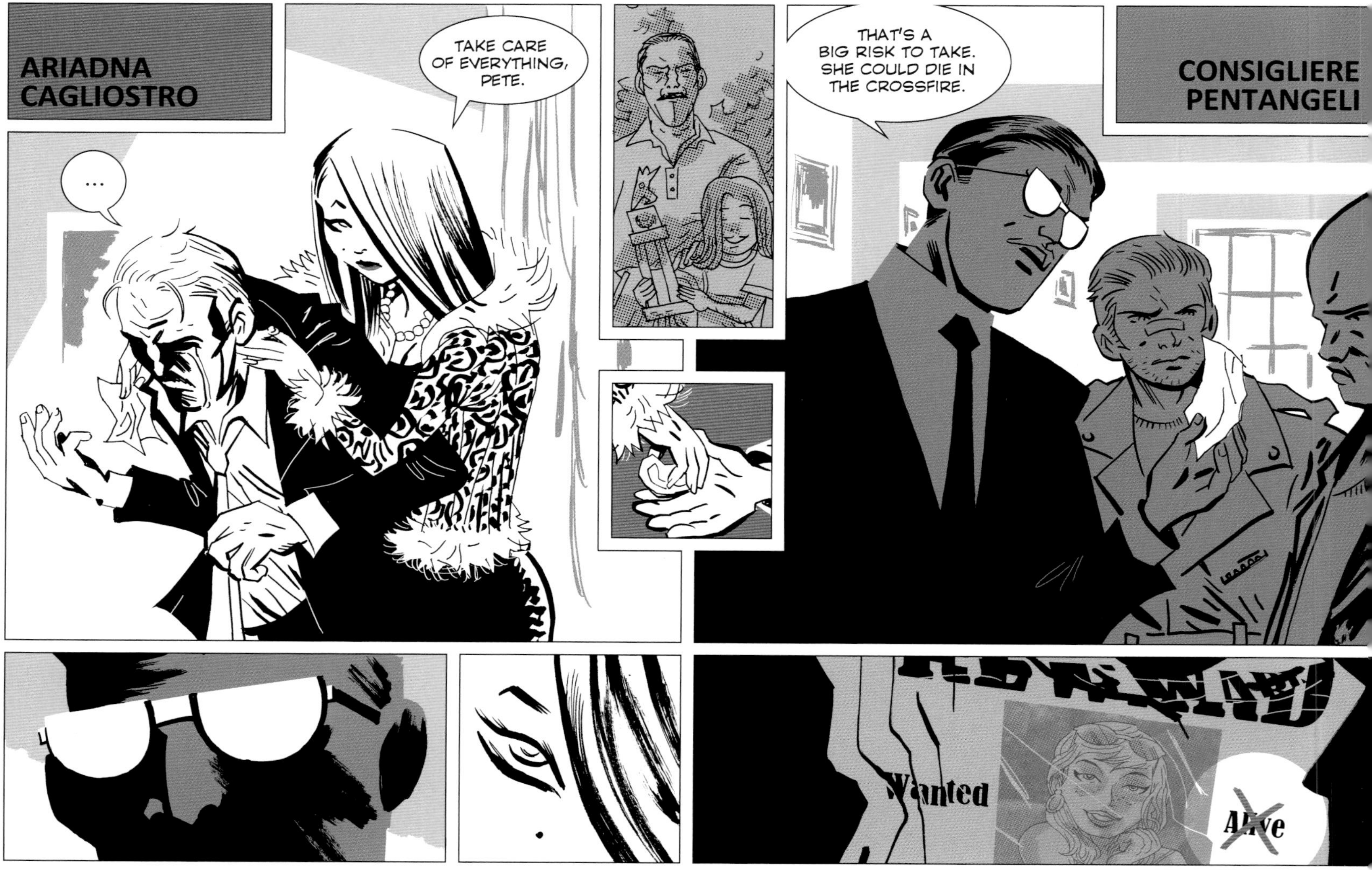
ARIADNA CAGLIOSTRO
TAKE CARE OF EVERYTHING, PETE.
...
THAT'S A BIG RISK TO TAKE. SHE COULD DIE IN THE CROSSFIRE.
CONSIGLIERE PENTANGELI
Wanted
Alive

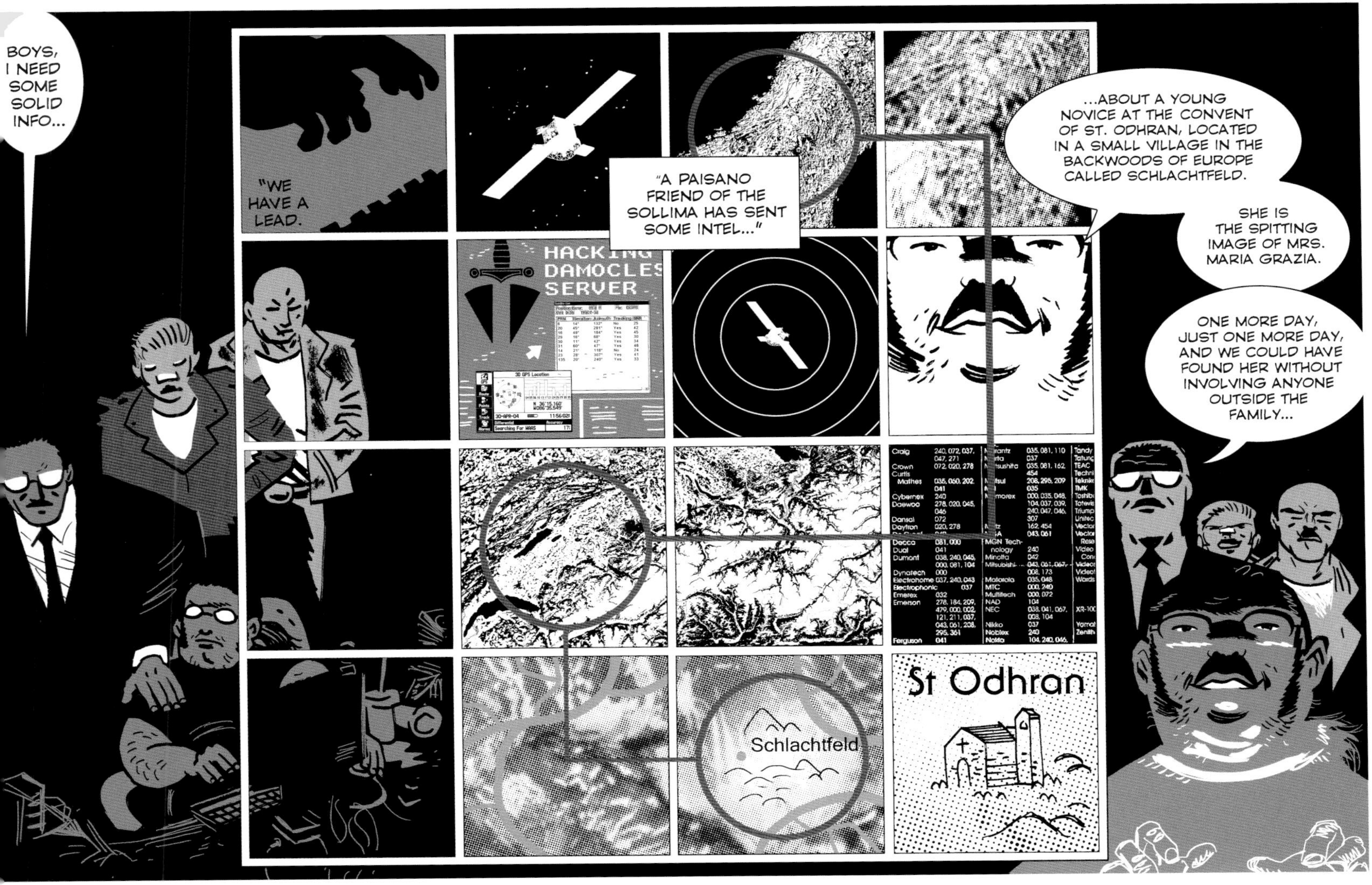

BOYS, I NEED SOME SOLID INFO...
"WE HAVE A LEAD.
"A PAISANO FRIEND OF THE SOLLIMA HAS SENT SOME INTEL..."
HACKING DAMOCLES SERVER
...ABOUT A YOUNG NOVICE AT THE CONVENT OF ST. ODHRAN, LOCATED IN A SMALL VILLAGE IN THE BACKWOODS OF EUROPE CALLED SCHLACHTFELD.
SHE IS THE SPITTING IMAGE OF MRS. MARIA GRAZIA.
ONE MORE DAY, JUST ONE MORE DAY, AND WE COULD HAVE FOUND HER WITHOUT INVOLVING ANYONE OUTSIDE THE FAMILY...
Schlachtfeld
St Odhran

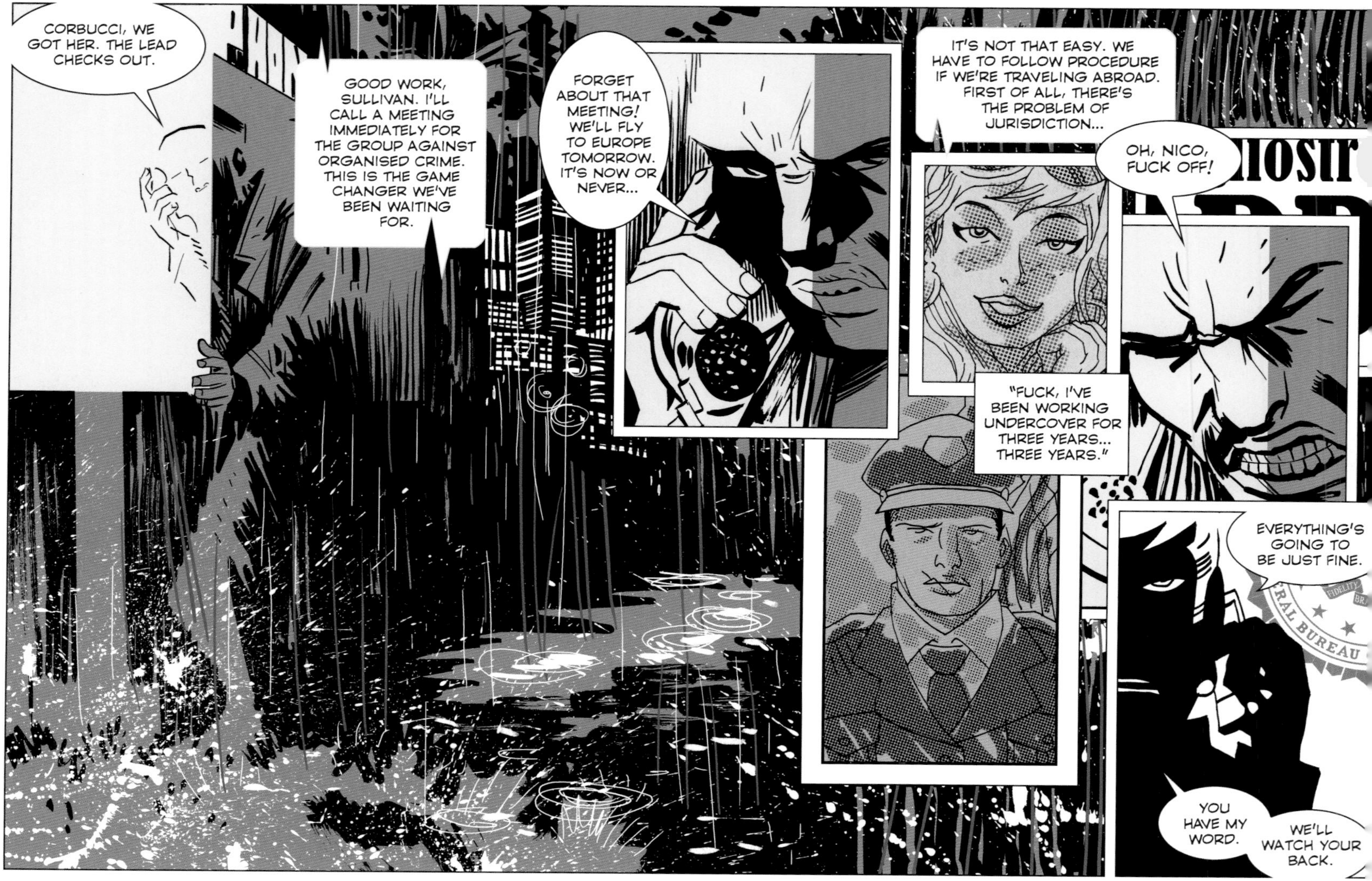
CORBUCCI, WE GOT HER. THE LEAD CHECKS OUT.
GOOD WORK, SULLIVAN. I'LL CALL A MEETING IMMEDIATELY FOR THE GROUP AGAINST ORGANISED CRIME. THIS IS THE GAME CHANGER WE'VE BEEN WAITING FOR.
FORGET ABOUT THAT MEETING! WE'LL FLY TO EUROPE TOMORROW. IT'S NOW OR NEVER...
IT'S NOT THAT EASY. WE HAVE TO FOLLOW PROCEDURE IF WE'RE TRAVELING ABROAD. FIRST OF ALL, THERE'S THE PROBLEM OF JURISDICTION...
OH, NICO, FUCK OFF!
"FUCK, I'VE BEEN WORKING UNDERCOVER FOR THREE YEARS... THREE YEARS."
EVERYTHING'S GOING TO BE JUST FINE.
YOU HAVE MY WORD.
WE'LL WATCH YOUR BACK.

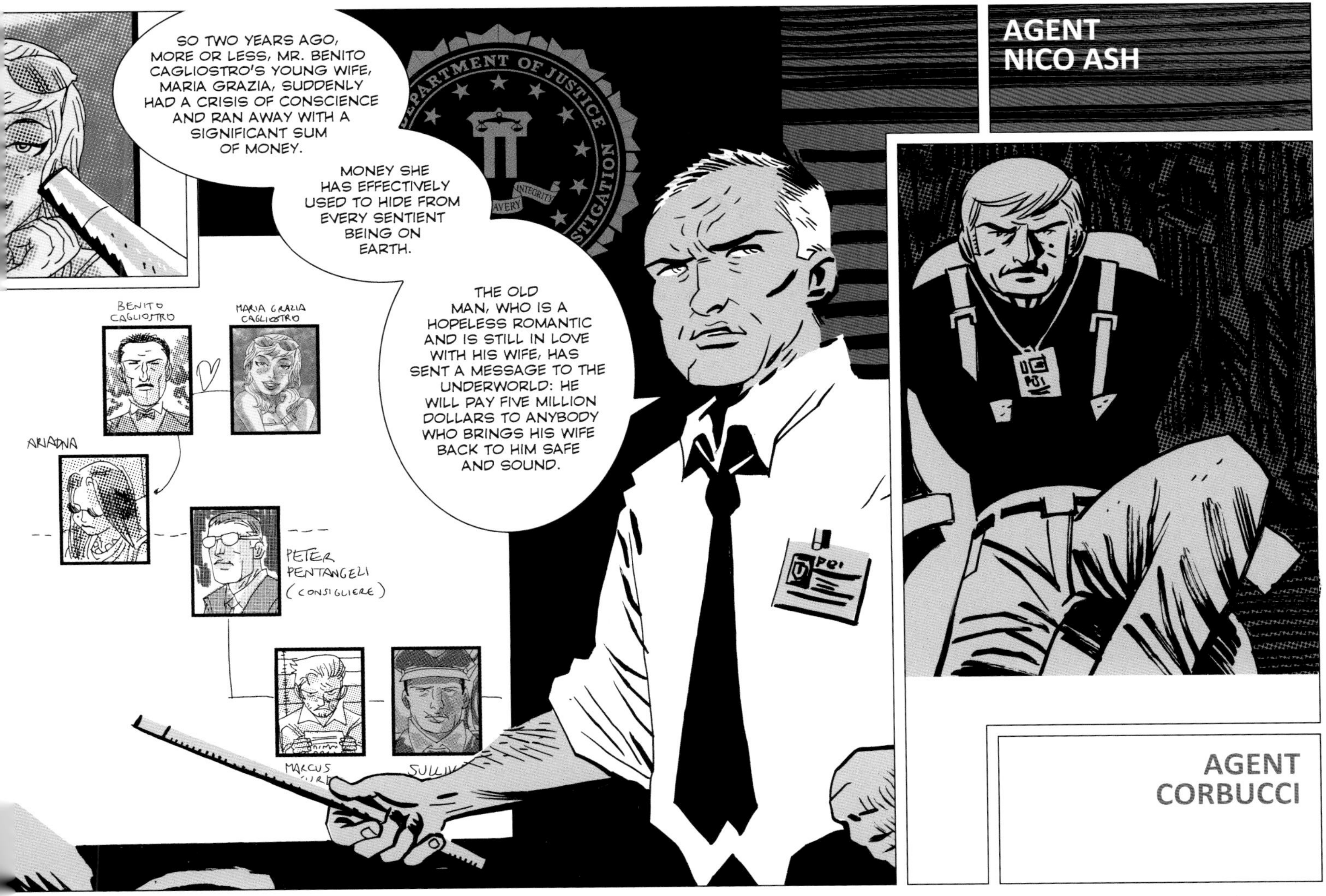
SO TWO YEARS AGO, MORE OR LESS, MR. BENITO CAGLIOSTRO'S YOUNG WIFE, MARIA GRAZIA, SUDDENLY HAD A CRISIS OF CONSCIENCE AND RAN AWAY WITH A SIGNIFICANT SUM OF MONEY.
MONEY SHE HAS EFFECTIVELY USED TO HIDE FROM EVERY SENTIENT BEING ON EARTH.
THE OLD MAN, WHO IS A HOPELESS ROMANTIC AND IS STILL IN LOVE WITH HIS WIFE, HAS SENT A MESSAGE TO THE UNDERWORLD: HE WILL PAY FIVE MILLION DOLLARS TO ANYBODY WHO BRINGS HIS WIFE BACK TO HIM SAFE AND SOUND.
BENITO CAGLIOSTRO
MARIA GRAZIA CAGLIOSTRO
ARIADNA
PETER PENTANGELI (CONSIGLIERE)
MARCUS
AGENT NICO ASH
AGENT CORBUCCI

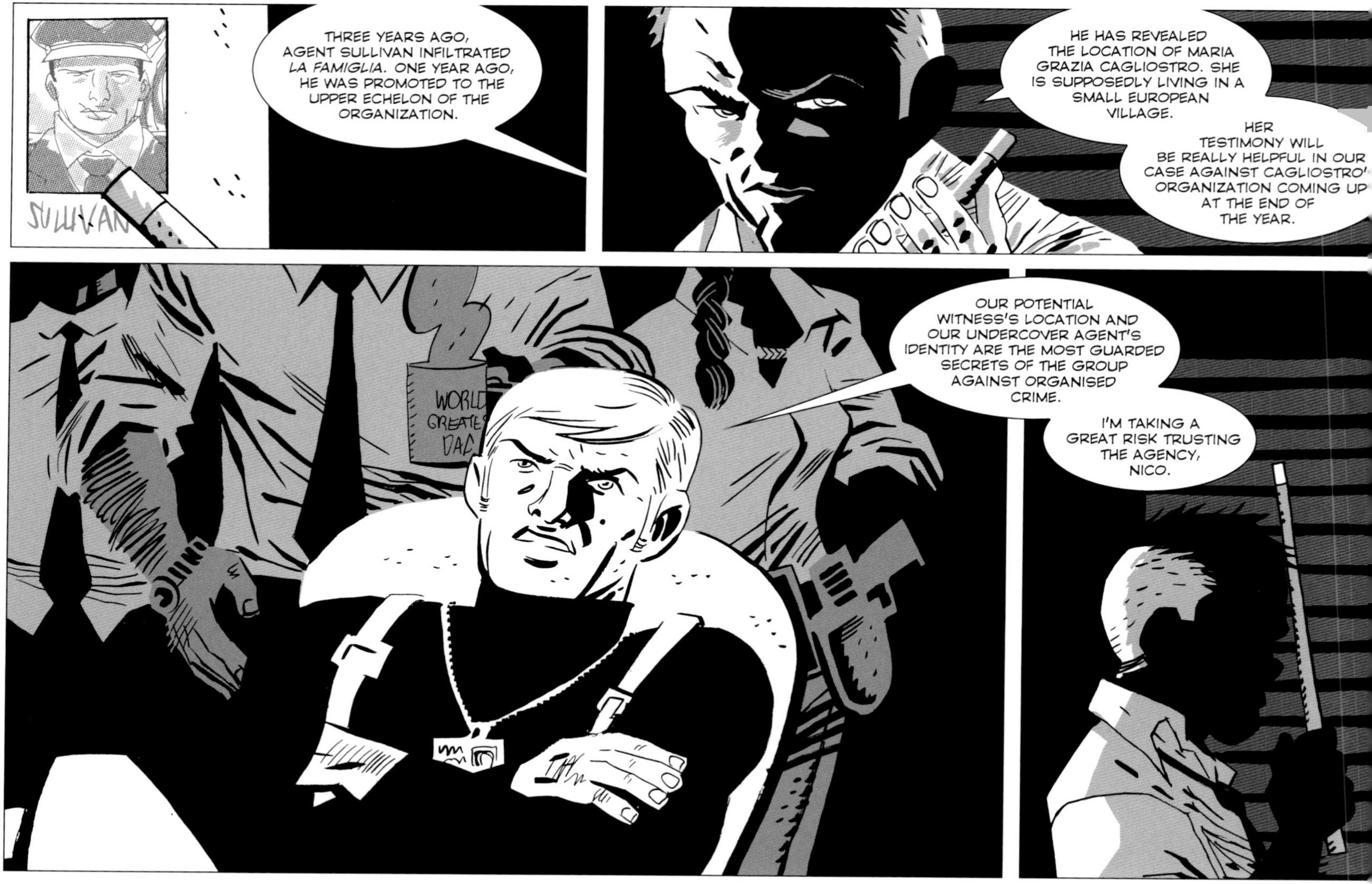

SULLIVAN
THREE YEARS AGO, AGENT SULLIVAN INFILTRATED *LA FAMIGLIA*. ONE YEAR AGO, HE WAS PROMOTED TO THE UPPER ECHELON OF THE ORGANIZATION.
HE HAS REVEALED THE LOCATION OF MARIA GRAZIA CAGLIOSTRO. SHE IS SUPPOSEDLY LIVING IN A SMALL EUROPEAN VILLAGE.
HER TESTIMONY WILL BE REALLY HELPFUL IN OUR CASE AGAINST CAGLIOSTRO' ORGANIZATION COMING UP AT THE END OF THE YEAR.
OUR POTENTIAL WITNESS'S LOCATION AND OUR UNDERCOVER AGENT'S IDENTITY ARE THE MOST GUARDED SECRETS OF THE GROUP AGAINST ORGANISED CRIME.
I'M TAKING A GREAT RISK TRUSTING THE AGENCY, NICO.

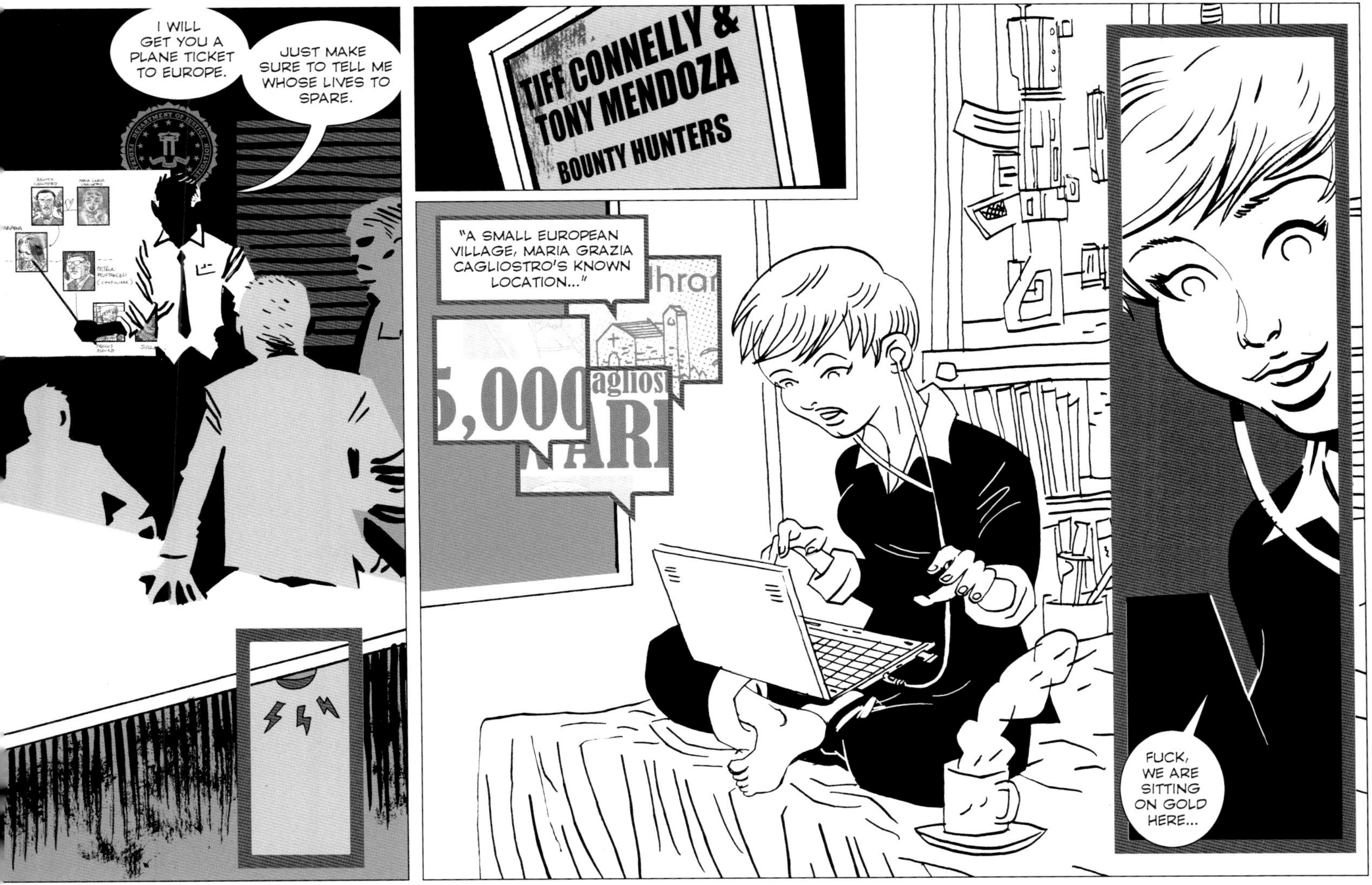
I WILL GET YOU A PLANE TICKET TO EUROPE.
JUST MAKE SURE TO TELL ME WHOSE LIVES TO SPARE.
TIFF CONNELLY & TONY MENDOZA
BOUNTY HUNTERS
"A SMALL EUROPEAN VILLAGE, MARIA GRAZIA CAGLIOSTRO'S KNOWN LOCATION..."
FUCK, WE ARE SITTING ON GOLD HERE...

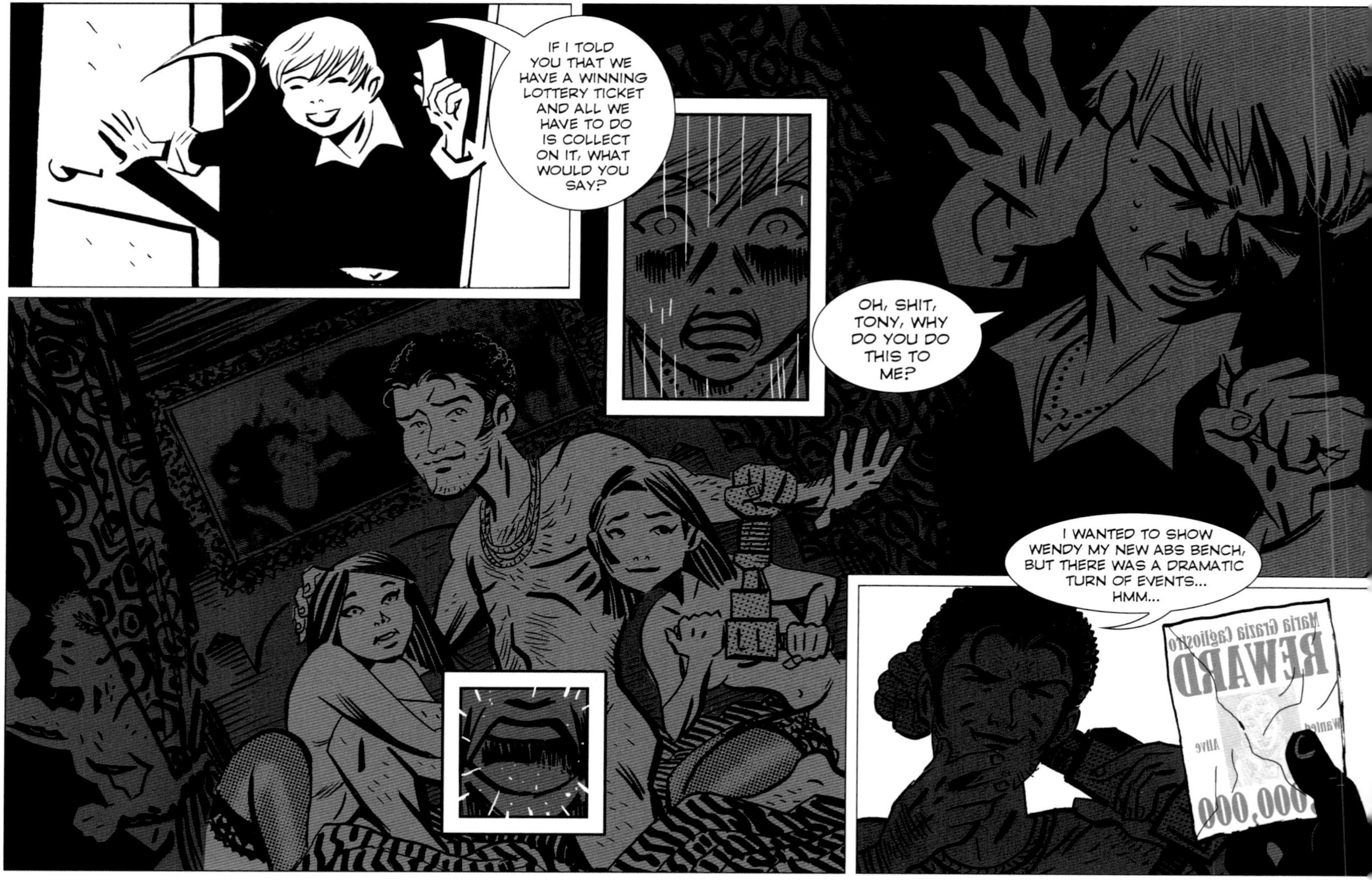
IF I TOLD YOU THAT WE HAVE A WINNING LOTTERY TICKET AND ALL WE HAVE TO DO IS COLLECT ON IT, WHAT WOULD YOU SAY?
OH, SHIT, TONY, WHY DO YOU DO THIS TO ME?
I WANTED TO SHOW WENDY MY NEW ABS BENCH, BUT THERE WAS A DRAMATIC TURN OF EVENTS... HMM...
Maria Grazia Cagliostro
REWARD
Wanted
Alive
000,000

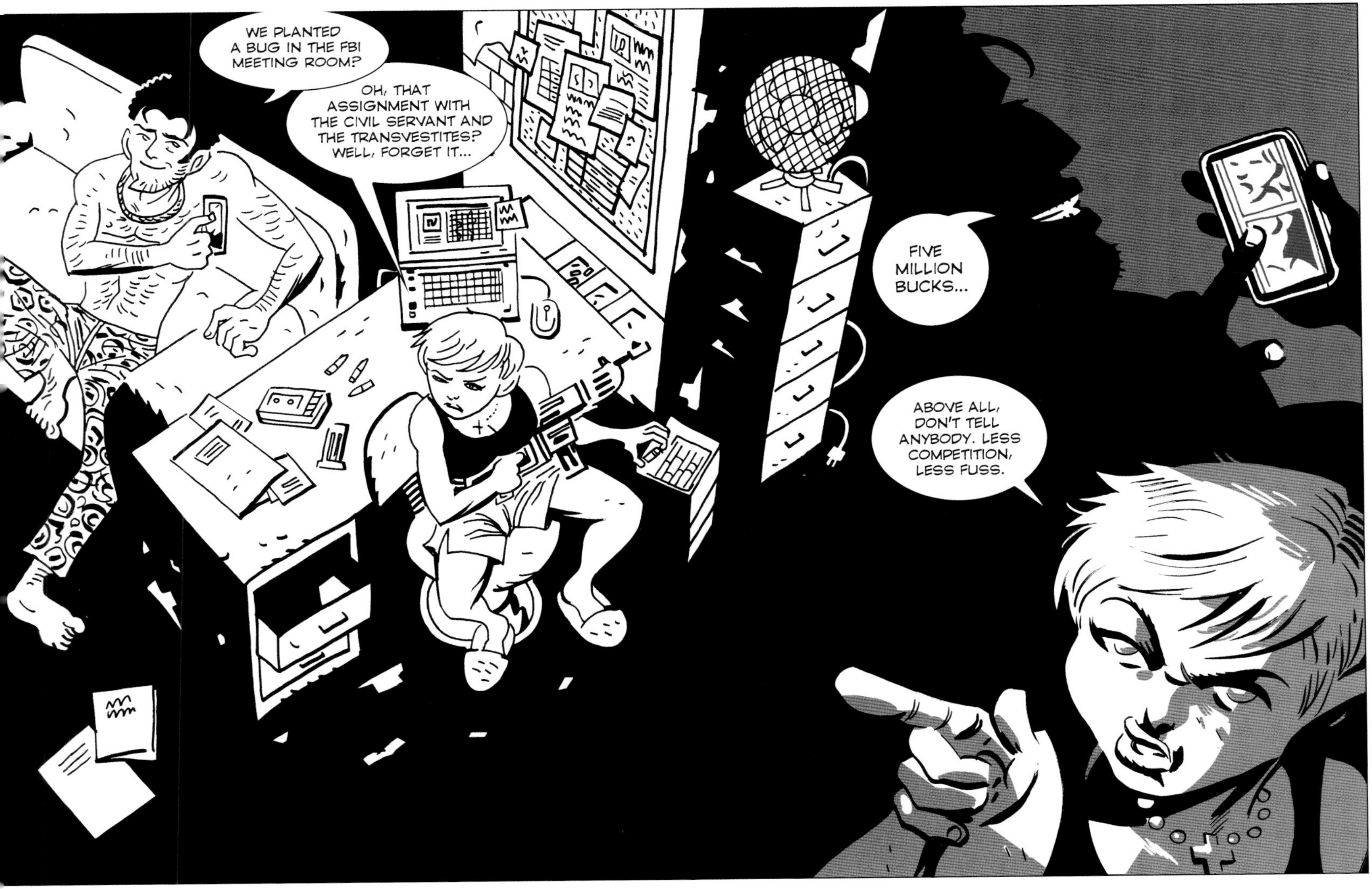
WE PLANTED A BUG IN THE FBI MEETING ROOM?
OH, THAT ASSIGNMENT WITH THE CIVIL SERVANT AND THE TRANSVESTITES? WELL, FORGET IT...
FIVE MILLION BUCKS...
ABOVE ALL, DON'T TELL ANYBODY. LESS COMPETITION, LESS FUSS.

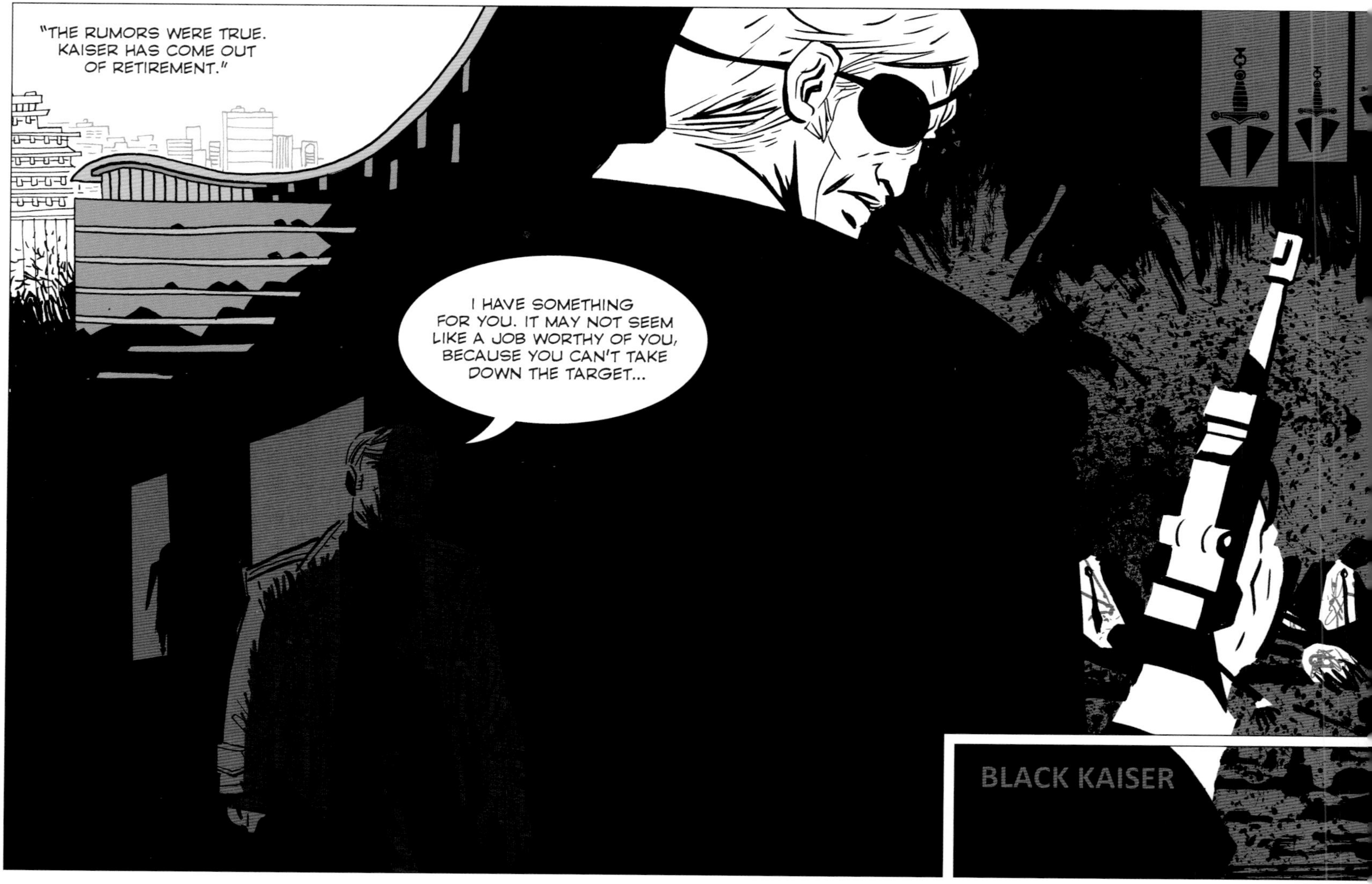
"THE RUMORS WERE TRUE. KAISER HAS COME OUT OF RETIREMENT."
I HAVE SOMETHING FOR YOU. IT MAY NOT SEEM LIKE A JOB WORTHY OF YOU, BECAUSE YOU CAN'T TAKE DOWN THE TARGET...
BLACK KAISER

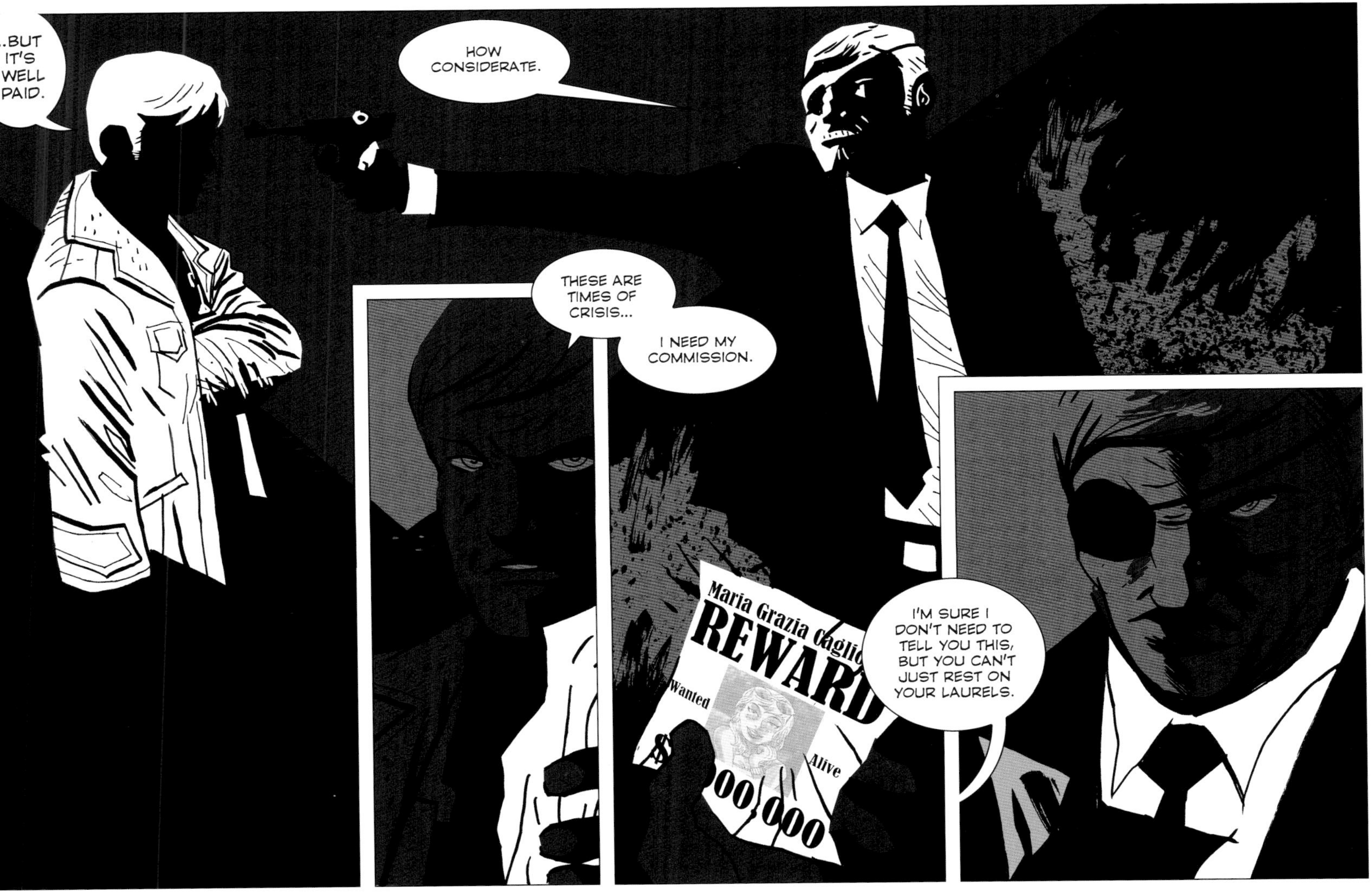

...BUT IT'S WELL PAID.
HOW CONSIDERATE.
THESE ARE TIMES OF CRISIS...
I NEED MY COMMISSION.
Maria Grazia Caglio
REWARD
Wanted
Alive
I'M SURE I DON'T NEED TO TELL YOU THIS, BUT YOU CAN'T JUST REST ON YOUR LAURELS.

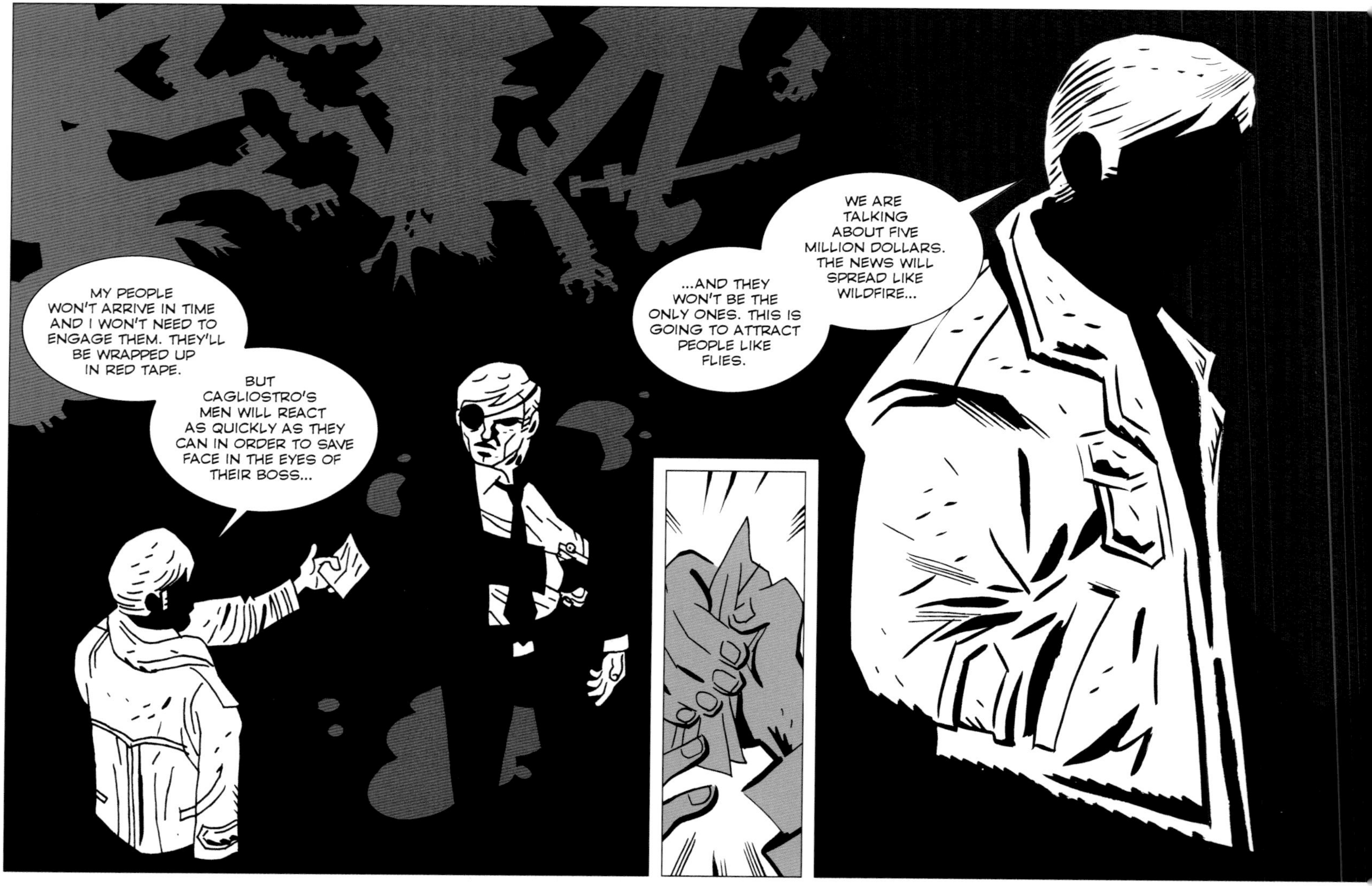
MY PEOPLE WON'T ARRIVE IN TIME AND I WON'T NEED TO ENGAGE THEM. THEY'LL BE WRAPPED UP IN RED TAPE.
BUT CAGLIOSTRO'S MEN WILL REACT AS QUICKLY AS THEY CAN IN ORDER TO SAVE FACE IN THE EYES OF THEIR BOSS...
...AND THEY WON'T BE THE ONLY ONES. THIS IS GOING TO ATTRACT PEOPLE LIKE FLIES.
WE ARE TALKING ABOUT FIVE MILLION DOLLARS. THE NEWS WILL SPREAD LIKE WILDFIRE...

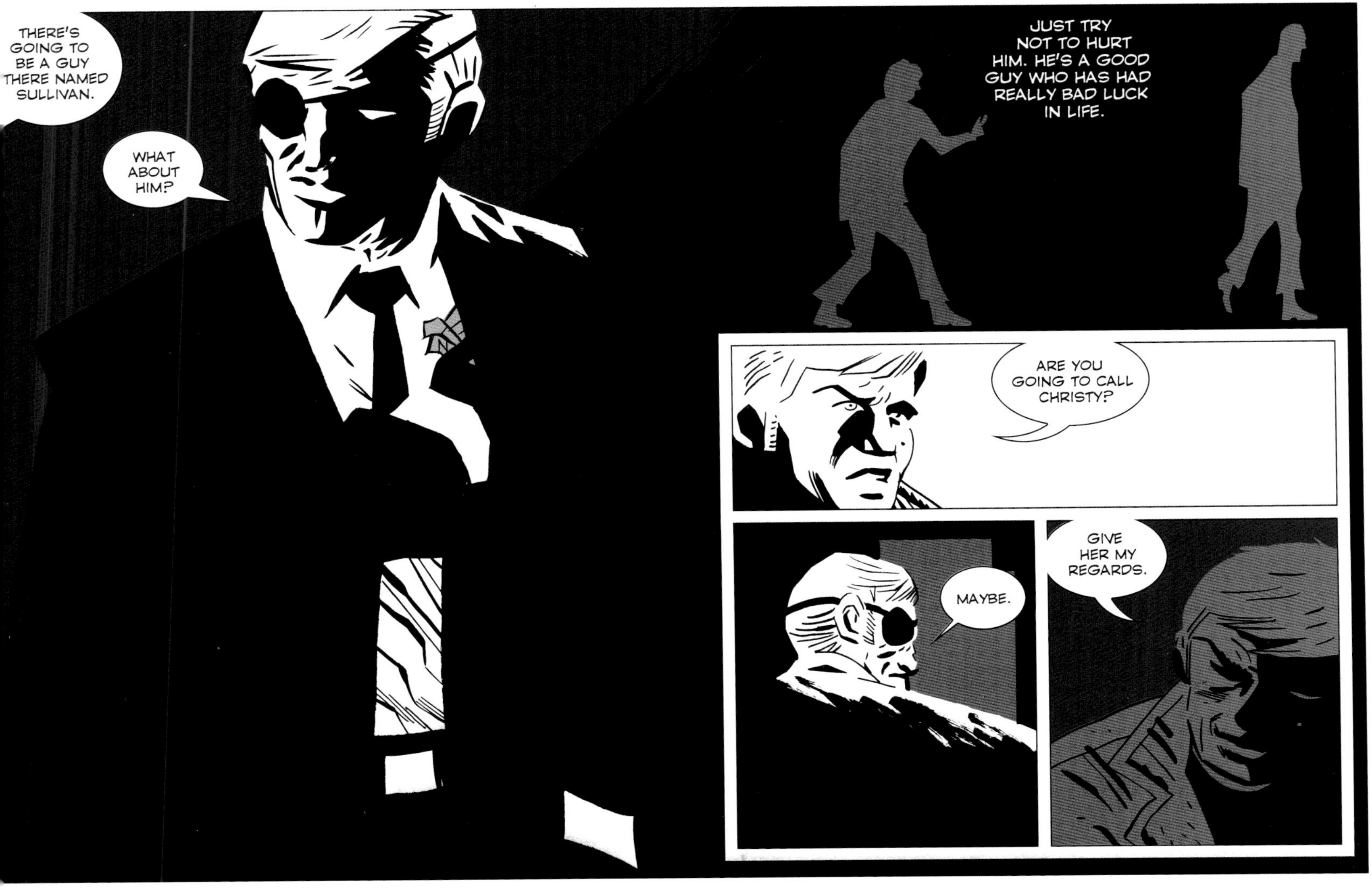
THERE'S GOING TO BE A GUY THERE NAMED SULLIVAN.
WHAT ABOUT HIM?
JUST TRY NOT TO HURT HIM. HE'S A GOOD GUY WHO HAS HAD REALLY BAD LUCK IN LIFE.
ARE YOU GOING TO CALL CHRISTY?
MAYBE.
GIVE HER MY REGARDS.

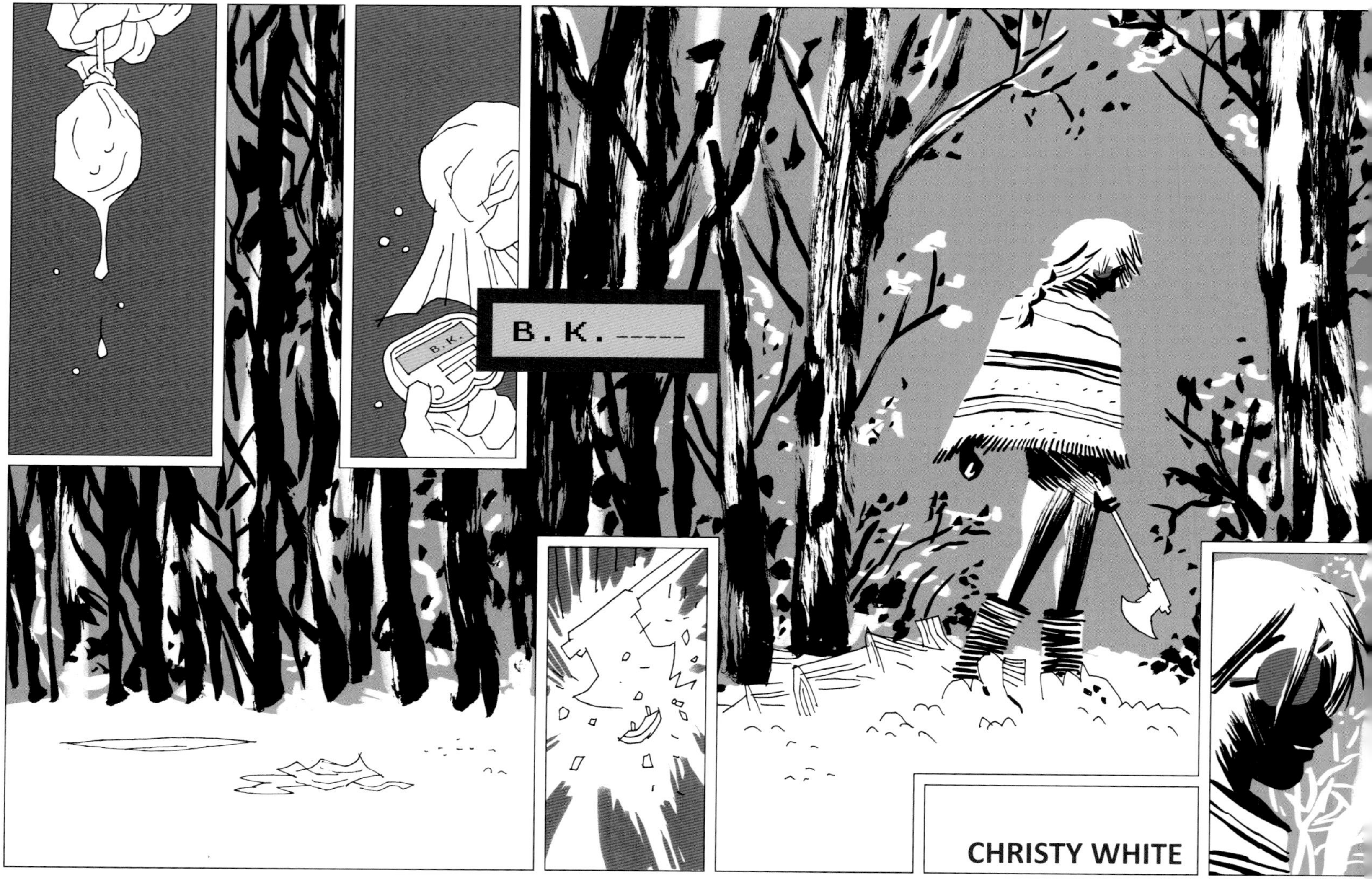
B.K.
B. K. -----
CHRISTY WHITE

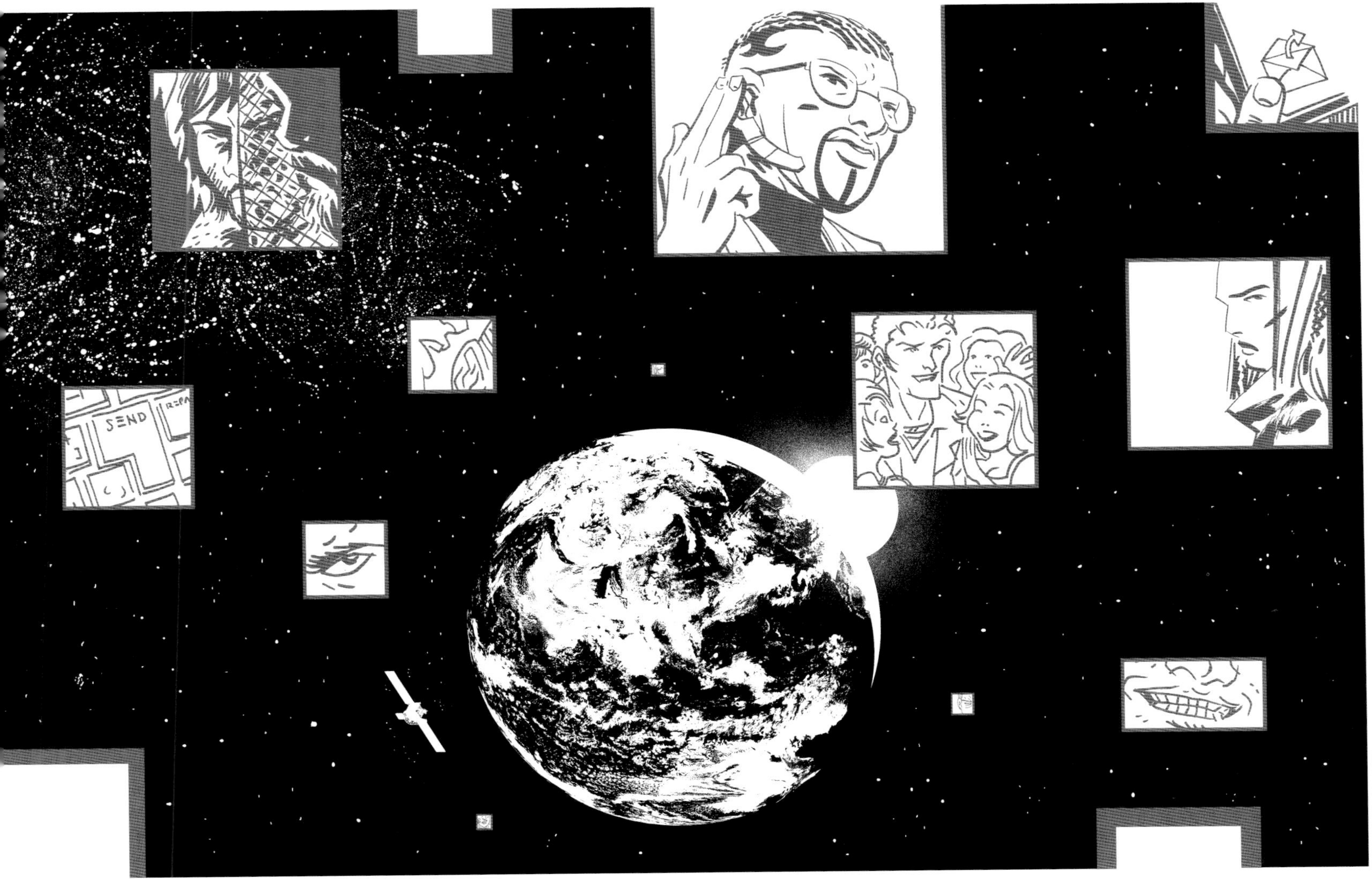
SEND

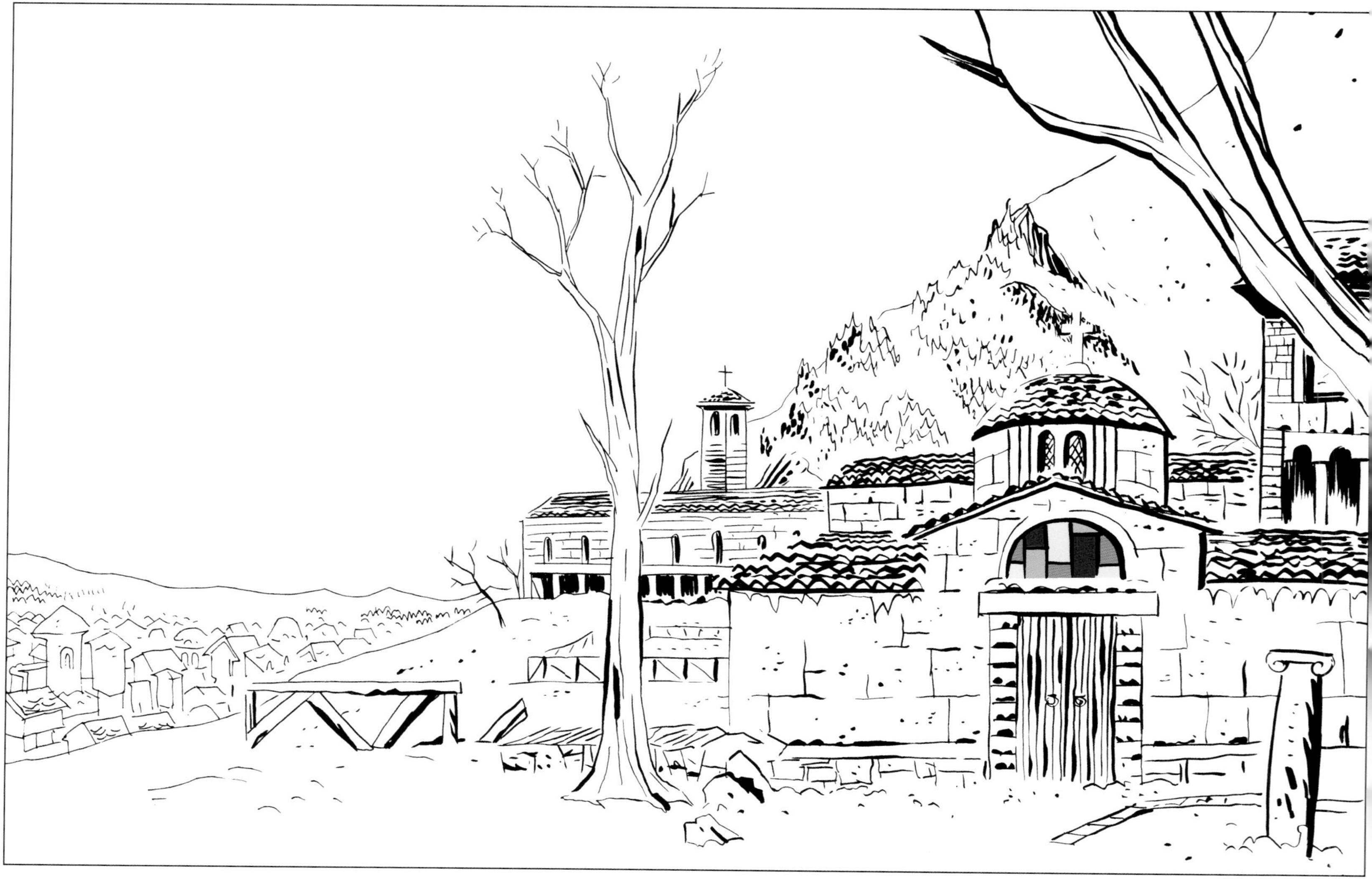

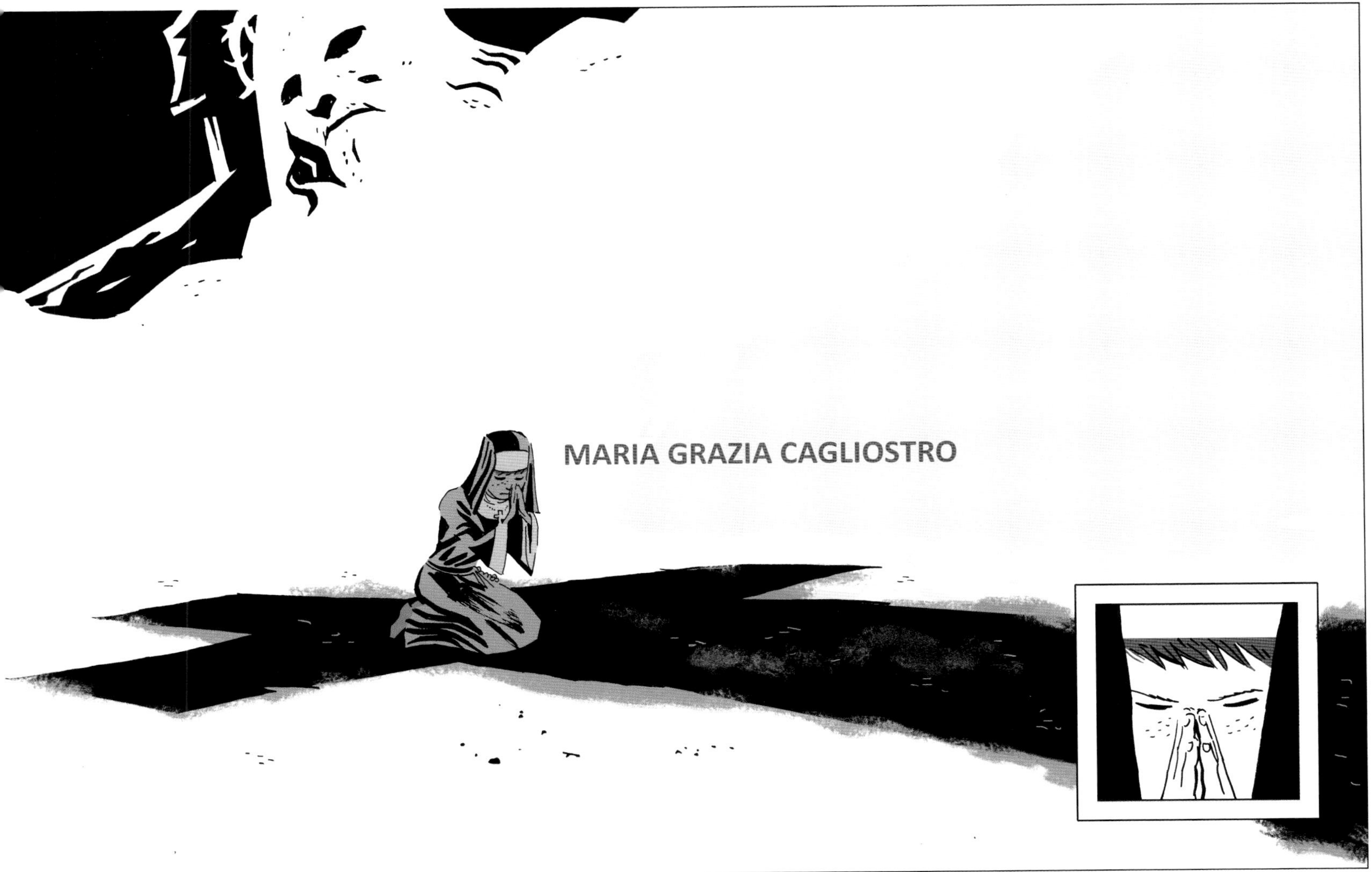
MARIA GRAZIA CAGLIOSTRO

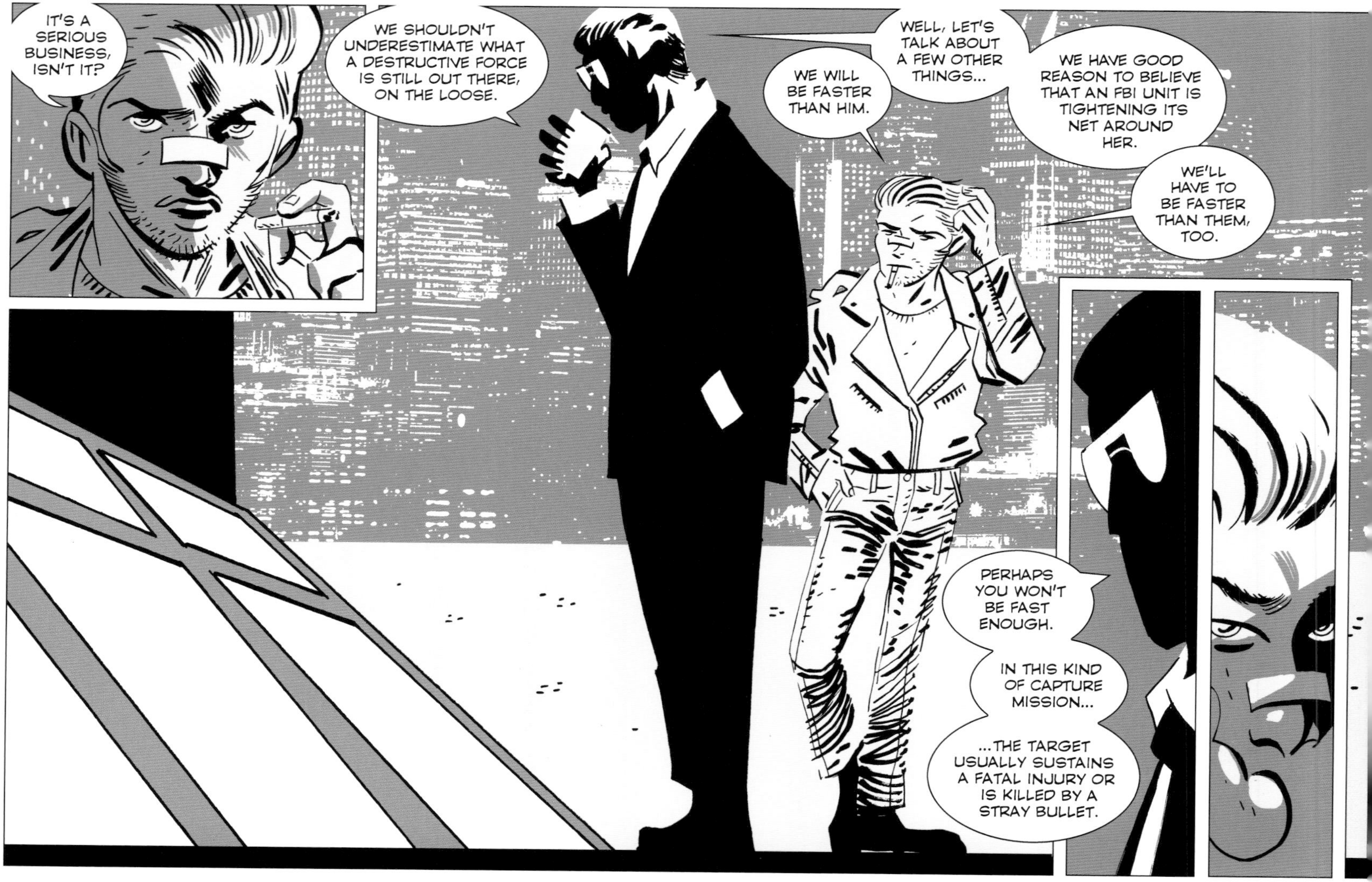

IT'S A SERIOUS BUSINESS, ISN'T IT?
WE SHOULDN'T UNDERESTIMATE WHAT A DESTRUCTIVE FORCE IS STILL OUT THERE, ON THE LOOSE.
WE WILL BE FASTER THAN HIM.
WELL, LET'S TALK ABOUT A FEW OTHER THINGS...
WE HAVE GOOD REASON TO BELIEVE THAT AN FBI UNIT IS TIGHTENING ITS NET AROUND HER.
WE'LL HAVE TO BE FASTER THAN THEM, TOO.
PERHAPS YOU WON'T BE FAST ENOUGH.
IN THIS KIND OF CAPTURE MISSION...
...THE TARGET USUALLY SUSTAINS A FATAL INJURY OR IS KILLED BY A STRAY BULLET.

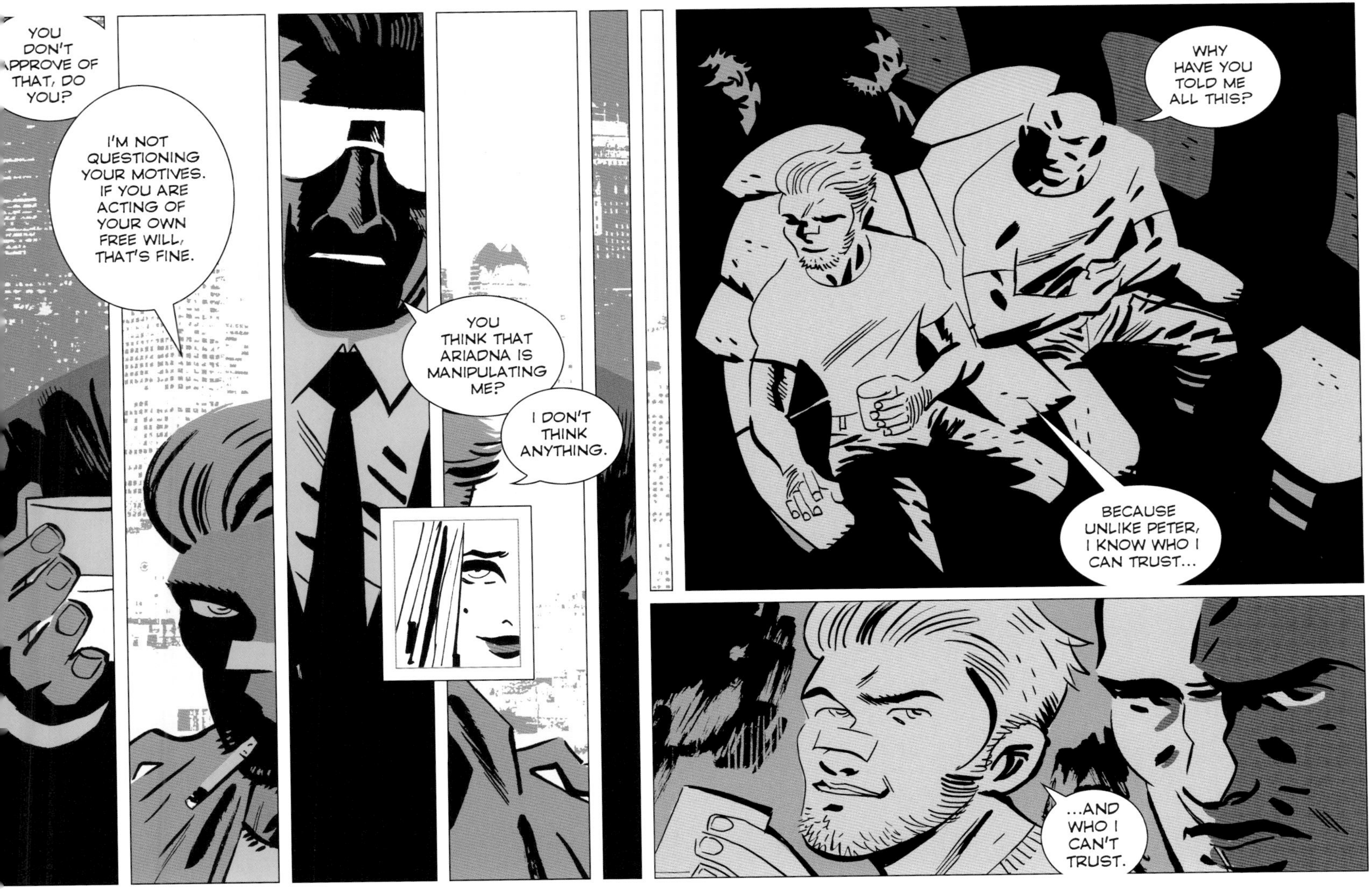
YOU DON'T APPROVE OF THAT, DO YOU?
I'M NOT QUESTIONING YOUR MOTIVES. IF YOU ARE ACTING OF YOUR OWN FREE WILL, THAT'S FINE.
YOU THINK THAT ARIADNA IS MANIPULATING ME?
I DON'T THINK ANYTHING.
WHY HAVE YOU TOLD ME ALL THIS?
BECAUSE UNLIKE PETER, I KNOW WHO I CAN TRUST...
...AND WHO I CAN'T TRUST.

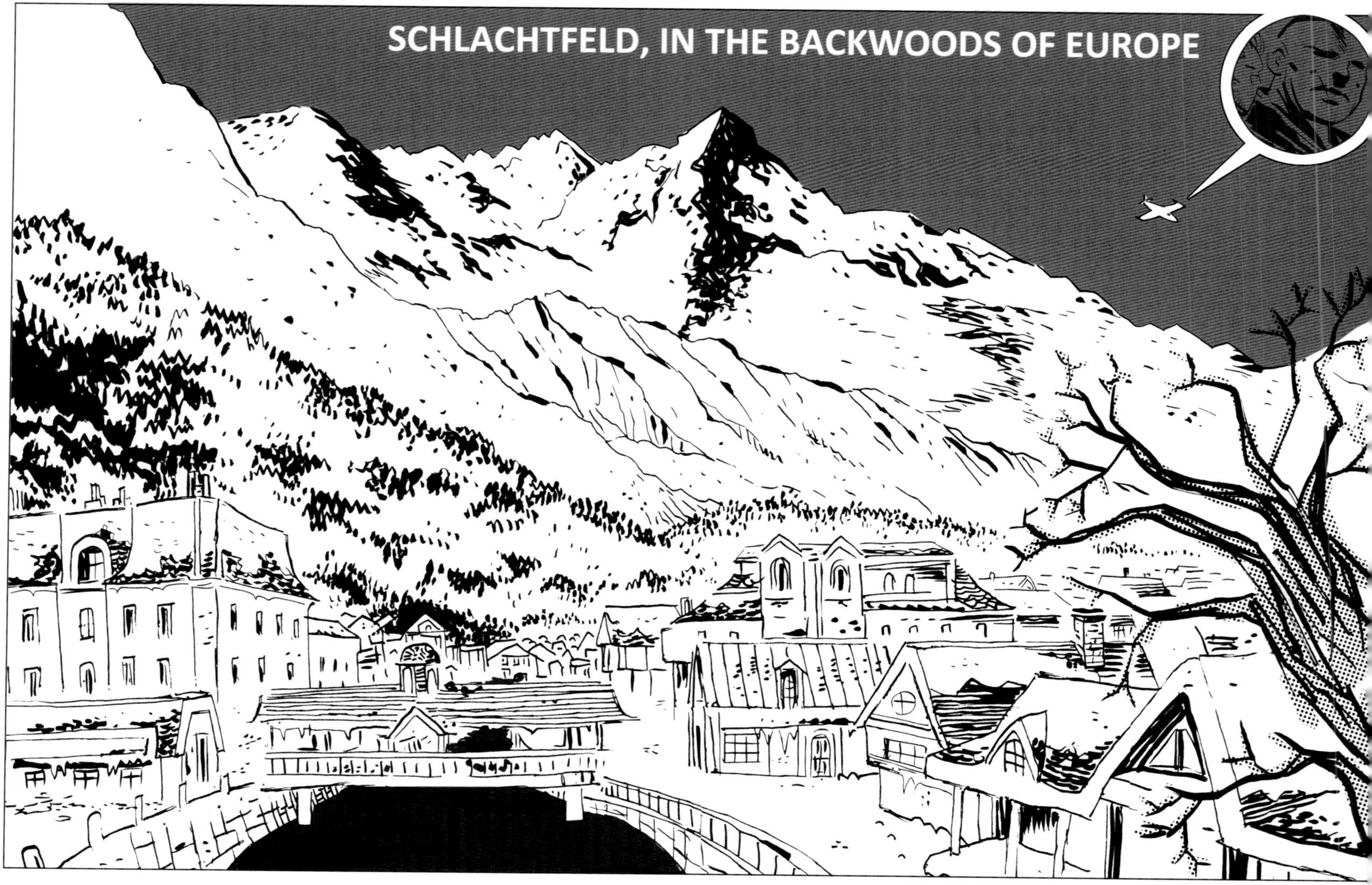
SCHLACHTFELD, IN THE BACKWOODS OF EUROPE

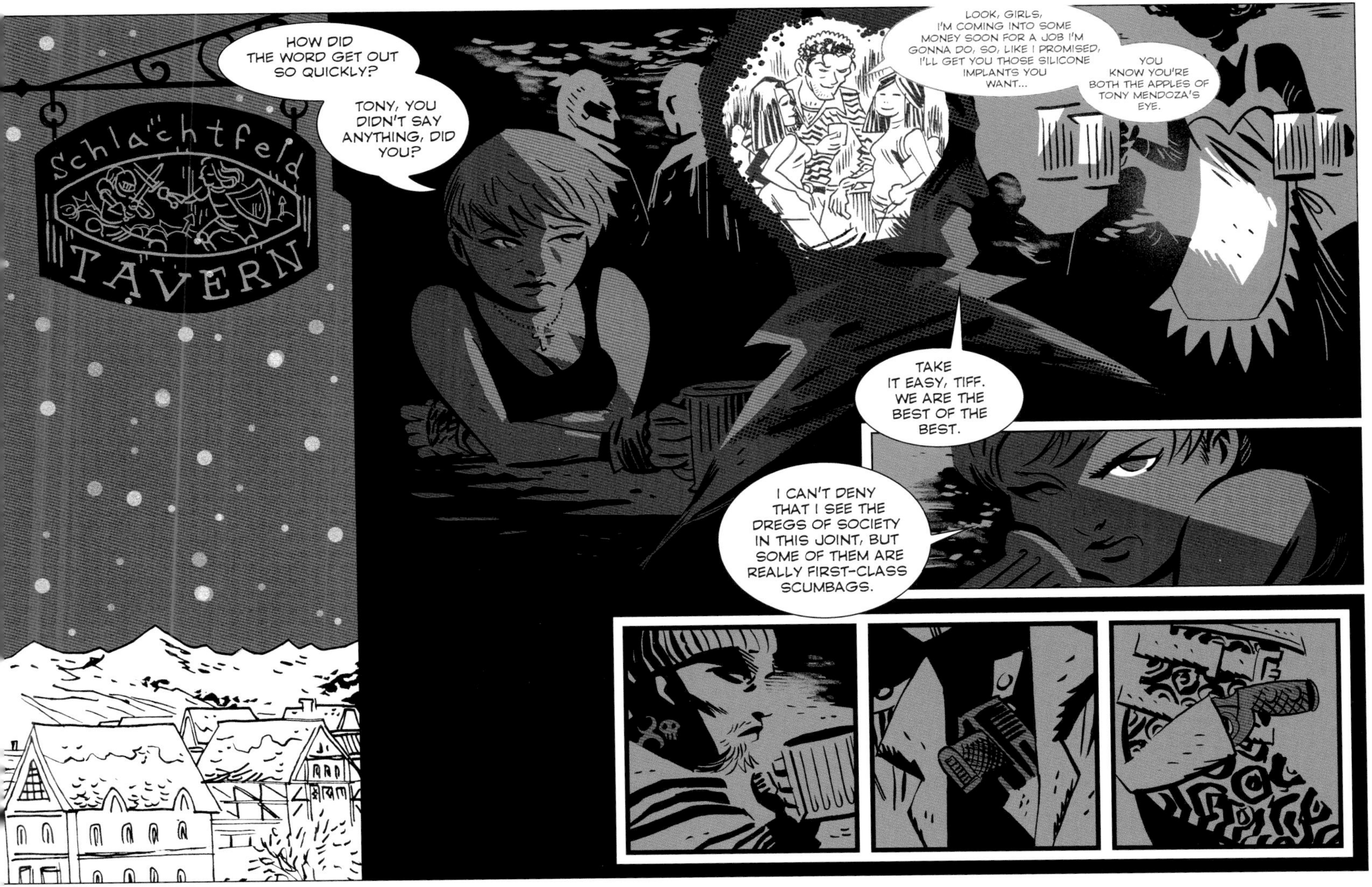
Schlachtfeld TAVERN
HOW DID THE WORD GET OUT SO QUICKLY?
TONY, YOU DIDN'T SAY ANYTHING, DID YOU?
LOOK, GIRLS, I'M COMING INTO SOME MONEY SOON FOR A JOB I'M GONNA DO, SO, LIKE I PROMISED, I'LL GET YOU THOSE SILICONE IMPLANTS YOU WANT...
YOU KNOW YOU'RE BOTH THE APPLES OF TONY MENDOZA'S EYE.
TAKE IT EASY, TIFF. WE ARE THE BEST OF THE BEST.
I CAN'T DENY THAT I SEE THE DREGS OF SOCIETY IN THIS JOINT, BUT SOME OF THEM ARE REALLY FIRST-CLASS SCUMBAGS.

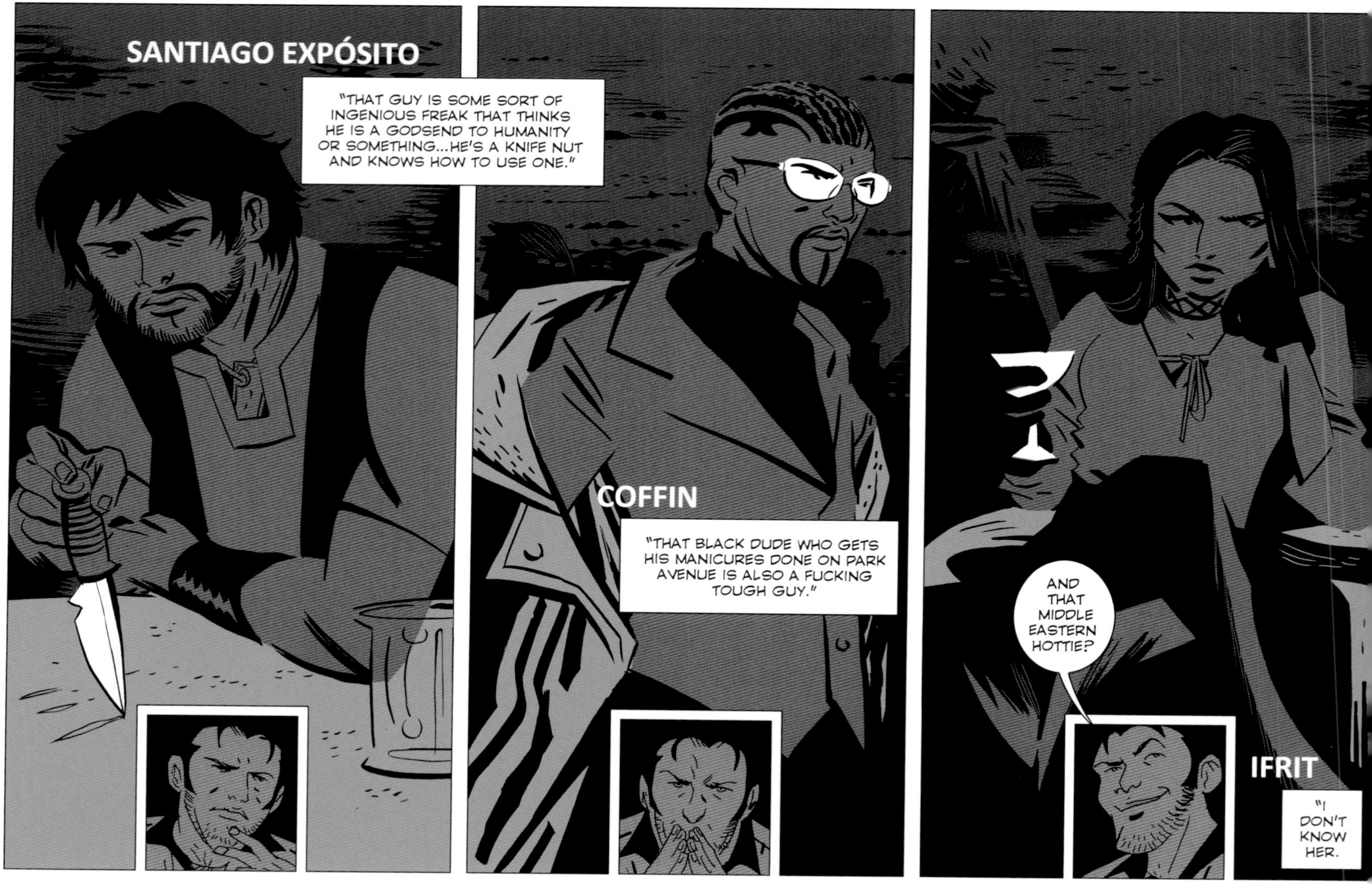

SANTIAGO EXPÓSITO
"THAT GUY IS SOME SORT OF INGENIOUS FREAK THAT THINKS HE IS A GODSEND TO HUMANITY OR SOMETHING...HE'S A KNIFE NUT AND KNOWS HOW TO USE ONE."
COFFIN
"THAT BLACK DUDE WHO GETS HIS MANICURES DONE ON PARK AVENUE IS ALSO A FUCKING TOUGH GUY."
AND THAT MIDDLE EASTERN HOTTIE?
IFRIT
"I DON'T KNOW HER.

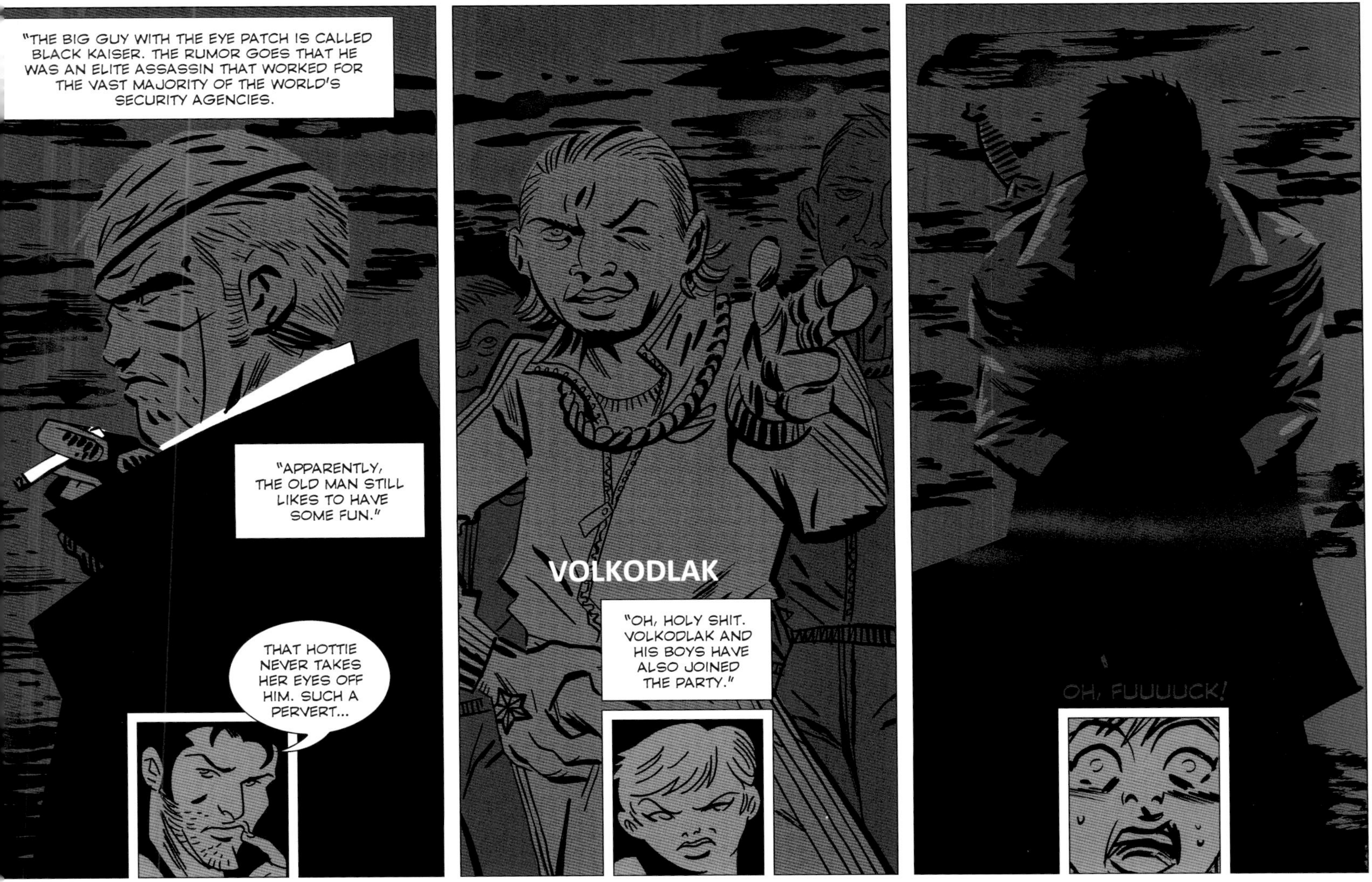
"THE BIG GUY WITH THE EYE PATCH IS CALLED BLACK KAISER. THE RUMOR GOES THAT HE WAS AN ELITE ASSASSIN THAT WORKED FOR THE VAST MAJORITY OF THE WORLD'S SECURITY AGENCIES.
"APPARENTLY, THE OLD MAN STILL LIKES TO HAVE SOME FUN."
THAT HOTTIE NEVER TAKES HER EYES OFF HIM. SUCH A PERVERT...
VOLKODLAK
"OH, HOLY SHIT. VOLKODLAK AND HIS BOYS HAVE ALSO JOINED THE PARTY."
OH, FUUUUCK!

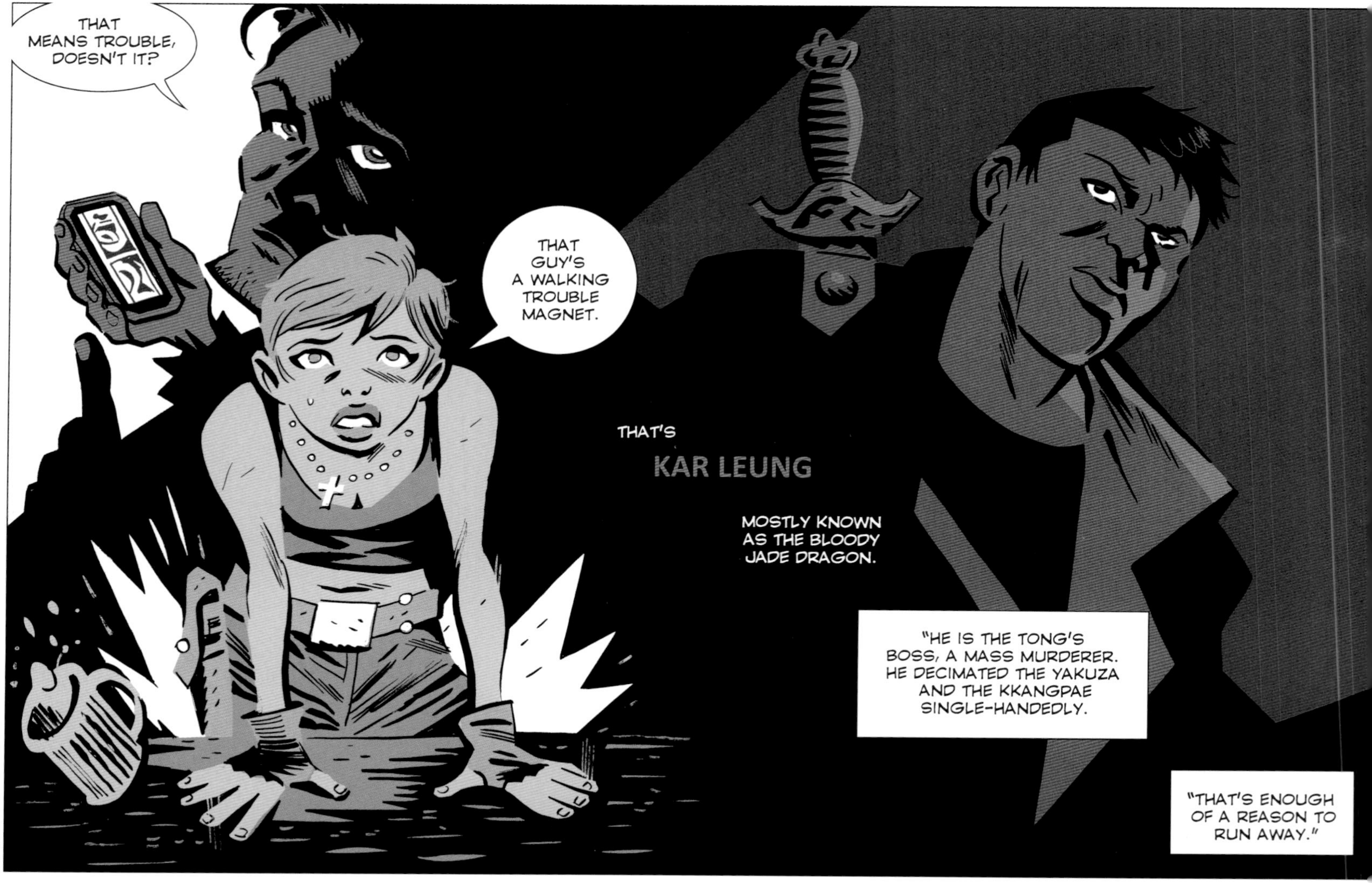
THAT MEANS TROUBLE, DOESN'T IT?
THAT GUY'S A WALKING TROUBLE MAGNET.
THAT'S
KAR LEUNG
MOSTLY KNOWN AS THE BLOODY JADE DRAGON.
"HE IS THE TONG'S BOSS, A MASS MURDERER. HE DECIMATED THE YAKUZA AND THE KKANGPAE SINGLE-HANDEDLY.
"THAT'S ENOUGH OF A REASON TO RUN AWAY."

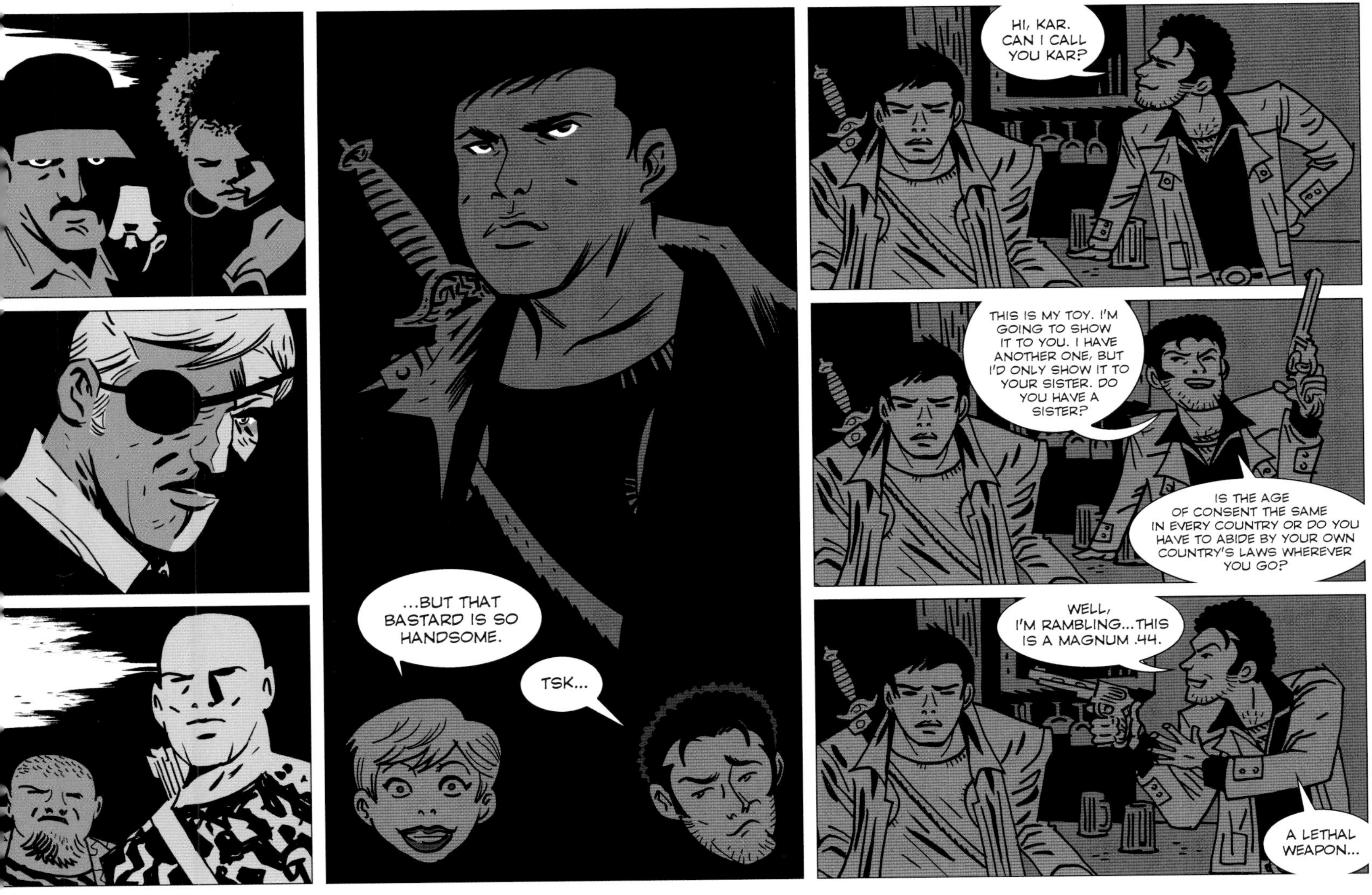
...BUT THAT BASTARD IS SO HANDSOME.
TSK...
HI, KAR. CAN I CALL YOU KAR?
THIS IS MY TOY. I'M GOING TO SHOW IT TO YOU. I HAVE ANOTHER ONE, BUT I'D ONLY SHOW IT TO YOUR SISTER. DO YOU HAVE A SISTER?
IS THE AGE OF CONSENT THE SAME IN EVERY COUNTRY OR DO YOU HAVE TO ABIDE BY YOUR OWN COUNTRY'S LAWS WHEREVER YOU GO?
WELL, I'M RAMBLING...THIS IS A MAGNUM .44.
A LETHAL WEAPON...

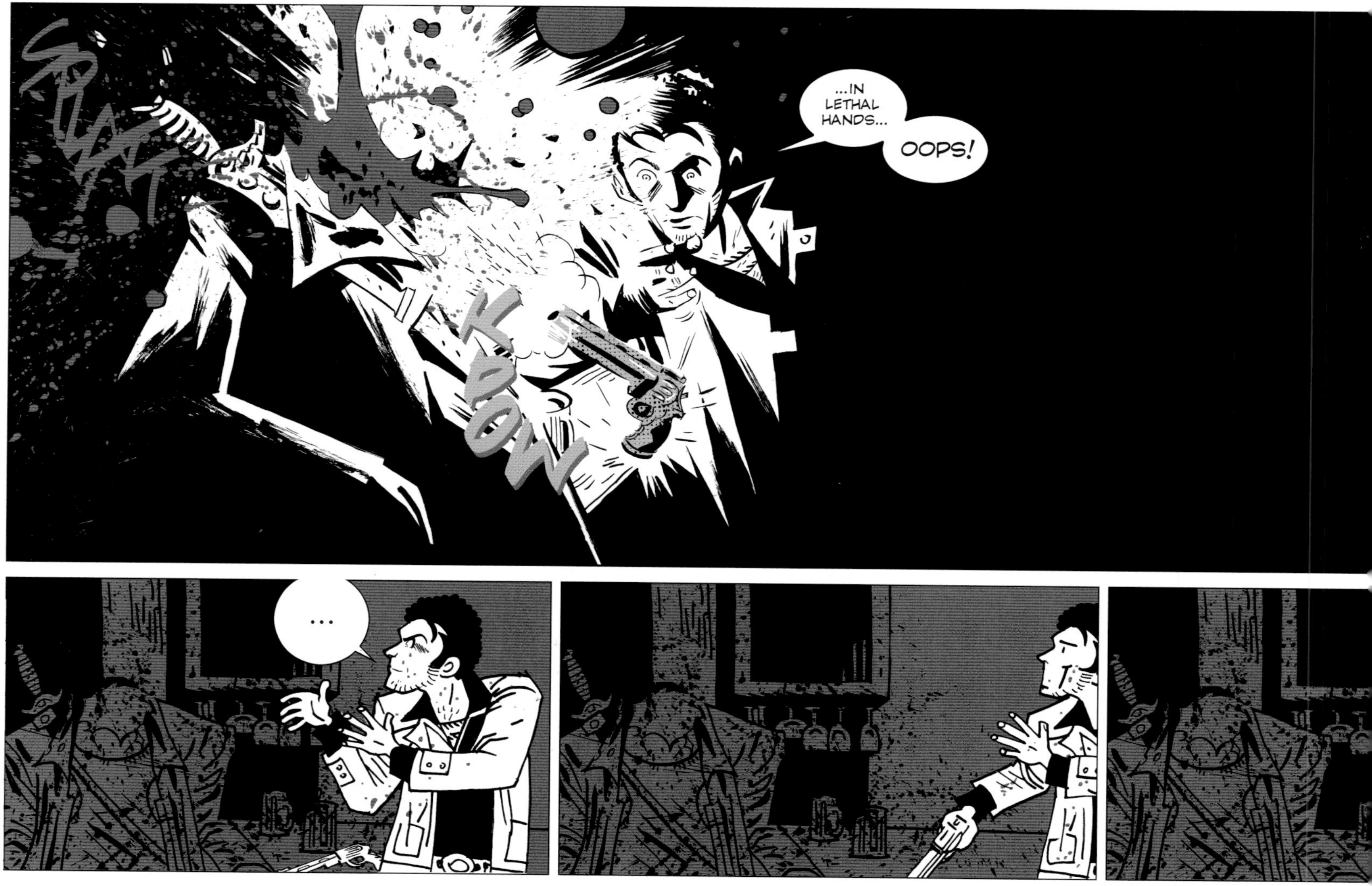
...IN LETHAL HANDS...
OOPS!
...

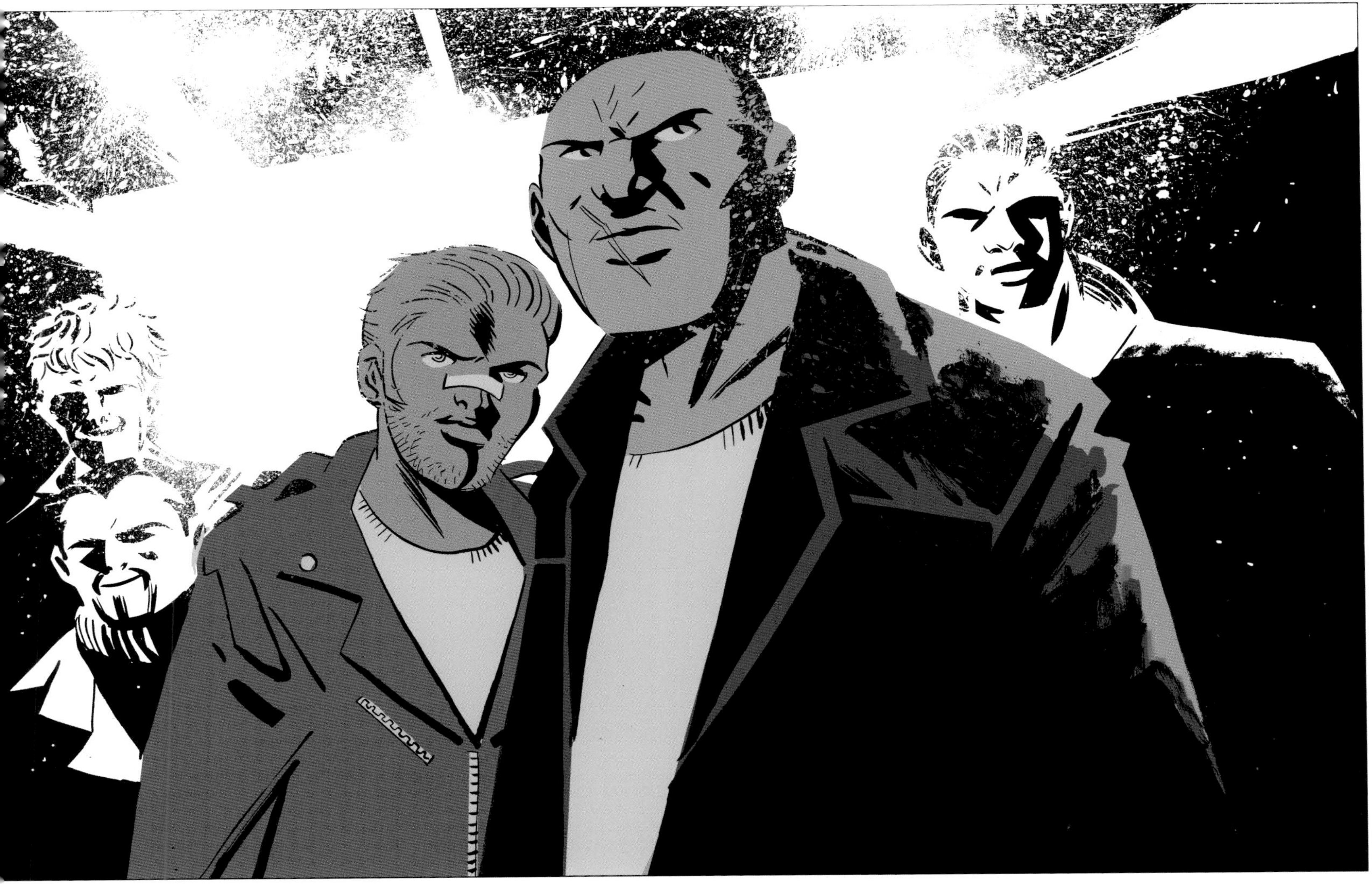

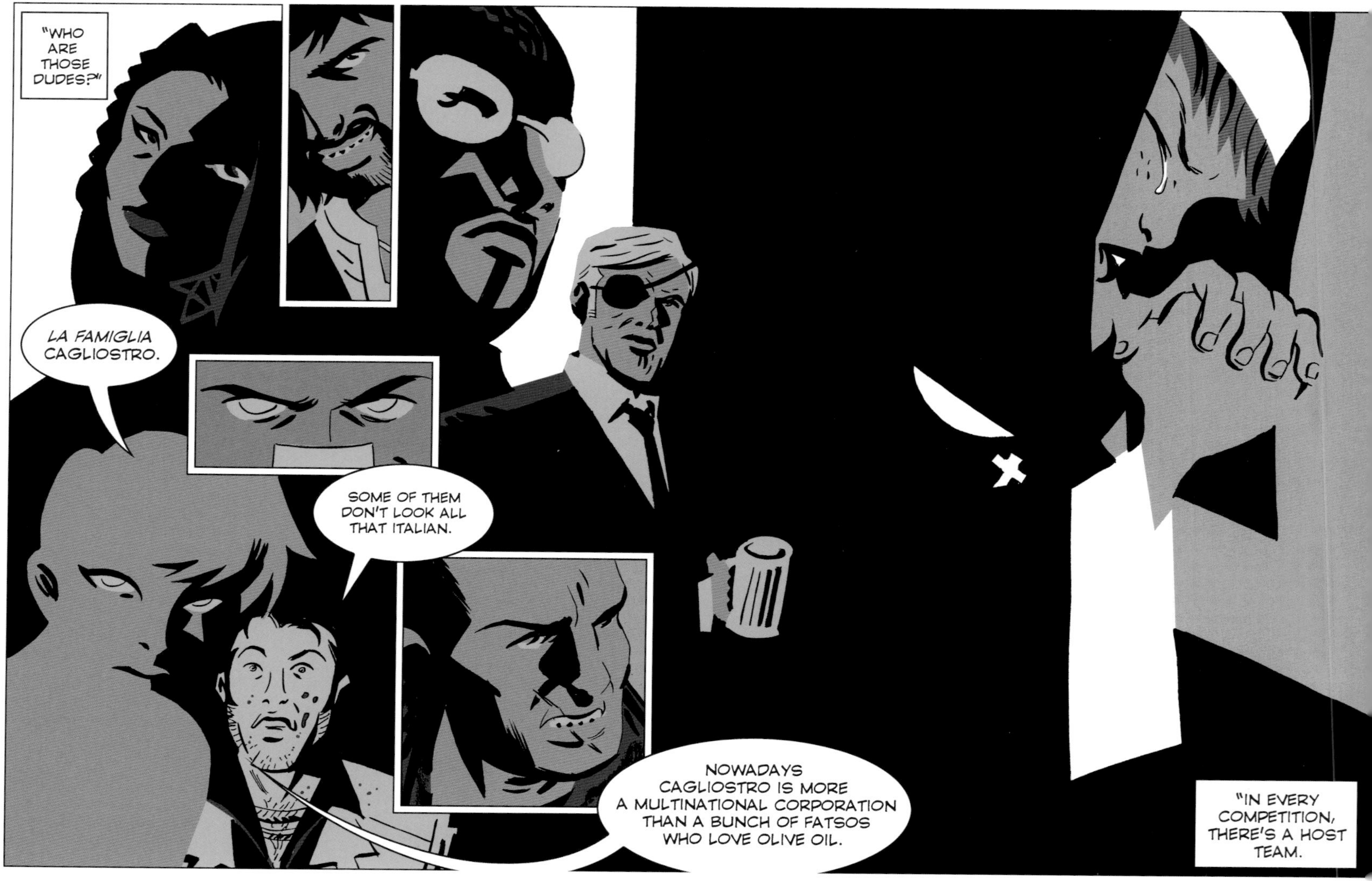
"WHO ARE THOSE DUDES?"
LA FAMIGLIA CAGLIOSTRO.
SOME OF THEM DON'T LOOK ALL THAT ITALIAN.
NOWADAYS CAGLIOSTRO IS MORE A MULTINATIONAL CORPORATION THAN A BUNCH OF FATSOS WHO LOVE OLIVE OIL.
"IN EVERY COMPETITION, THERE'S A HOST TEAM.

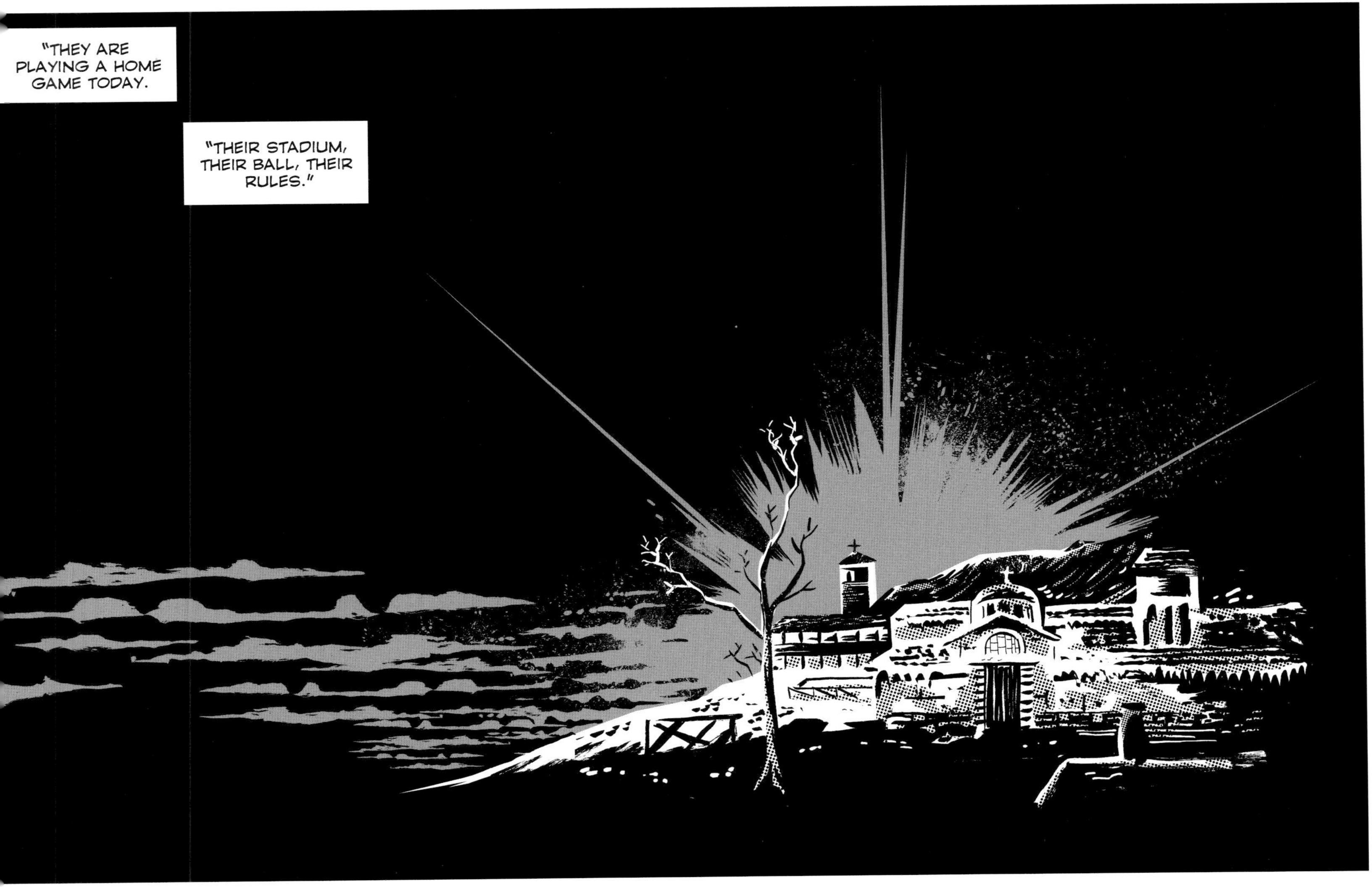
"THEY ARE PLAYING A HOME GAME TODAY.
"THEIR STADIUM, THEIR BALL, THEIR RULES."

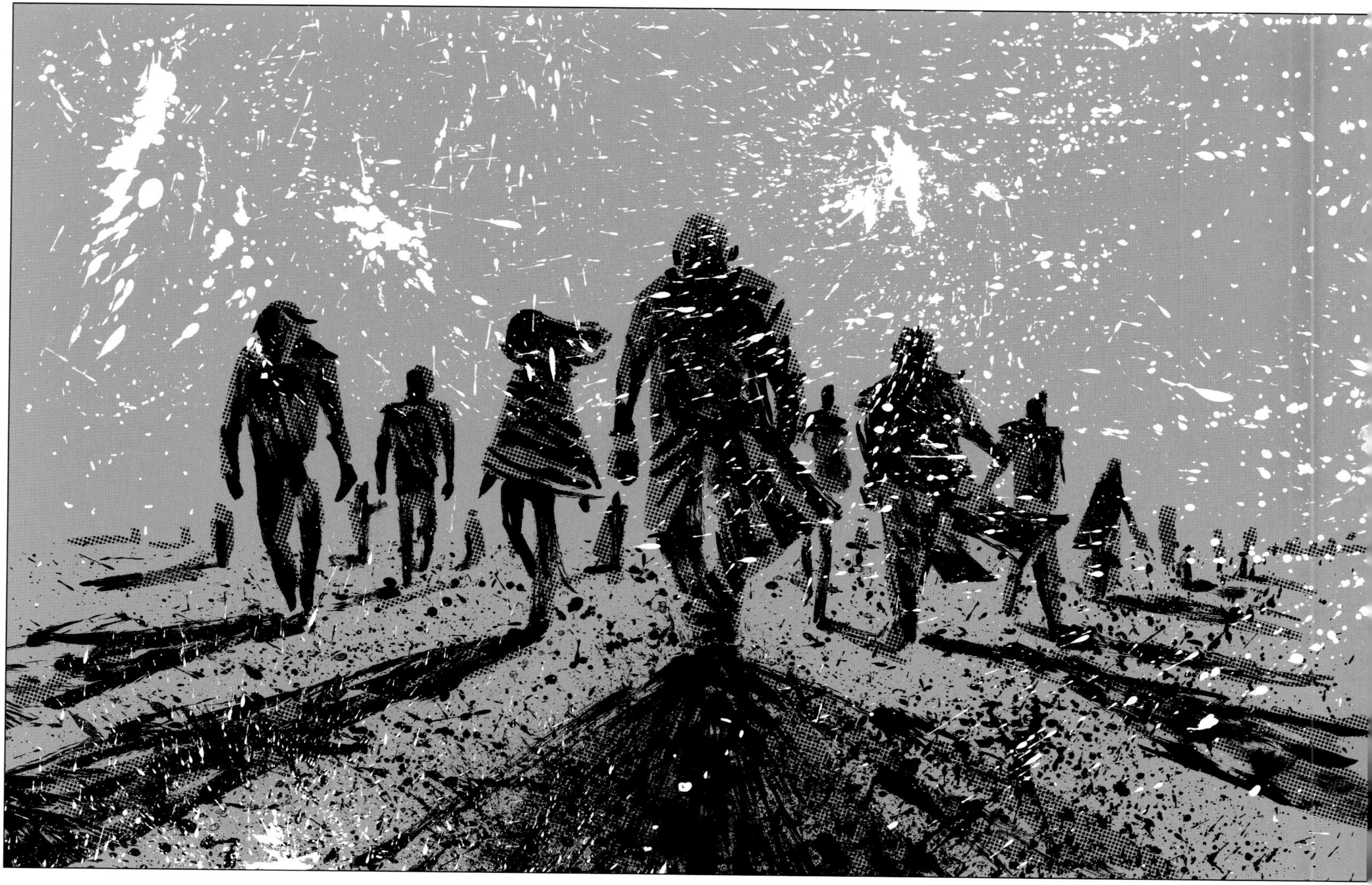

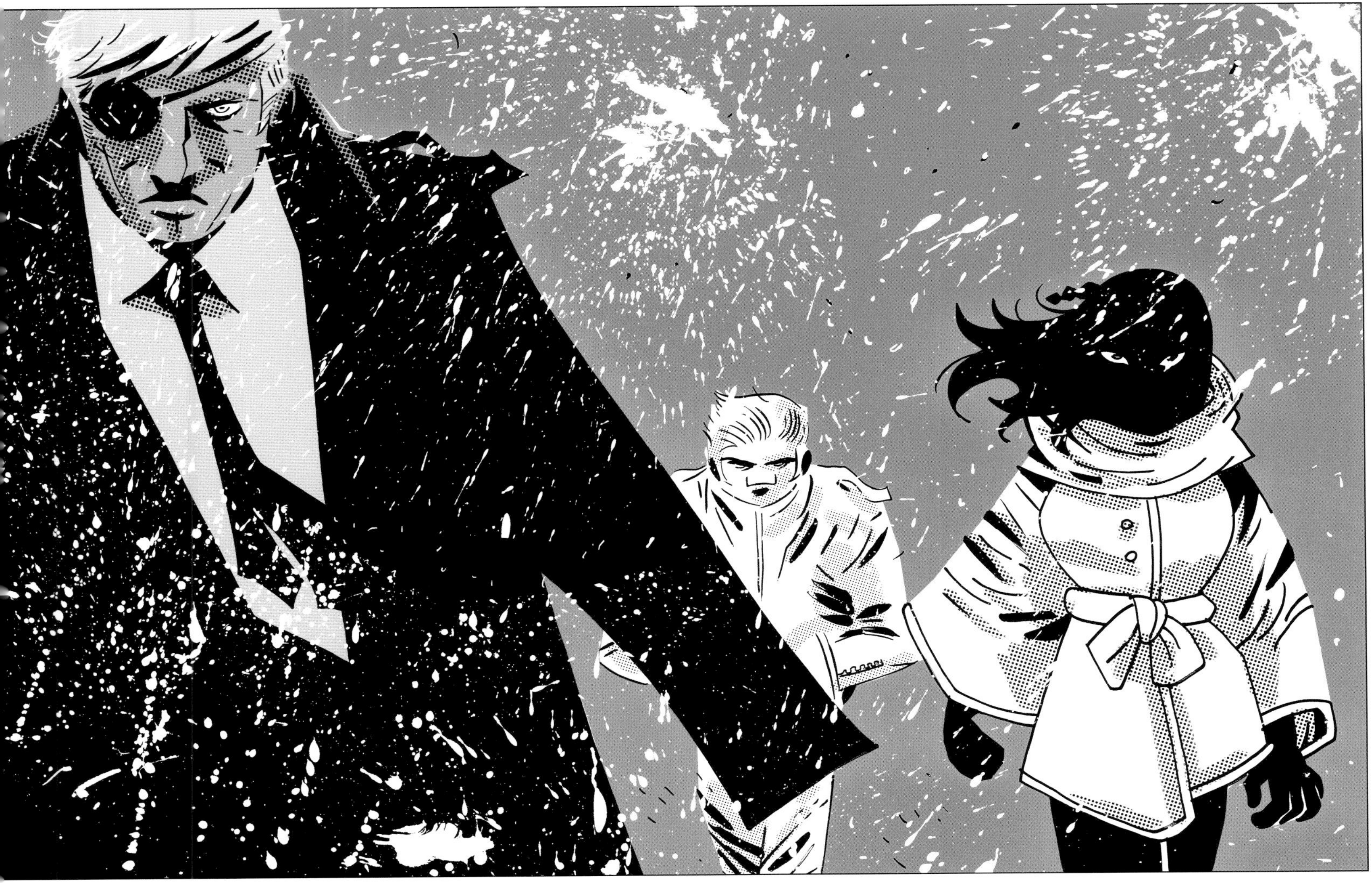

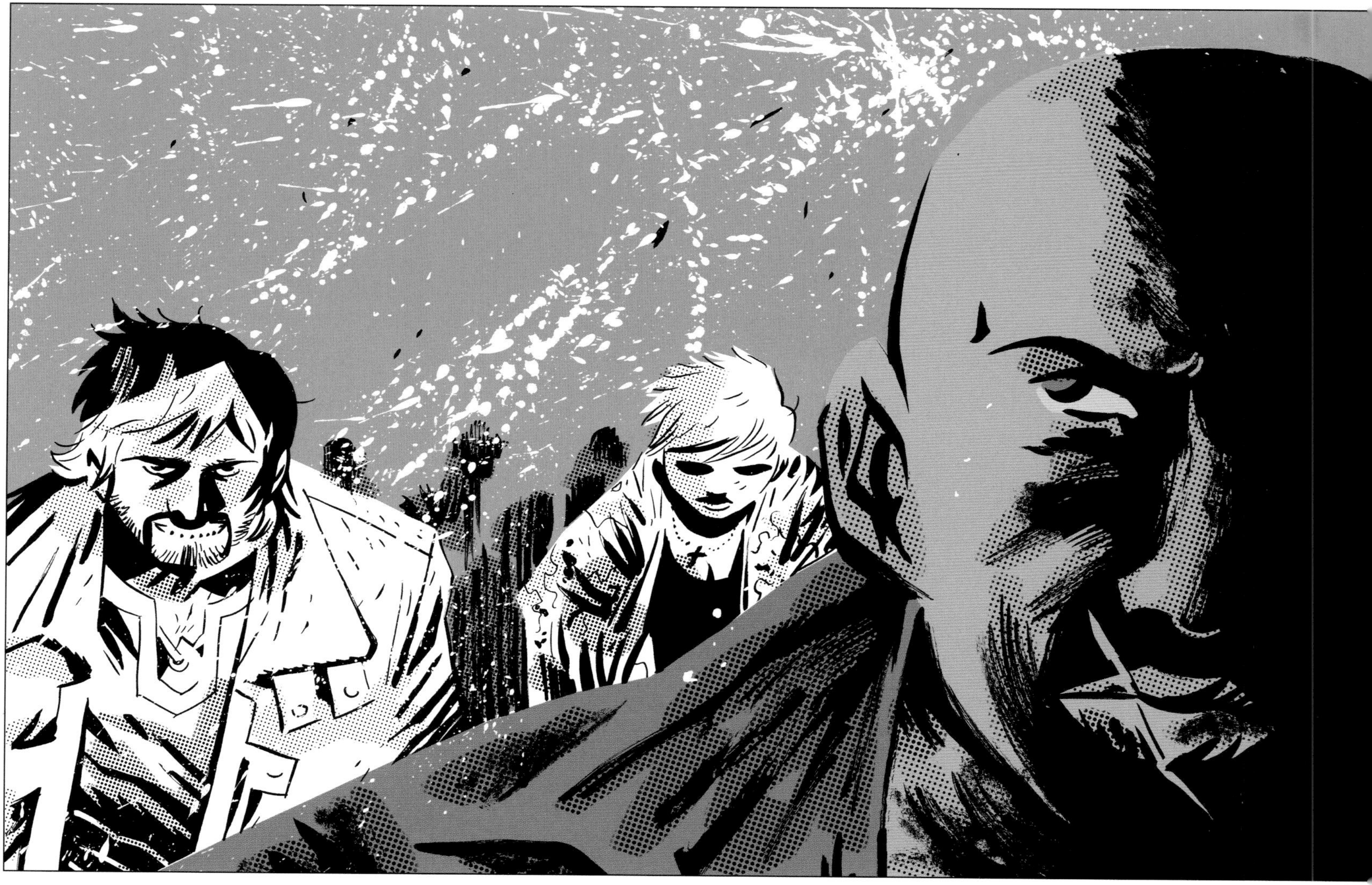

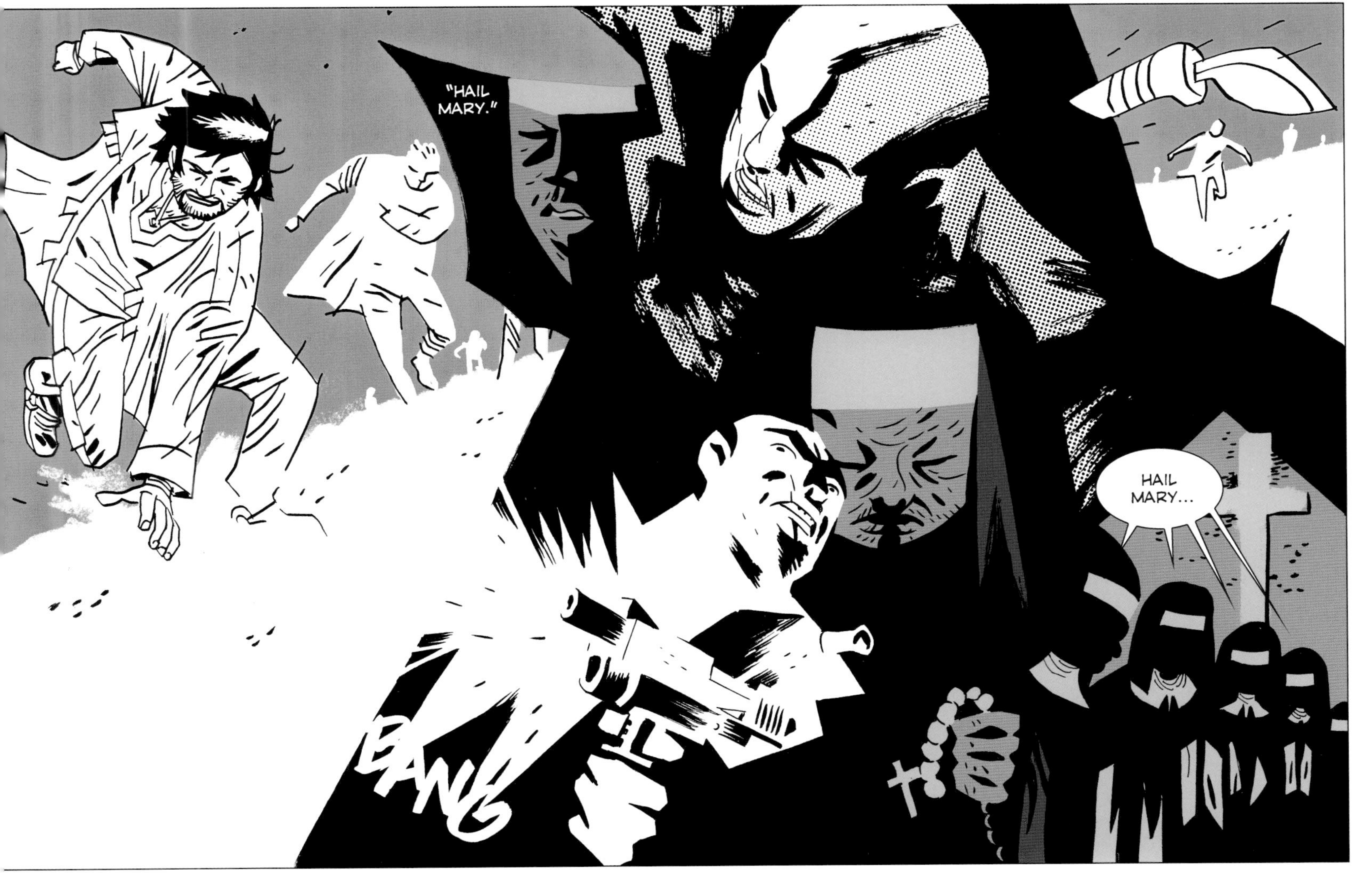

"HAIL MARY."
HAIL MARY...
BANG

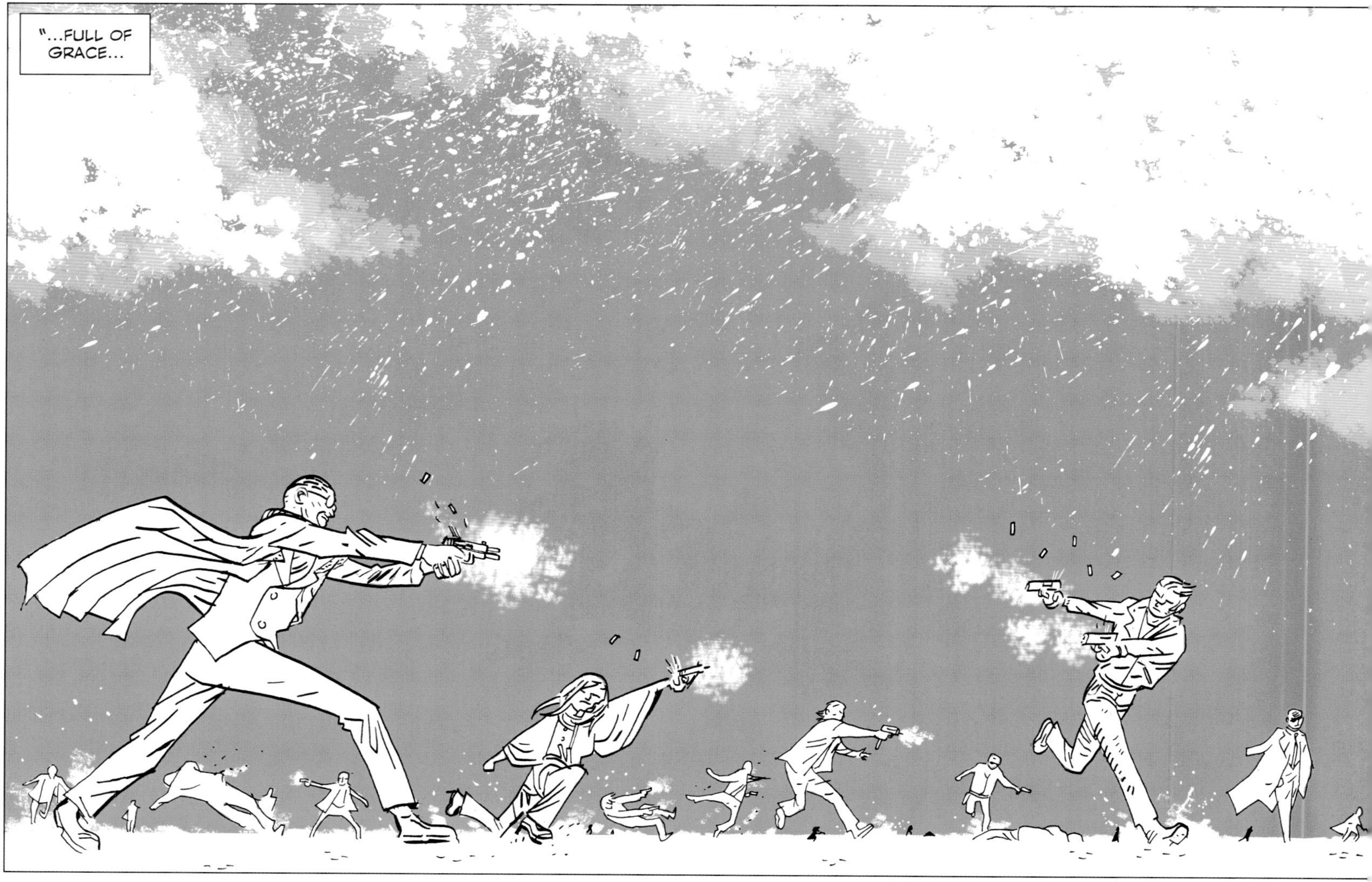
"...FULL OF
GRACE...

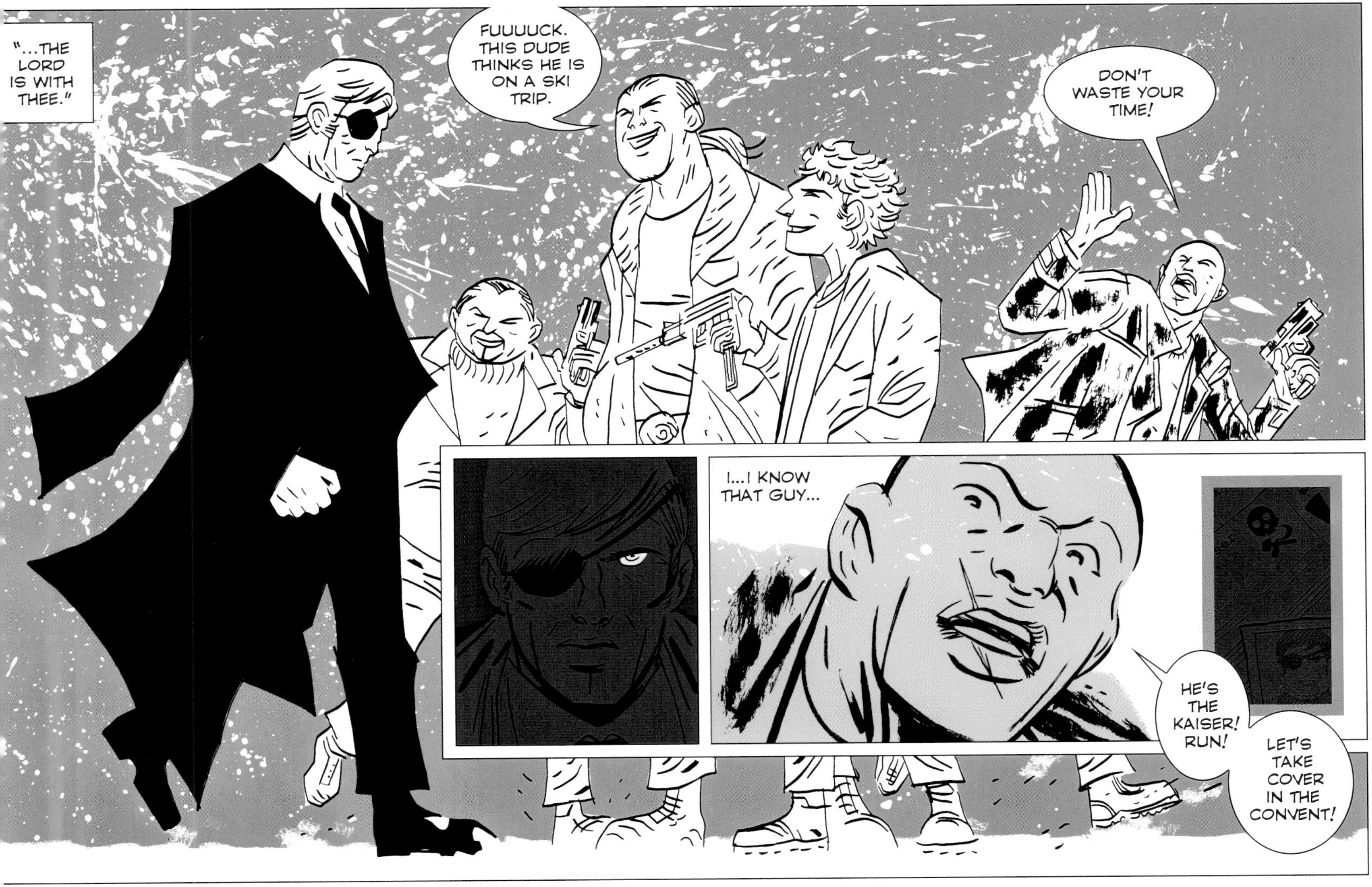
"...THE LORD IS WITH THEE."
FUUUUCK. THIS DUDE THINKS HE IS ON A SKI TRIP.
DON'T WASTE YOUR TIME!
I...I KNOW THAT GUY...
HE'S THE KAISER! RUN!
LET'S TAKE COVER IN THE CONVENT!

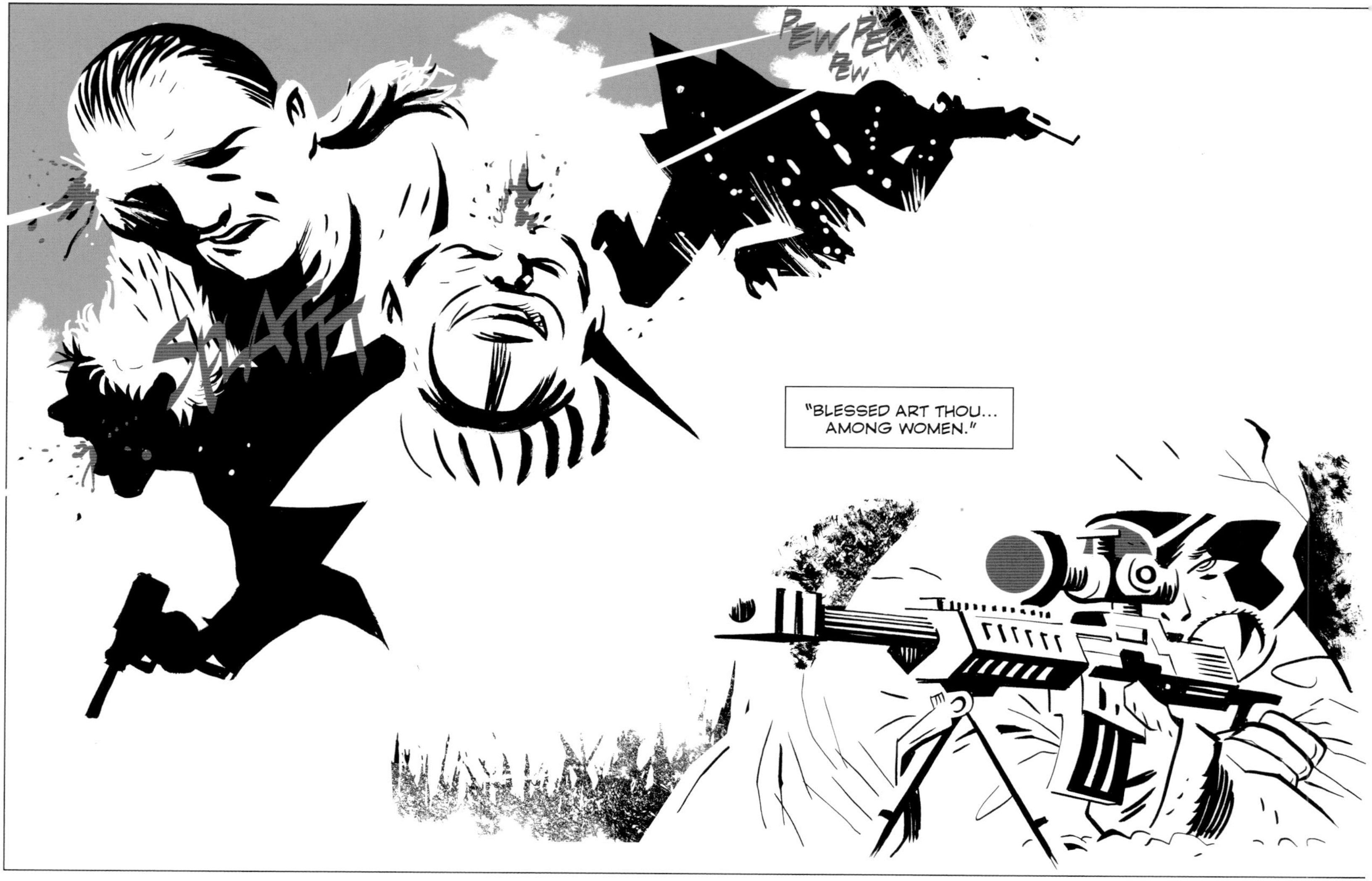
PEW PEW
PEW
SPLATT
"BLESSED ART THOU...
AMONG WOMEN."

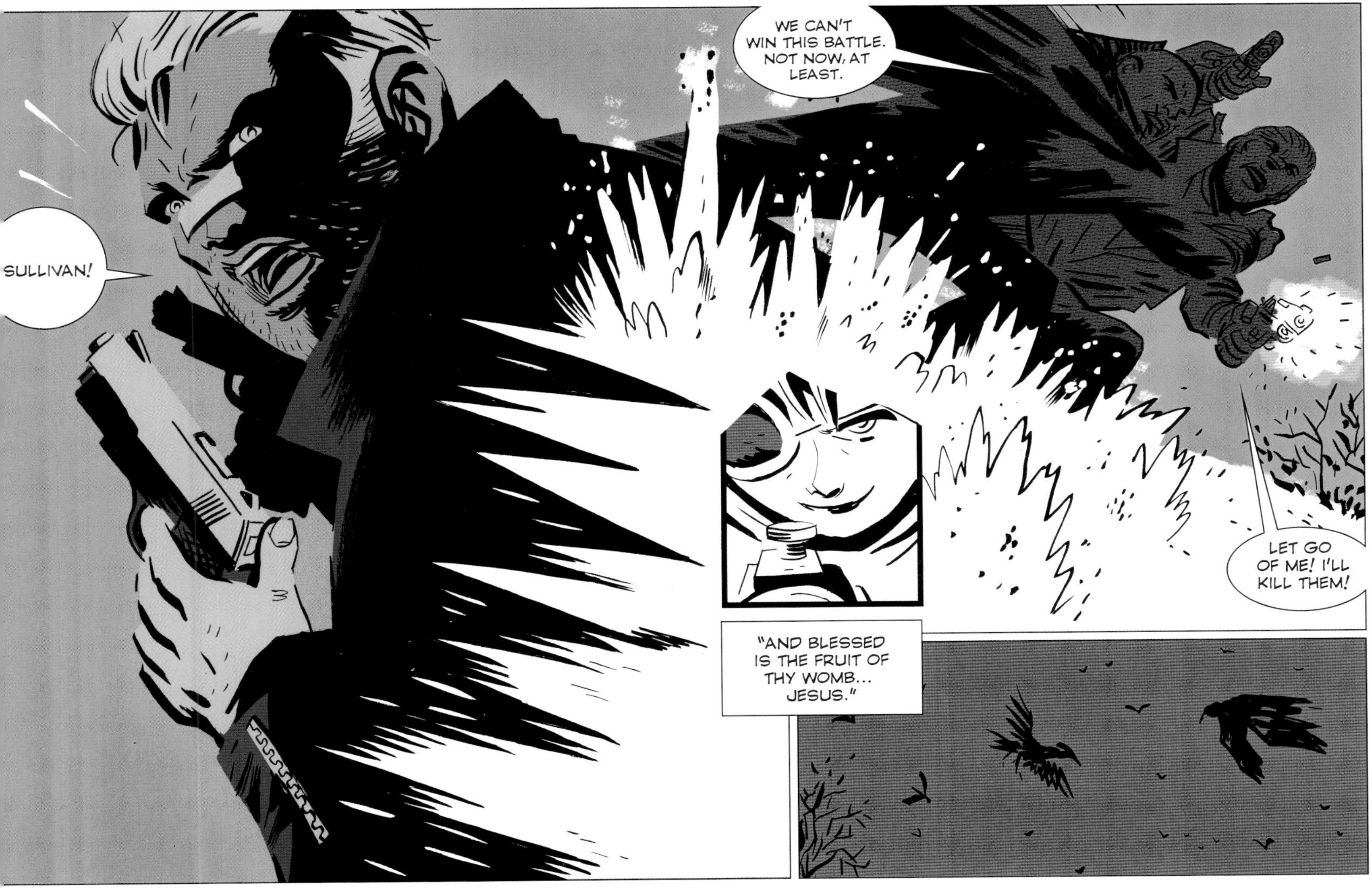
SULLIVAN!
WE CAN'T WIN THIS BATTLE. NOT NOW, AT LEAST.
LET GO OF ME! I'LL KILL THEM!
"AND BLESSED IS THE FRUIT OF THY WOMB... JESUS."

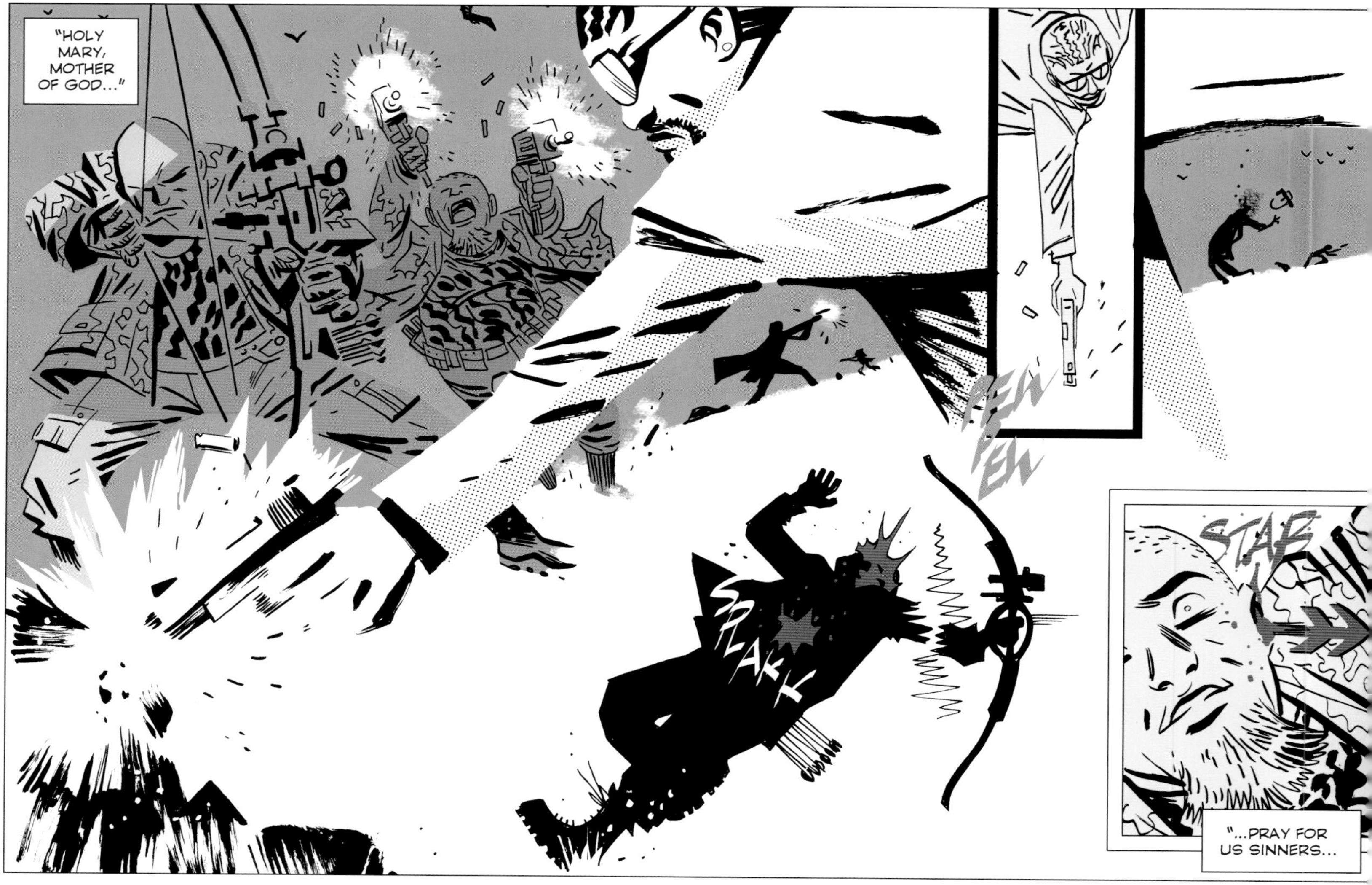
"HOLY MARY, MOTHER OF GOD..."
PEW PEW PEW
SPLAK
STAB
"...PRAY FOR US SINNERS...

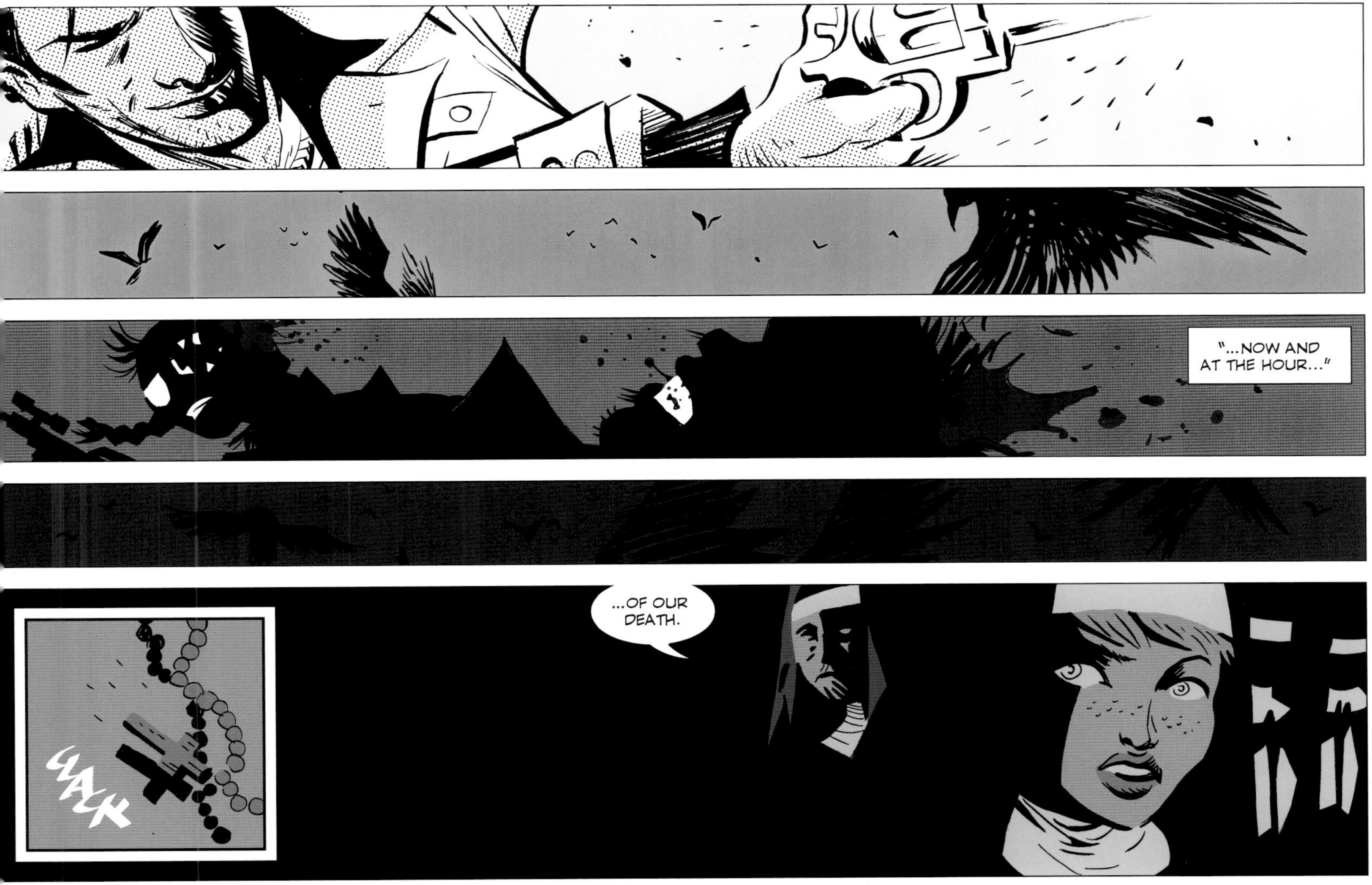
"...NOW AND AT THE HOUR..."
WACK
...OF OUR DEATH.

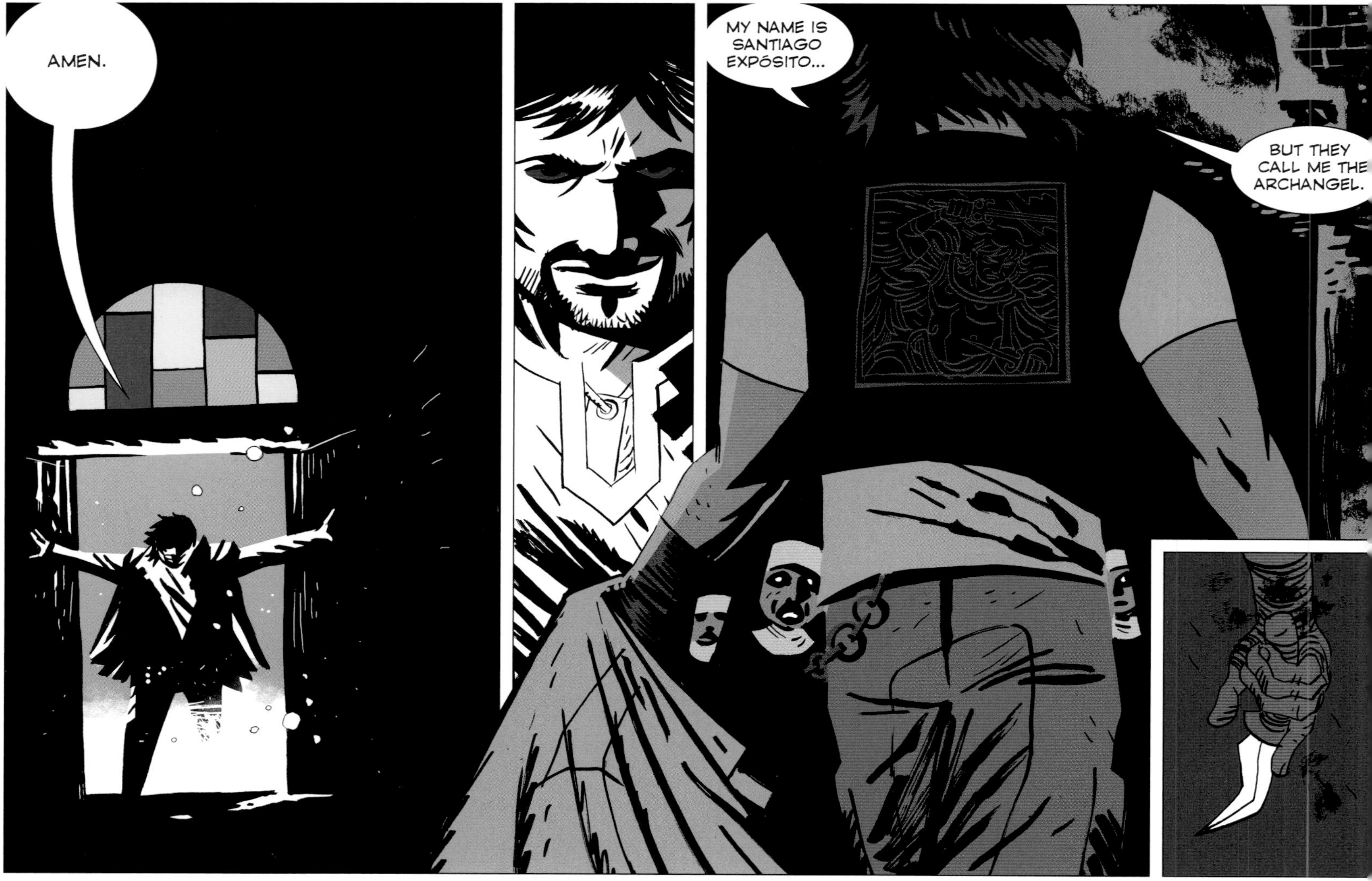
AMEN.
MY NAME IS SANTIAGO EXPÓSITO...
BUT THEY CALL ME THE ARCHANGEL.

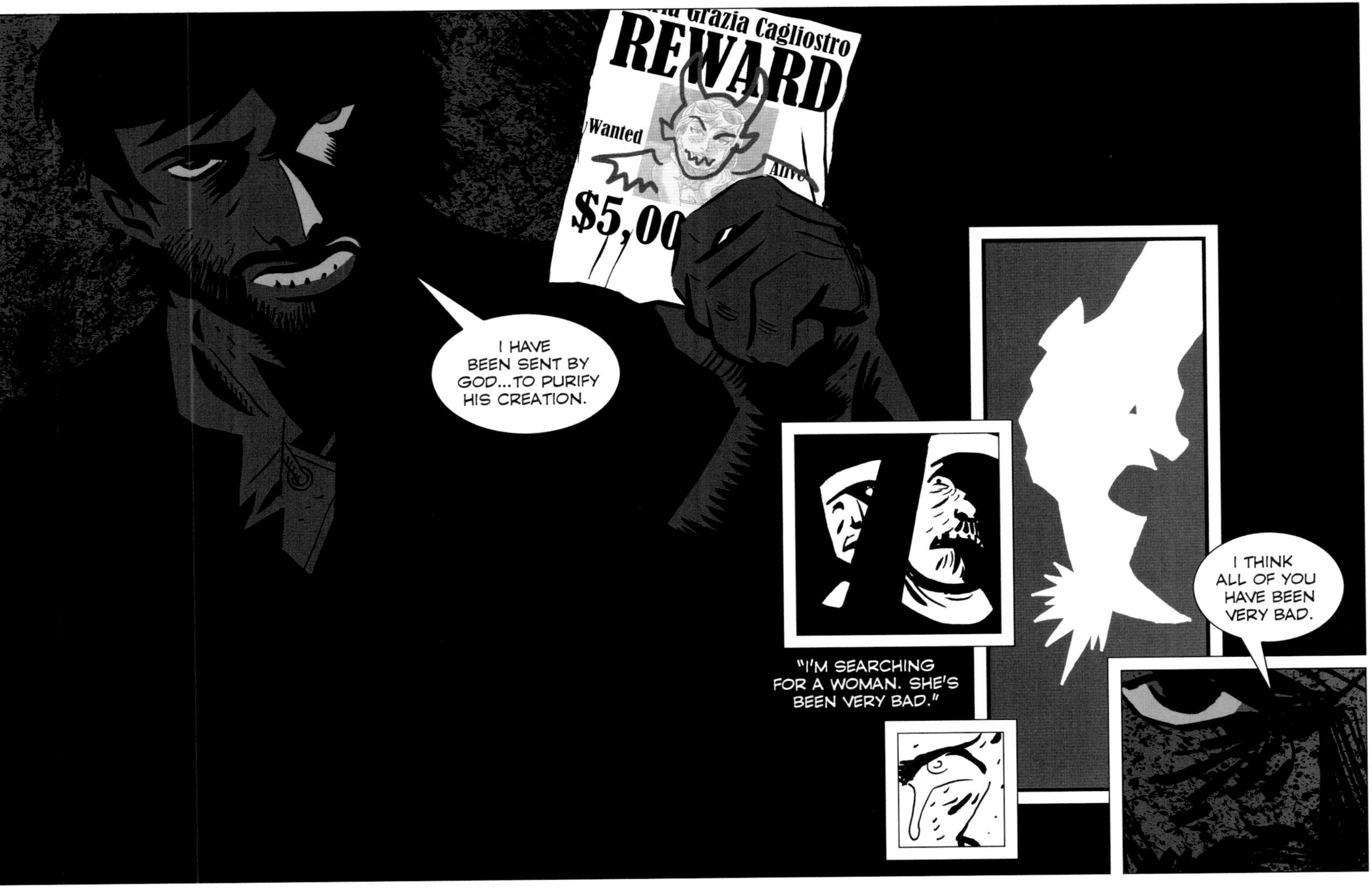
Grazia Cagliostro
REWARD
Wanted
Alive
$5,00
I HAVE BEEN SENT BY GOD...TO PURIFY HIS CREATION.
"I'M SEARCHING FOR A WOMAN. SHE'S BEEN VERY BAD."
I THINK ALL OF YOU HAVE BEEN VERY BAD.

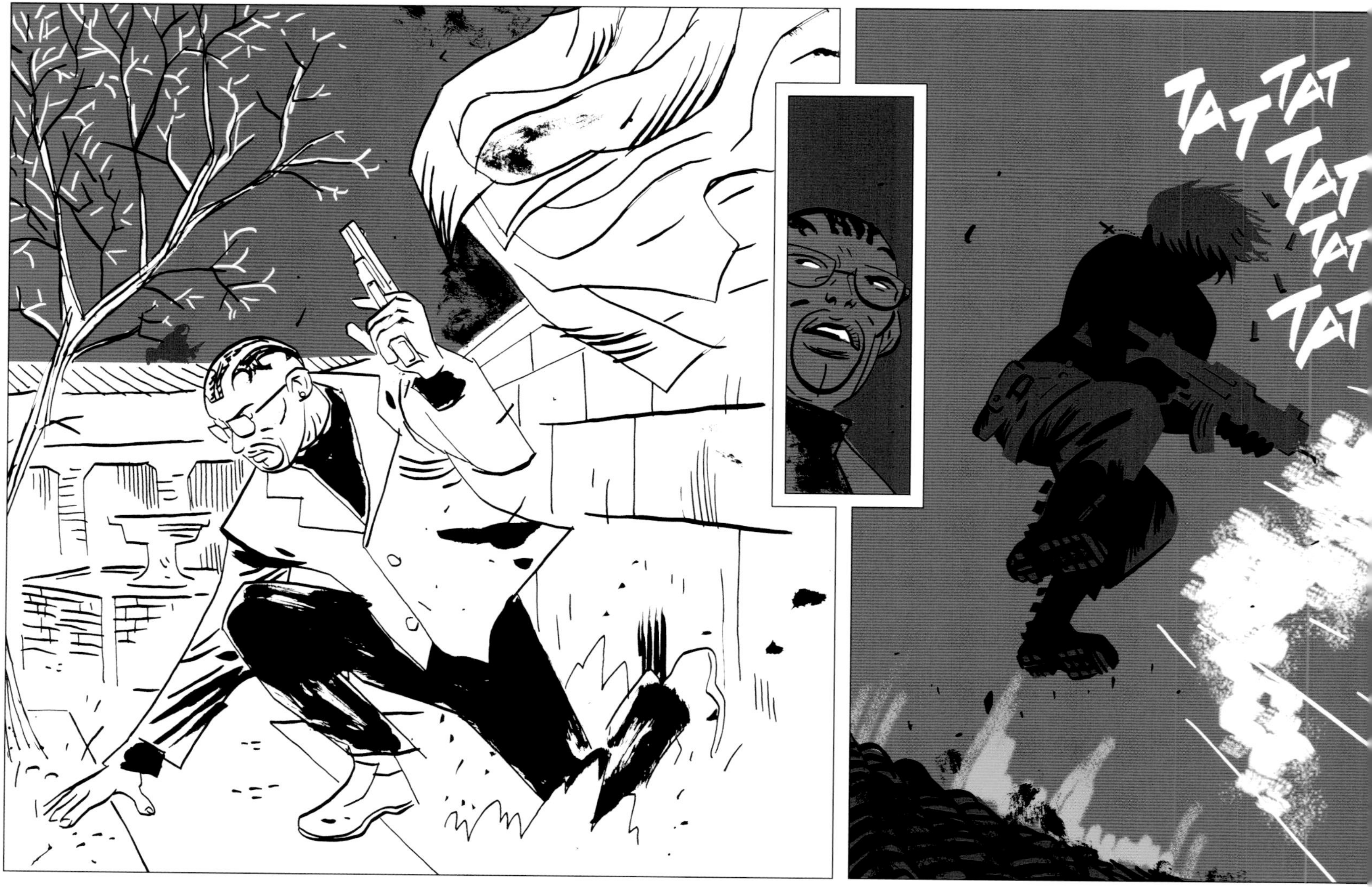
TAT TAT TAT TAT TAT TAT

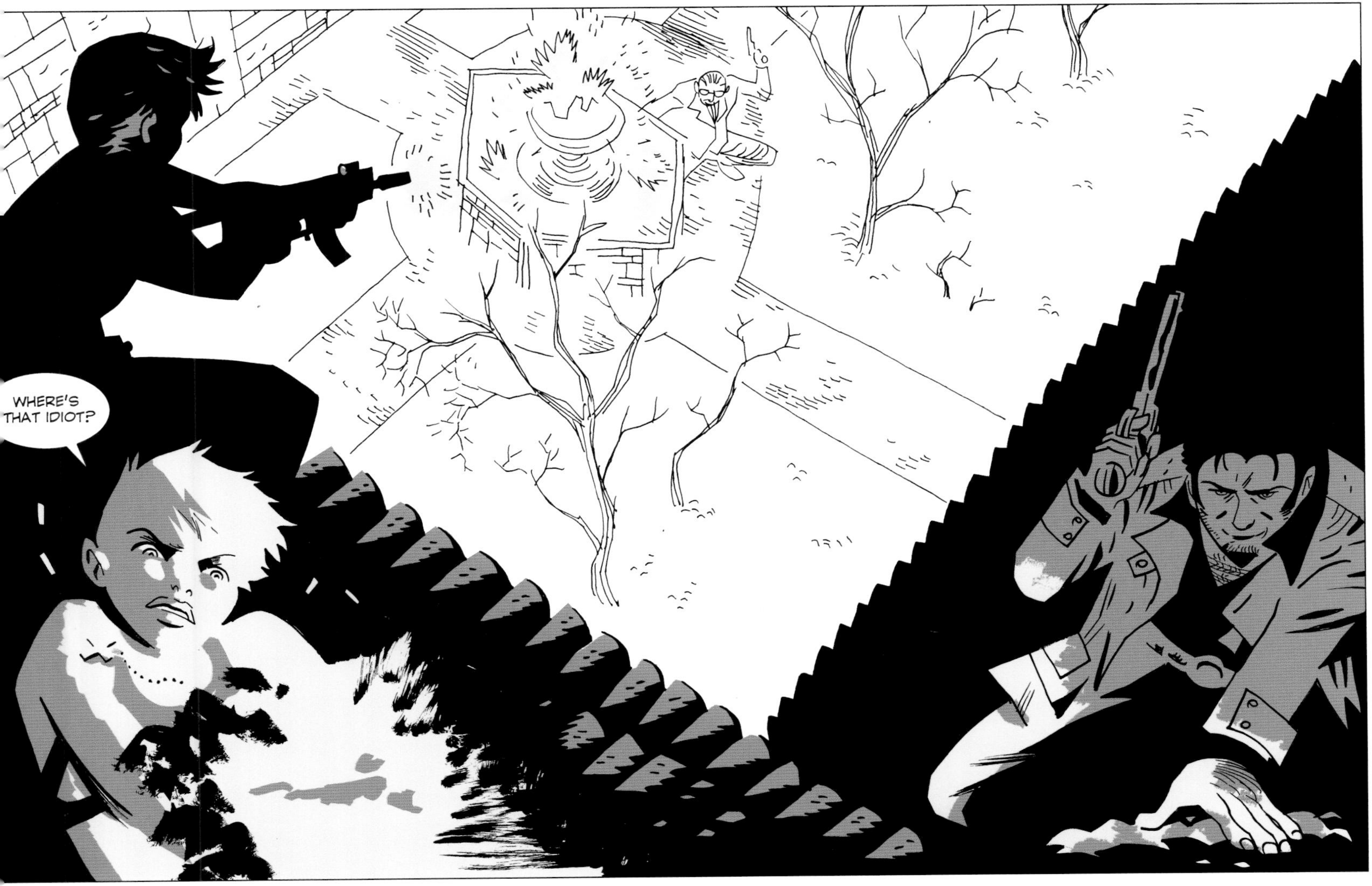
WHERE'S THAT IDIOT?

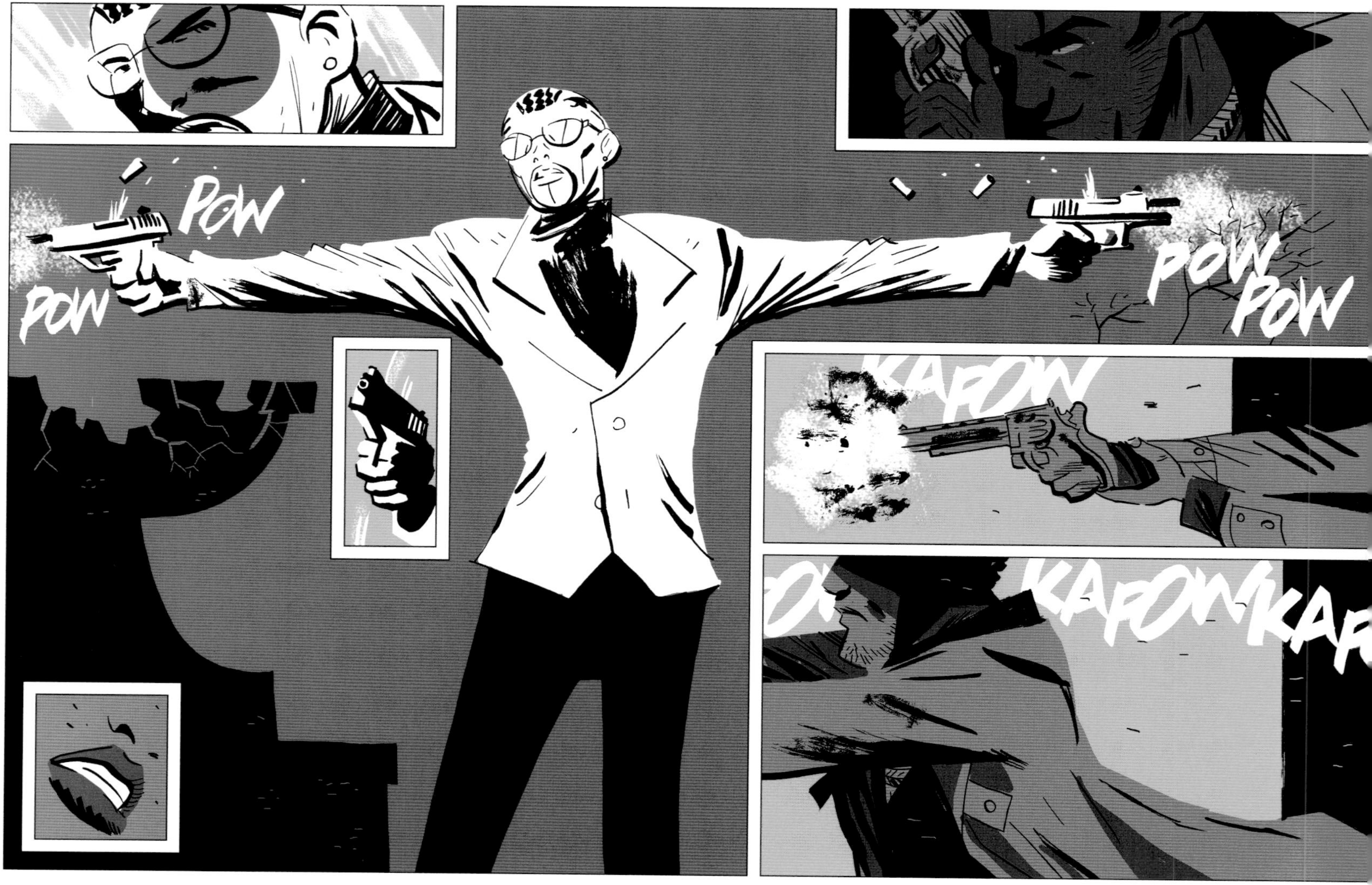
POW
POW
POW
POW
KAPOW
KAPOW
KAP

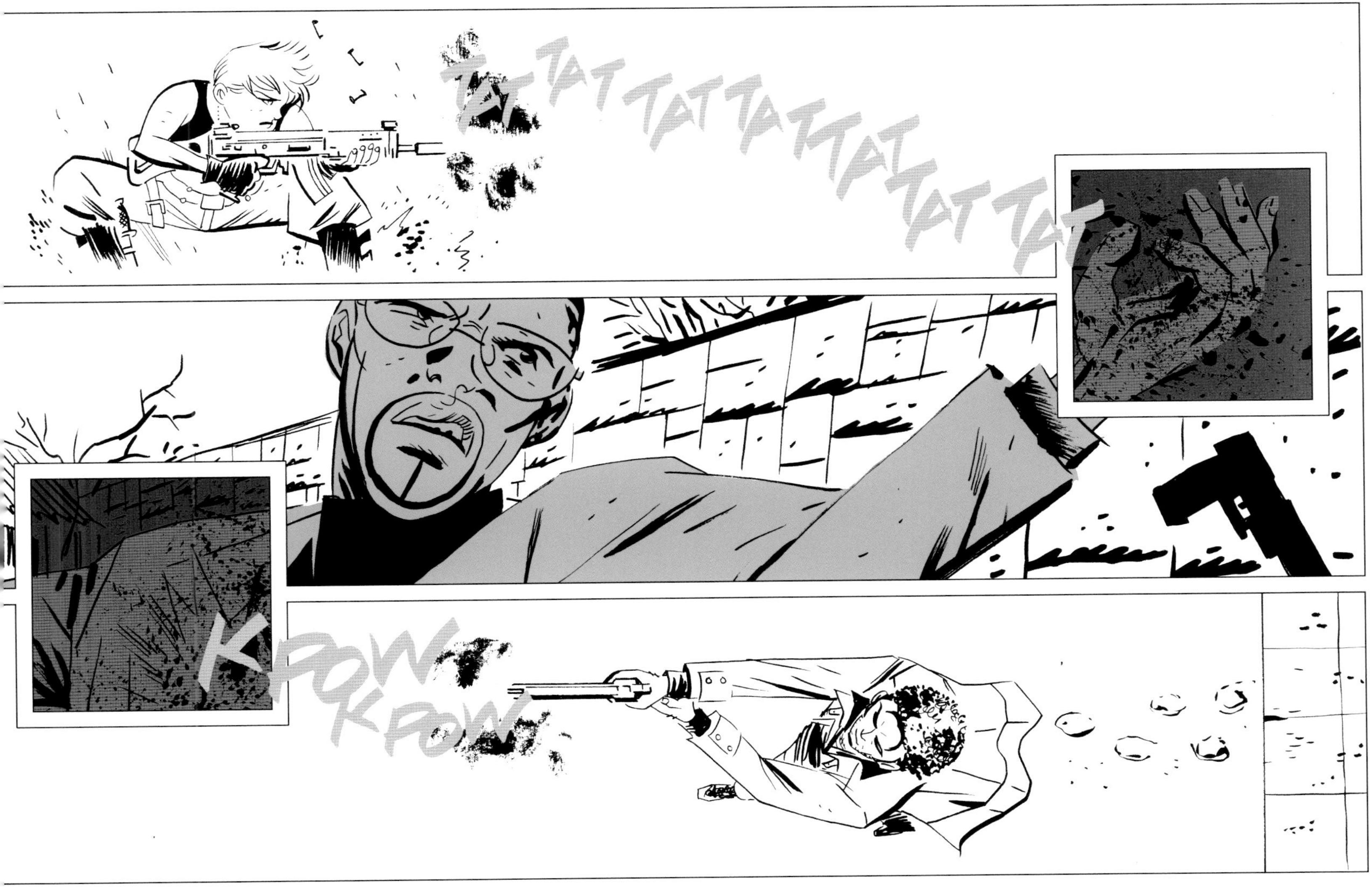
TAT TAT TAT TAT TAT TAT TAT TAT
KPOW
KPOW

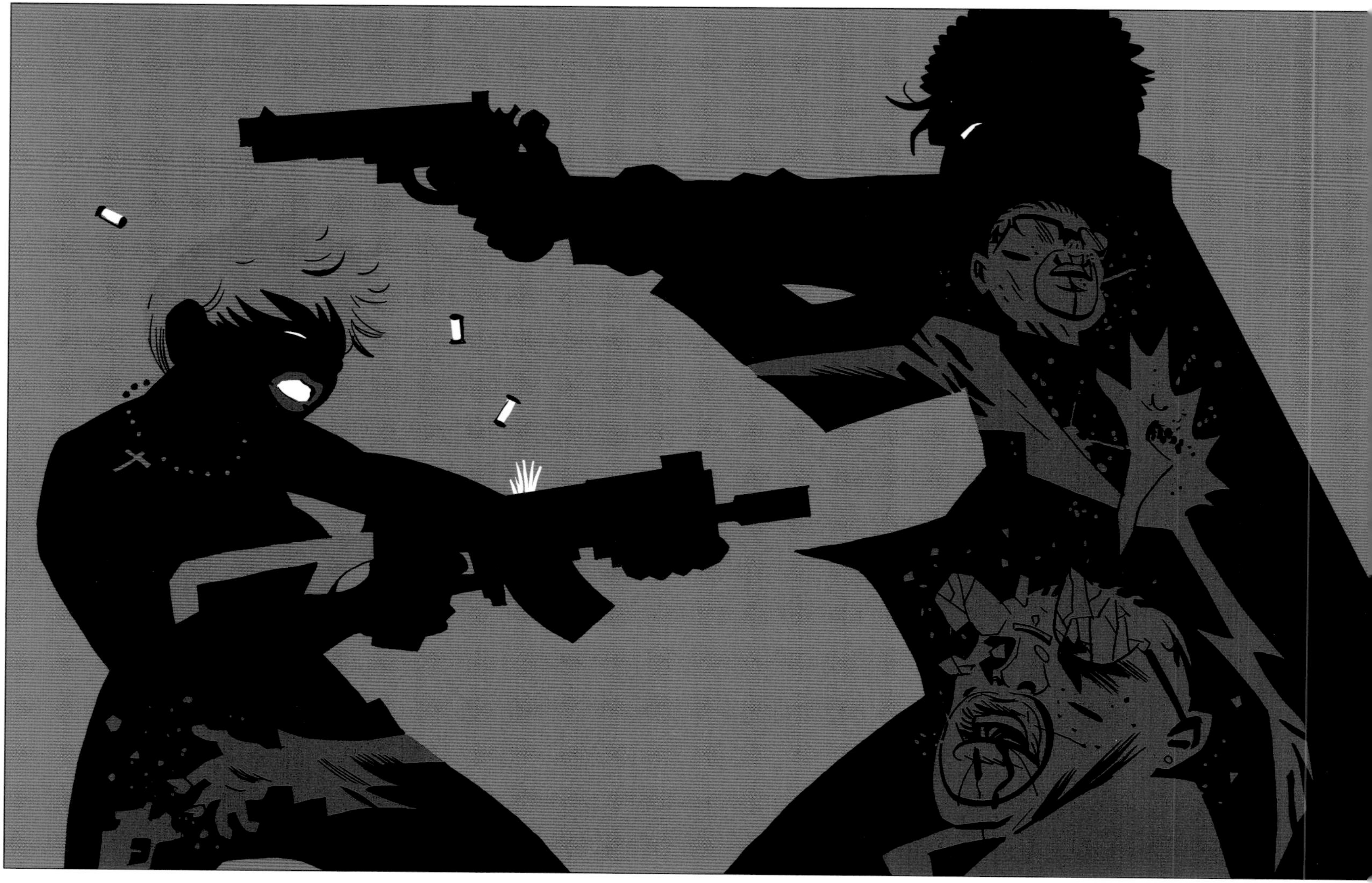

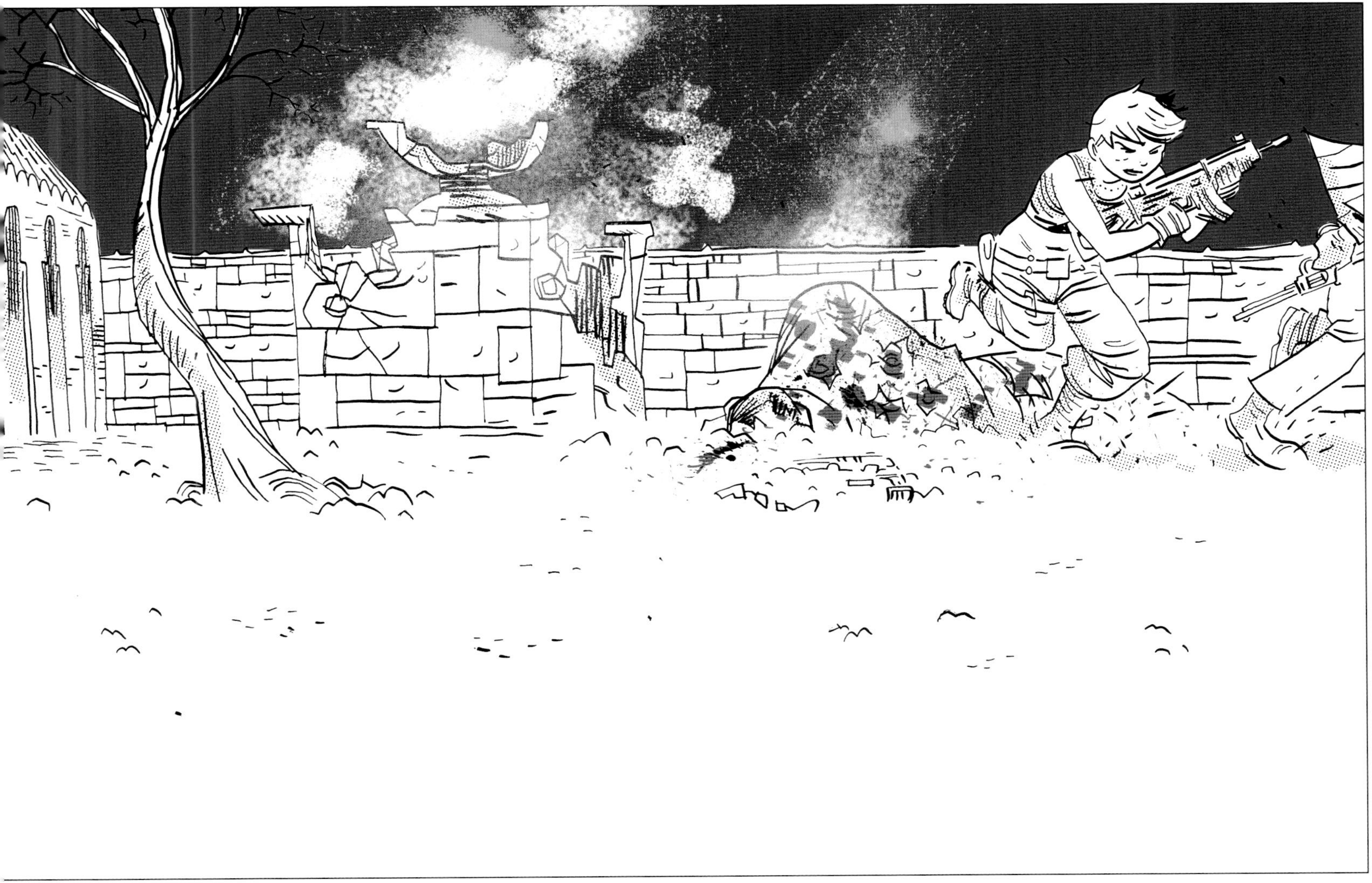

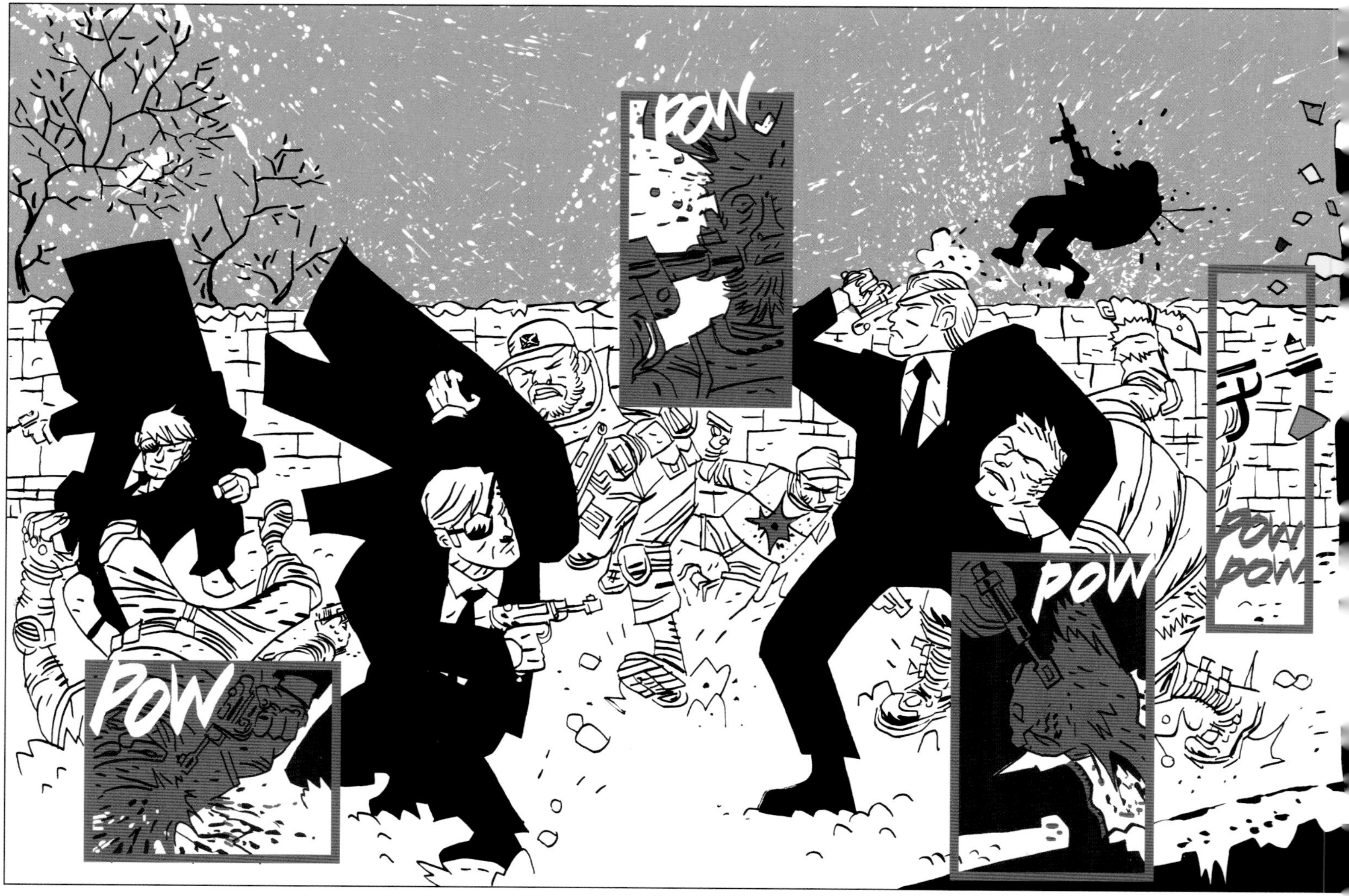
POW
POW
POW
POW POW

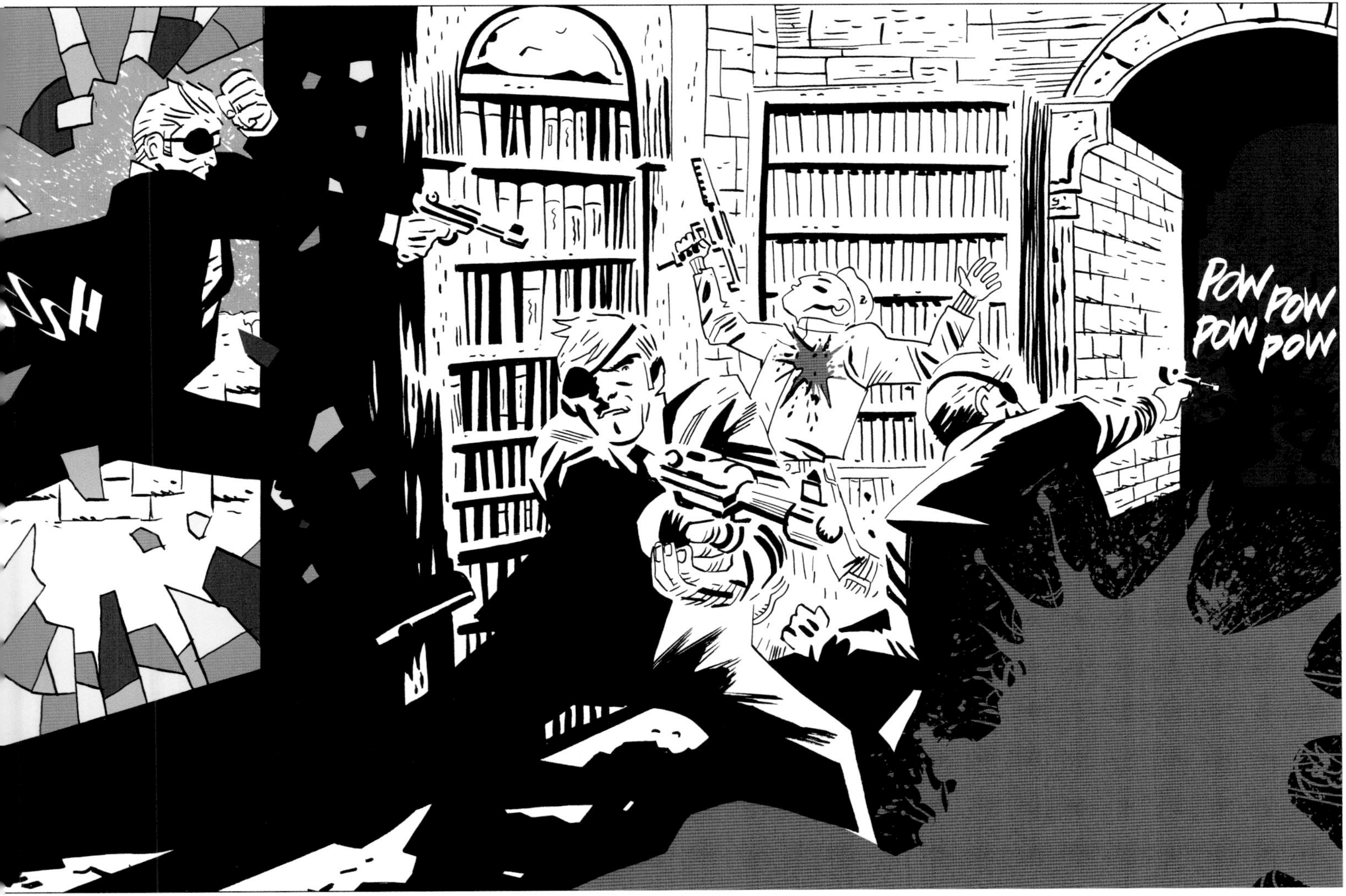
POW POW
POW POW

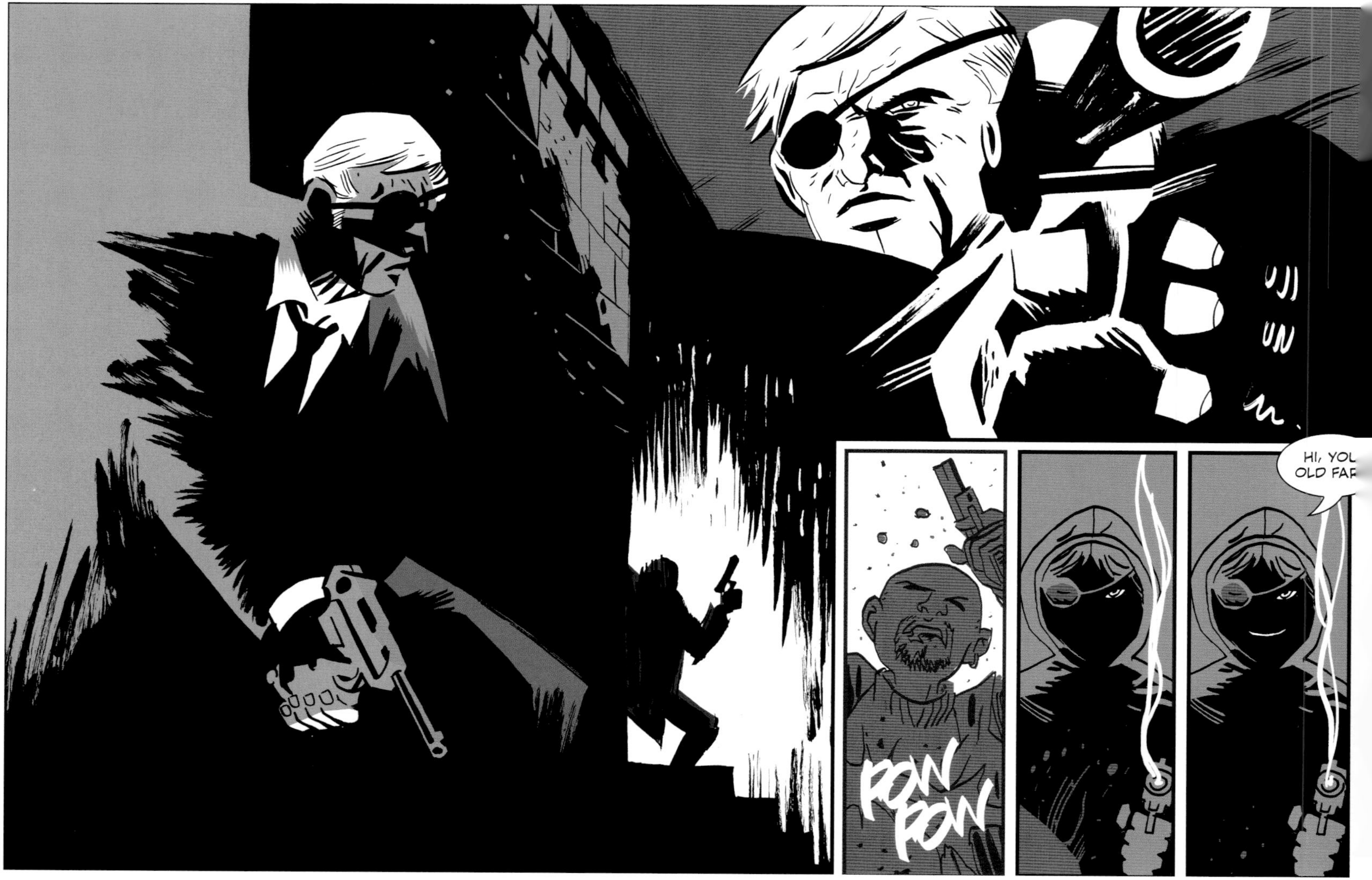
POW POW
HI, YOU OLD FAR

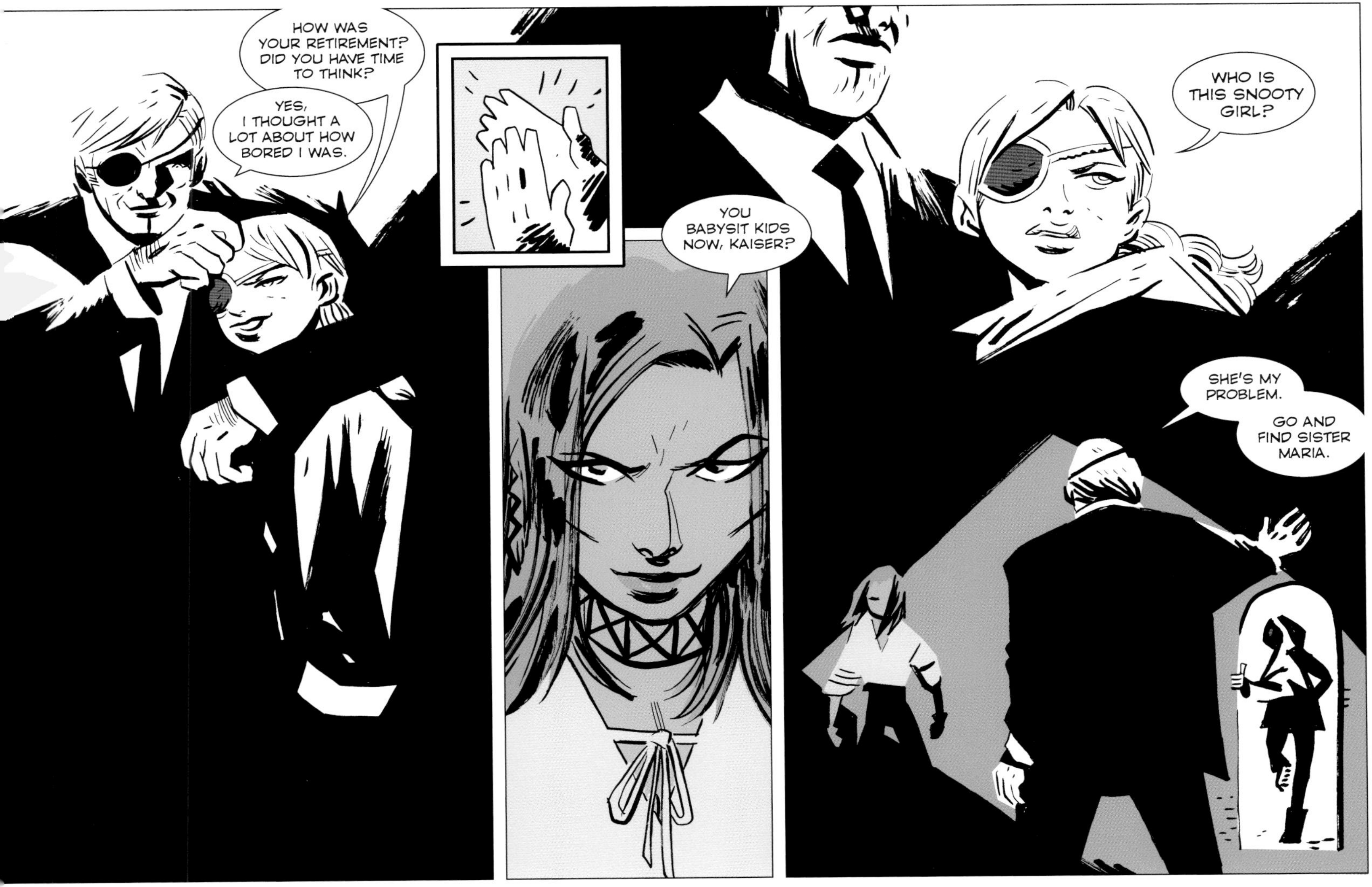
HOW WAS YOUR RETIREMENT? DID YOU HAVE TIME TO THINK?
YES, I THOUGHT A LOT ABOUT HOW BORED I WAS.
YOU BABYSIT KIDS NOW, KAISER?
WHO IS THIS SNOOTY GIRL?
SHE'S MY PROBLEM.
GO AND FIND SISTER MARIA.

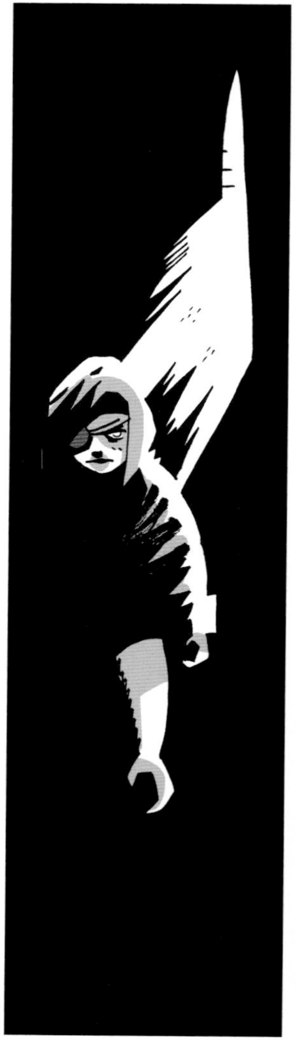

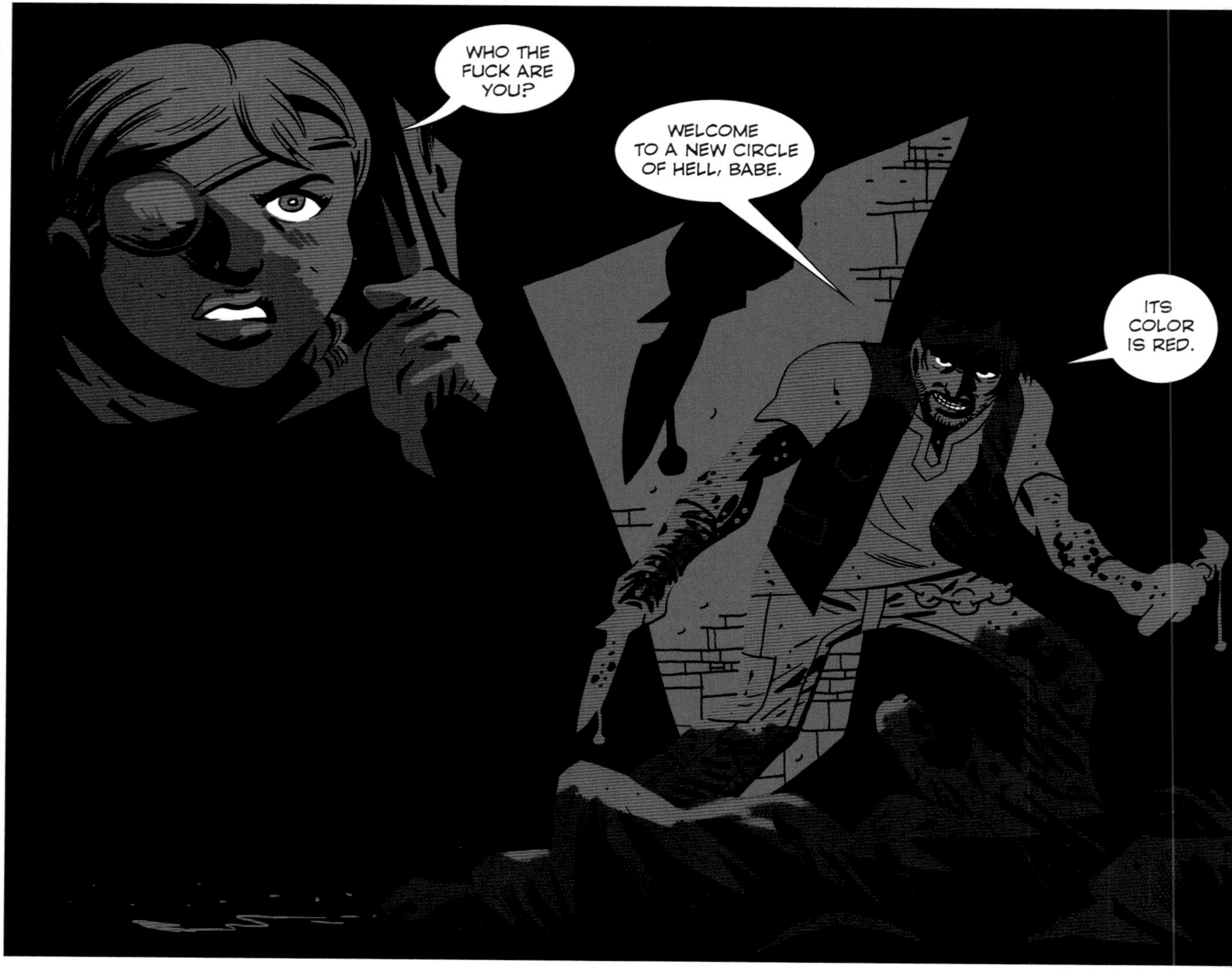
WHO THE FUCK ARE YOU?
WELCOME TO A NEW CIRCLE OF HELL, BABE.
ITS COLOR IS RED.

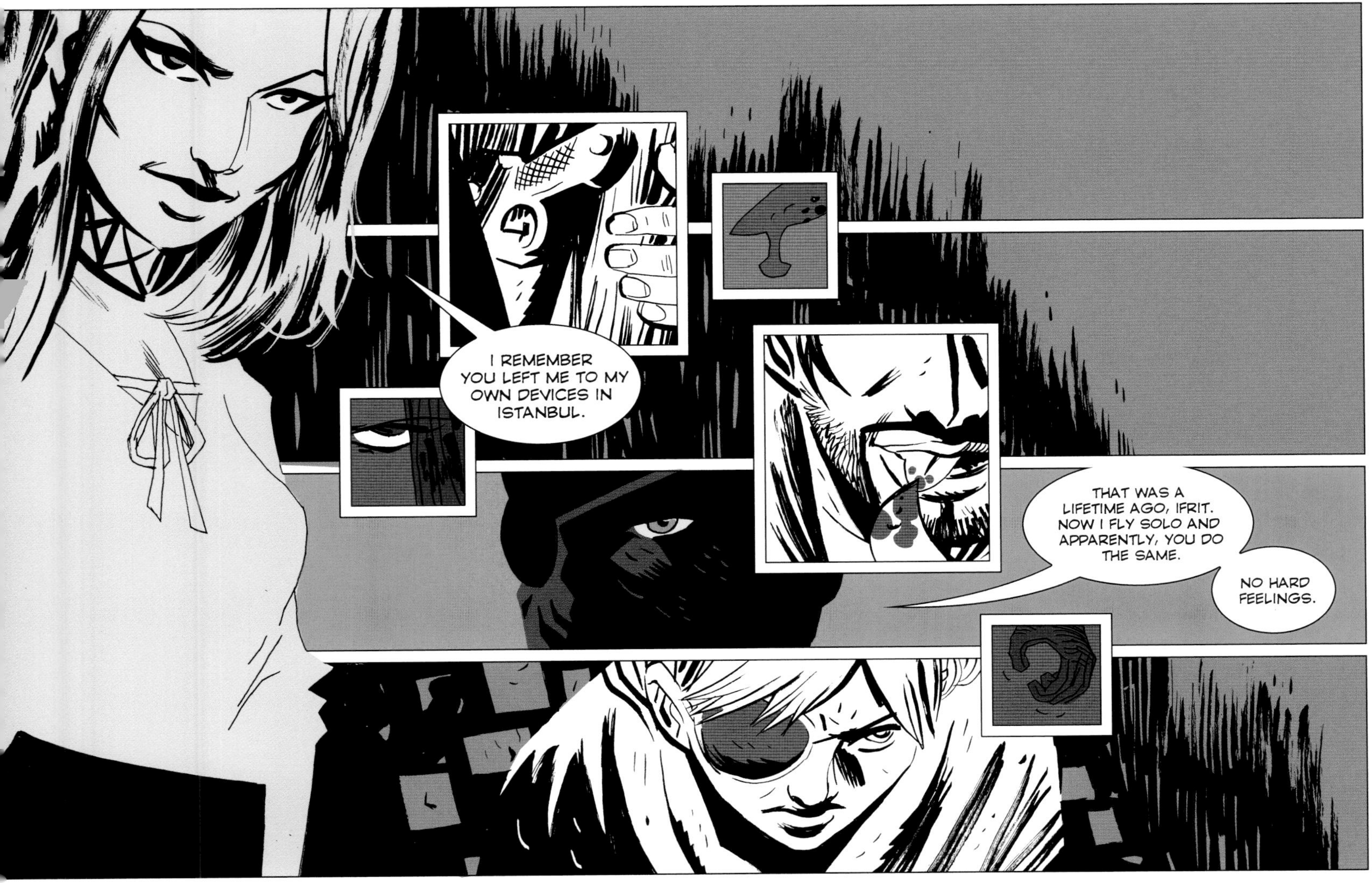
I REMEMBER YOU LEFT ME TO MY OWN DEVICES IN ISTANBUL.
THAT WAS A LIFETIME AGO, IFRIT. NOW I FLY SOLO AND APPARENTLY, YOU DO THE SAME.
NO HARD FEELINGS.

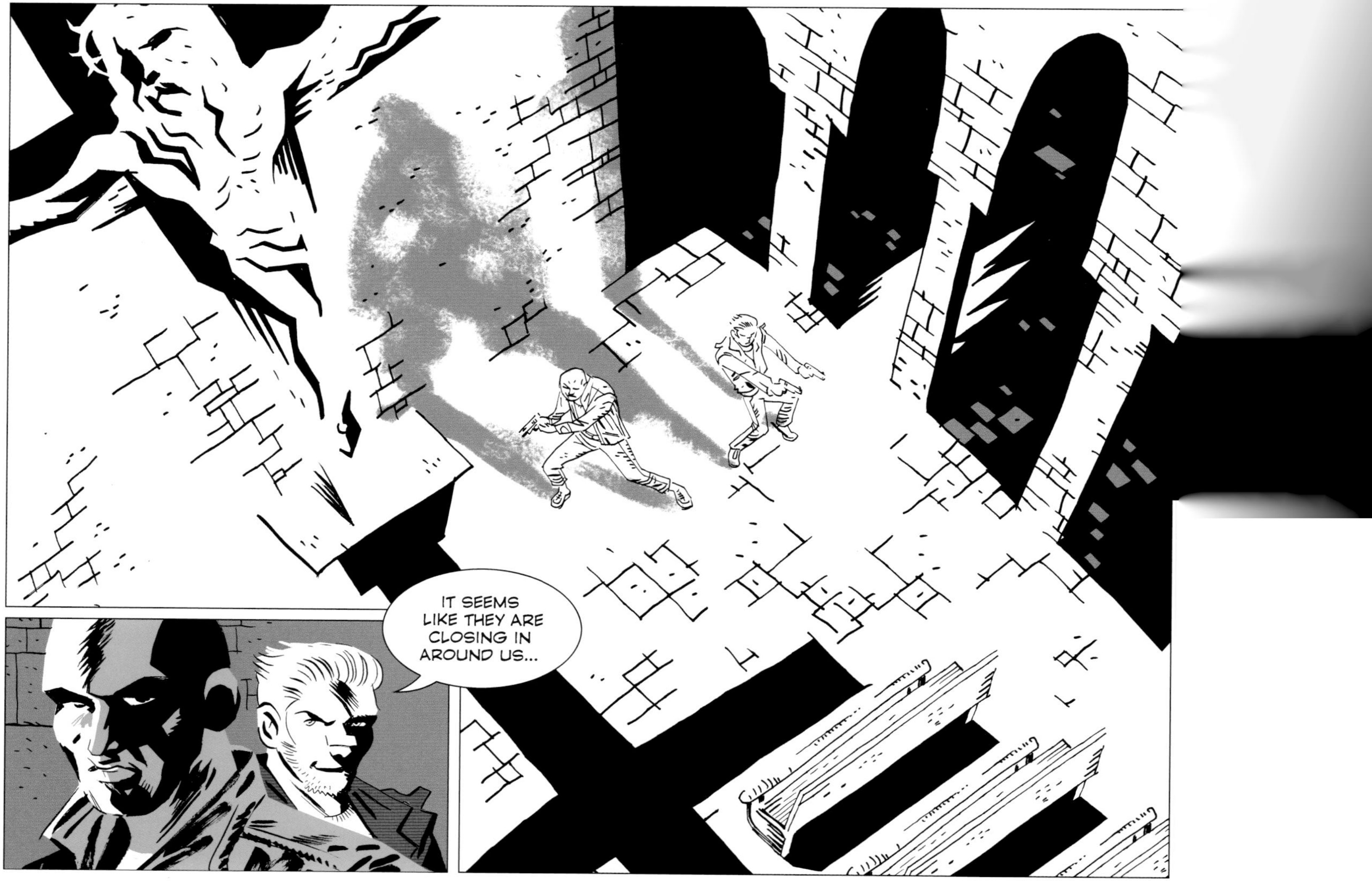
IT SEEMS LIKE THEY ARE CLOSING IN AROUND US...

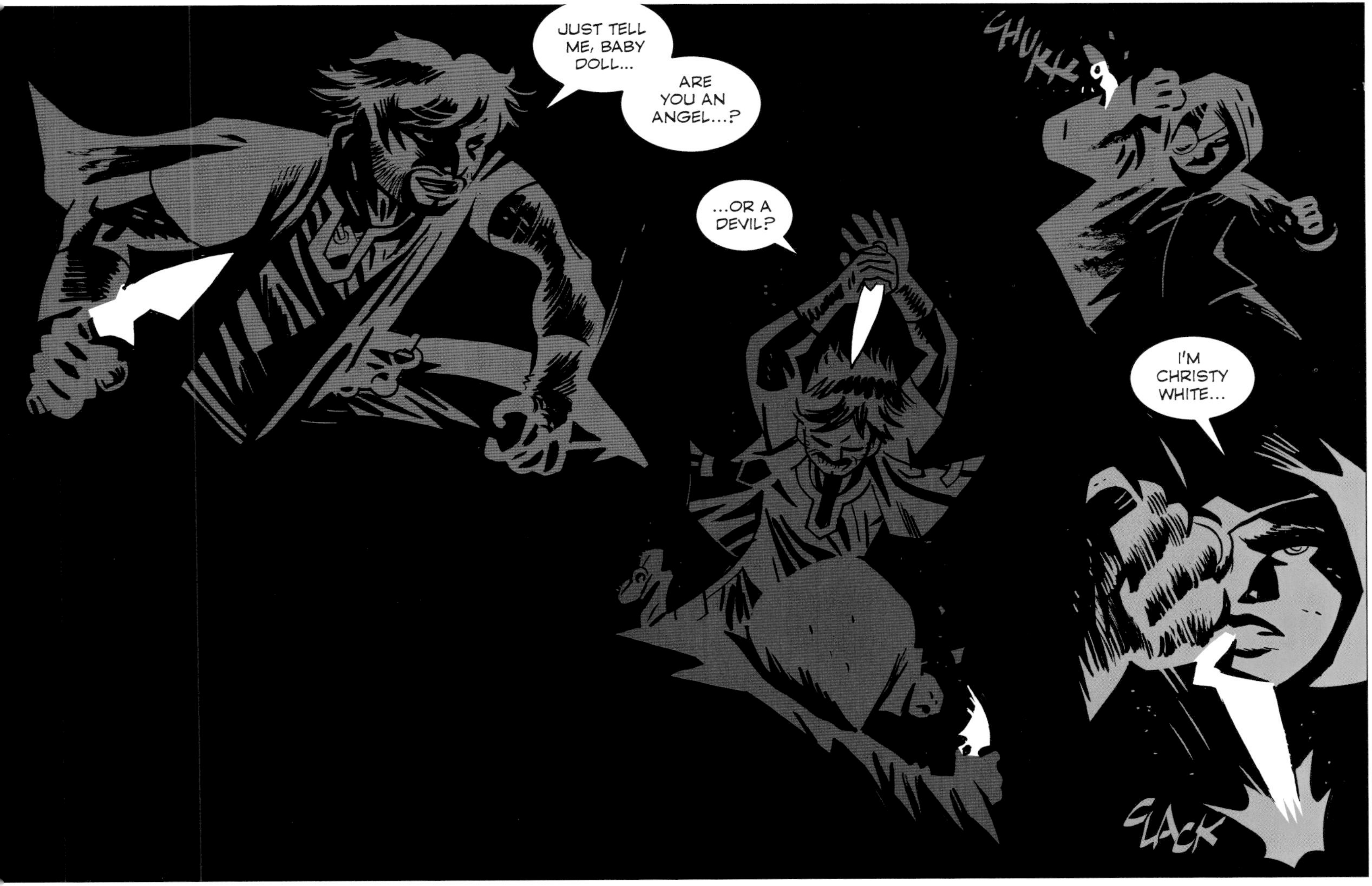
JUST TELL ME, BABY DOLL...
ARE YOU AN ANGEL...?
...OR A DEVIL?
CHUKK
I'M CHRISTY WHITE...
CLACK

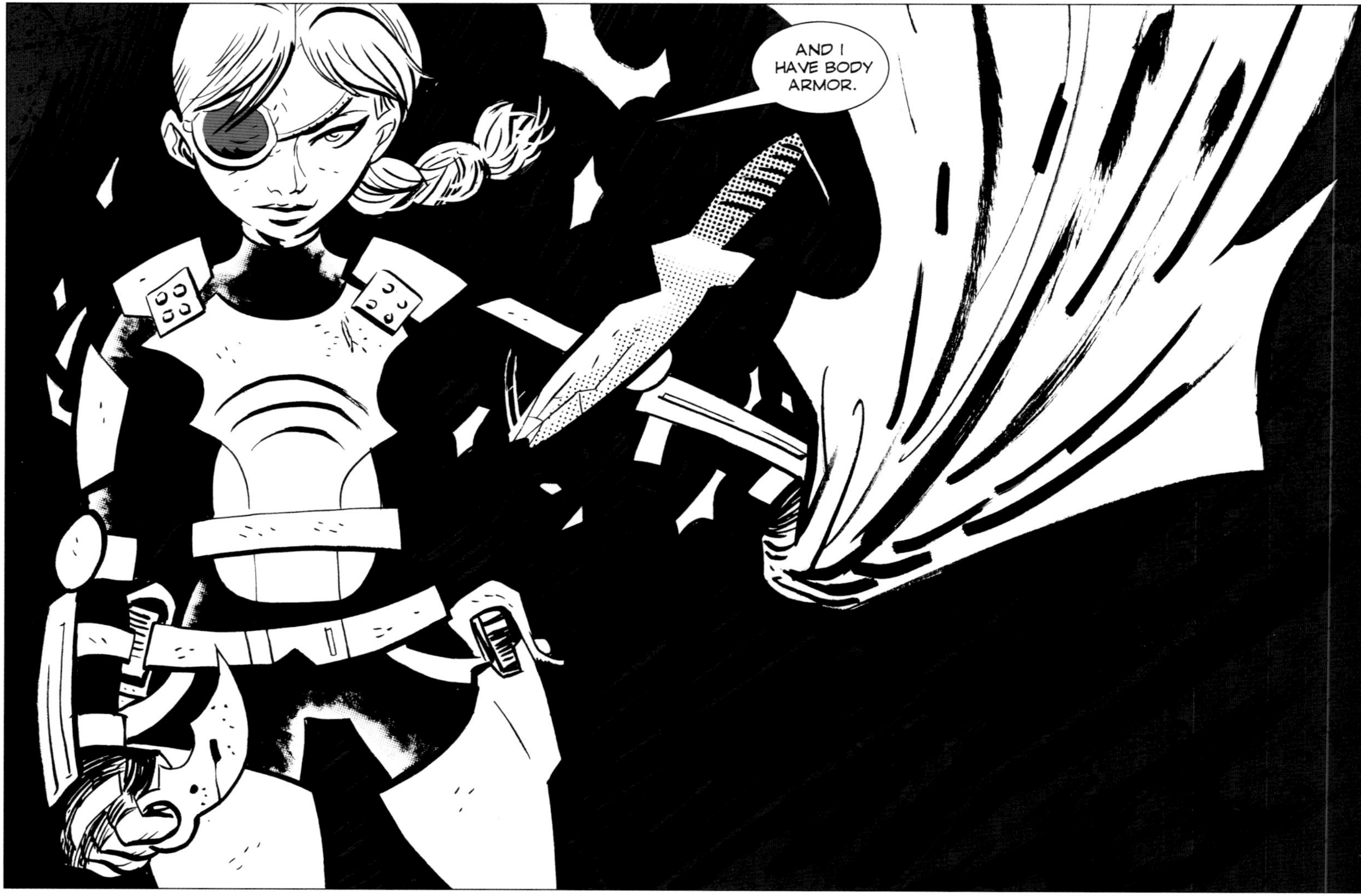
AND I HAVE BODY ARMOR.

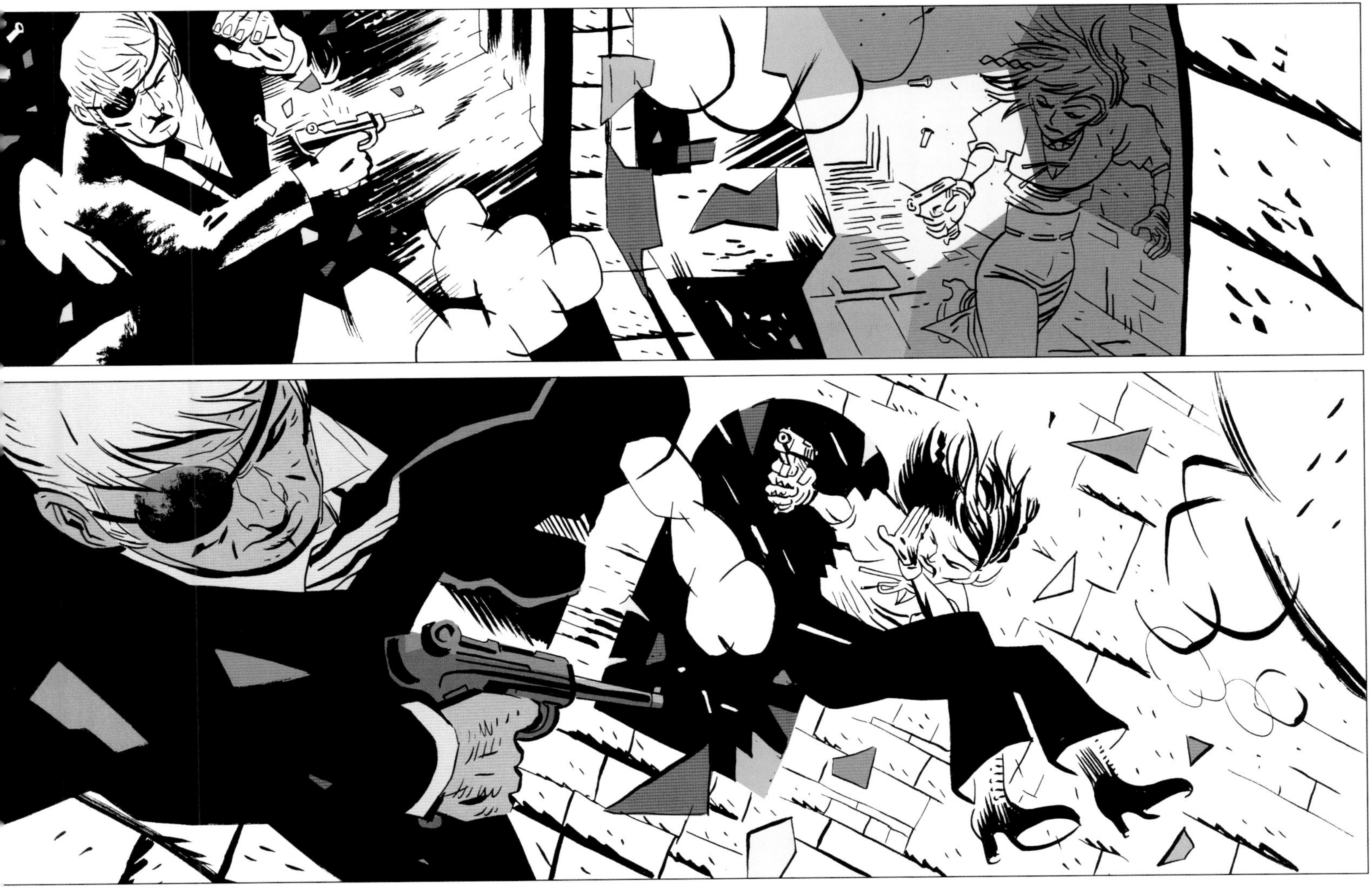

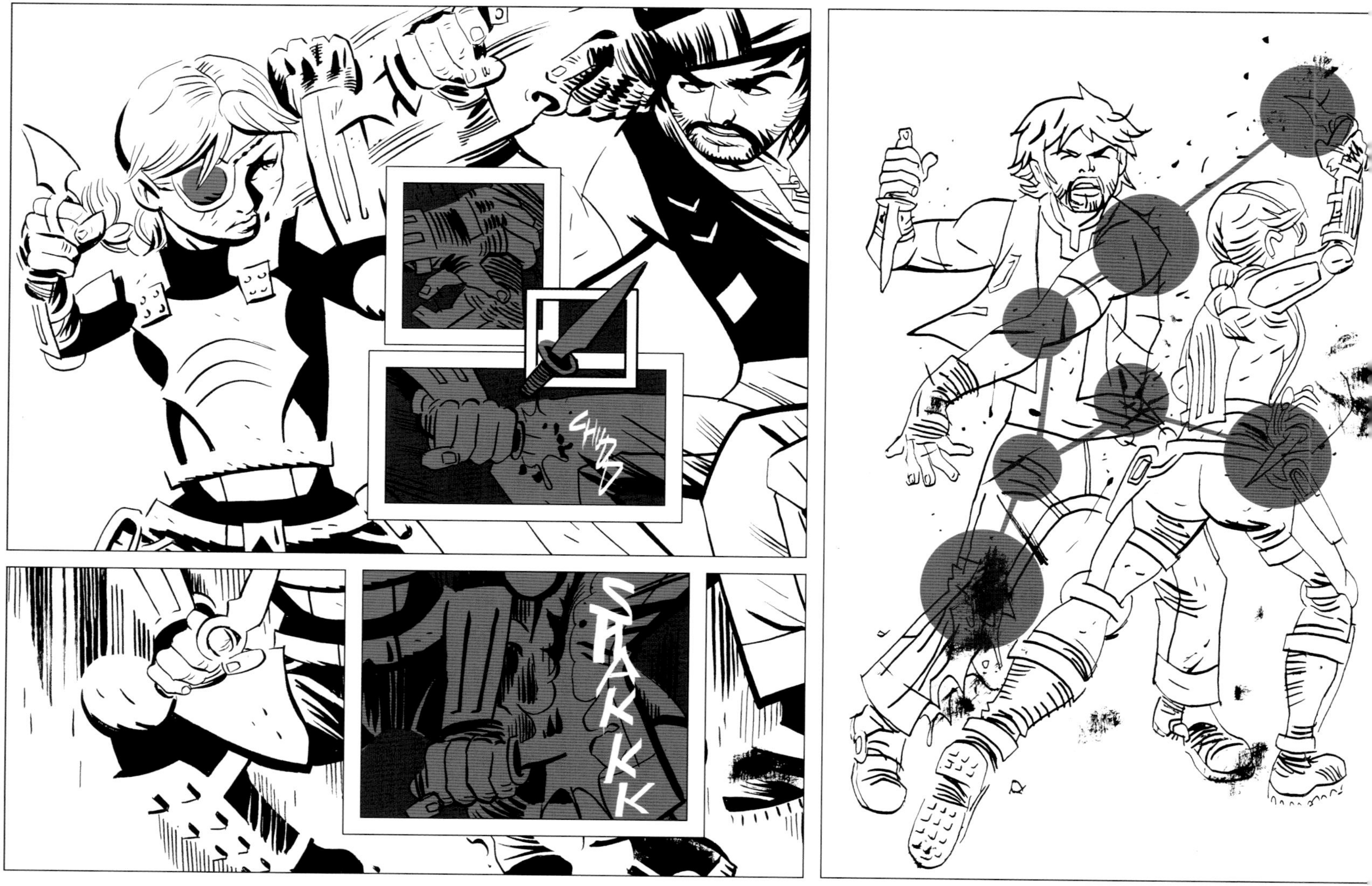

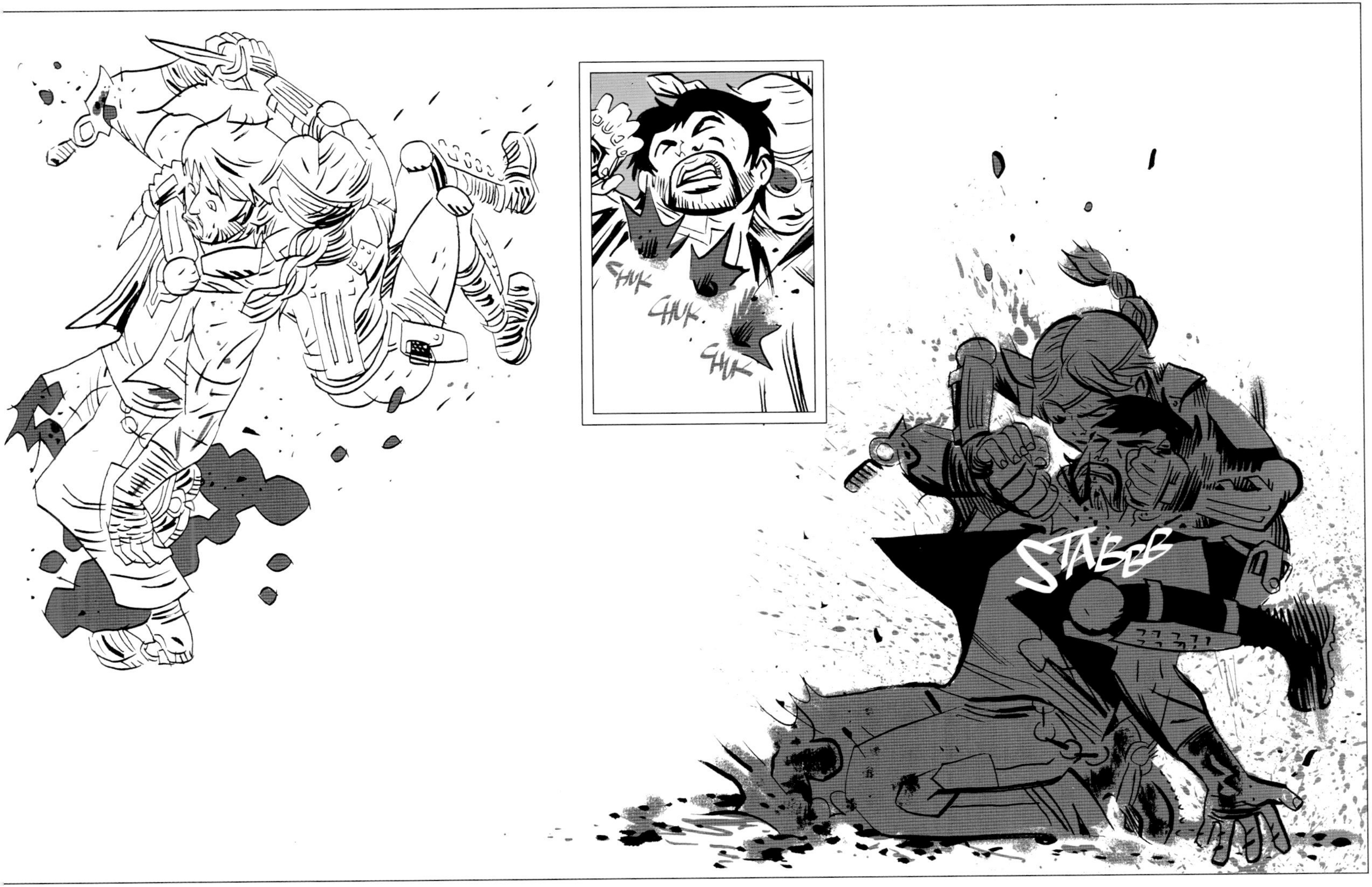
CHUK
CHUK
CHUK
STABBB

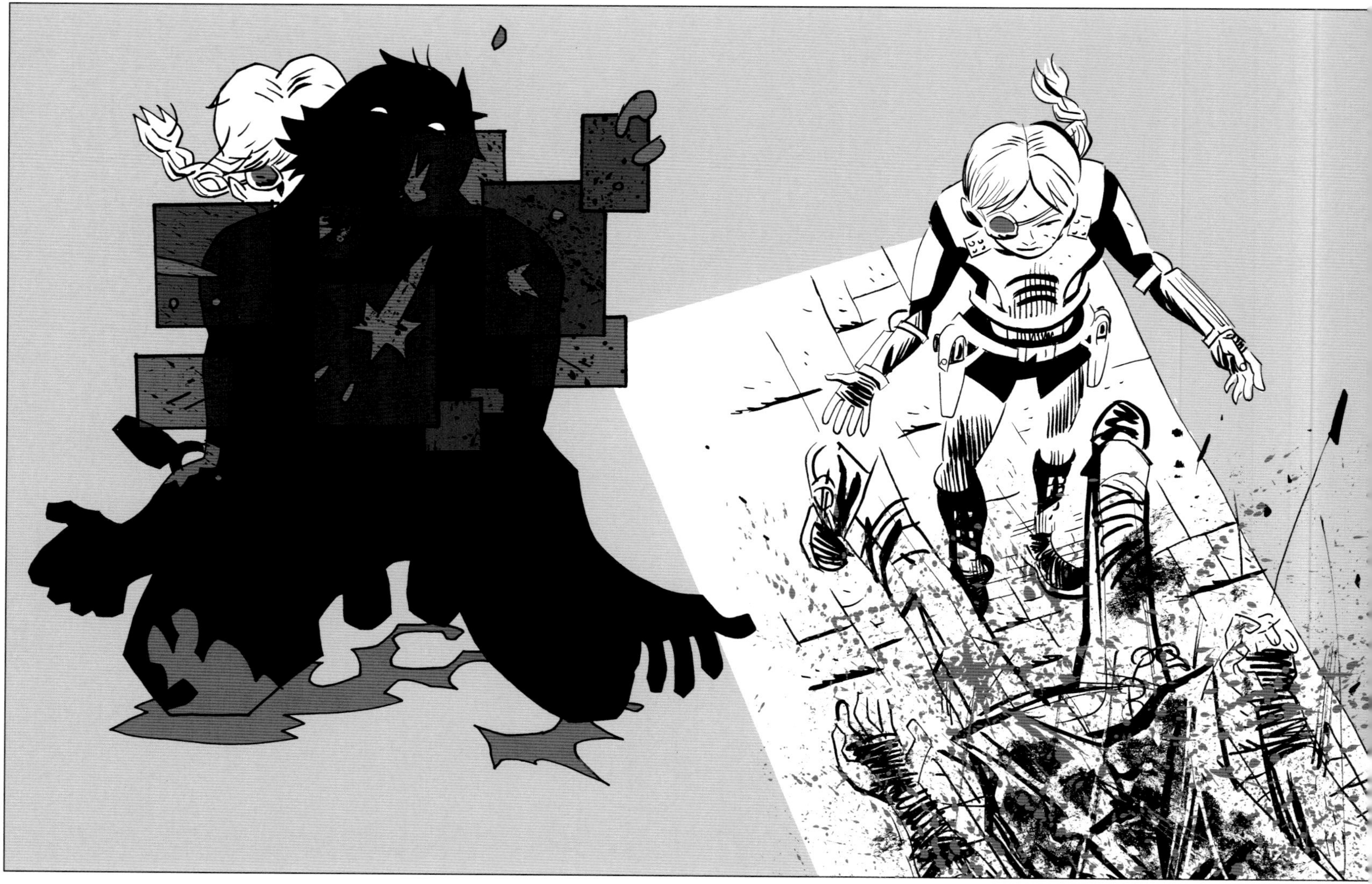

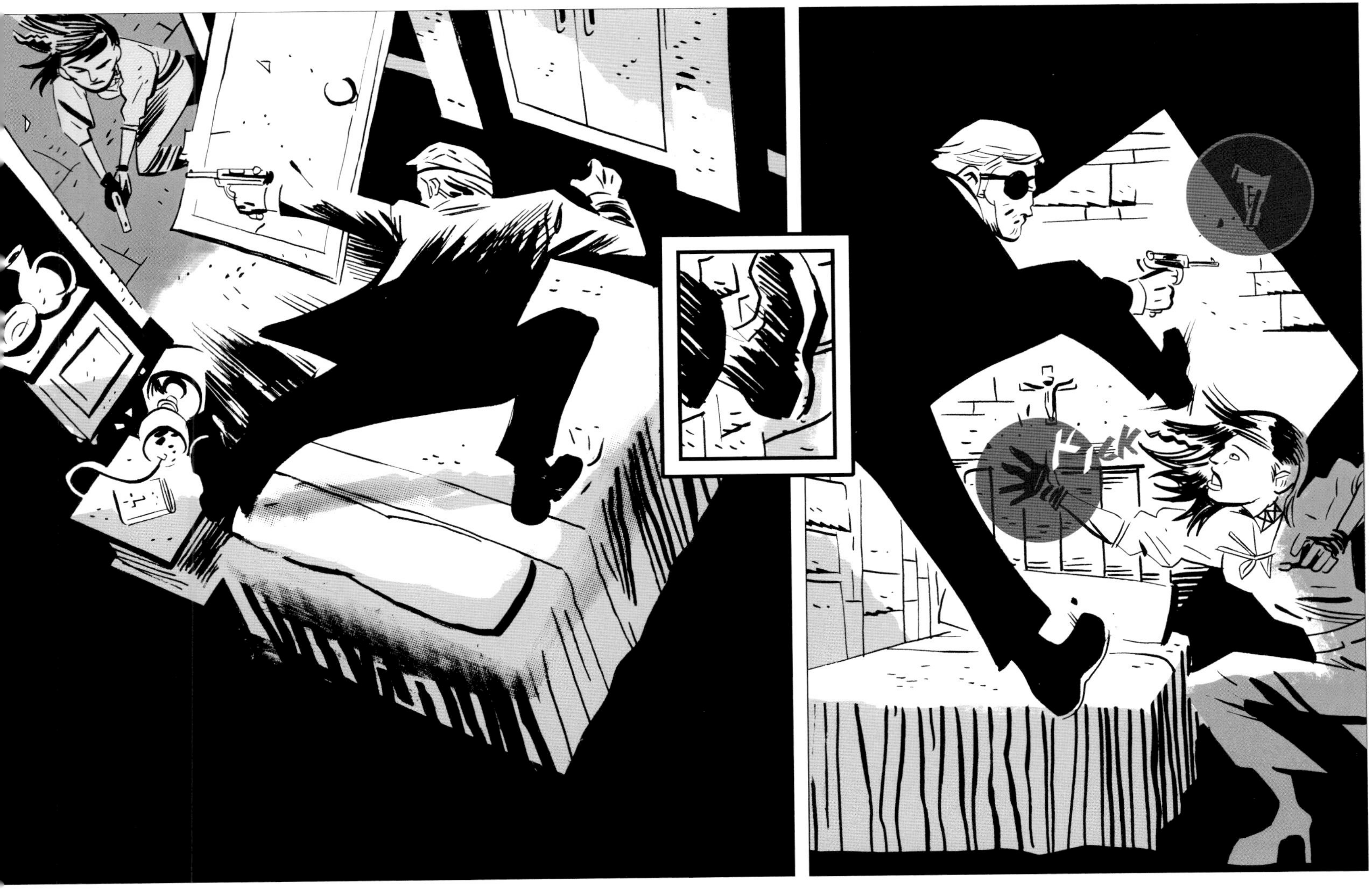
KICK

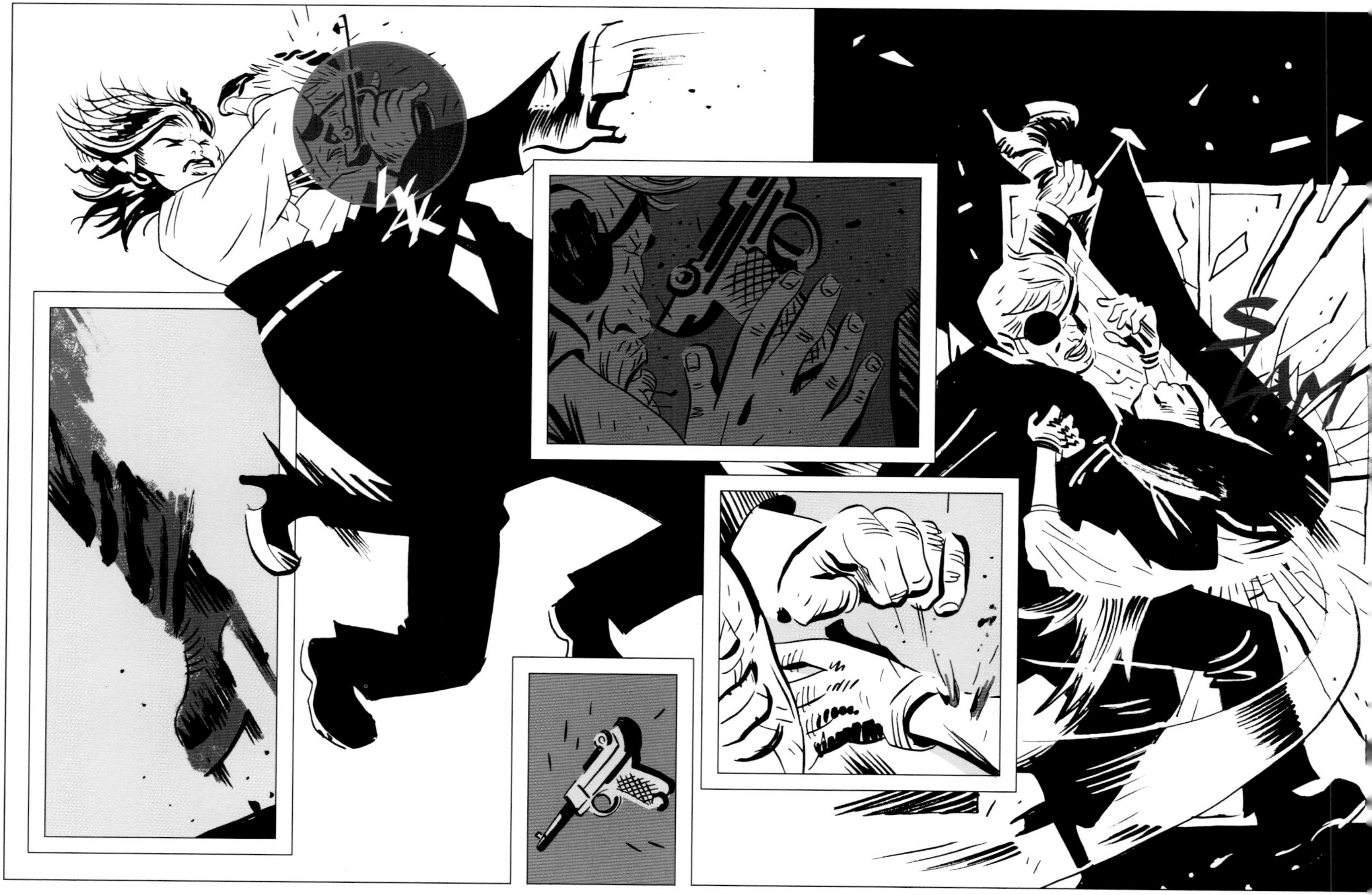
WAK
SLAM

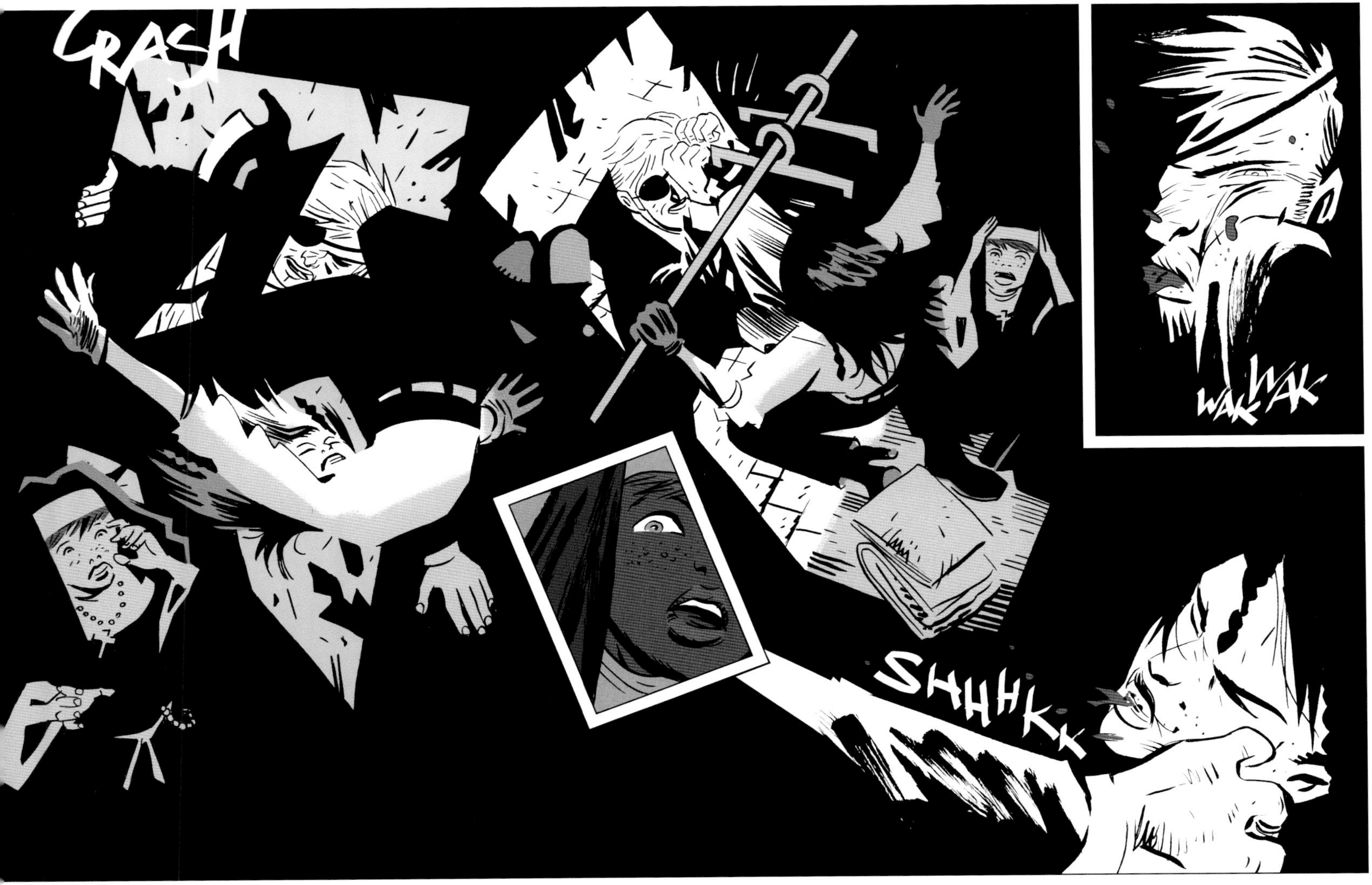
CRASH
WAK WAK
SHHHKK

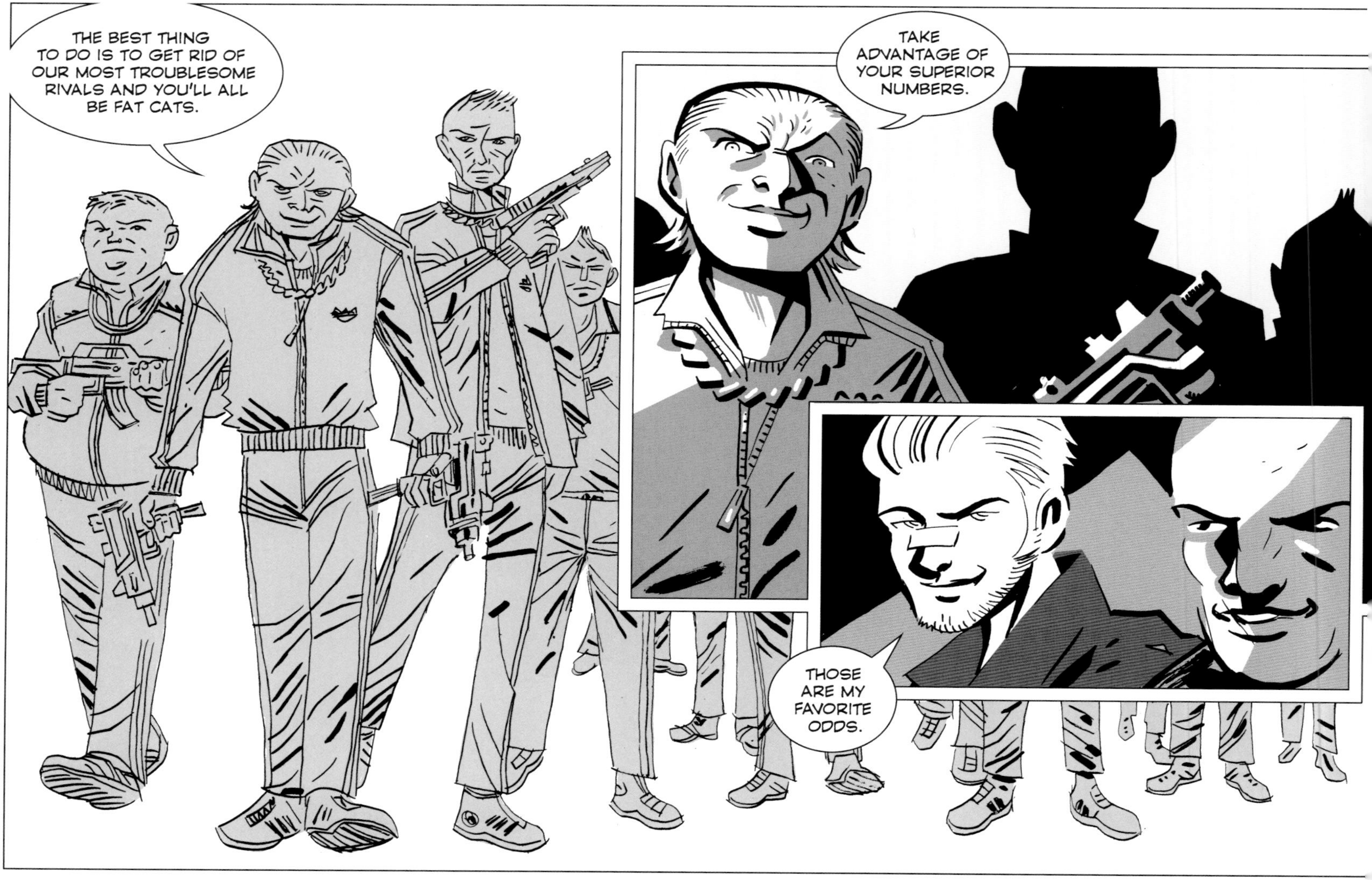
THE BEST THING TO DO IS TO GET RID OF OUR MOST TROUBLESOME RIVALS AND YOU'LL ALL BE FAT CATS.
TAKE ADVANTAGE OF YOUR SUPERIOR NUMBERS.
THOSE ARE MY FAVORITE ODDS.

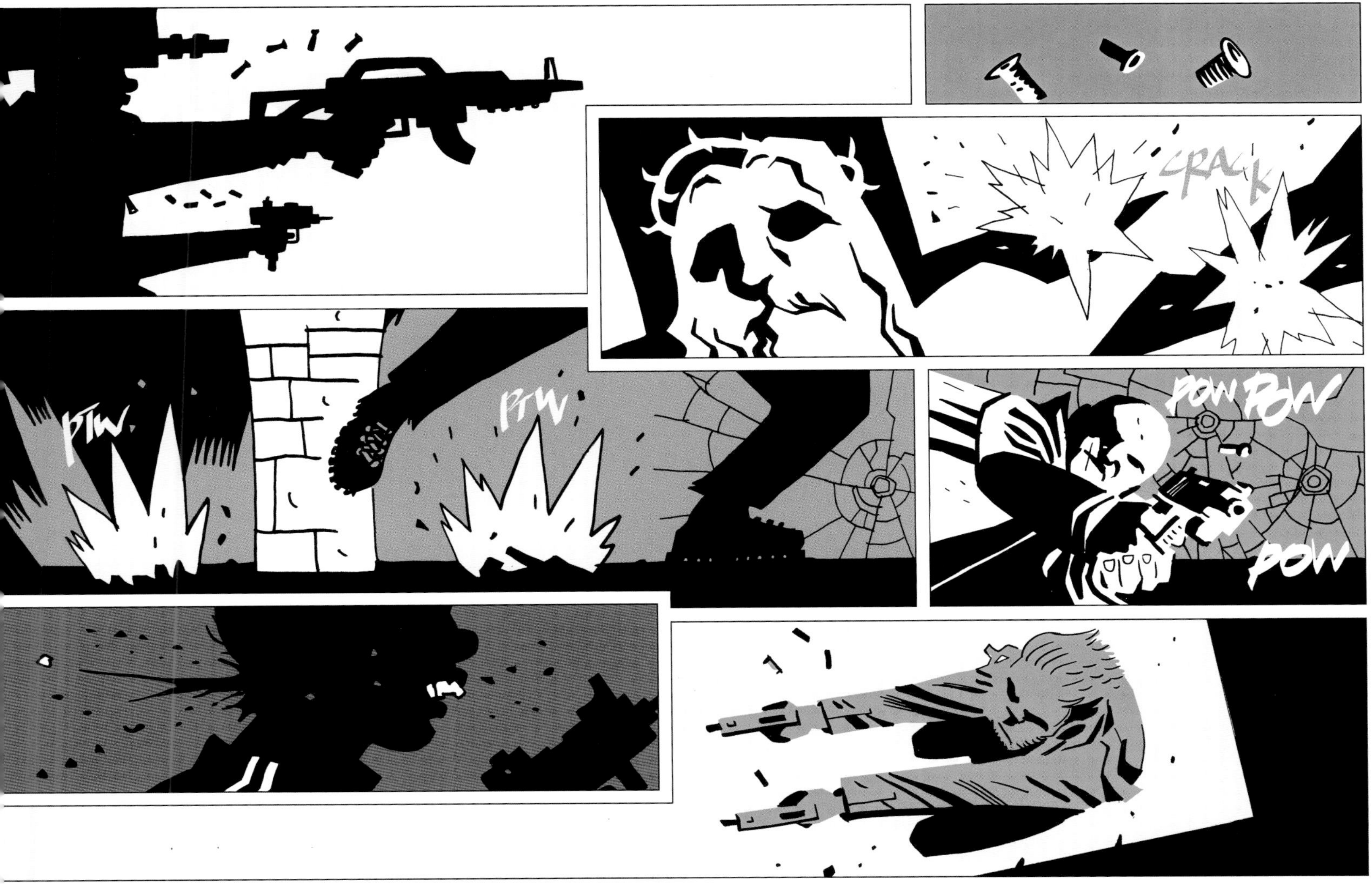
CRACK
PTW
PTW
POW POW
POW

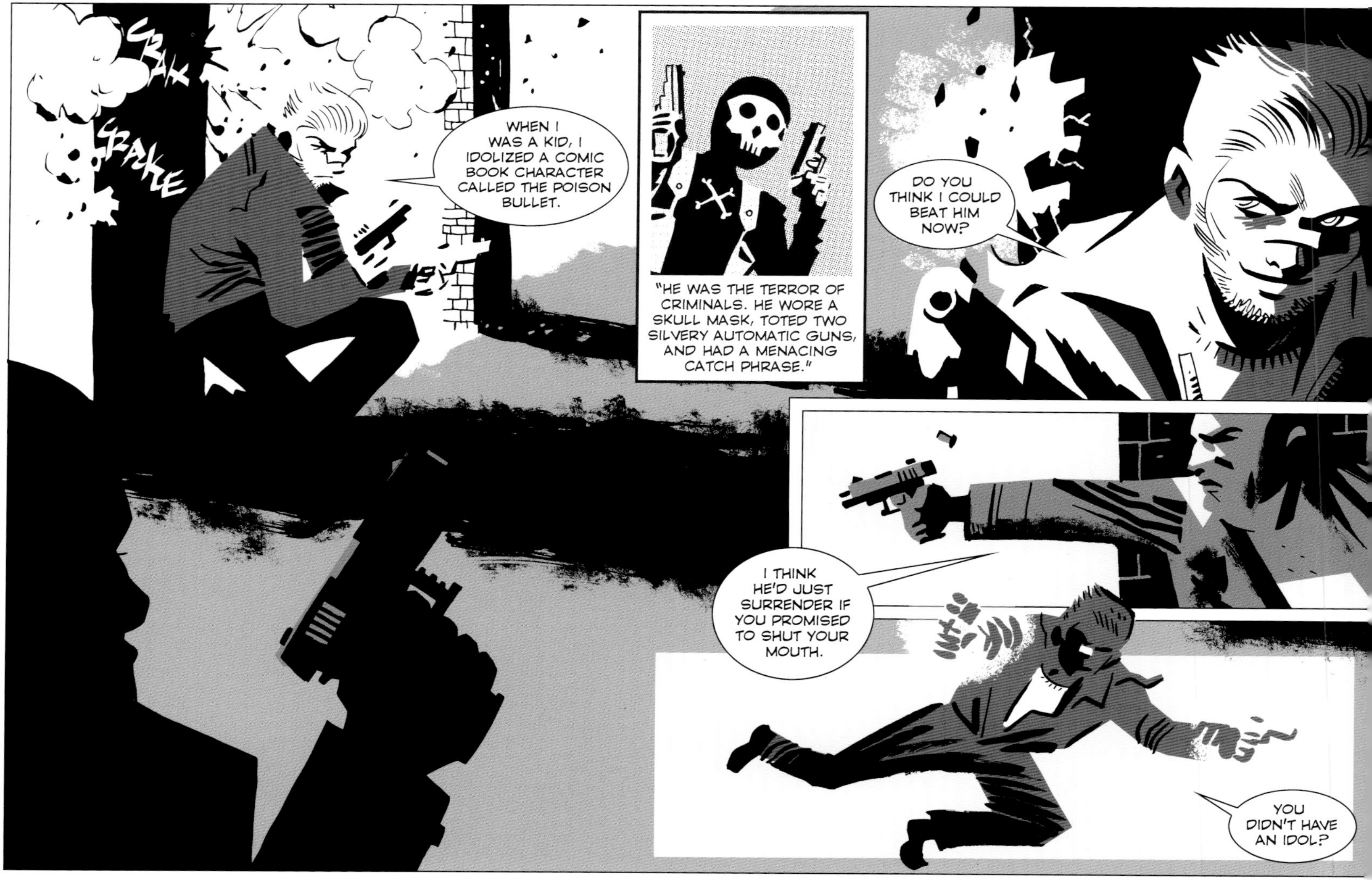
CRAK
CRAKKE
WHEN I WAS A KID, I IDOLIZED A COMIC BOOK CHARACTER CALLED THE POISON BULLET.
"HE WAS THE TERROR OF CRIMINALS. HE WORE A SKULL MASK, TOTED TWO SILVERY AUTOMATIC GUNS, AND HAD A MENACING CATCH PHRASE."
DO YOU THINK I COULD BEAT HIM NOW?
I THINK HE'D JUST SURRENDER IF YOU PROMISED TO SHUT YOUR MOUTH.
YOU DIDN'T HAVE AN IDOL?

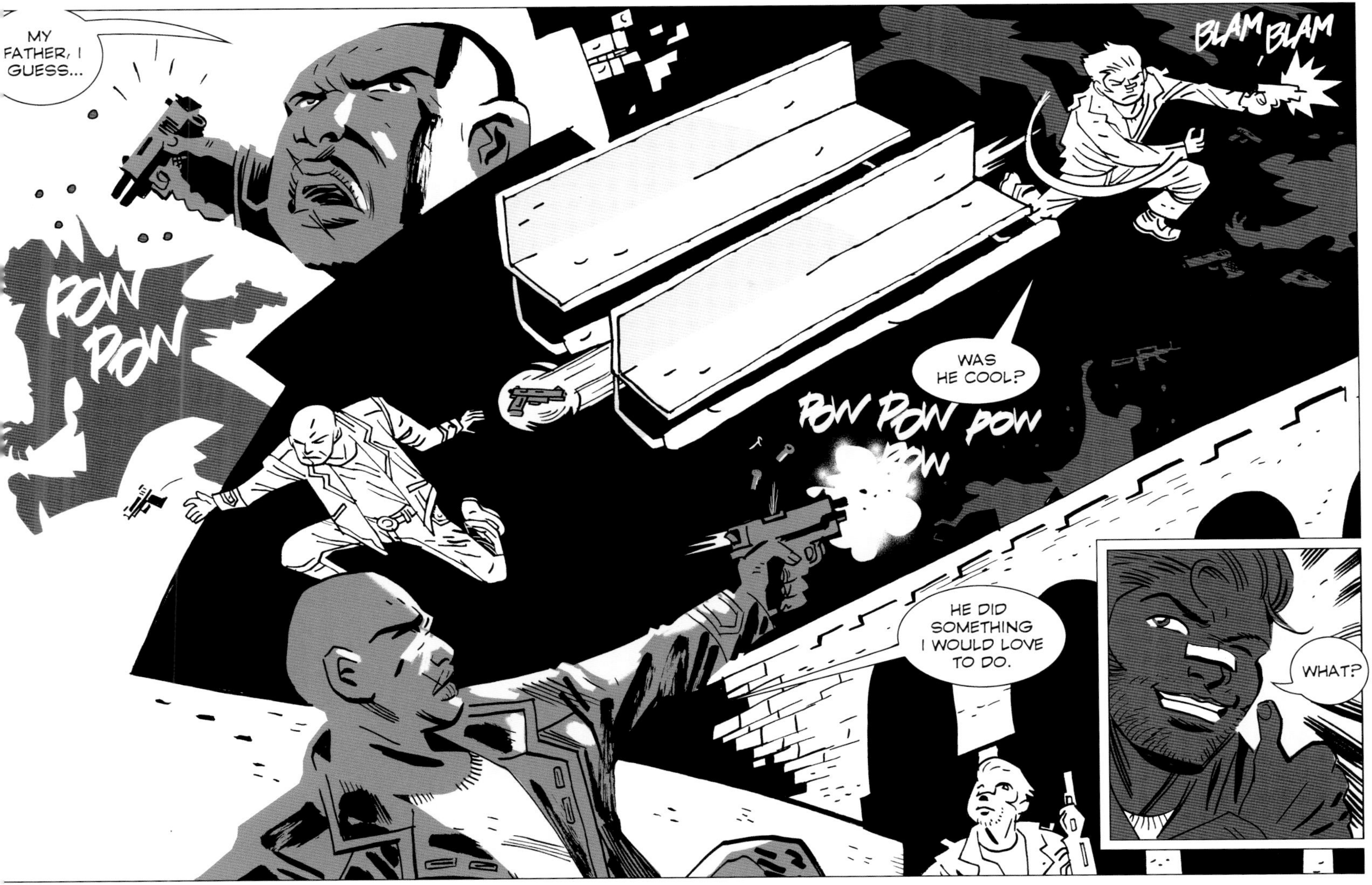
MY FATHER, I GUESS...
POW POW
BLAM BLAM
WAS HE COOL?
POW POW POW POW
HE DID SOMETHING I WOULD LOVE TO DO.
WHAT?

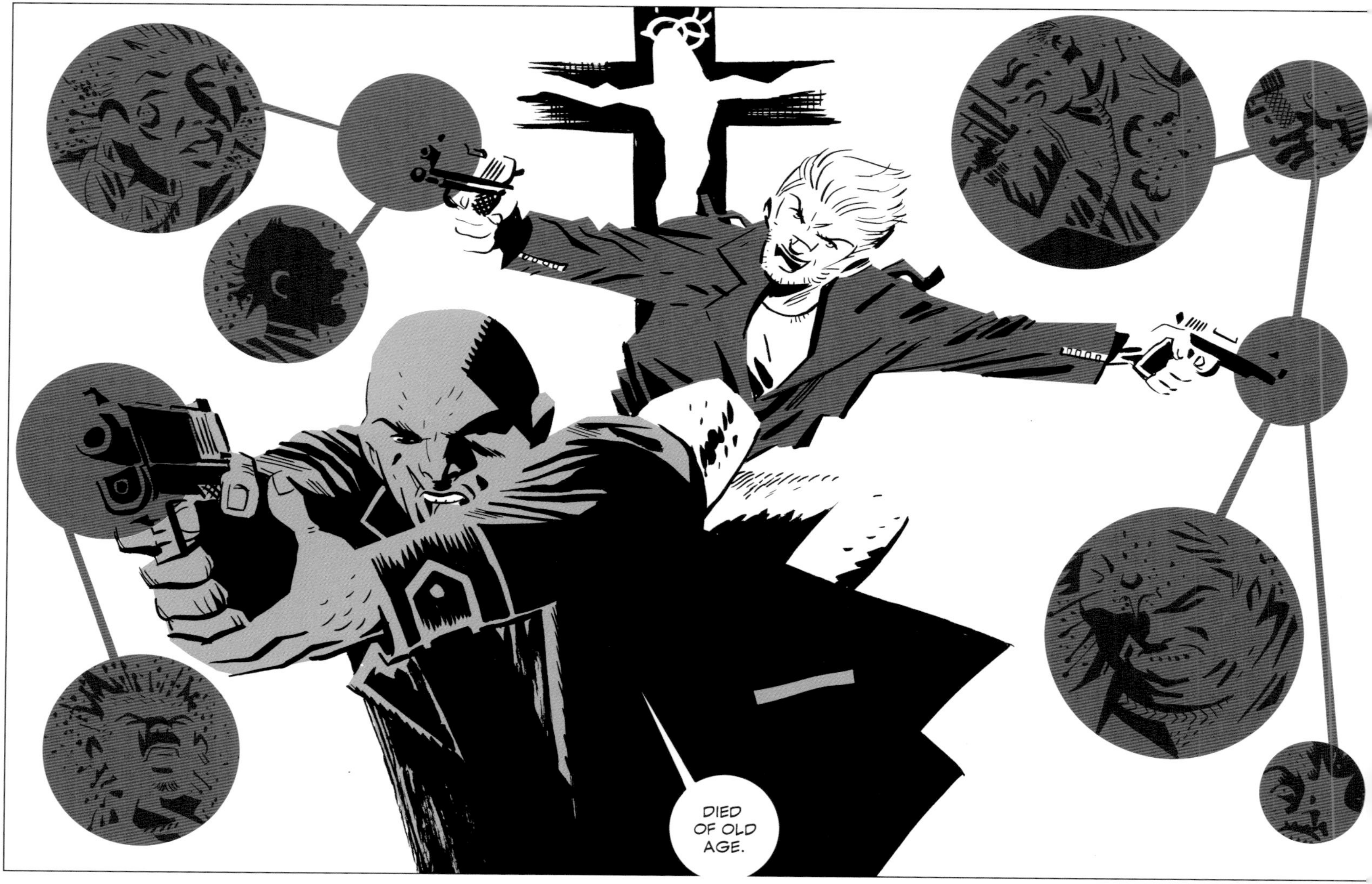
DIED OF OLD AGE.

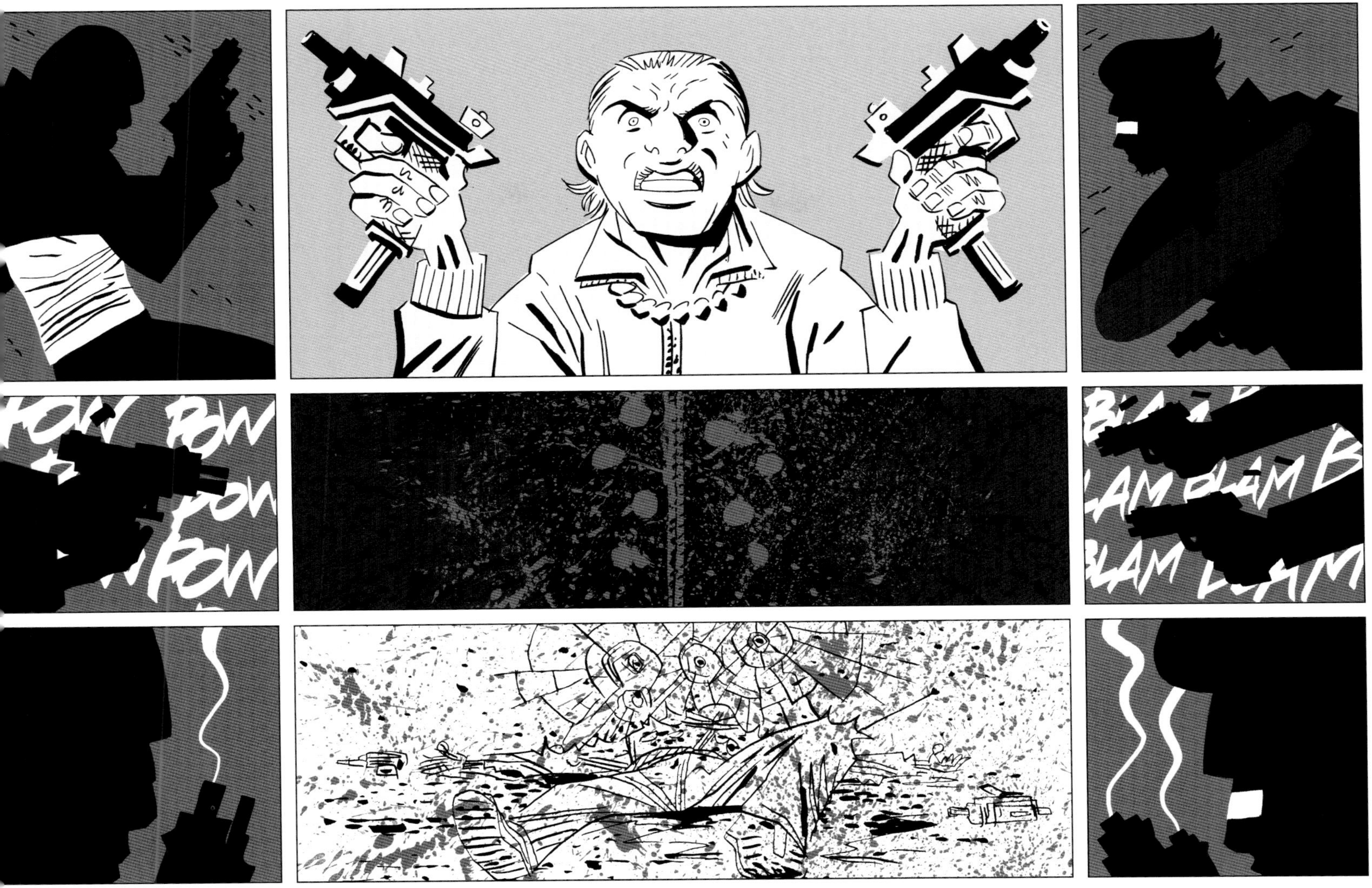
POW
POW
POW
BLAM BLAM
BLAM

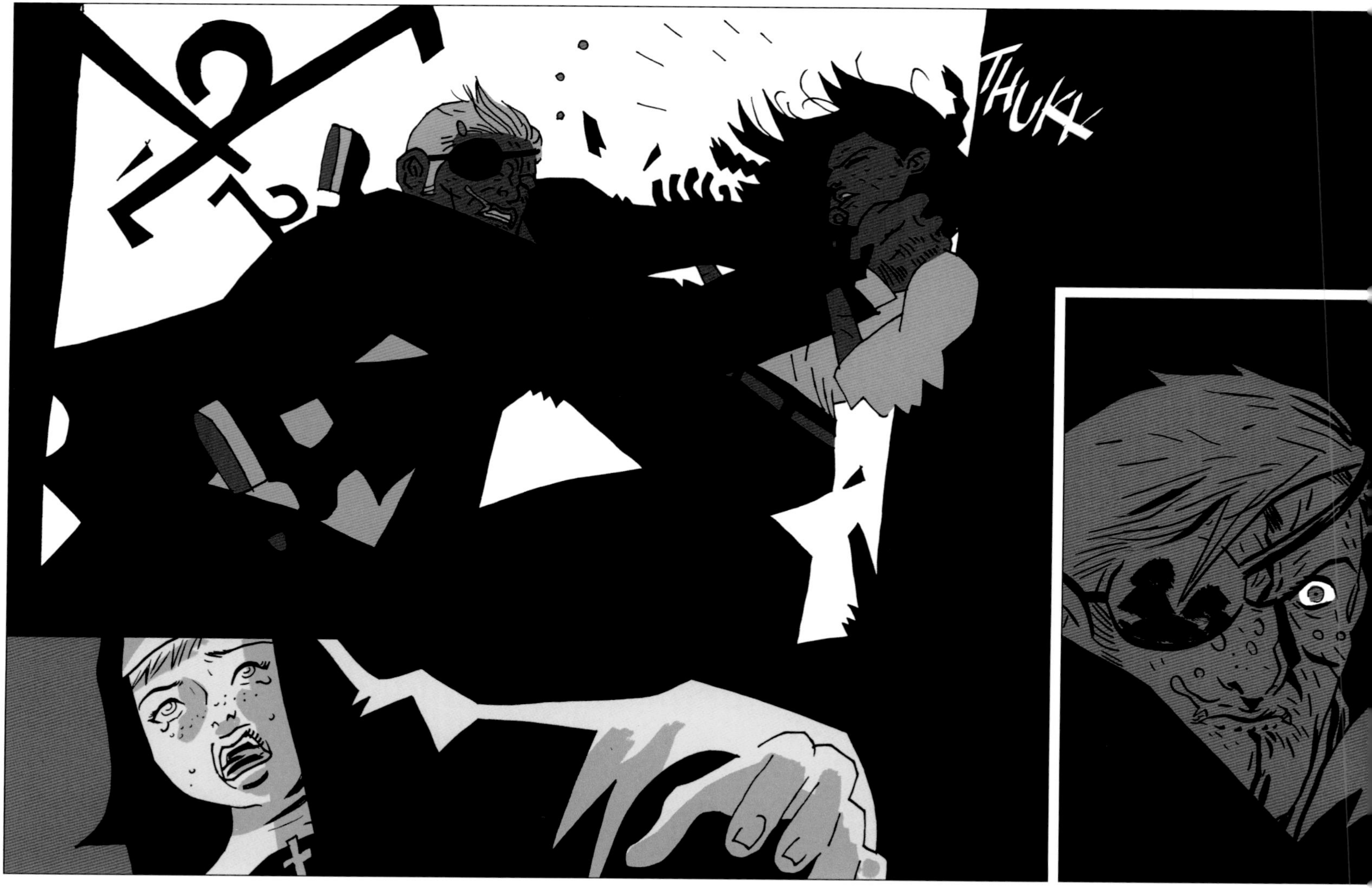
THUKK

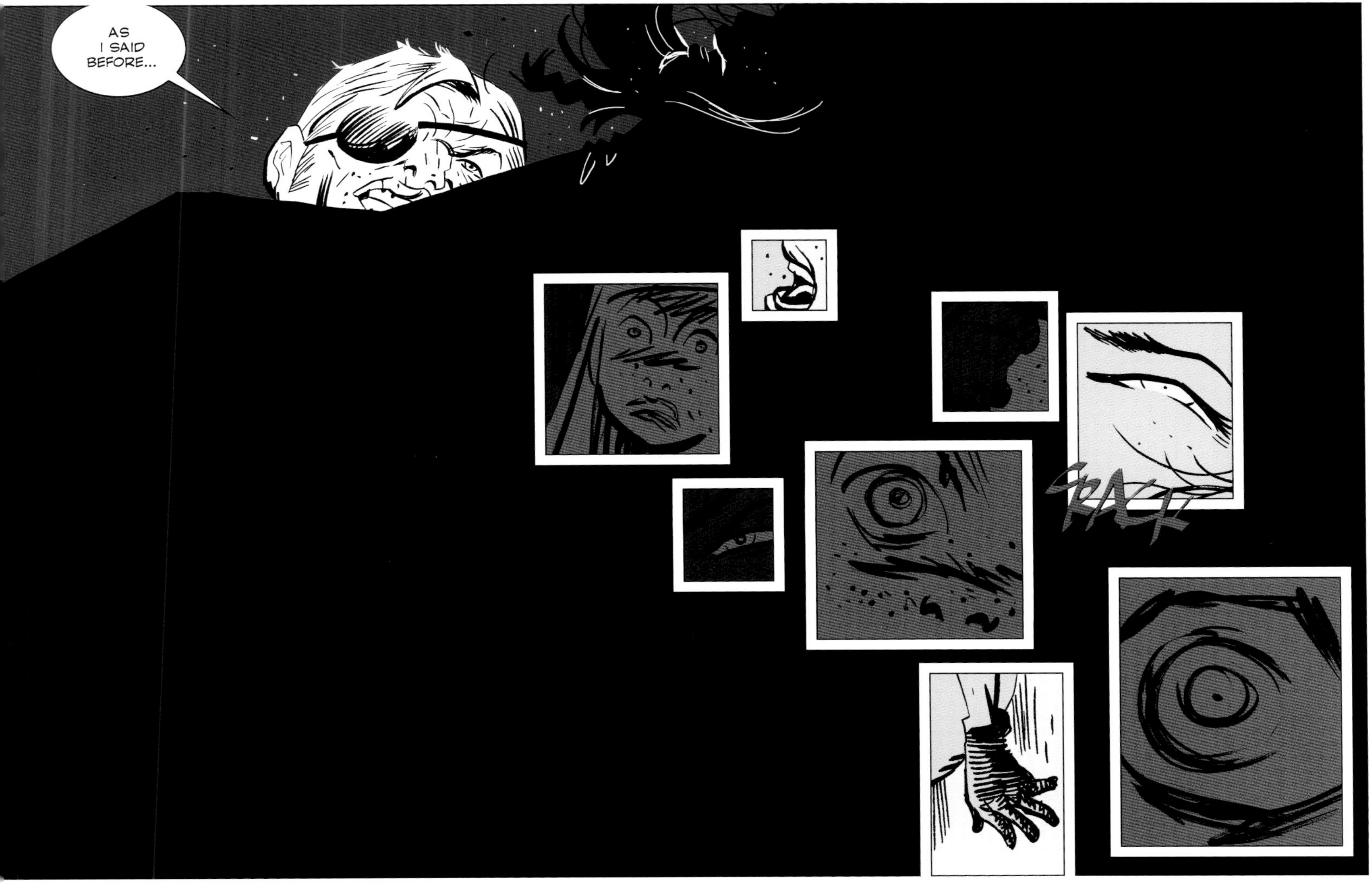
AS I SAID BEFORE...
CRACK!!

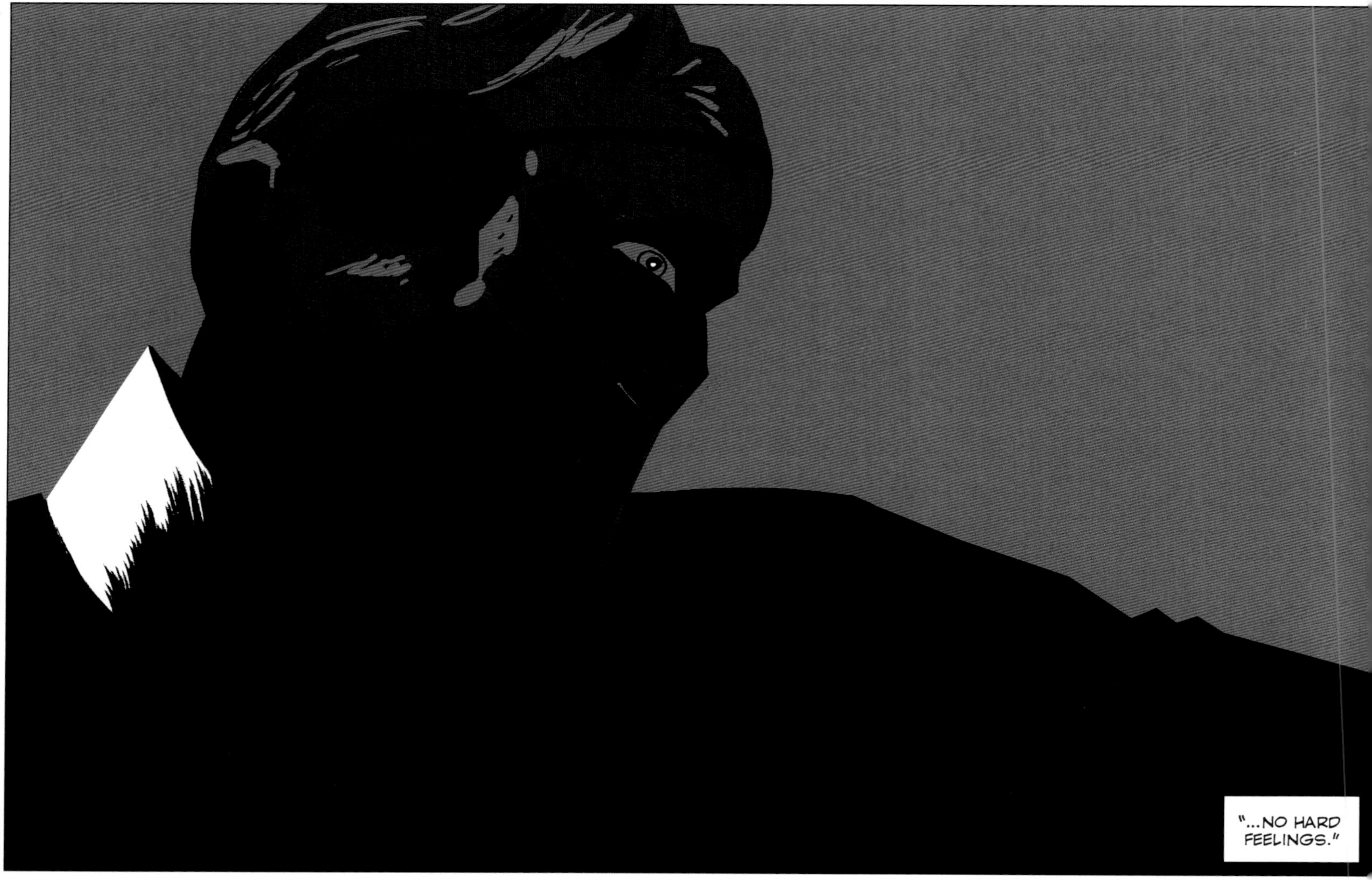
"...NO HARD FEELINGS."

PART TWO

THE GAMES AND THE PRIZE

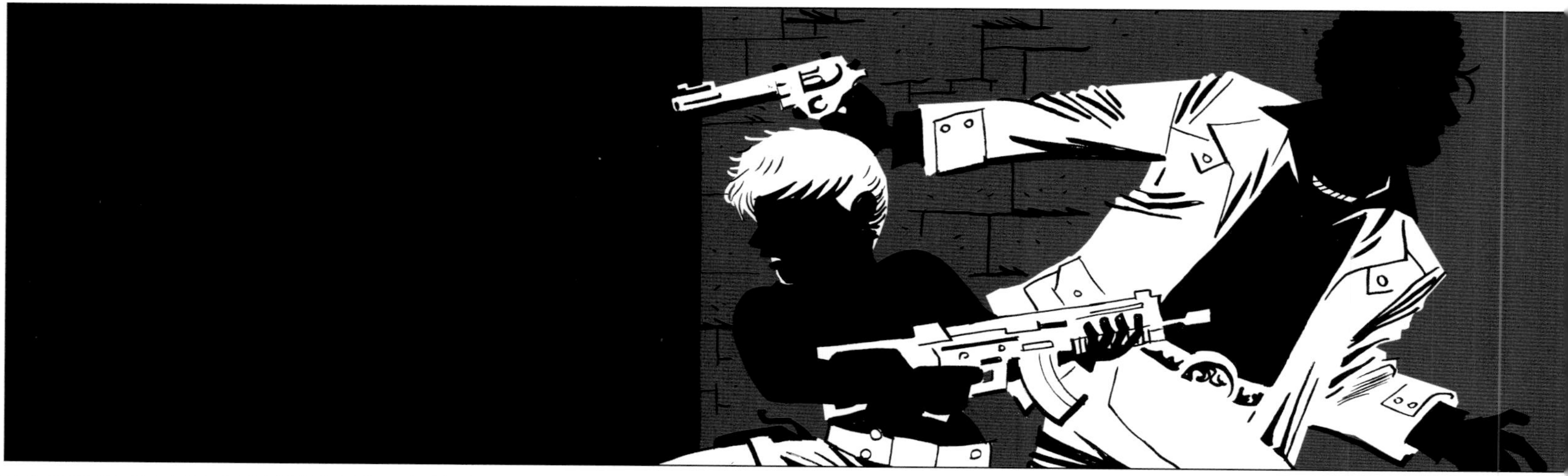

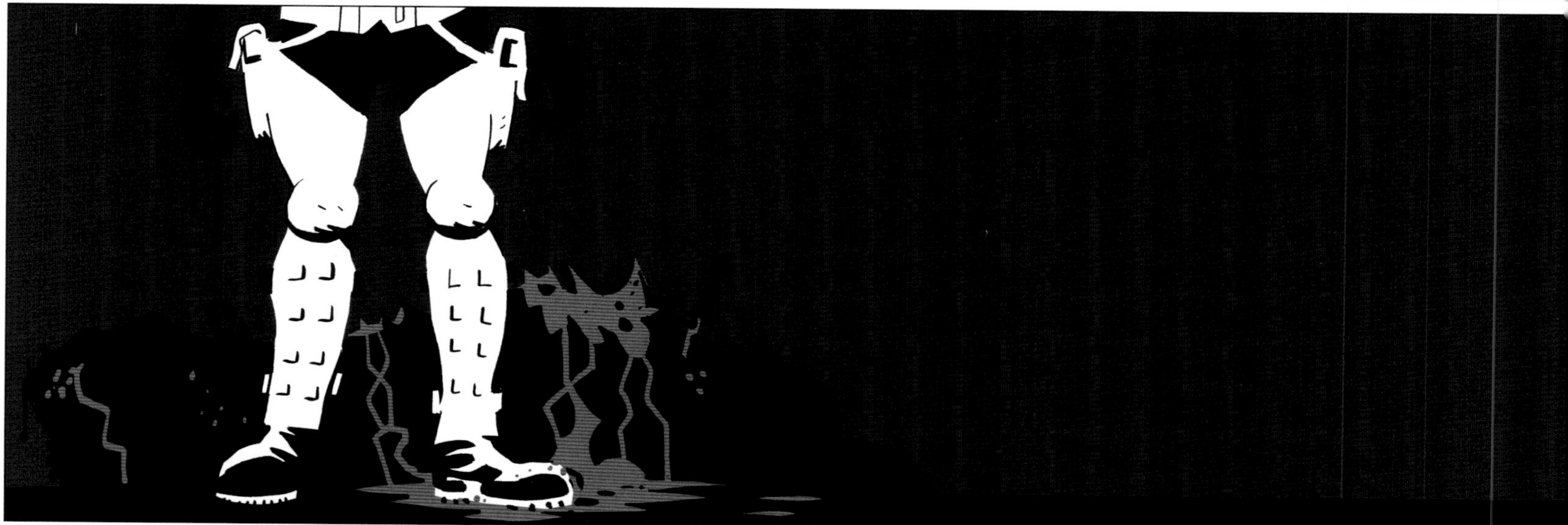

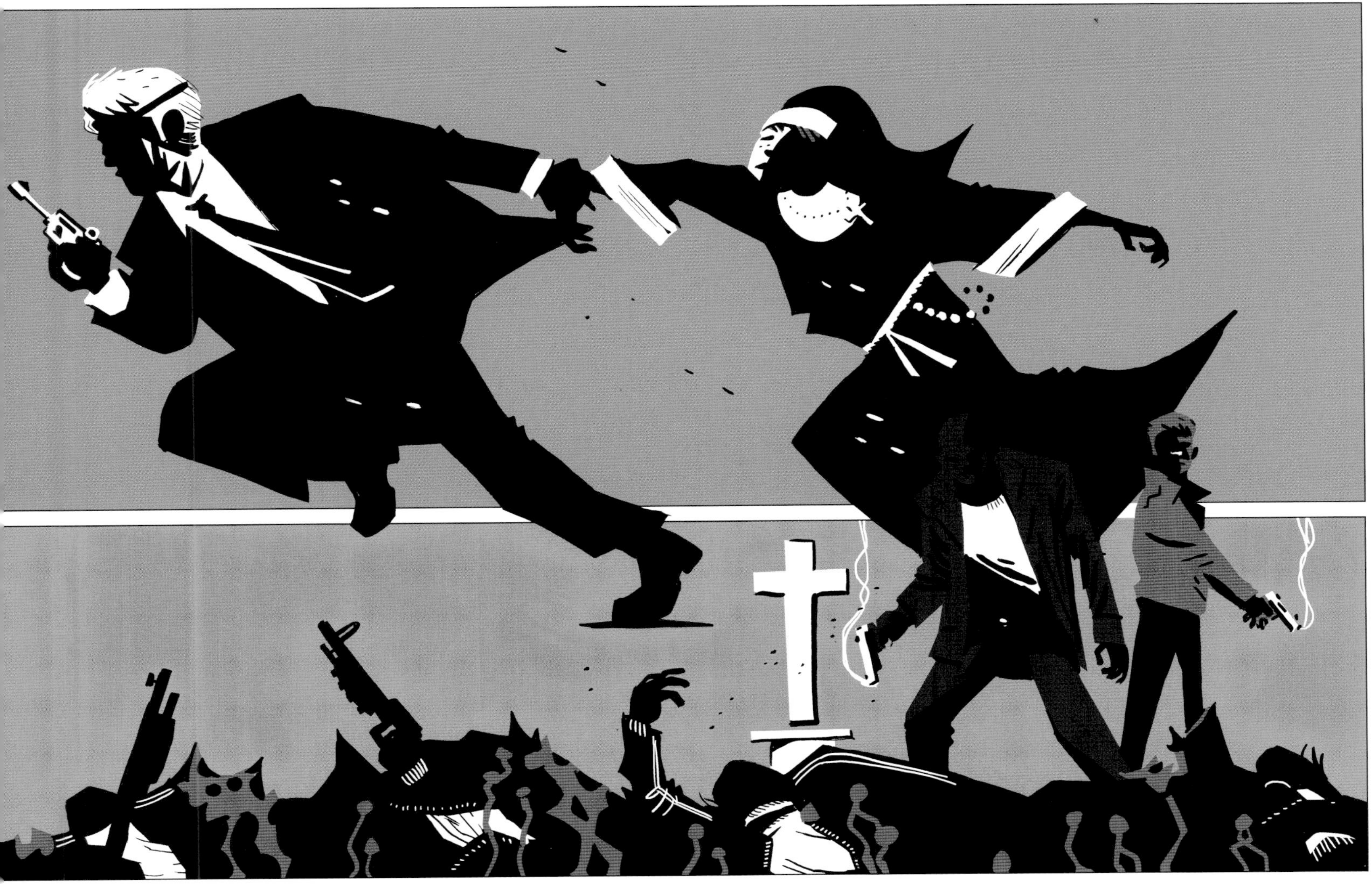

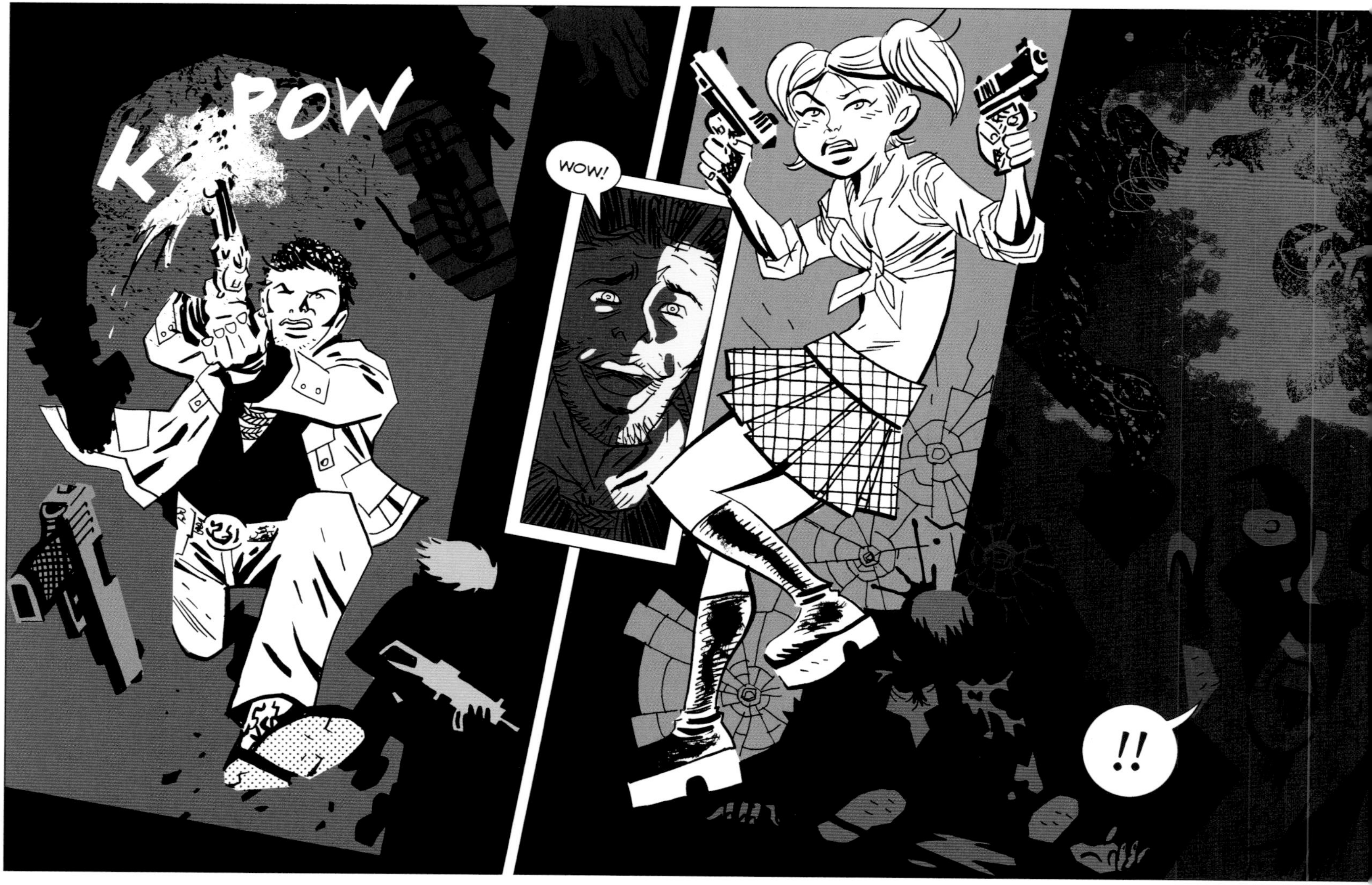

K-POW
WOW!
!!

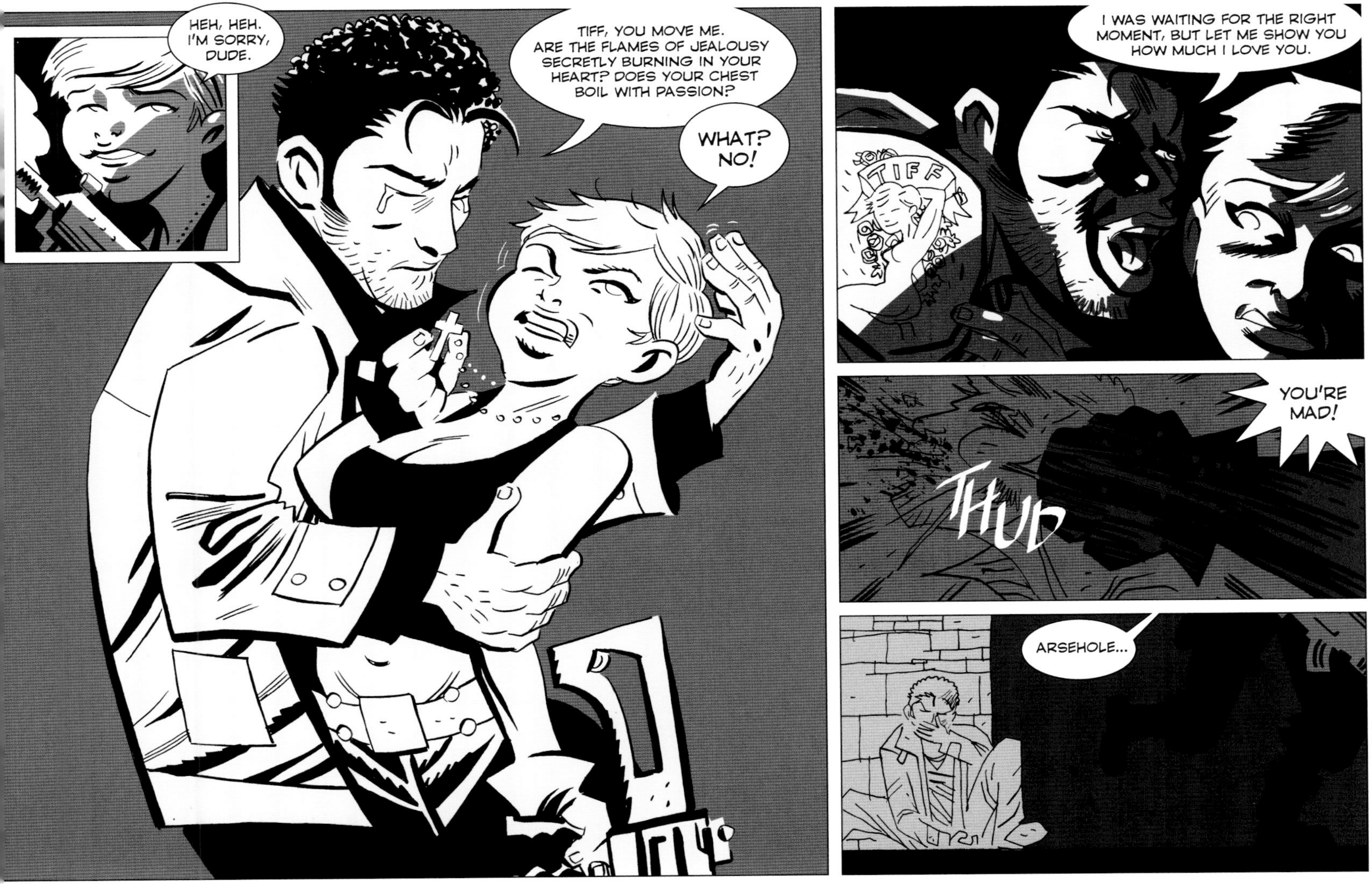
HEH, HEH. I'M SORRY, DUDE.
TIFF, YOU MOVE ME. ARE THE FLAMES OF JEALOUSY SECRETLY BURNING IN YOUR HEART? DOES YOUR CHEST BOIL WITH PASSION?
WHAT? NO!
I WAS WAITING FOR THE RIGHT MOMENT, BUT LET ME SHOW YOU HOW MUCH I LOVE YOU.
TIFF
YOU'RE MAD!
THUD
ARSEHOLE...

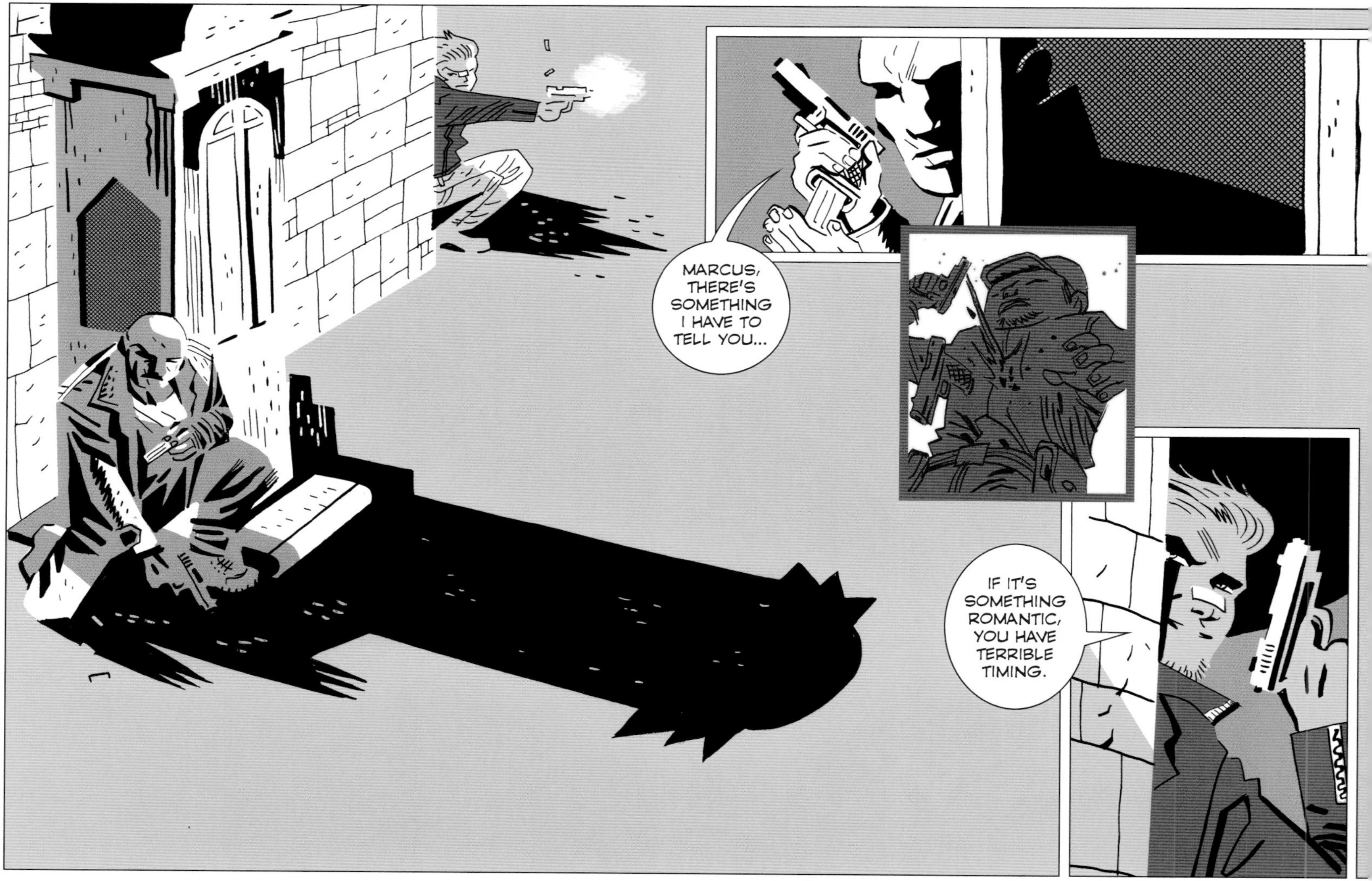
MARCUS, THERE'S SOMETHING I HAVE TO TELL YOU...
IF IT'S SOMETHING ROMANTIC, YOU HAVE TERRIBLE TIMING.

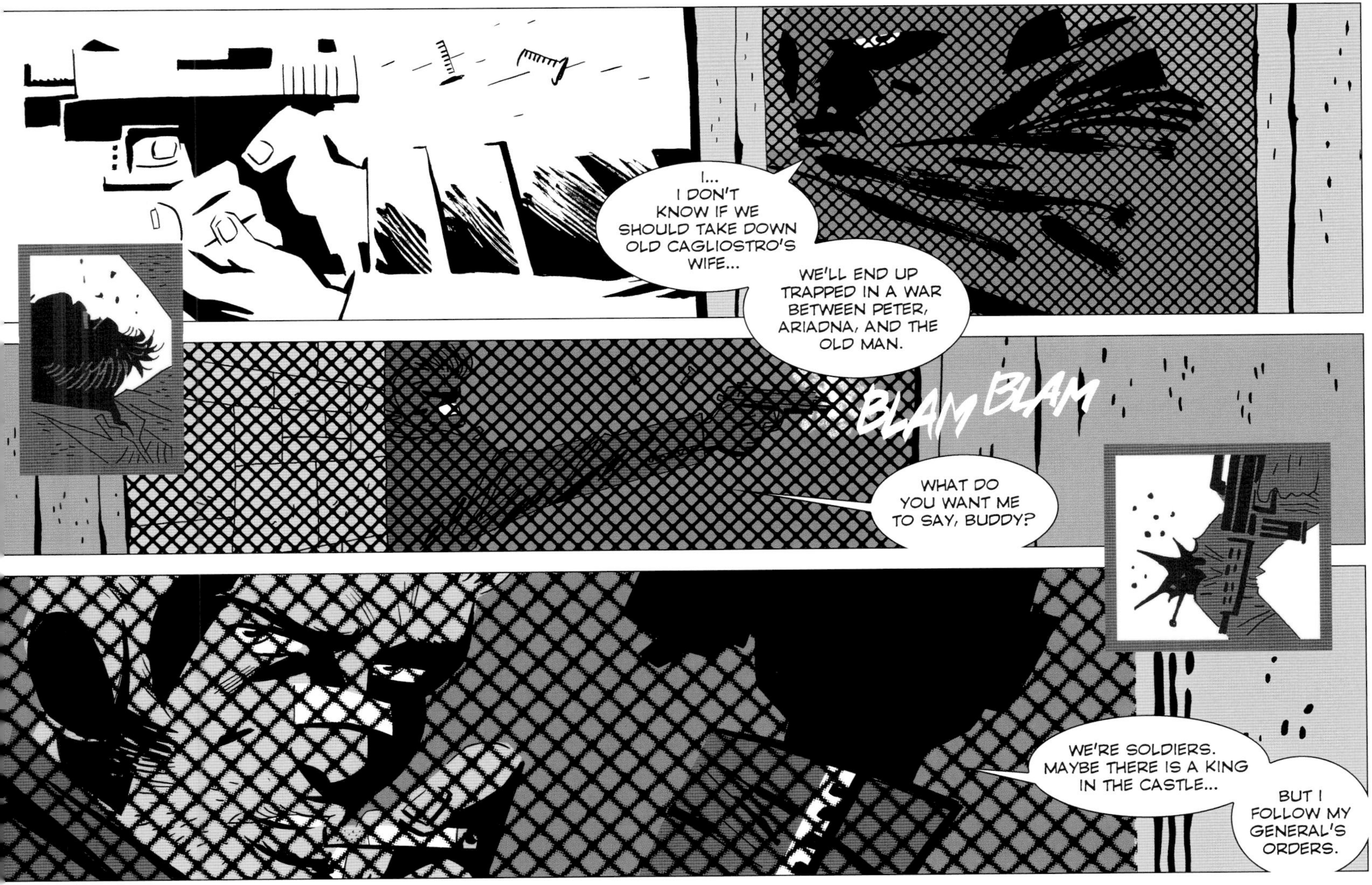

I... I DON'T KNOW IF WE SHOULD TAKE DOWN OLD CAGLIOSTRO'S WIFE...
WE'LL END UP TRAPPED IN A WAR BETWEEN PETER, ARIADNA, AND THE OLD MAN.
BLAM BLAM
WHAT DO YOU WANT ME TO SAY, BUDDY?
WE'RE SOLDIERS. MAYBE THERE IS A KING IN THE CASTLE...
BUT I FOLLOW MY GENERAL'S ORDERS.

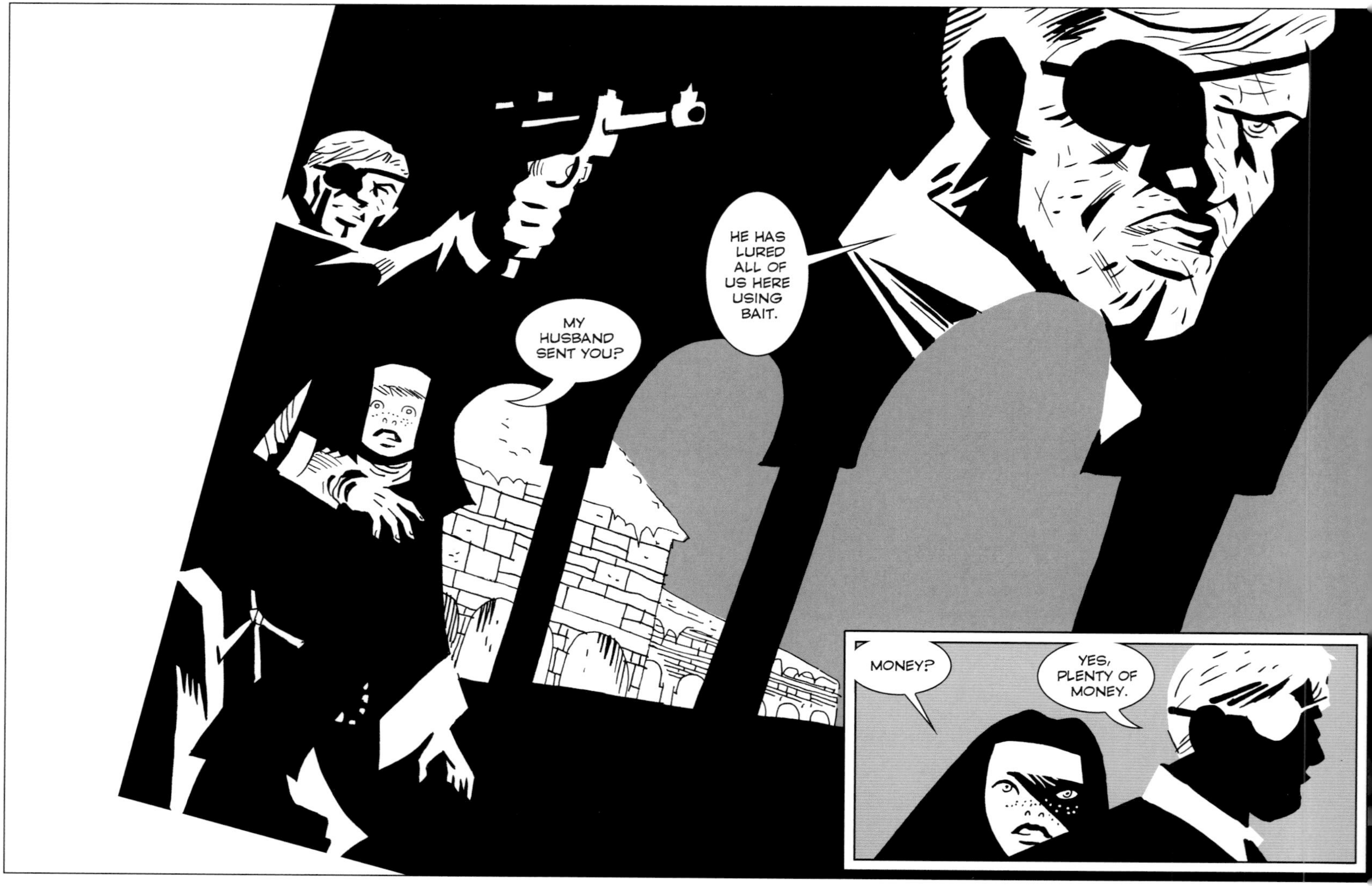
MY HUSBAND SENT YOU?
HE HAS LURED ALL OF US HERE USING BAIT.
MONEY?
YES, PLENTY OF MONEY.

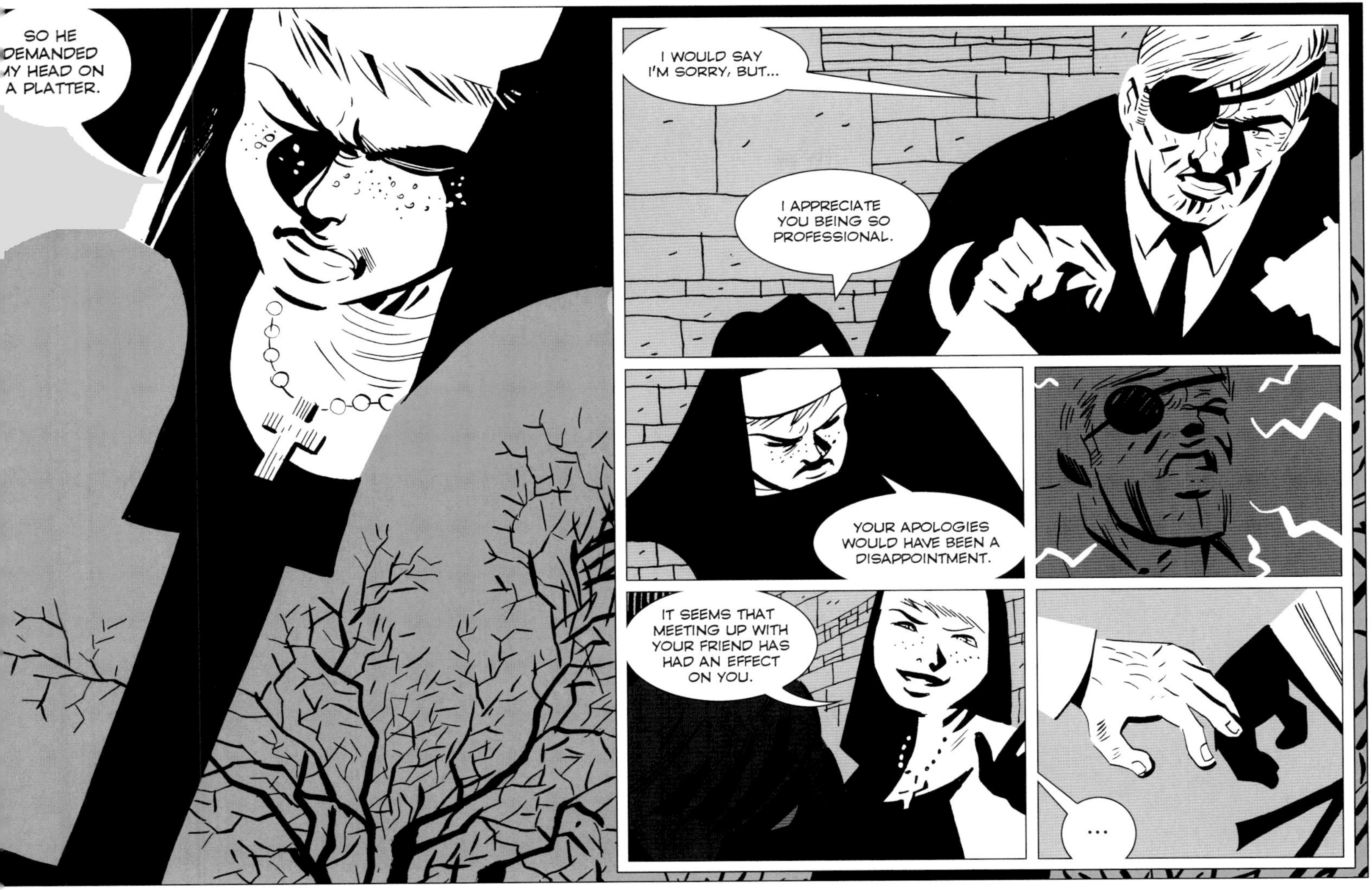

SO HE DEMANDED MY HEAD ON A PLATTER.
I WOULD SAY I'M SORRY, BUT...
I APPRECIATE YOU BEING SO PROFESSIONAL.
YOUR APOLOGIES WOULD HAVE BEEN A DISAPPOINTMENT.
IT SEEMS THAT MEETING UP WITH YOUR FRIEND HAS HAD AN EFFECT ON YOU.
...

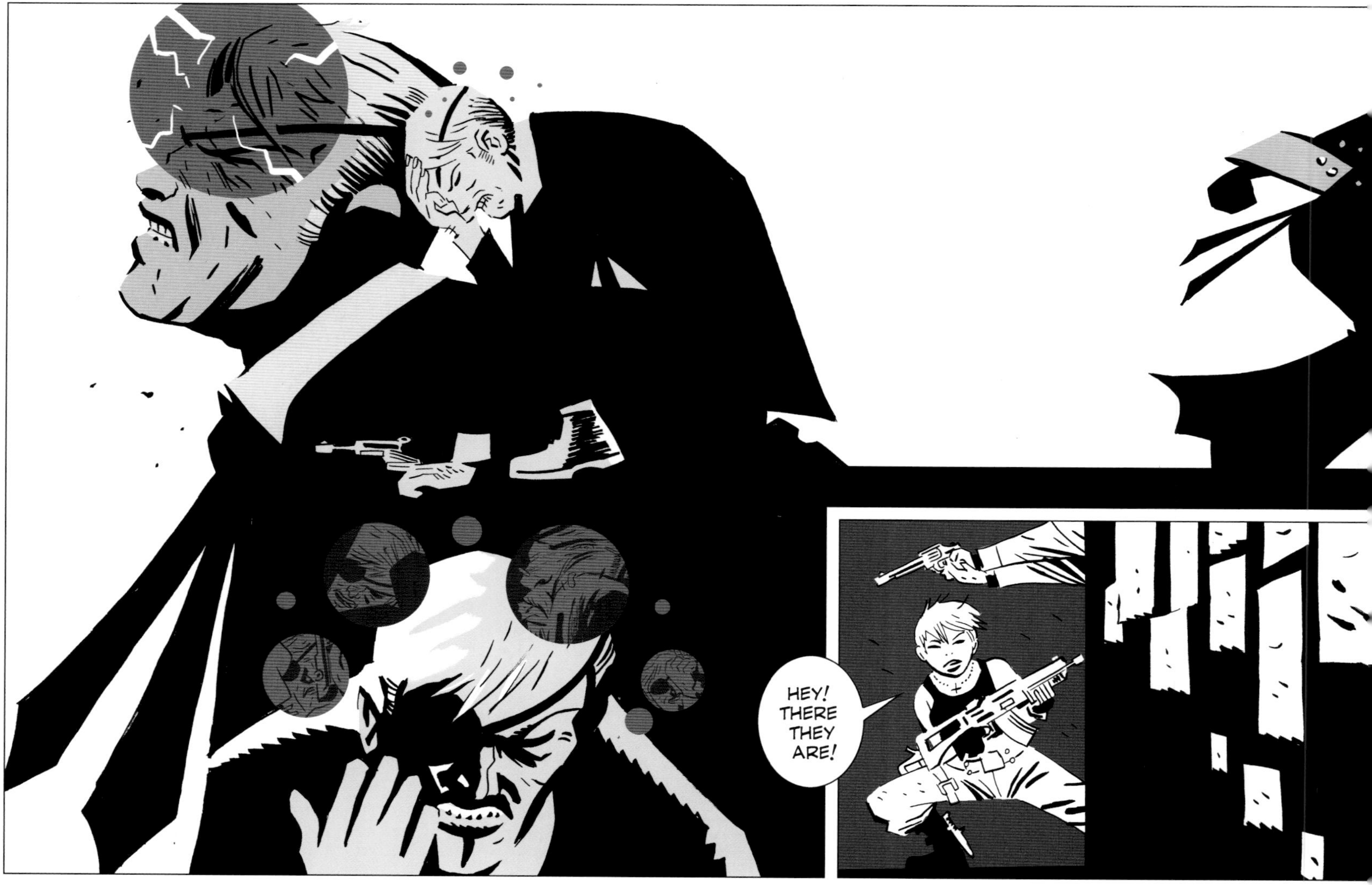
HEY! THERE THEY ARE!

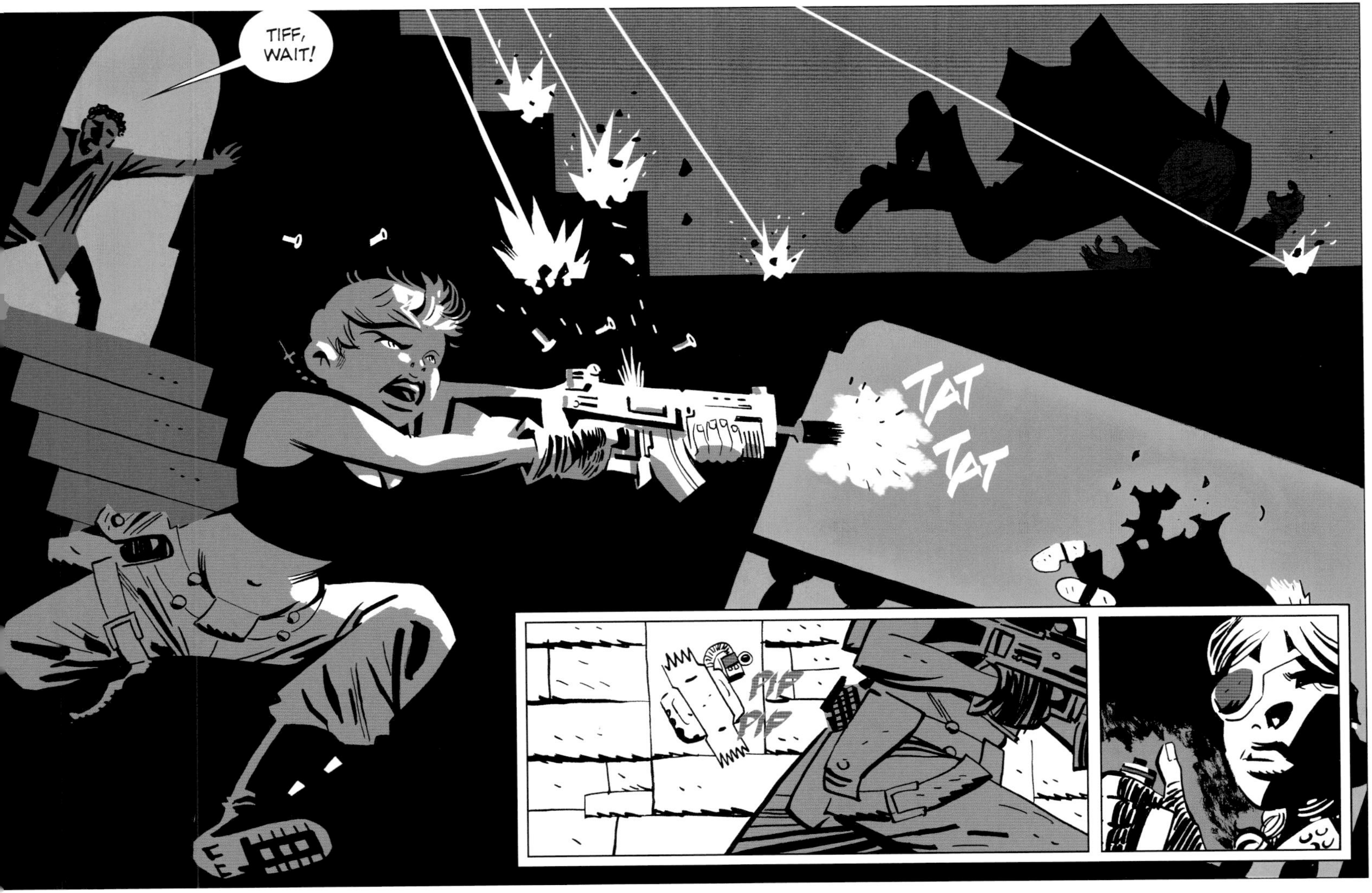

TIFF, WAIT!
TAT TAT
PIF PIF

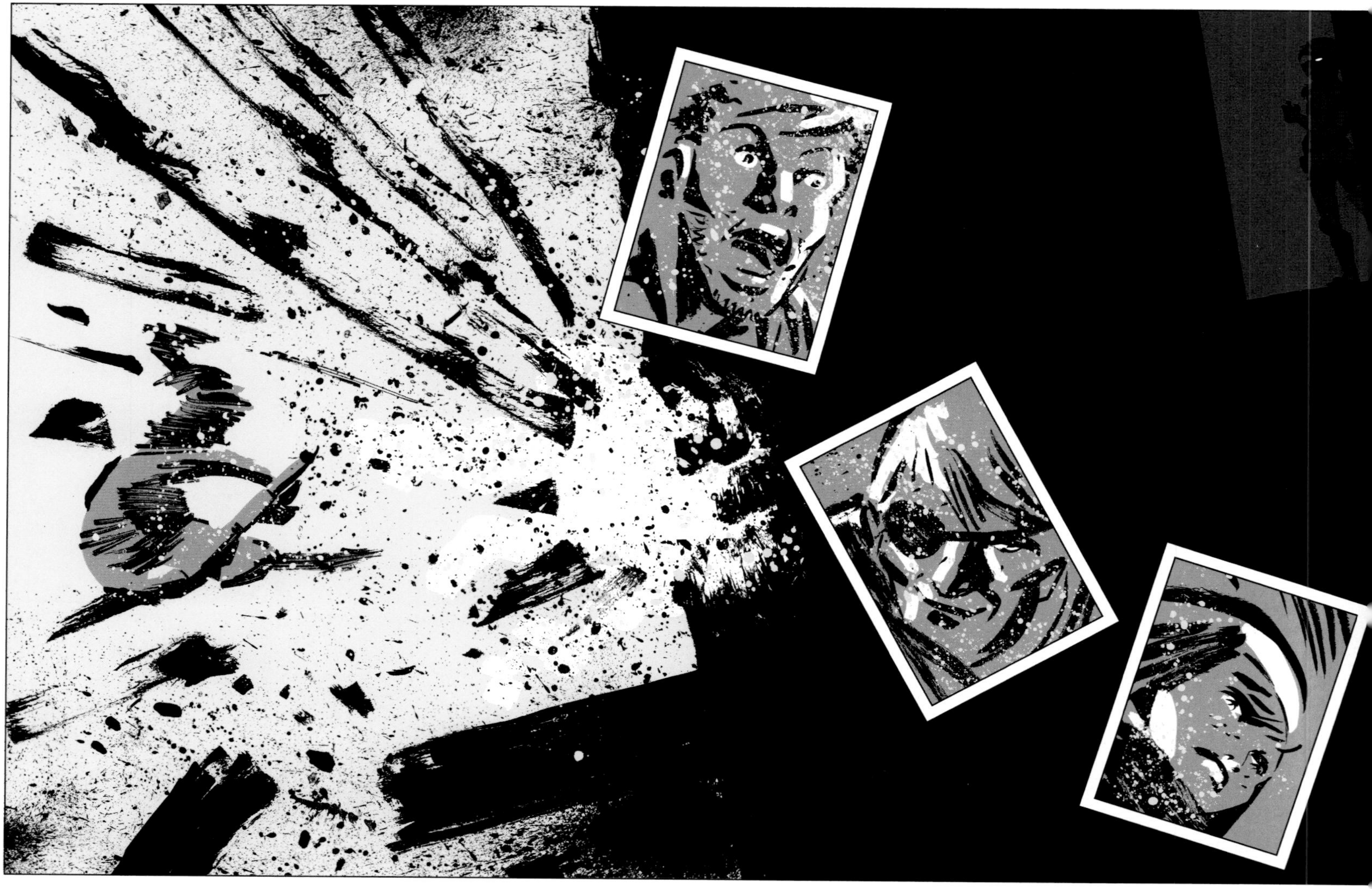

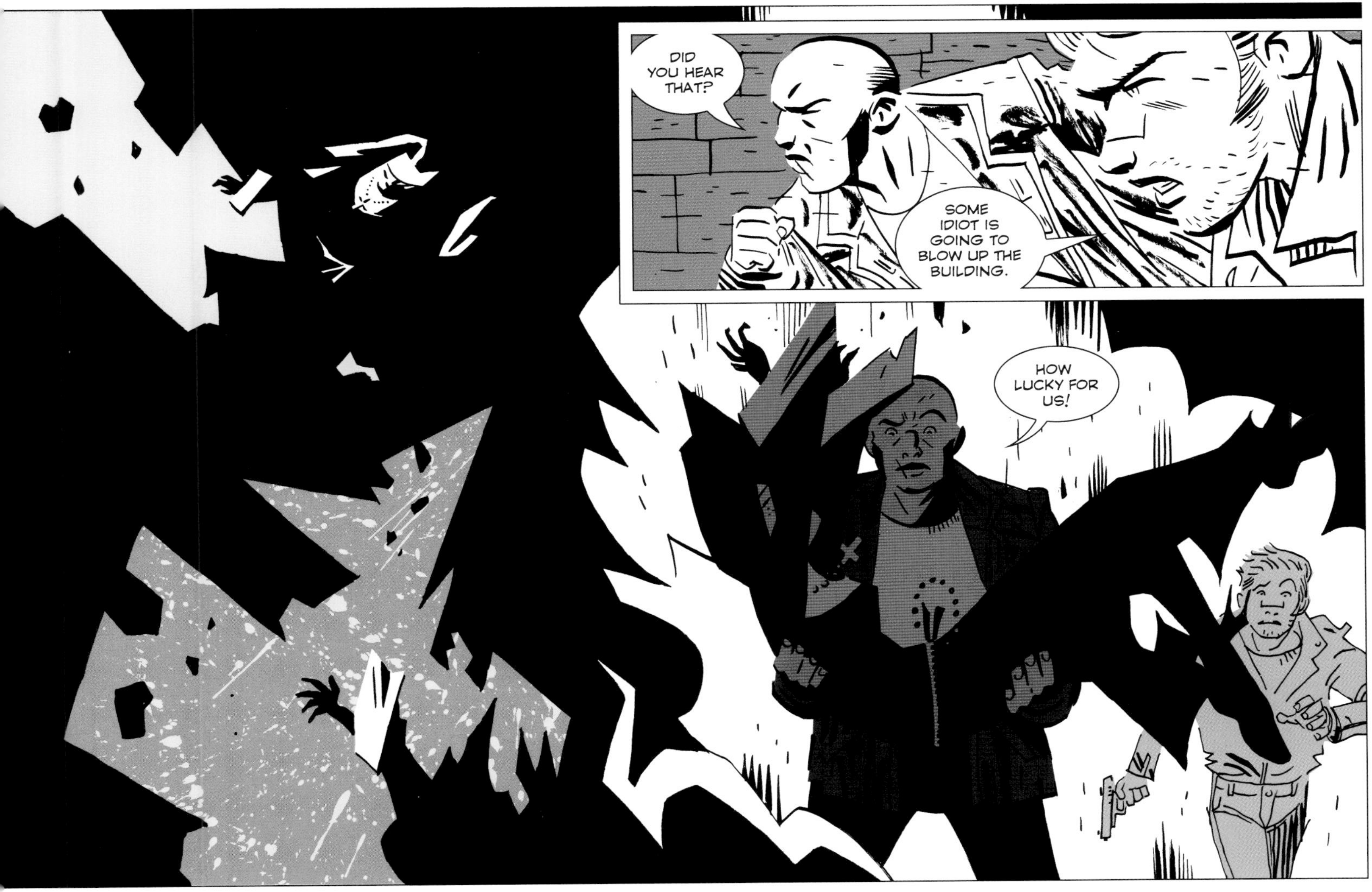

DID YOU HEAR THAT?
SOME IDIOT IS GOING TO BLOW UP THE BUILDING.
HOW LUCKY FOR US!

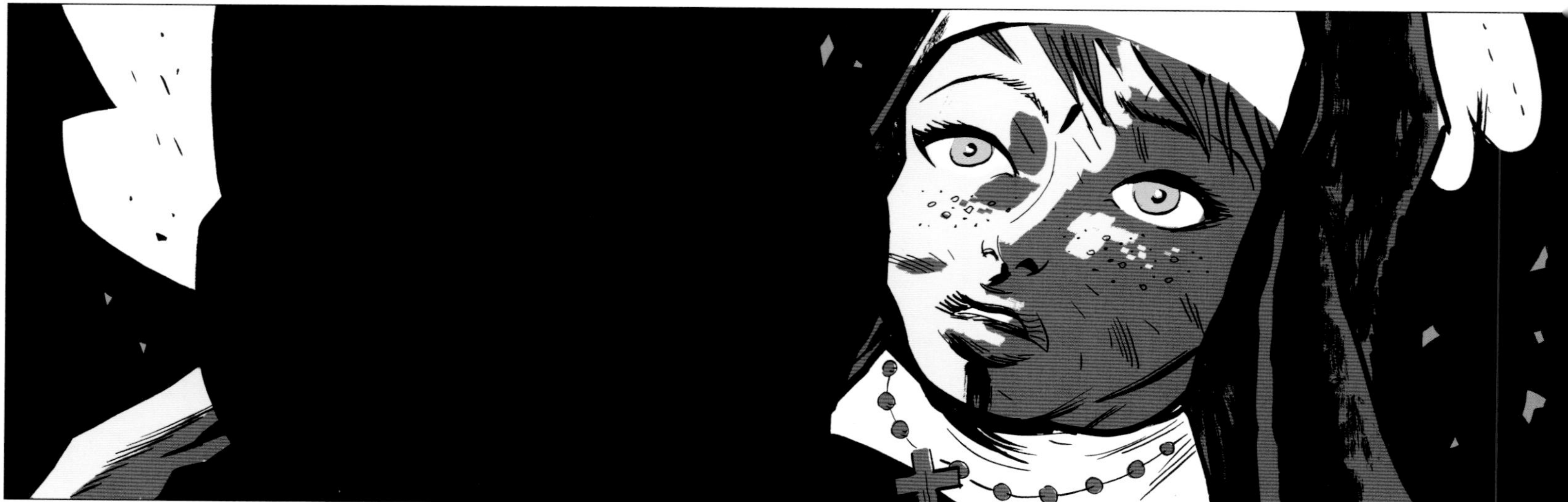

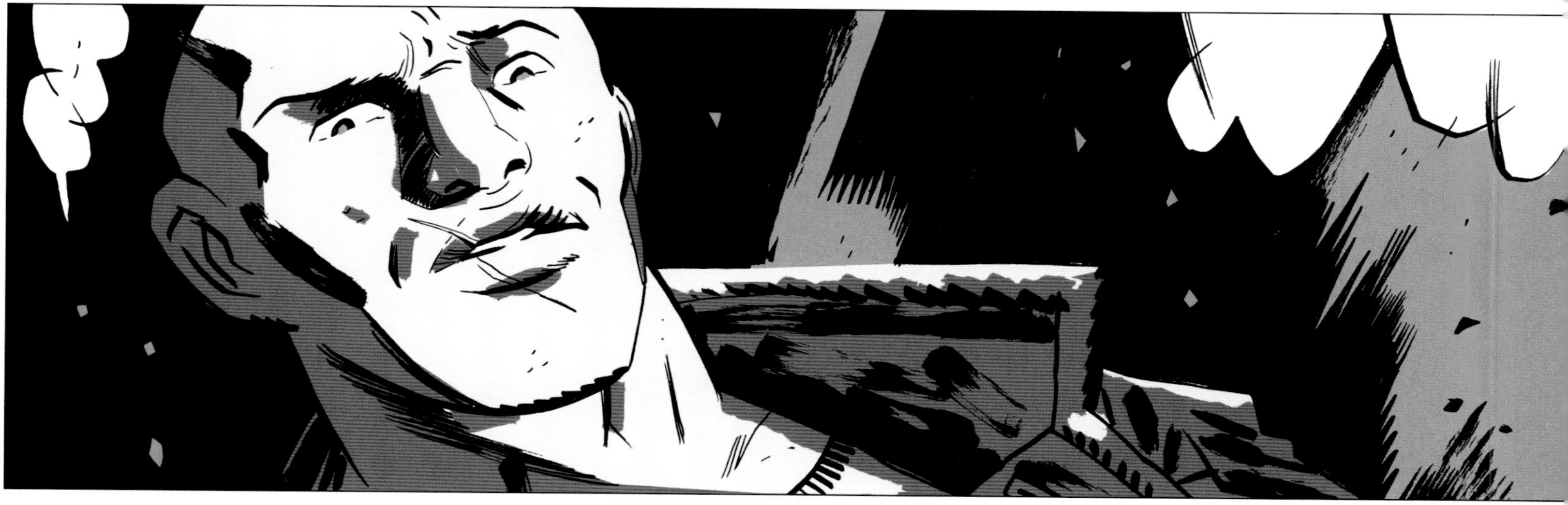

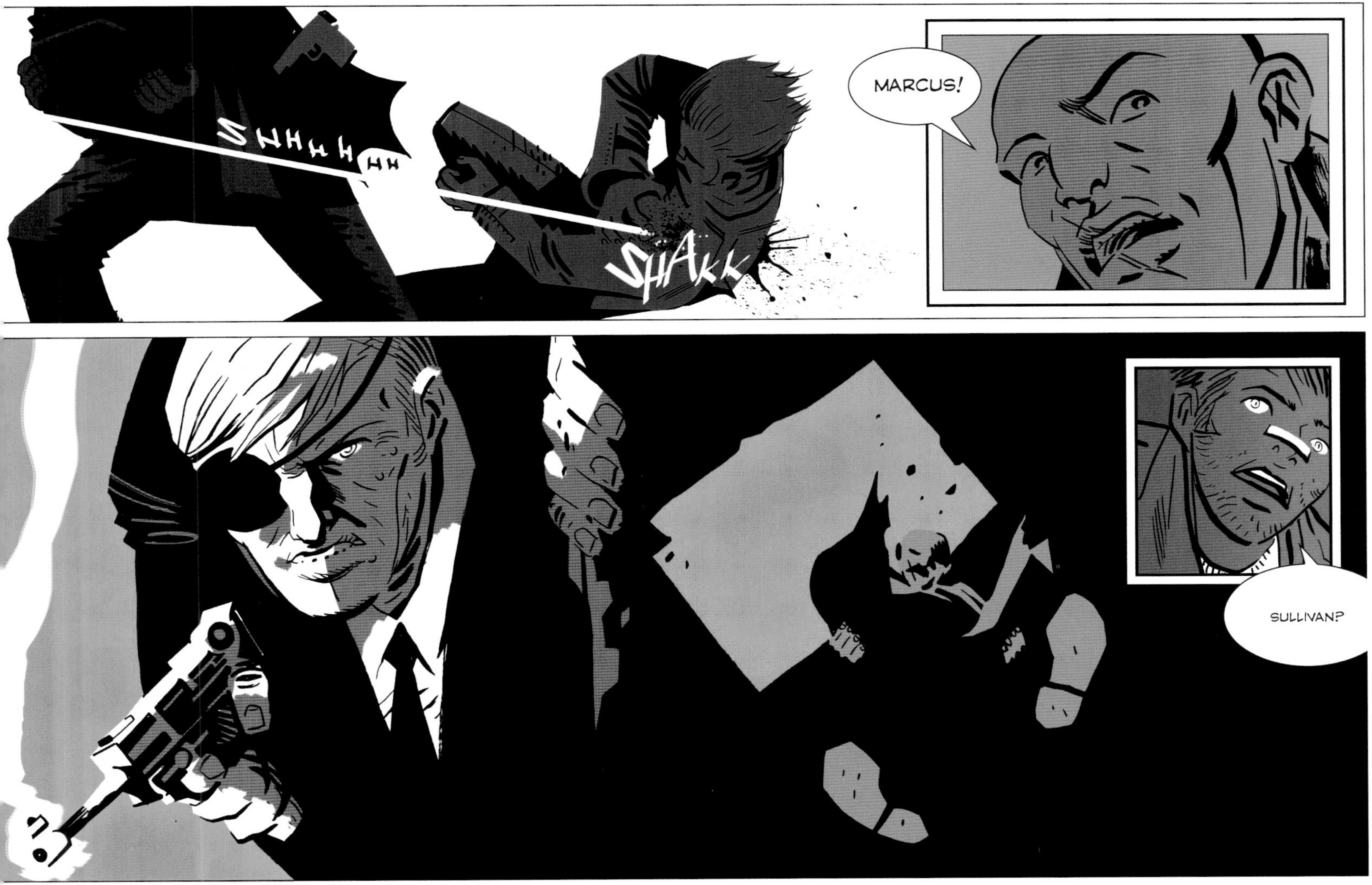
SHHHHHH
SHAKK
MARCUS!
SULLIVAN?

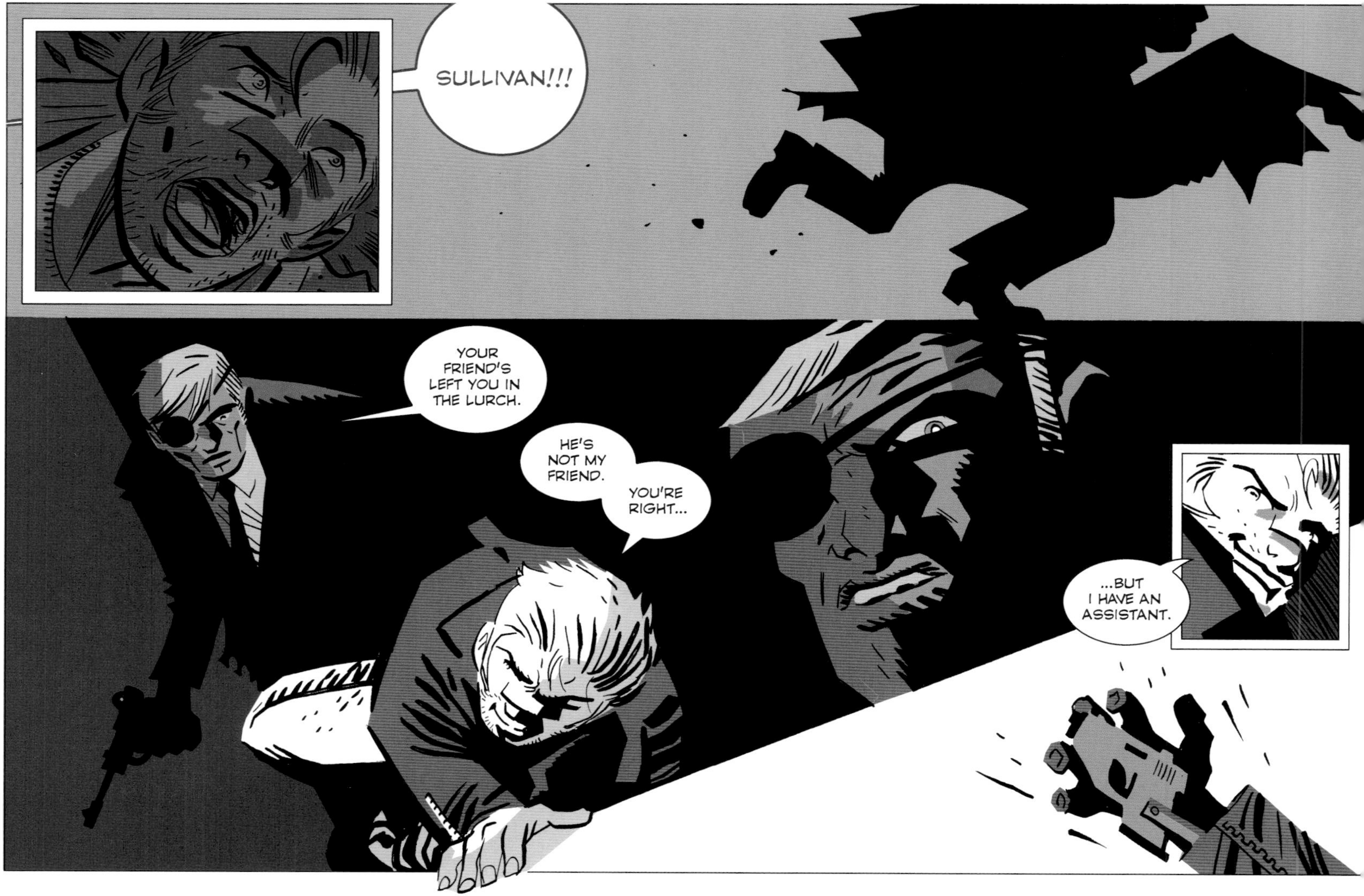

SULLIVAN!!!
YOUR FRIEND'S LEFT YOU IN THE LURCH.
HE'S NOT MY FRIEND.
YOU'RE RIGHT...
...BUT I HAVE AN ASSISTANT.

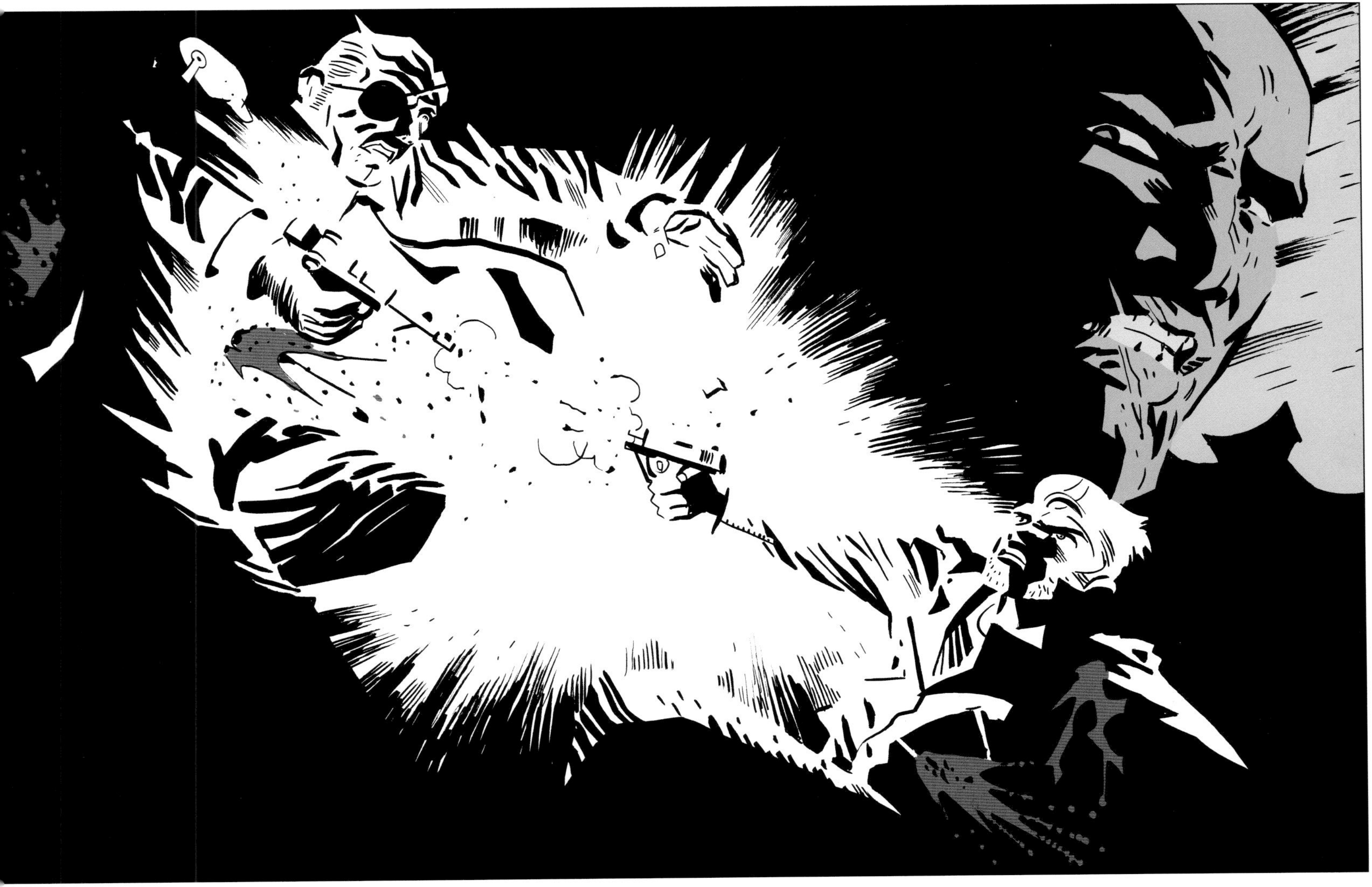

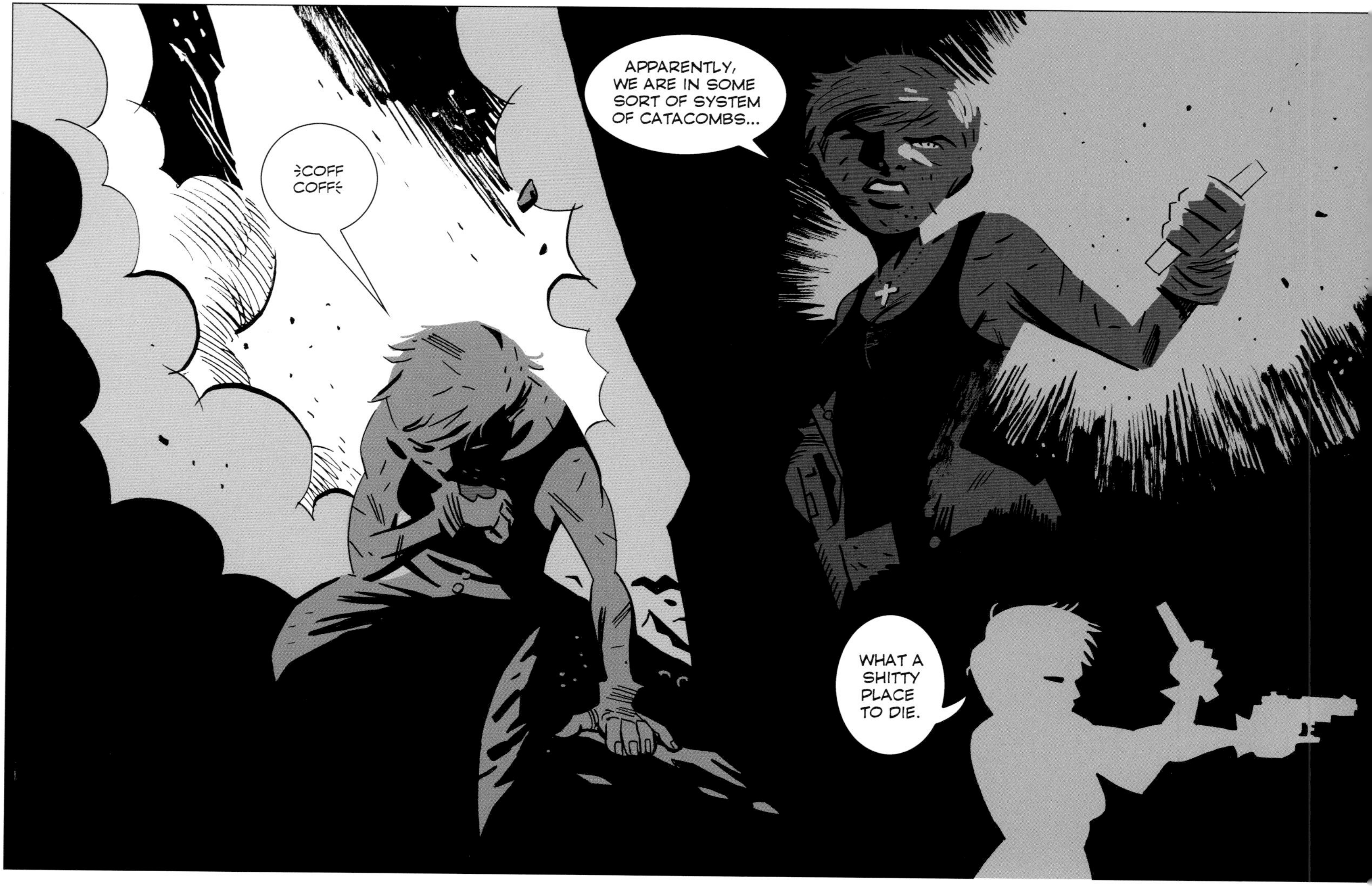

ƷCOFF COFFƸ
APPARENTLY, WE ARE IN SOME SORT OF SYSTEM OF CATACOMBS...
WHAT A SHITTY PLACE TO DIE.

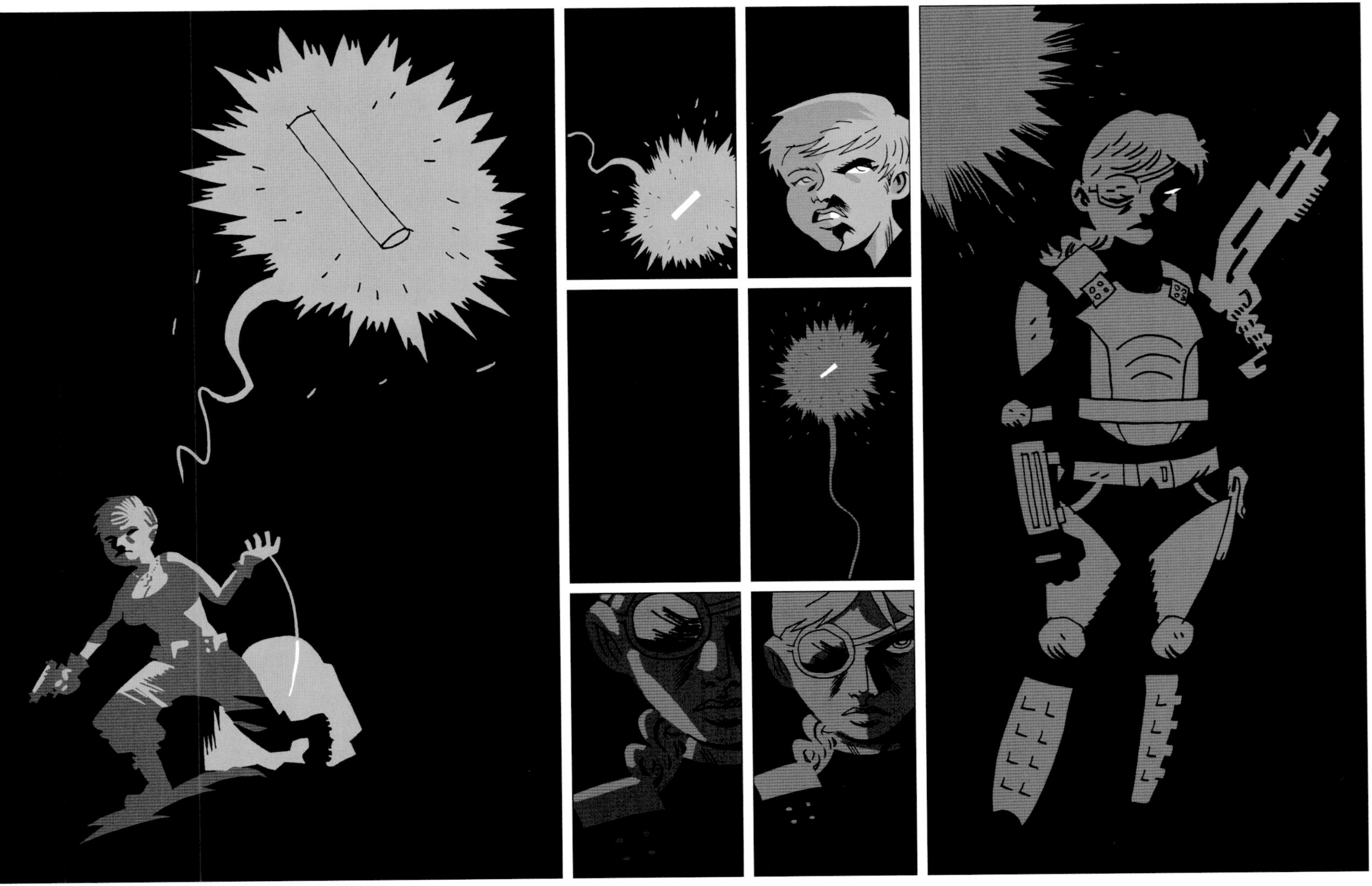

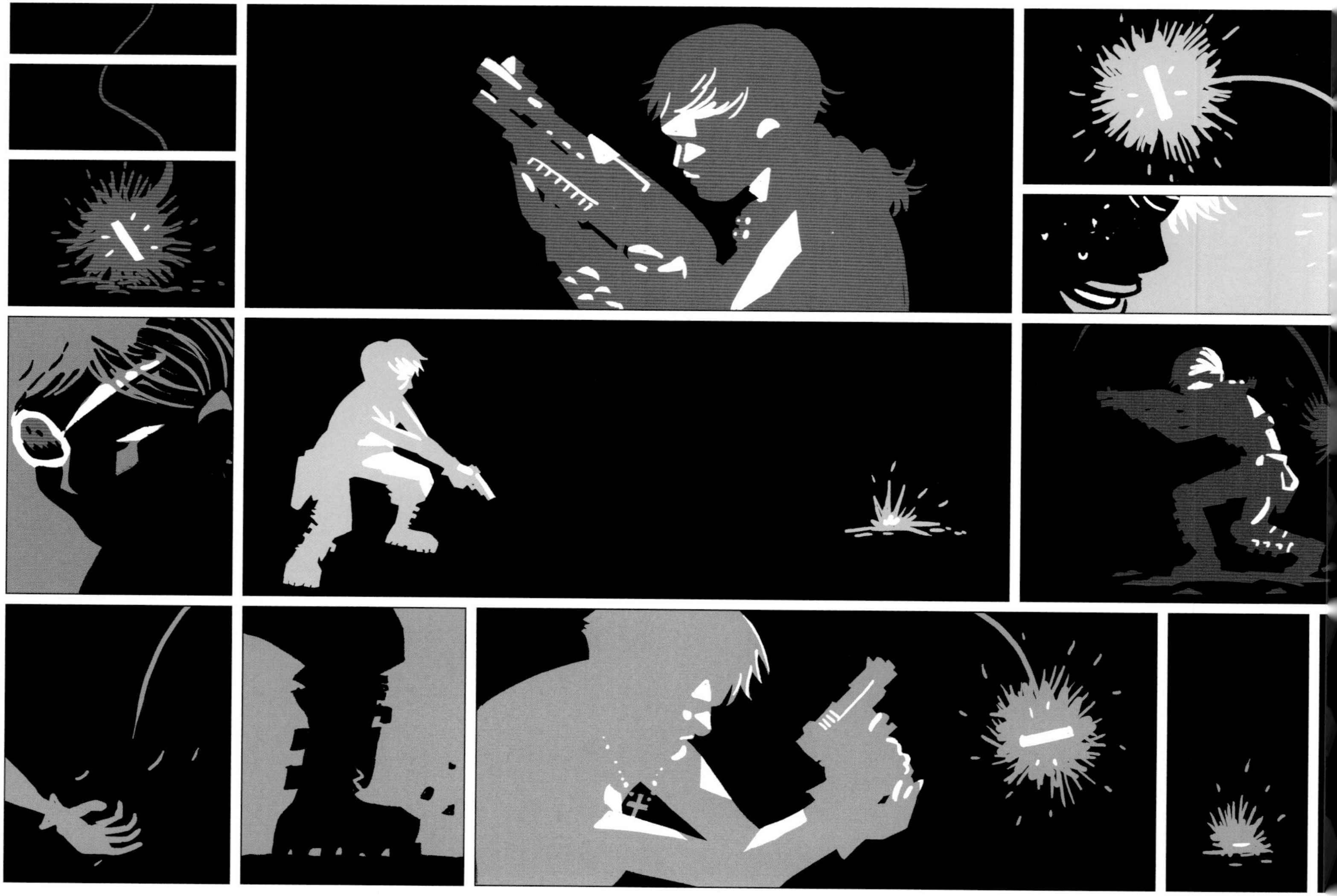

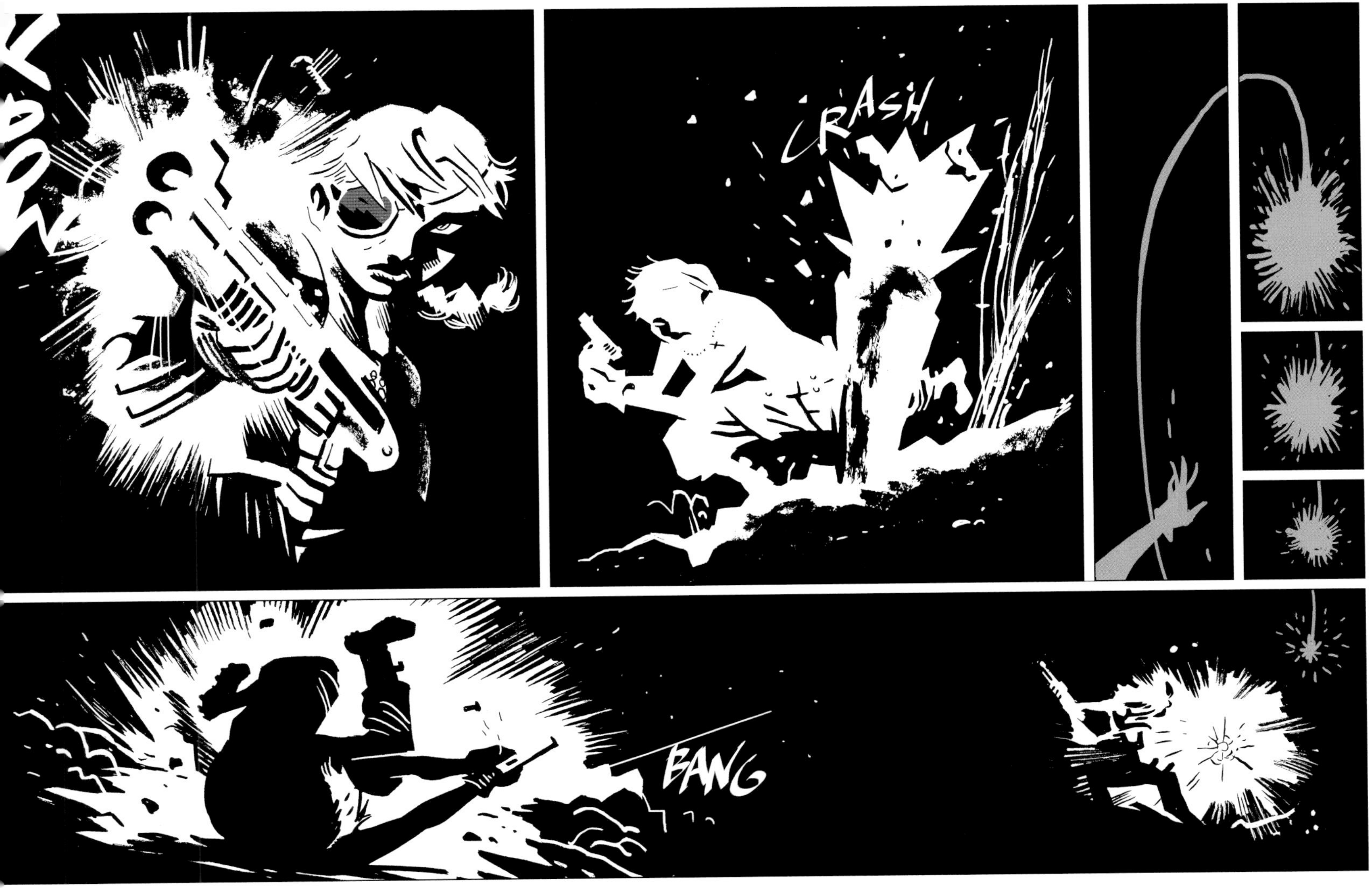
CRASH
BANG

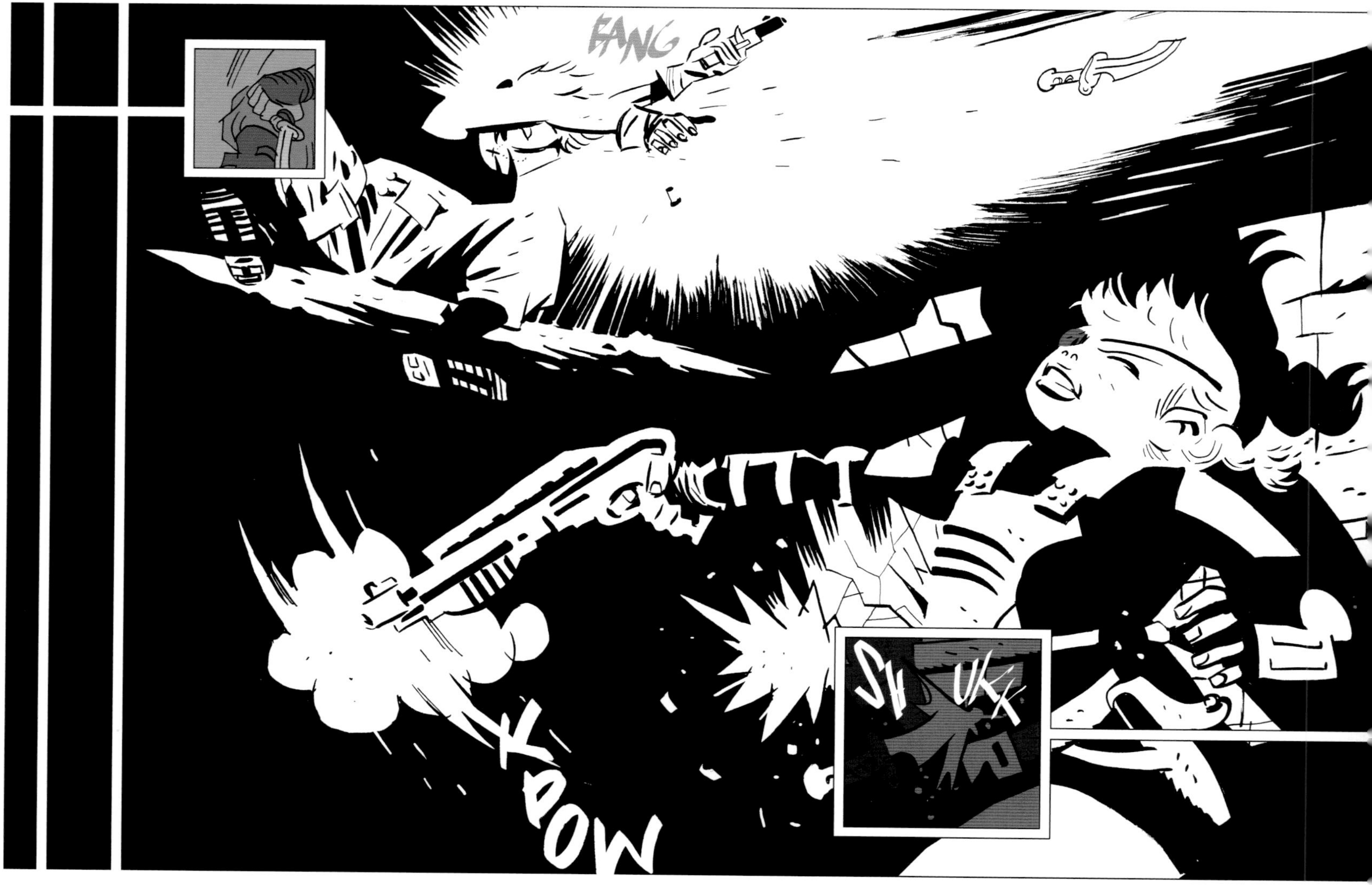
BANG

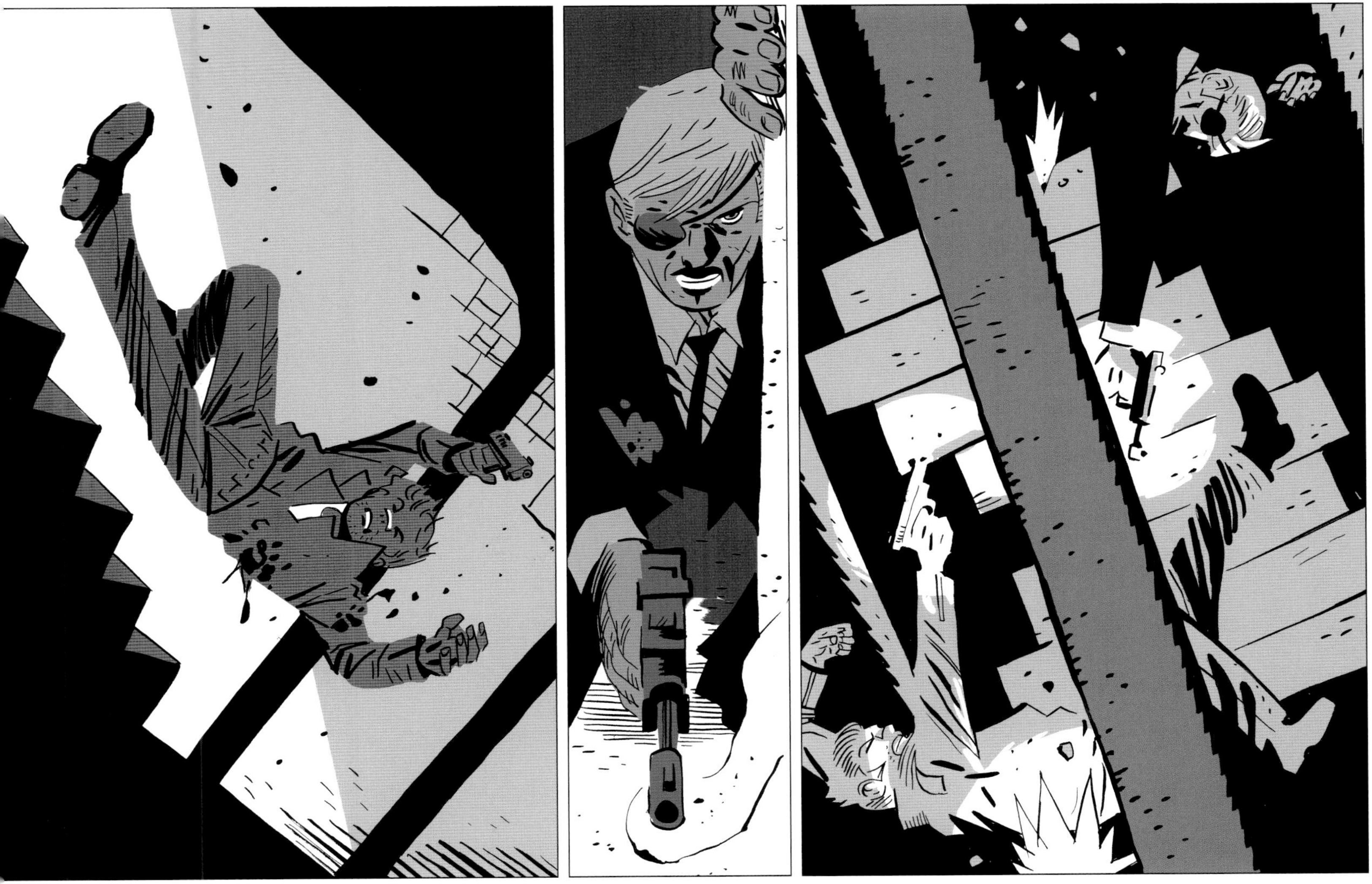

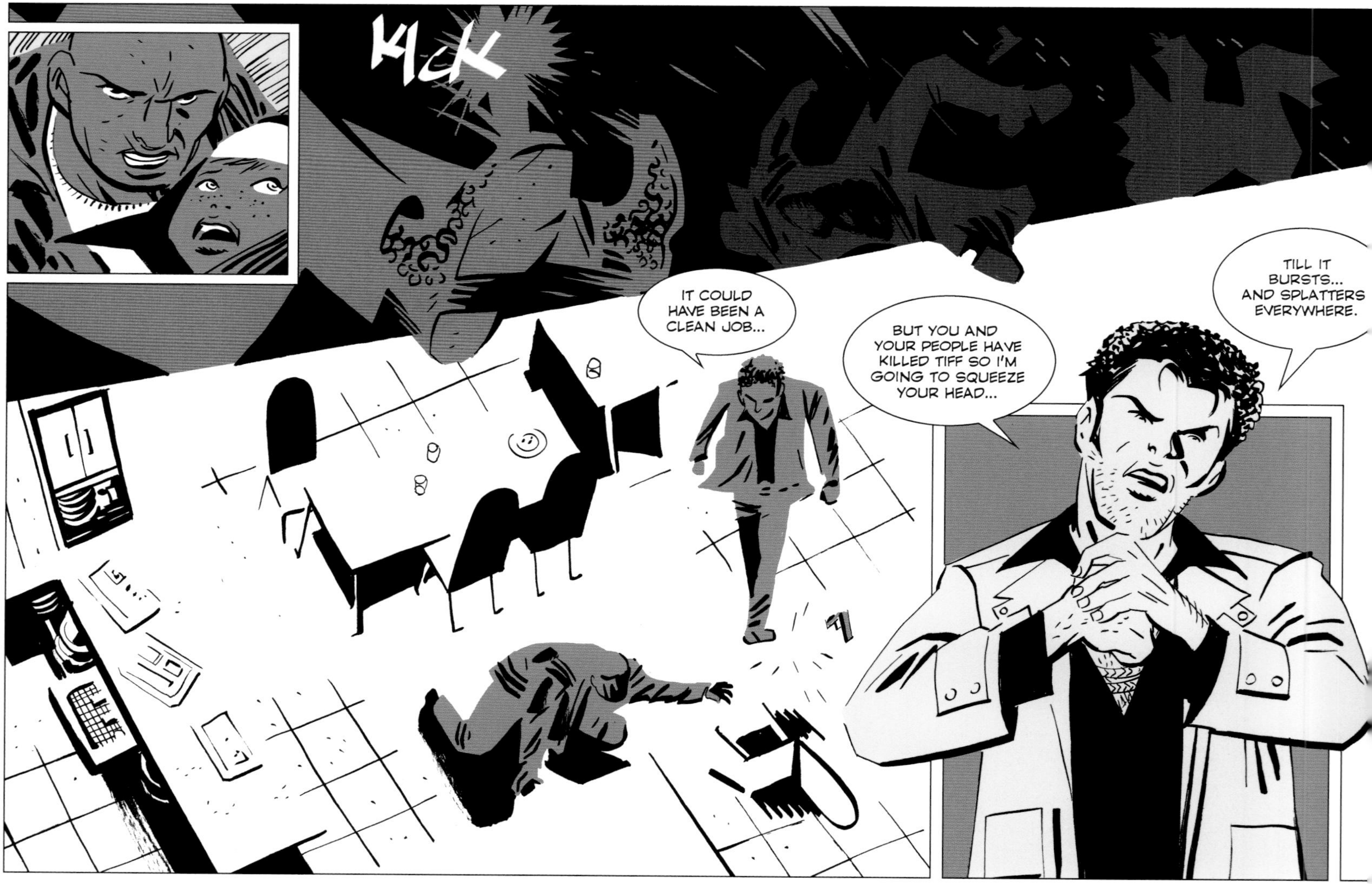
KICK
IT COULD HAVE BEEN A CLEAN JOB...
BUT YOU AND YOUR PEOPLE HAVE KILLED TIFF SO I'M GOING TO SQUEEZE YOUR HEAD...
TILL IT BURSTS... AND SPLATTERS EVERYWHERE.

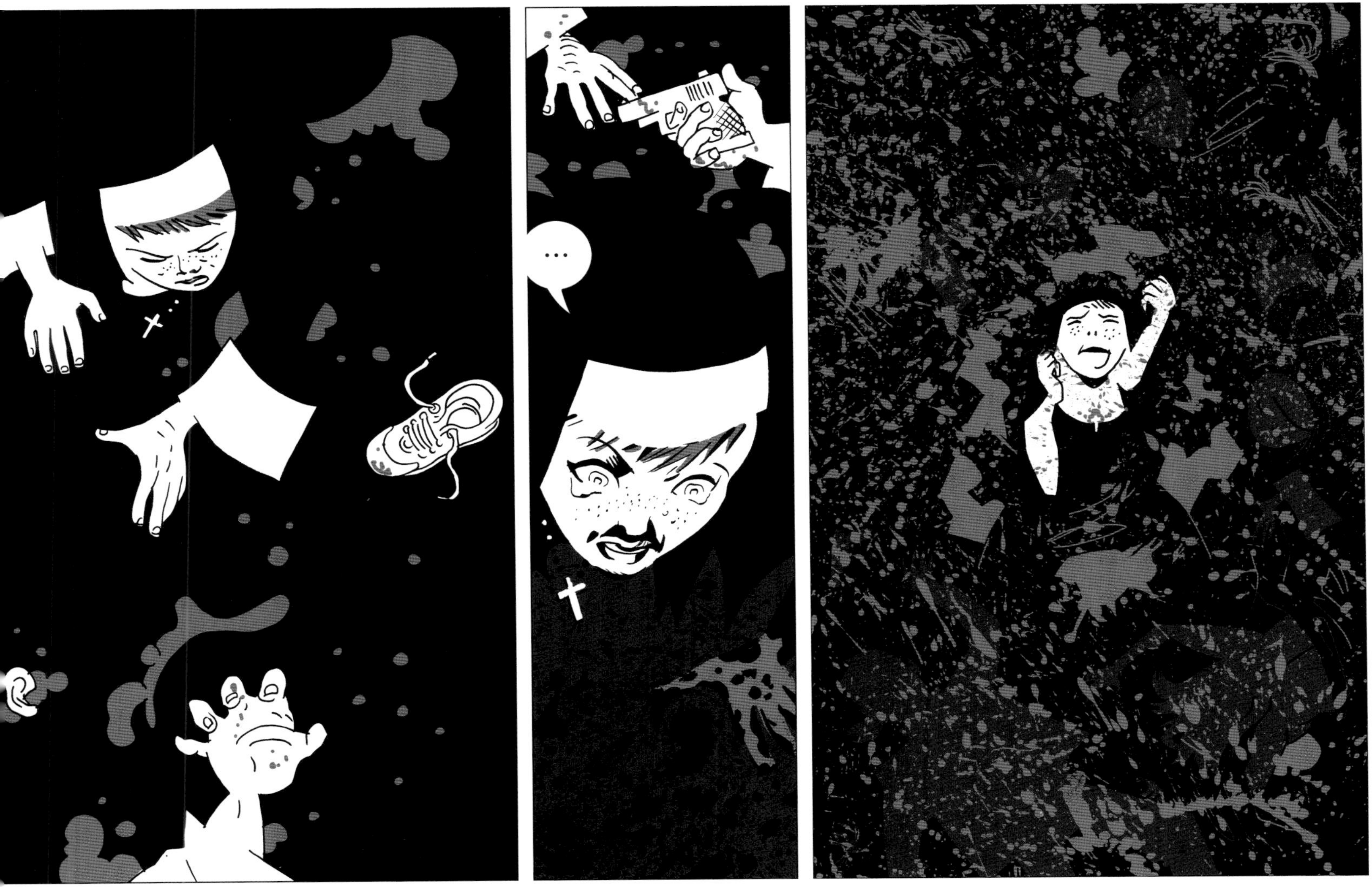
...

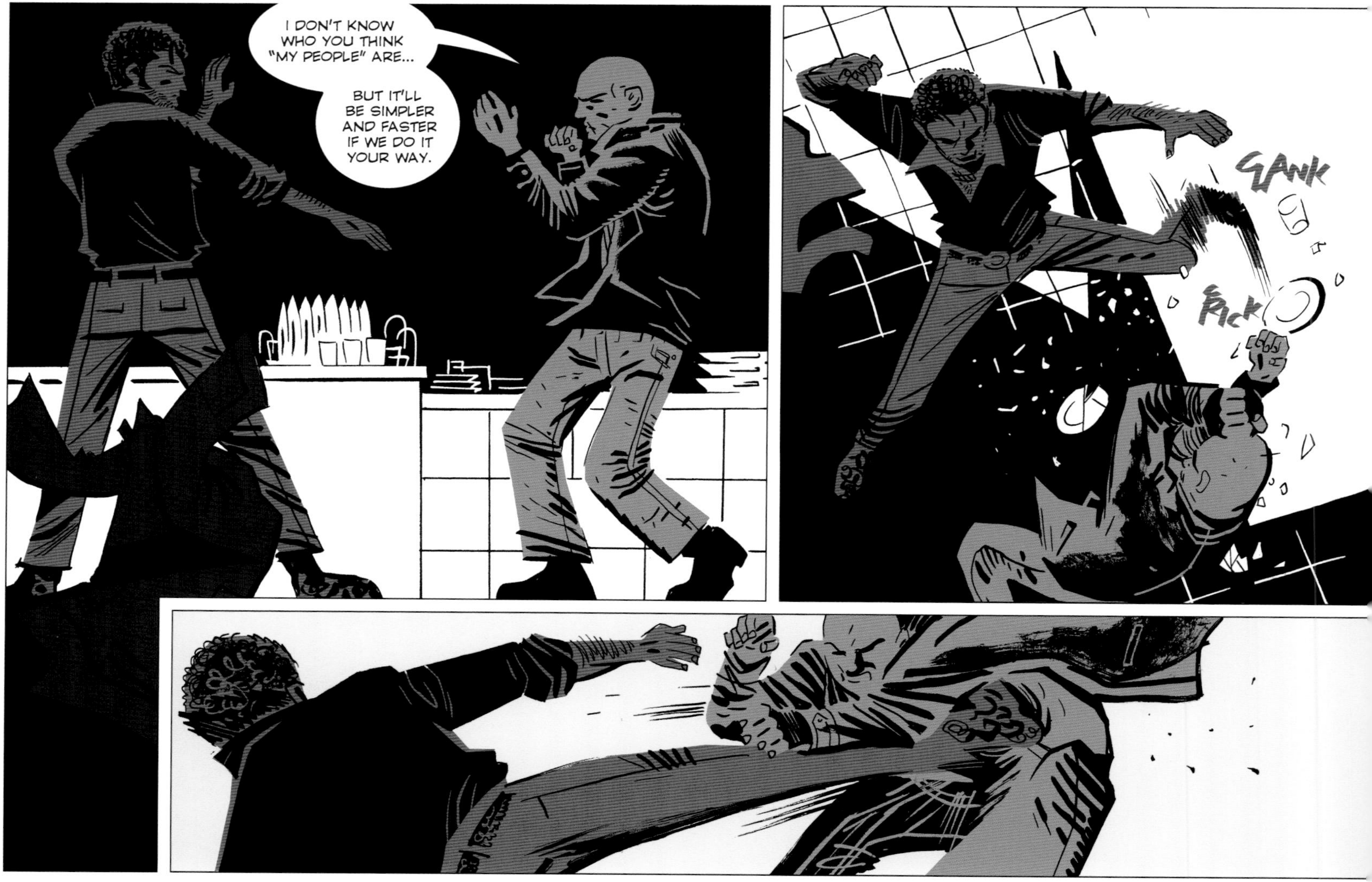
I DON'T KNOW WHO YOU THINK "MY PEOPLE" ARE...
BUT IT'LL BE SIMPLER AND FASTER IF WE DO IT YOUR WAY.
CLANK
CRICK

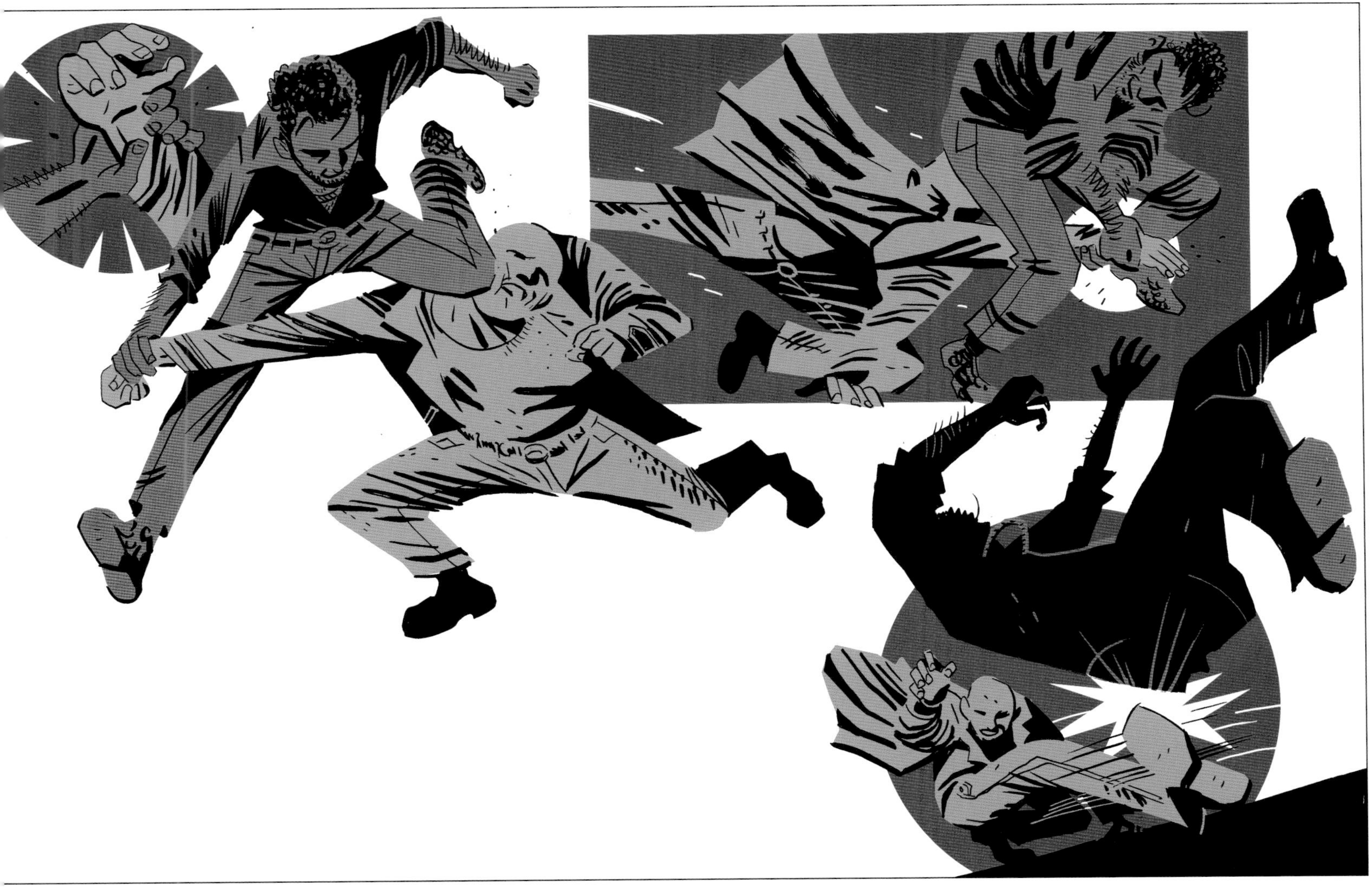

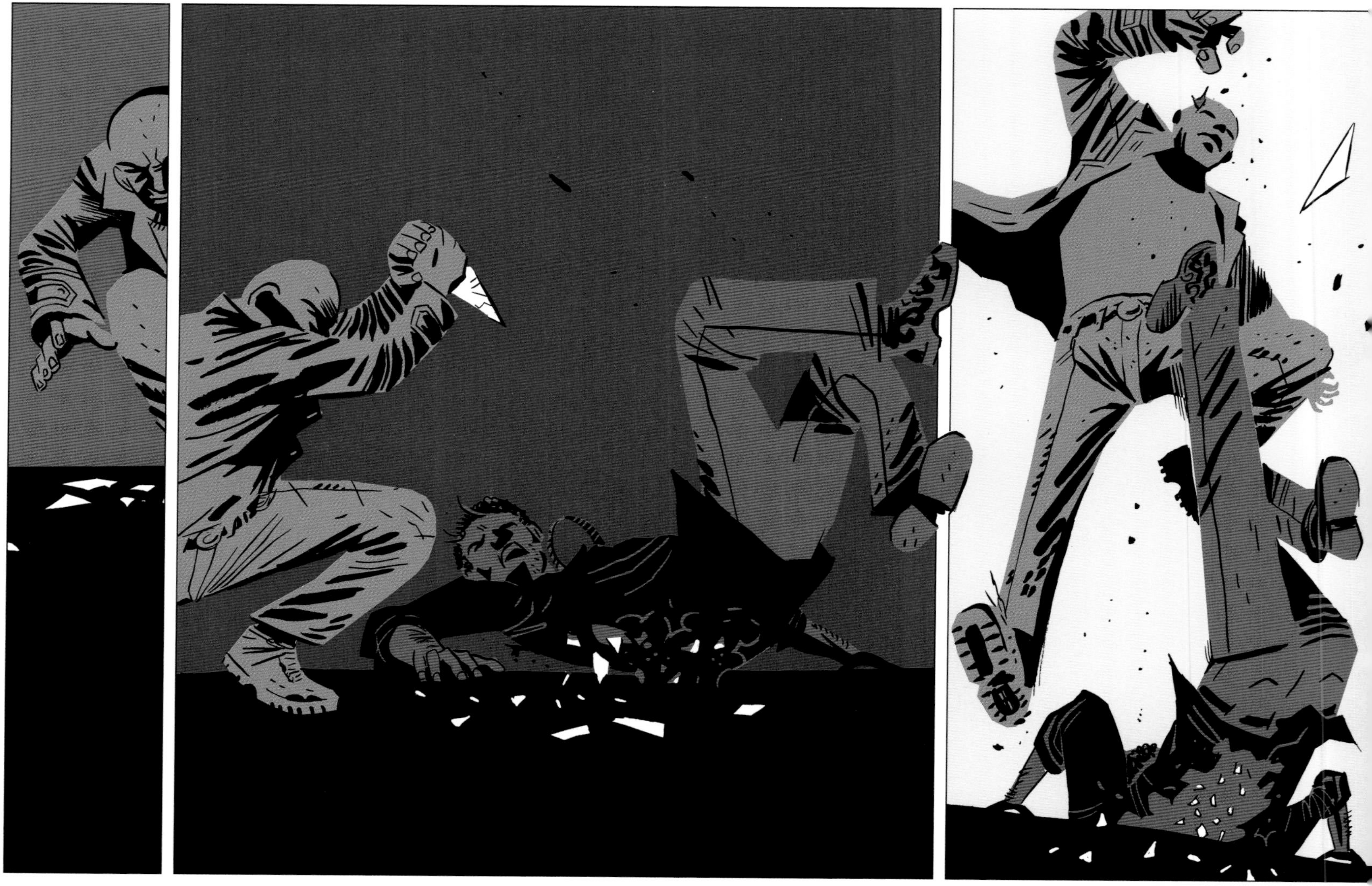

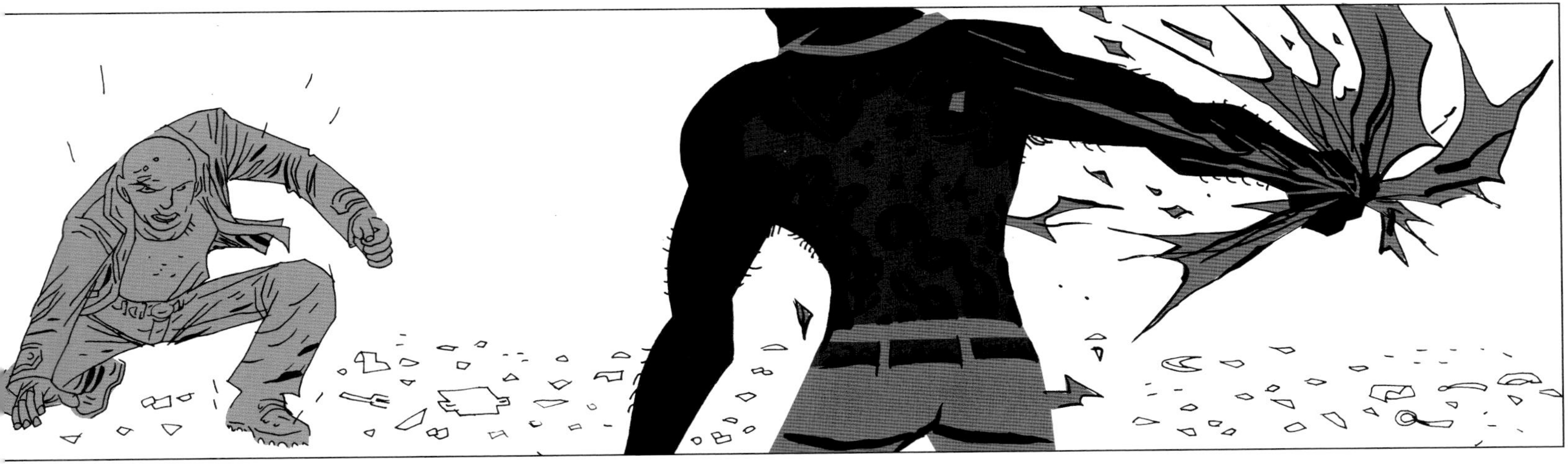

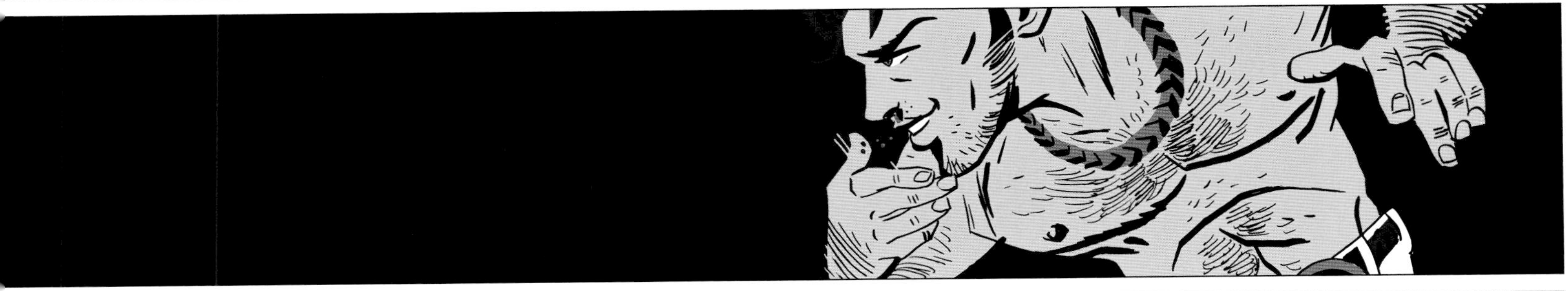

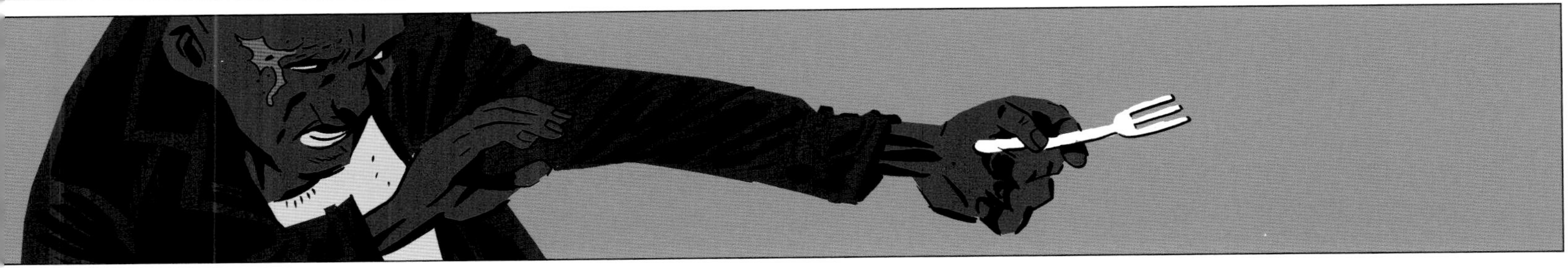

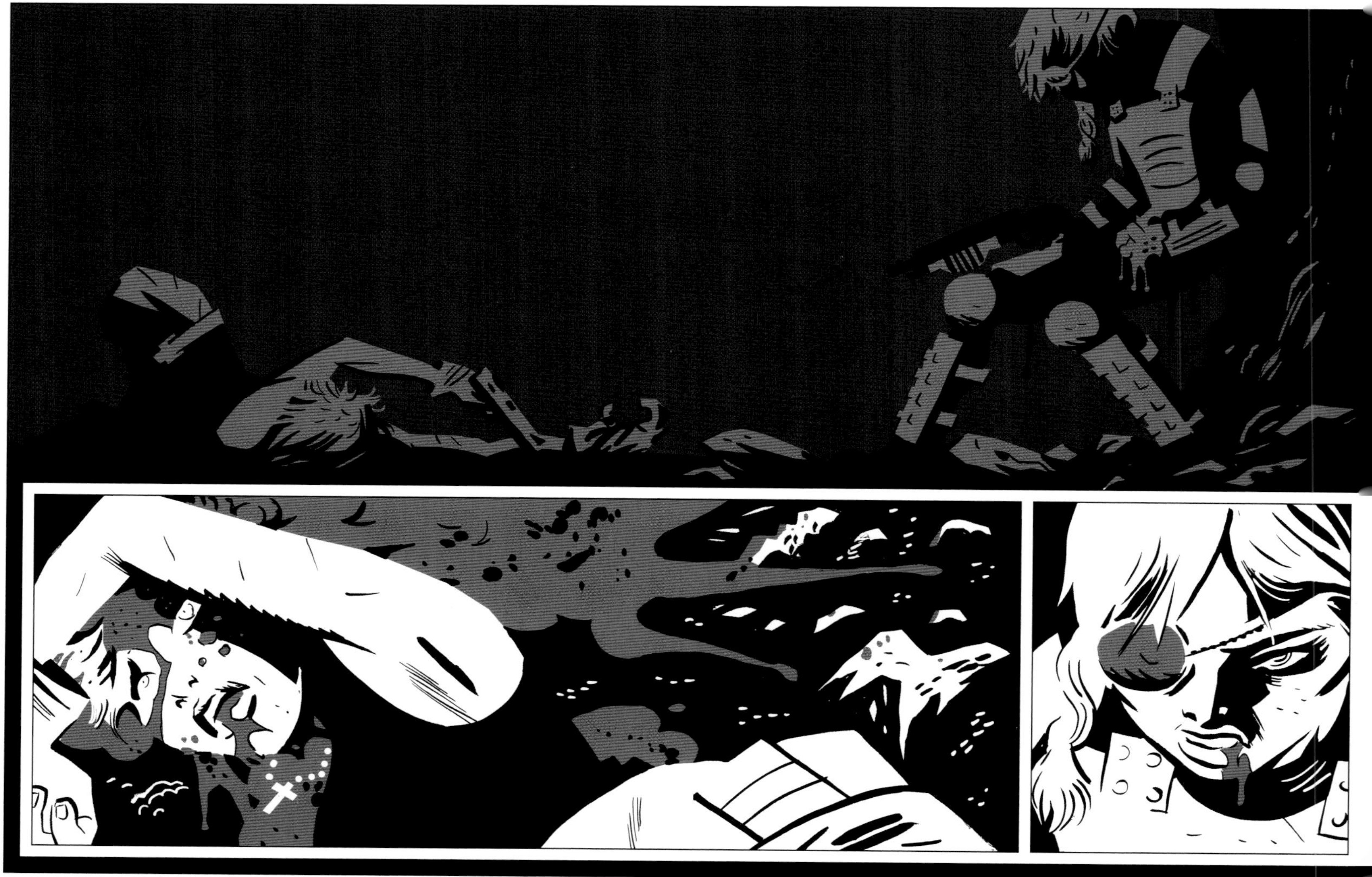

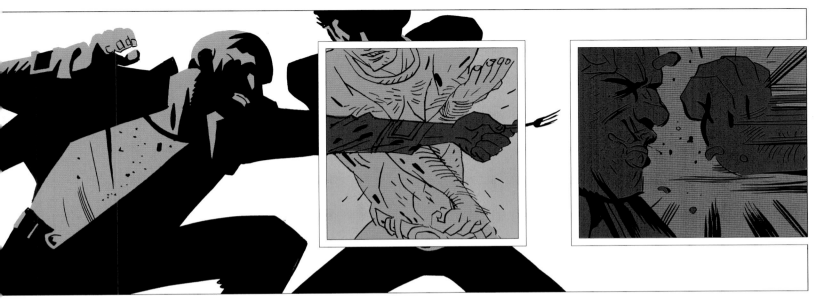

KRAK

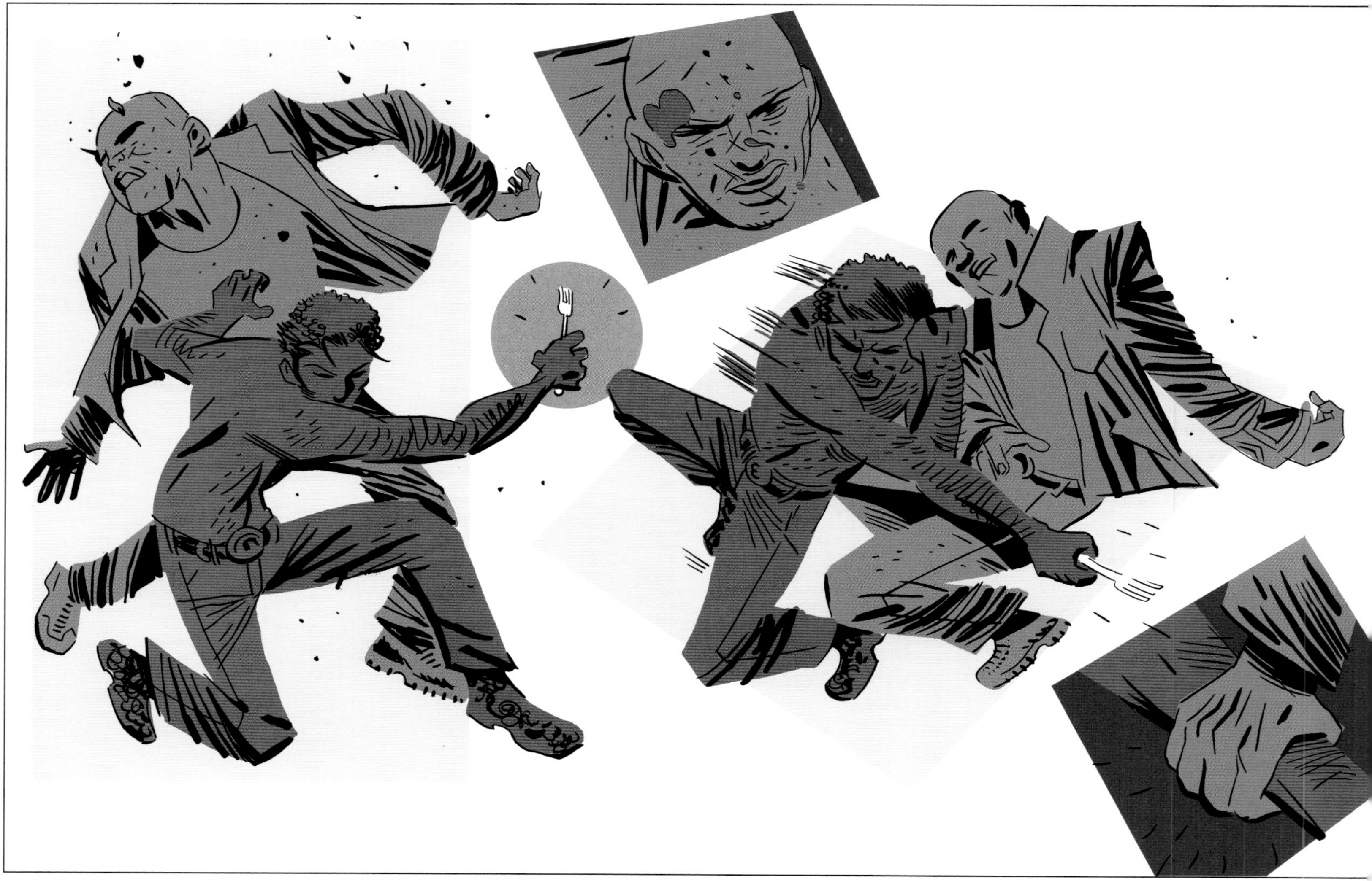

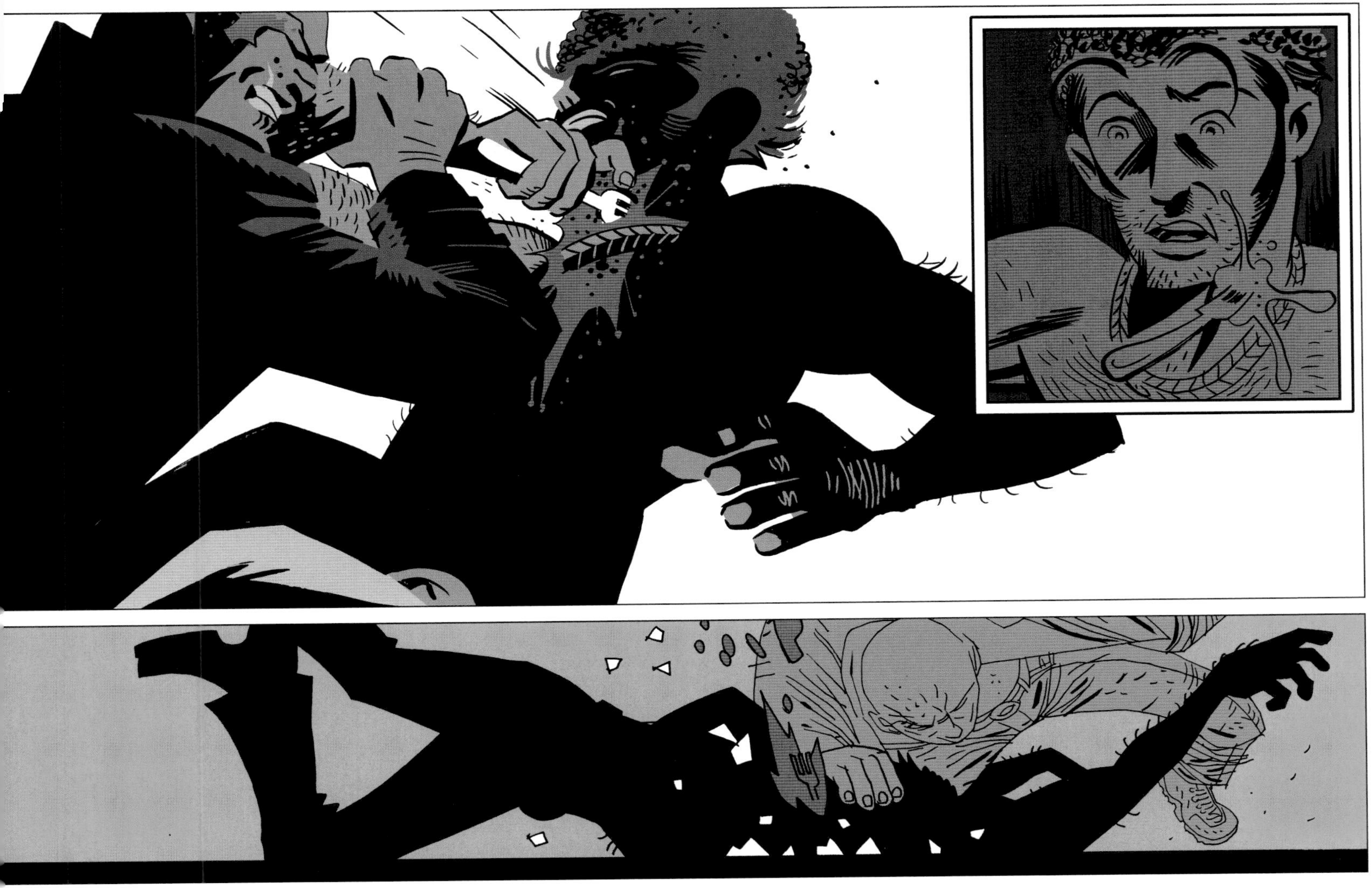

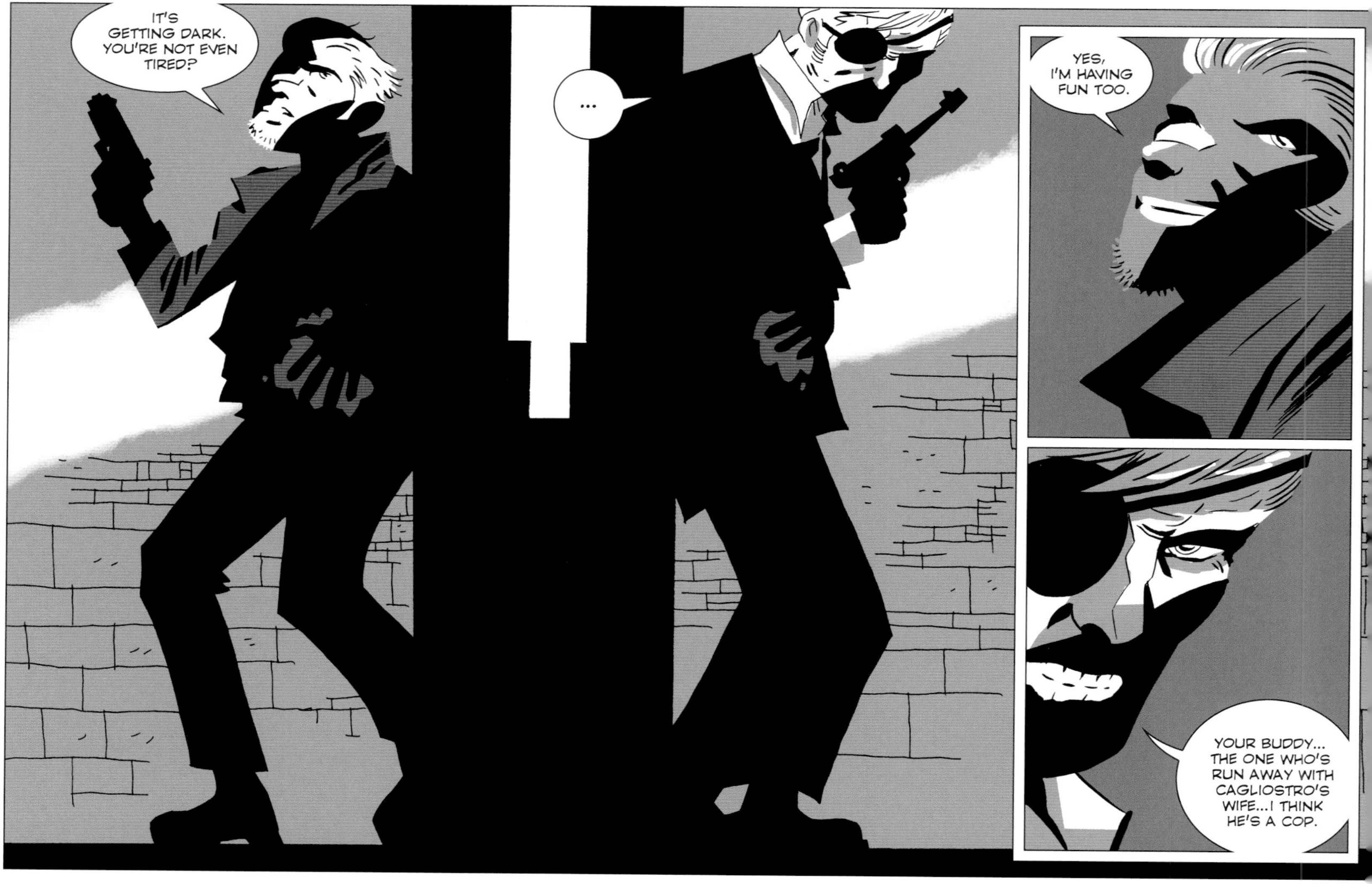
IT'S GETTING DARK. YOU'RE NOT EVEN TIRED?
...
YES, I'M HAVING FUN TOO.
YOUR BUDDY... THE ONE WHO'S RUN AWAY WITH CAGLIOSTRO'S WIFE...I THINK HE'S A COP.

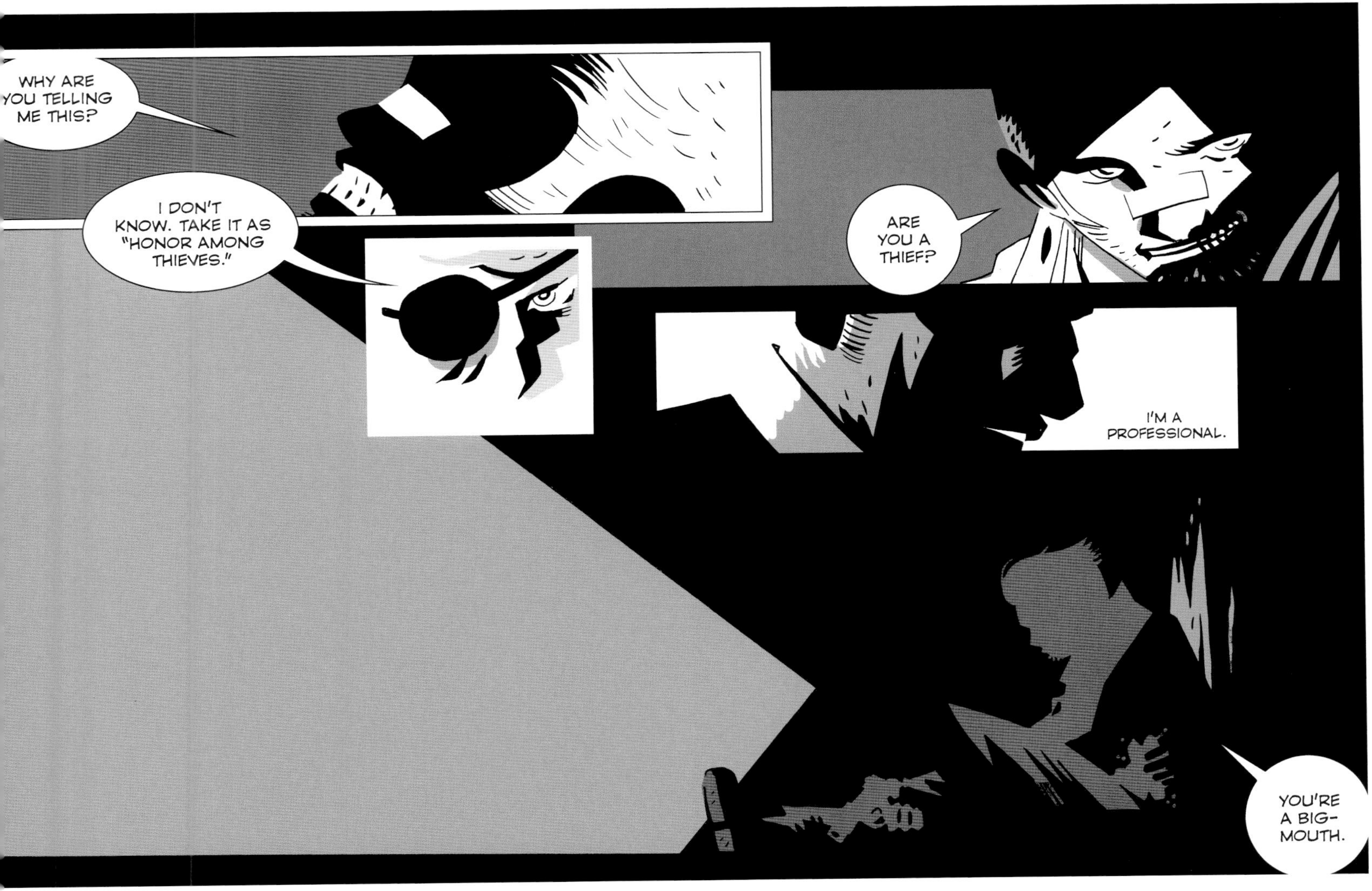
WHY ARE YOU TELLING ME THIS?
I DON'T KNOW. TAKE IT AS "HONOR AMONG THIEVES."
ARE YOU A THIEF?
I'M A PROFESSIONAL.
YOU'RE A BIG-MOUTH.

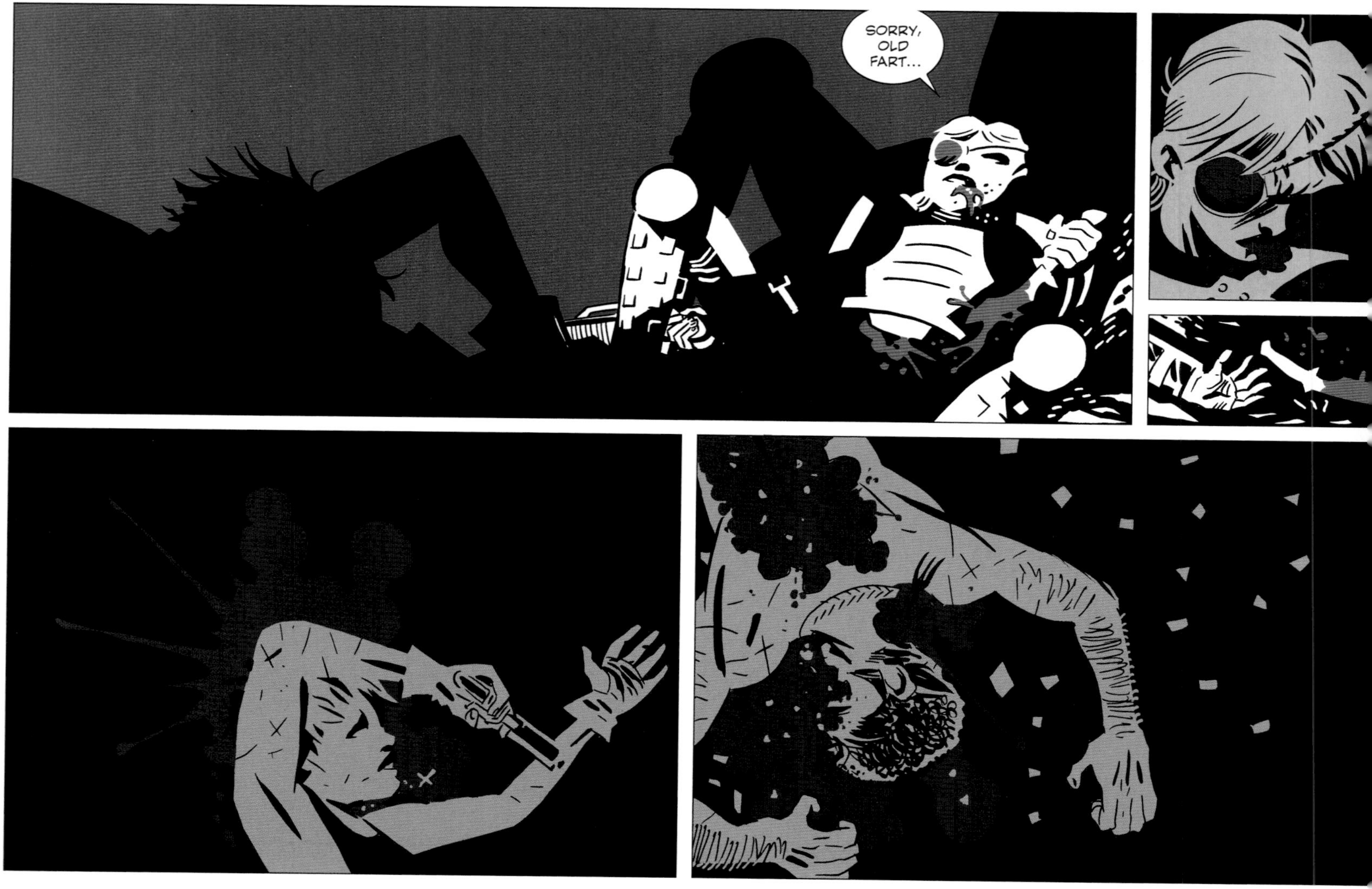
SORRY, OLD FART...

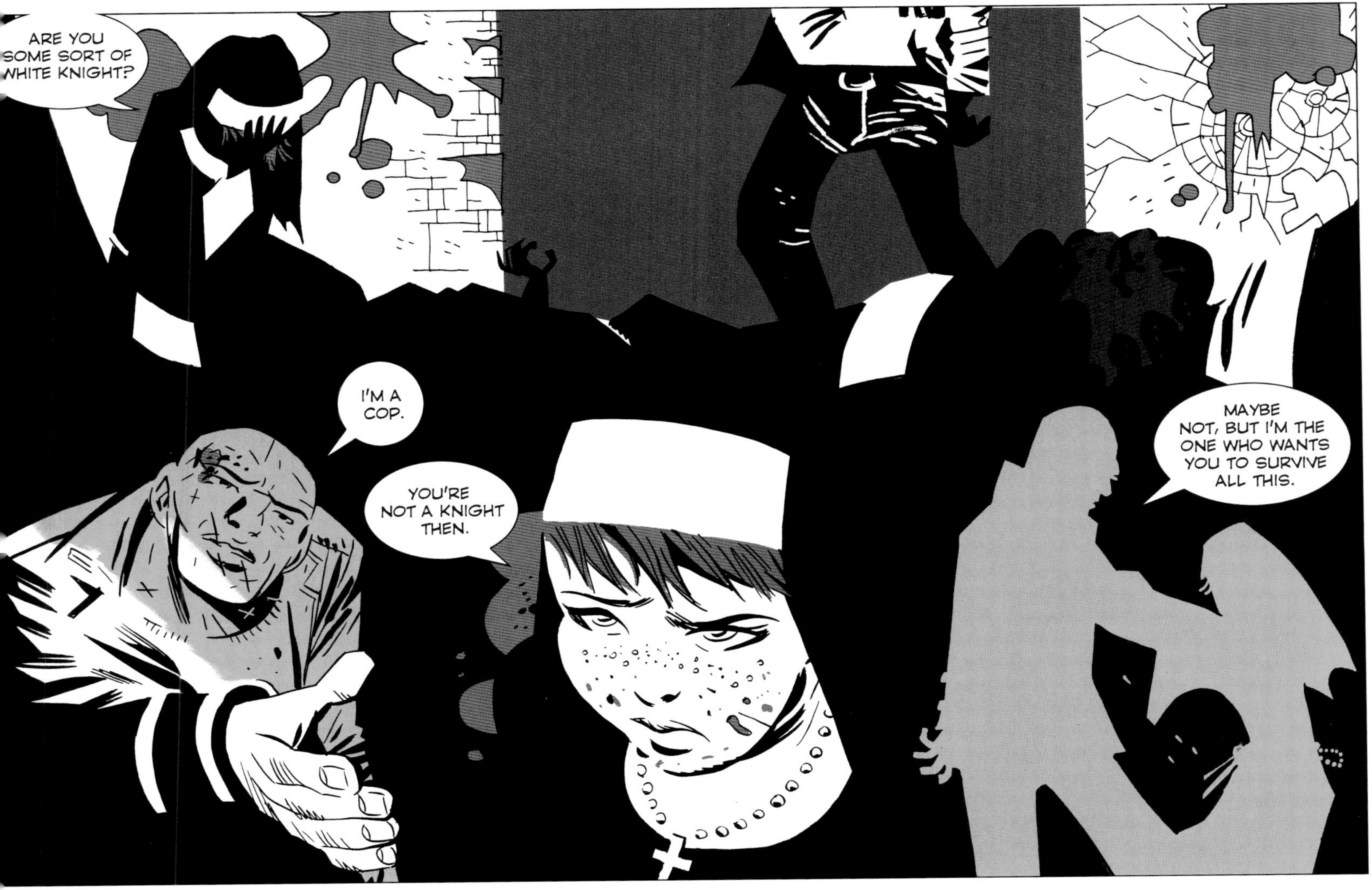
ARE YOU SOME SORT OF WHITE KNIGHT?
I'M A COP.
YOU'RE NOT A KNIGHT THEN.
MAYBE NOT, BUT I'M THE ONE WHO WANTS YOU TO SURVIVE ALL THIS.

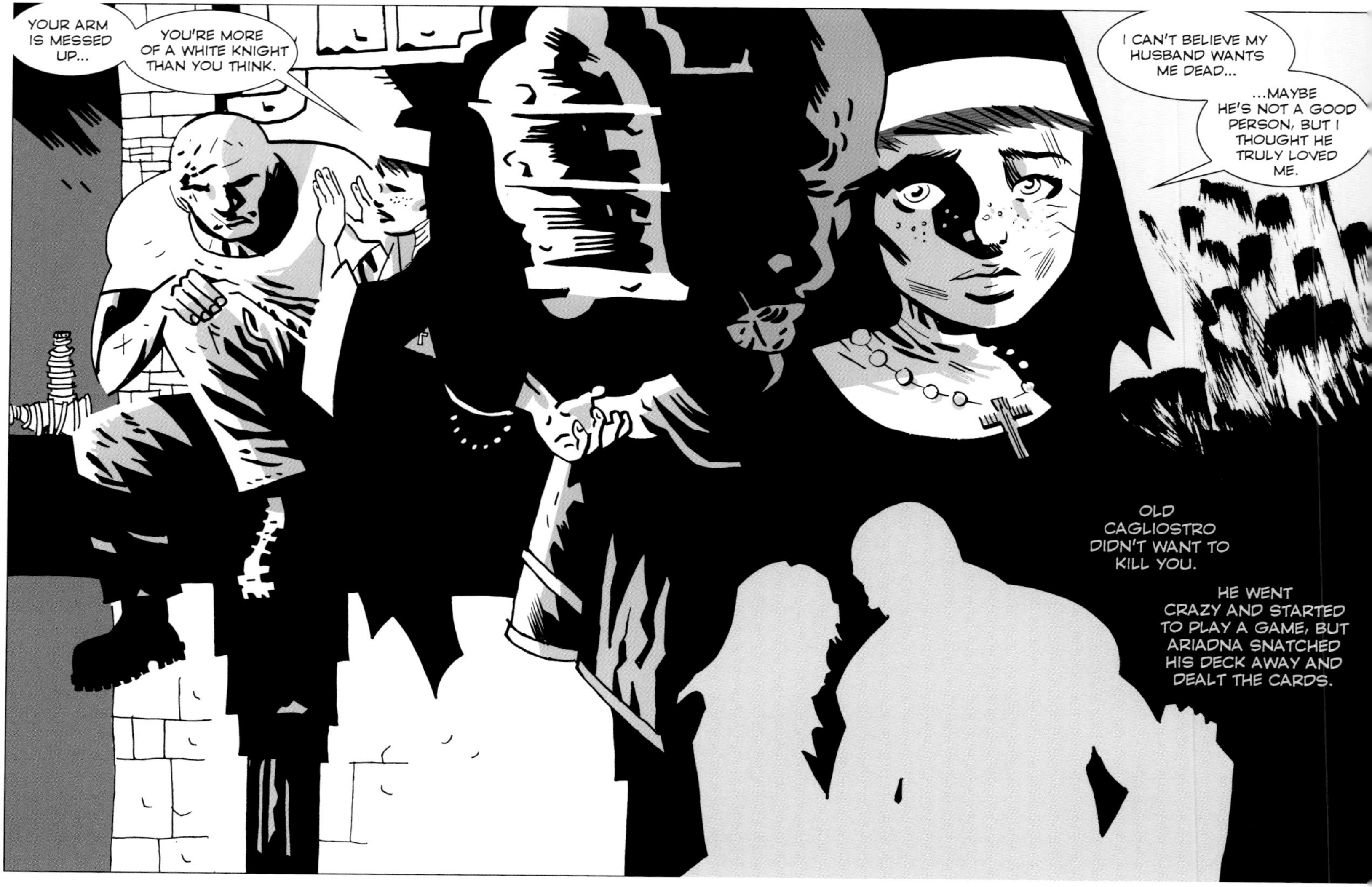
YOUR ARM IS MESSED UP...
YOU'RE MORE OF A WHITE KNIGHT THAN YOU THINK.
I CAN'T BELIEVE MY HUSBAND WANTS ME DEAD...
...MAYBE HE'S NOT A GOOD PERSON, BUT I THOUGHT HE TRULY LOVED ME.
OLD CAGLIOSTRO DIDN'T WANT TO KILL YOU.
HE WENT CRAZY AND STARTED TO PLAY A GAME, BUT ARIADNA SNATCHED HIS DECK AWAY AND DEALT THE CARDS.

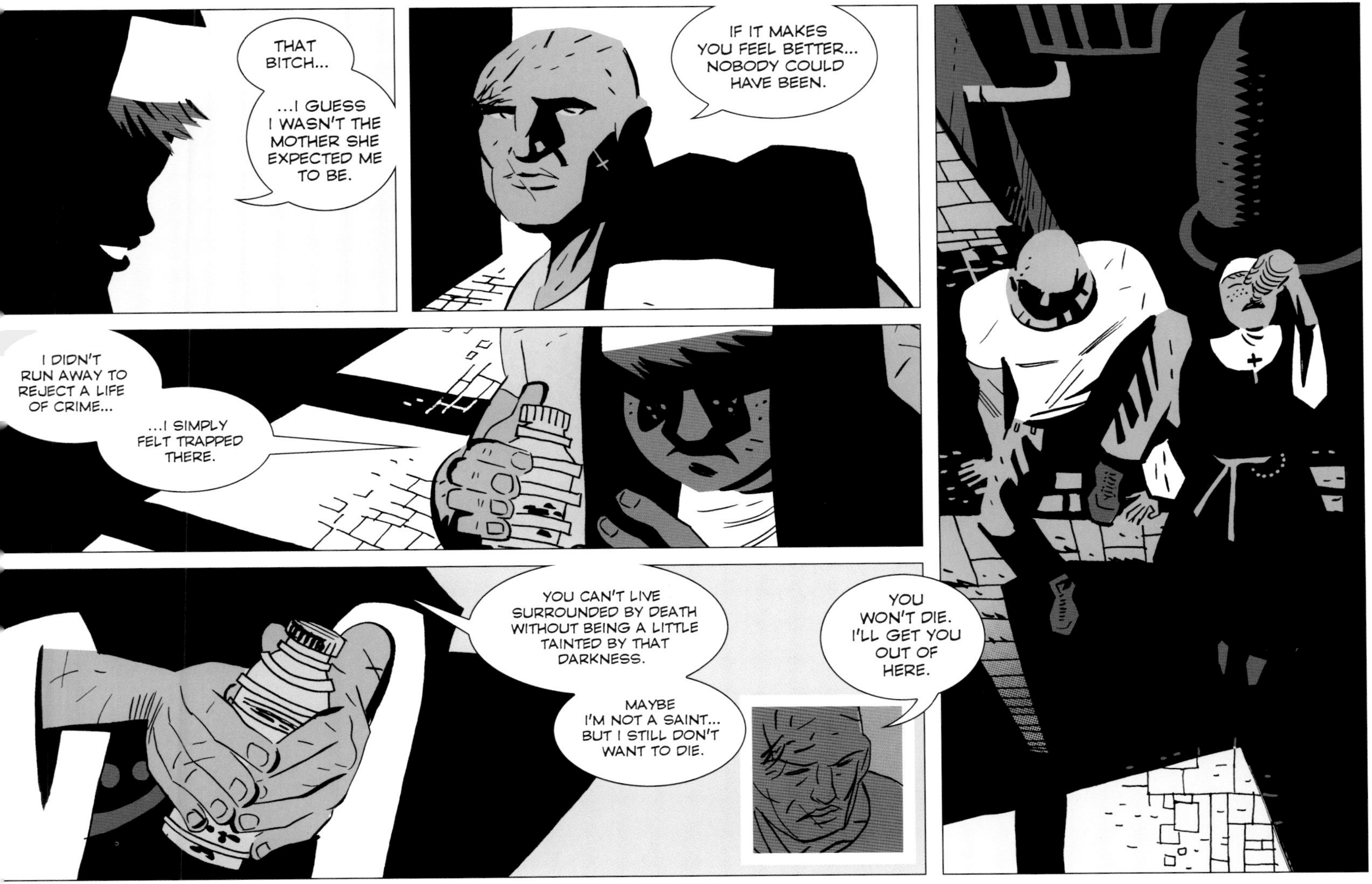
THAT BITCH...
...I GUESS I WASN'T THE MOTHER SHE EXPECTED ME TO BE.
IF IT MAKES YOU FEEL BETTER... NOBODY COULD HAVE BEEN.
I DIDN'T RUN AWAY TO REJECT A LIFE OF CRIME...
...I SIMPLY FELT TRAPPED THERE.
YOU CAN'T LIVE SURROUNDED BY DEATH WITHOUT BEING A LITTLE TAINTED BY THAT DARKNESS.
MAYBE I'M NOT A SAINT... BUT I STILL DON'T WANT TO DIE.
YOU WON'T DIE. I'LL GET YOU OUT OF HERE.

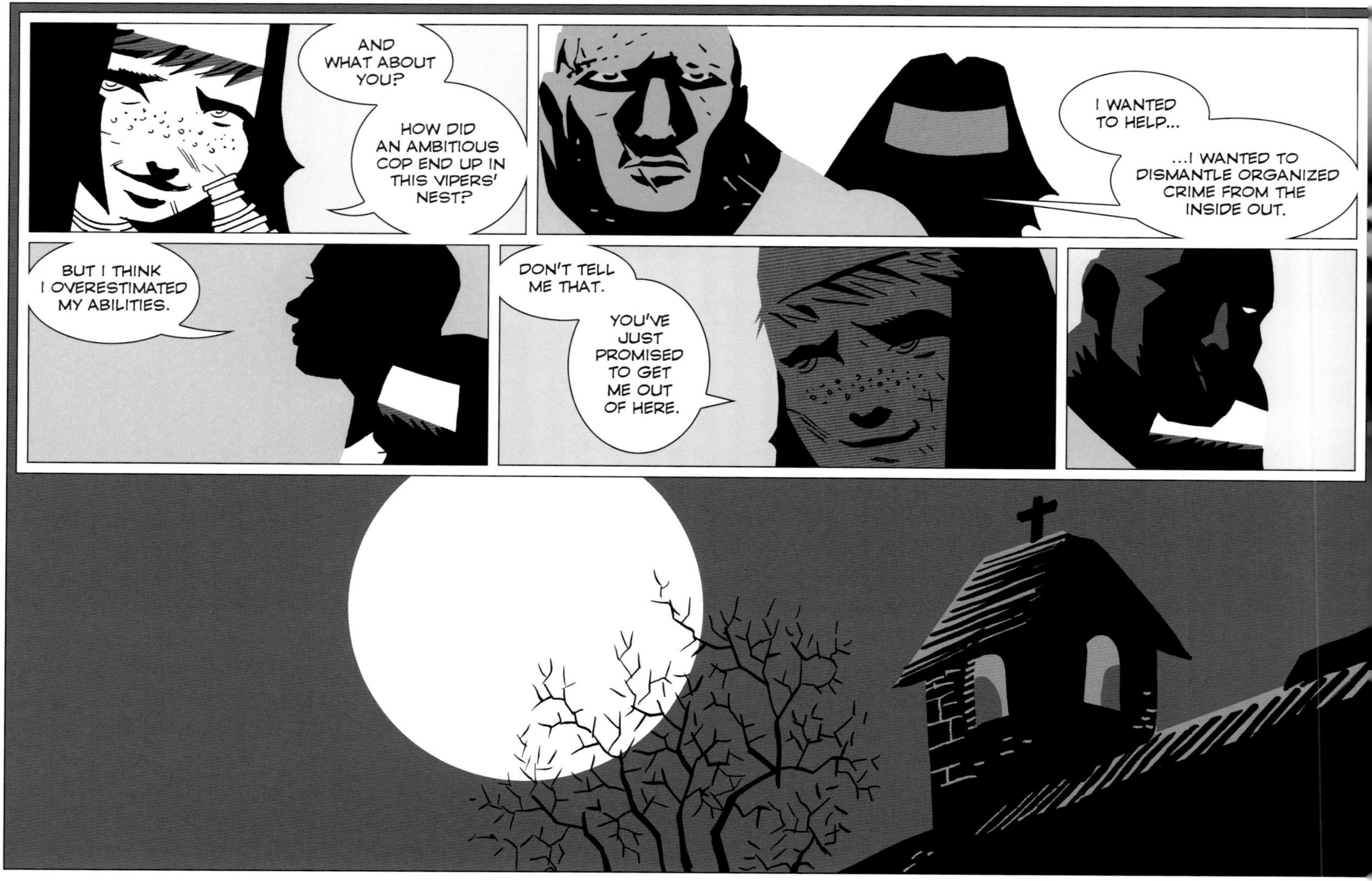
AND WHAT ABOUT YOU?
HOW DID AN AMBITIOUS COP END UP IN THIS VIPERS' NEST?
I WANTED TO HELP...
...I WANTED TO DISMANTLE ORGANIZED CRIME FROM THE INSIDE OUT.
BUT I THINK I OVERESTIMATED MY ABILITIES.
DON'T TELL ME THAT.
YOU'VE JUST PROMISED TO GET ME OUT OF HERE.

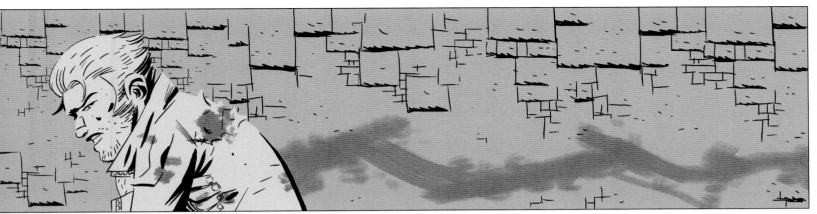

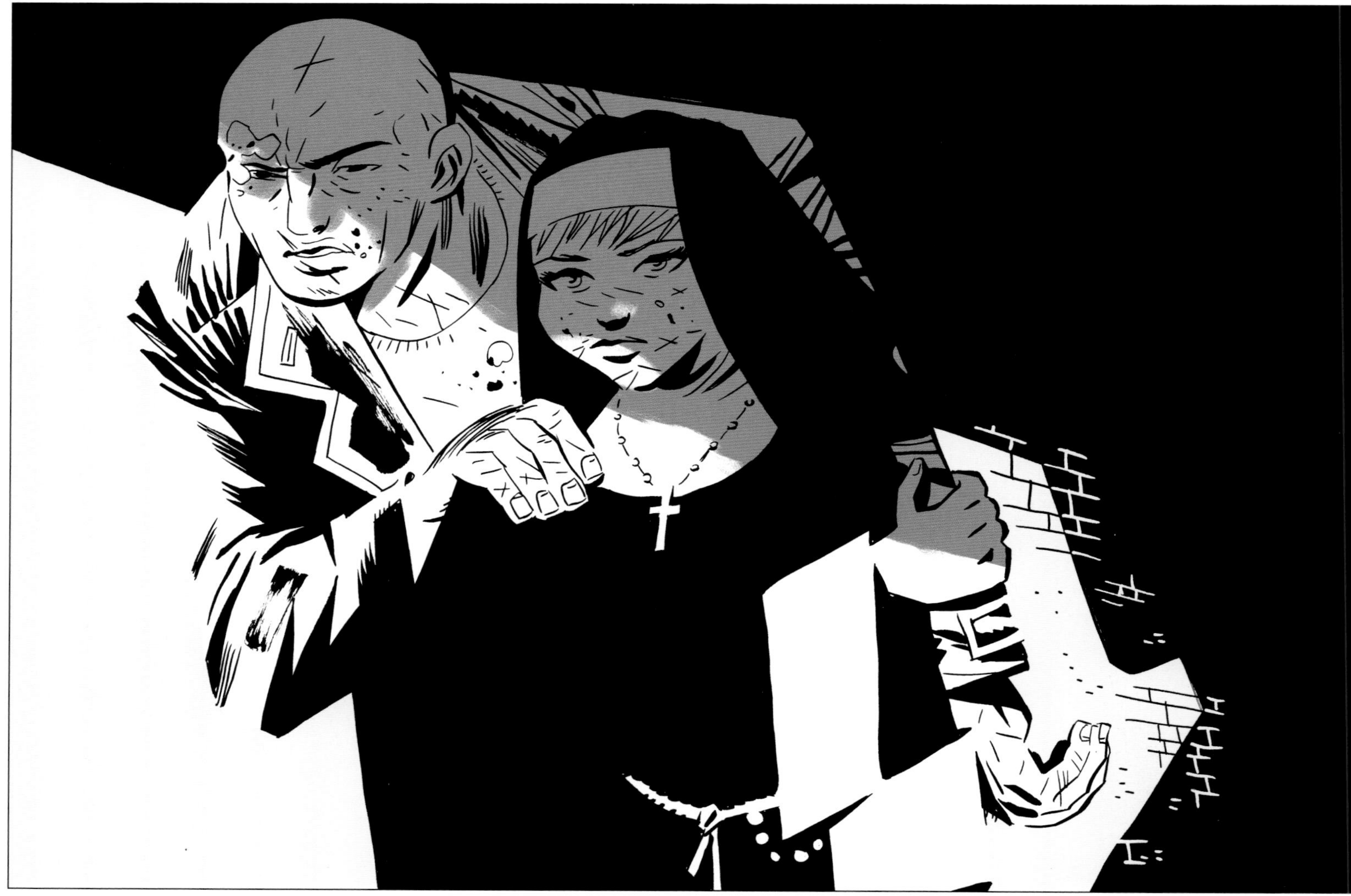

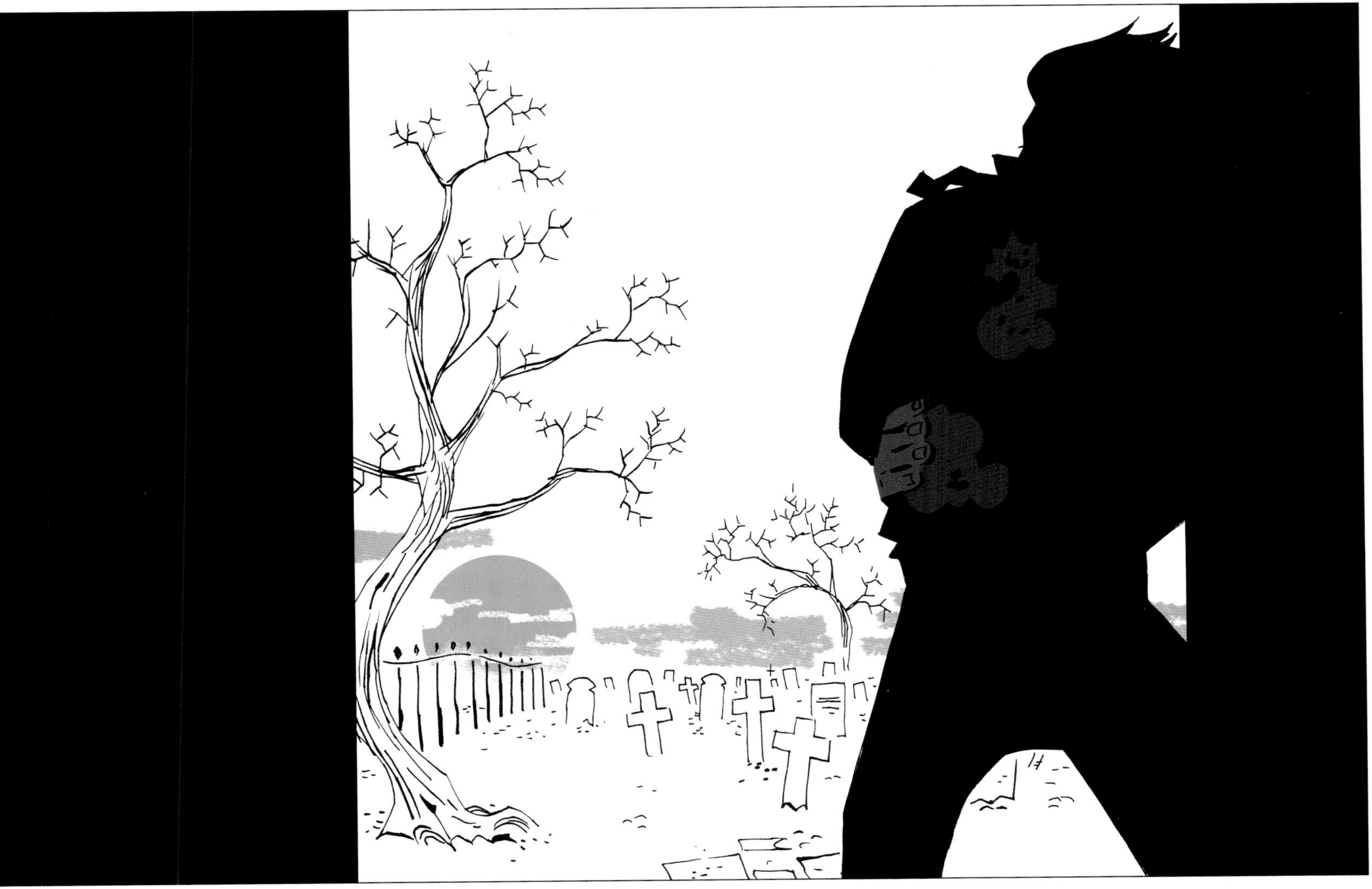

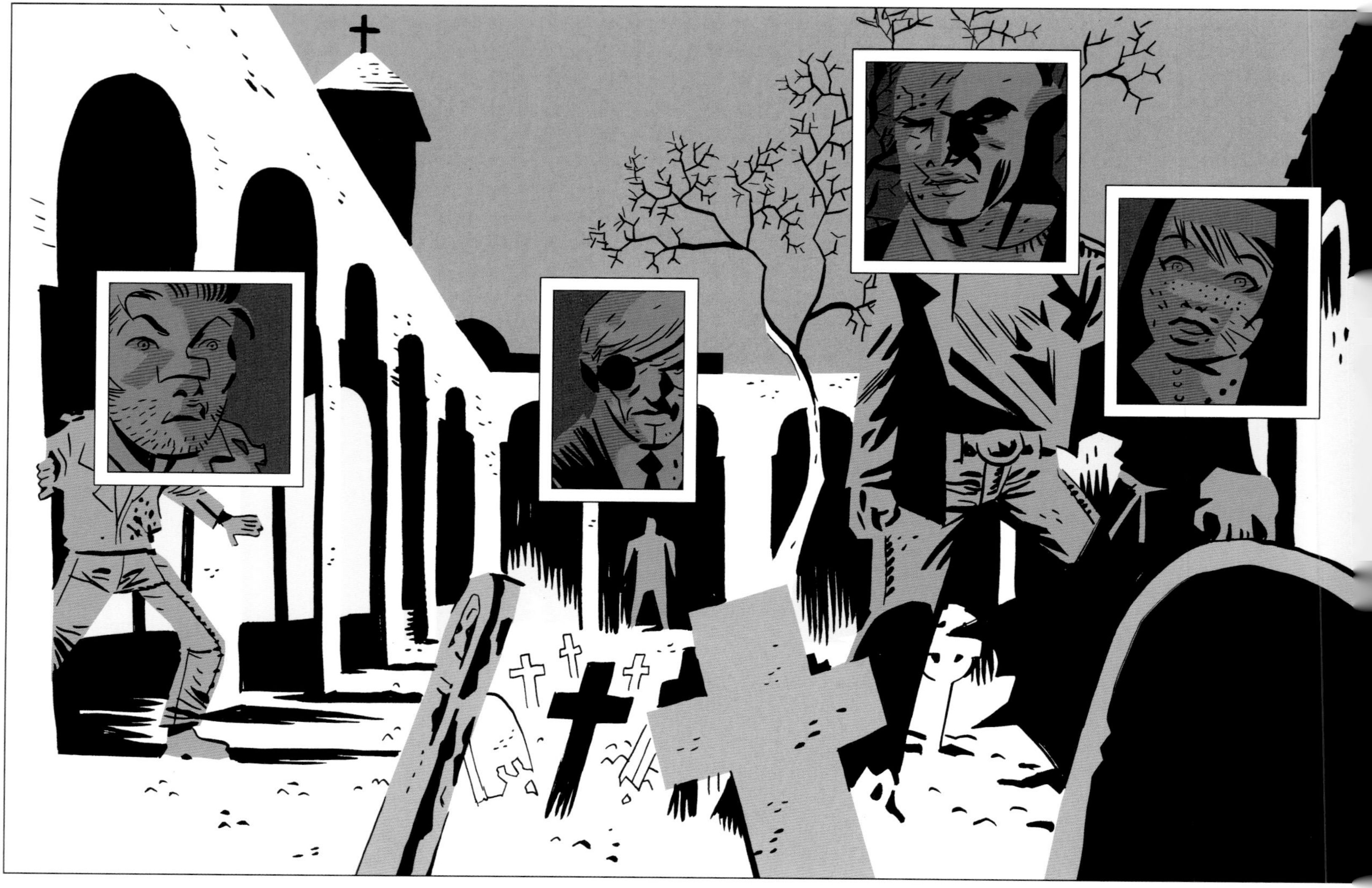

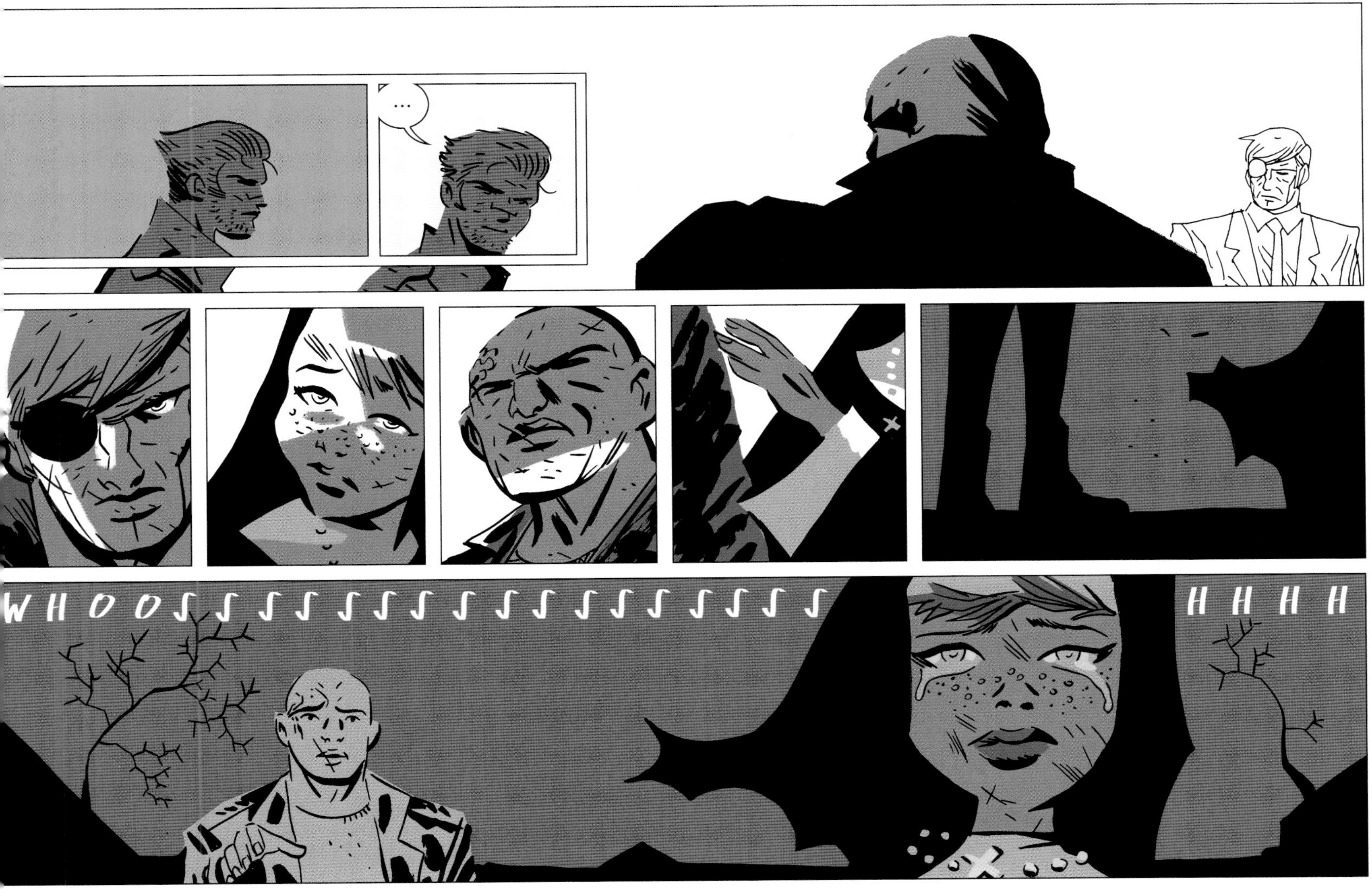
...
WHOOSSSSSSSSSSSSSSSSSS
HHHH

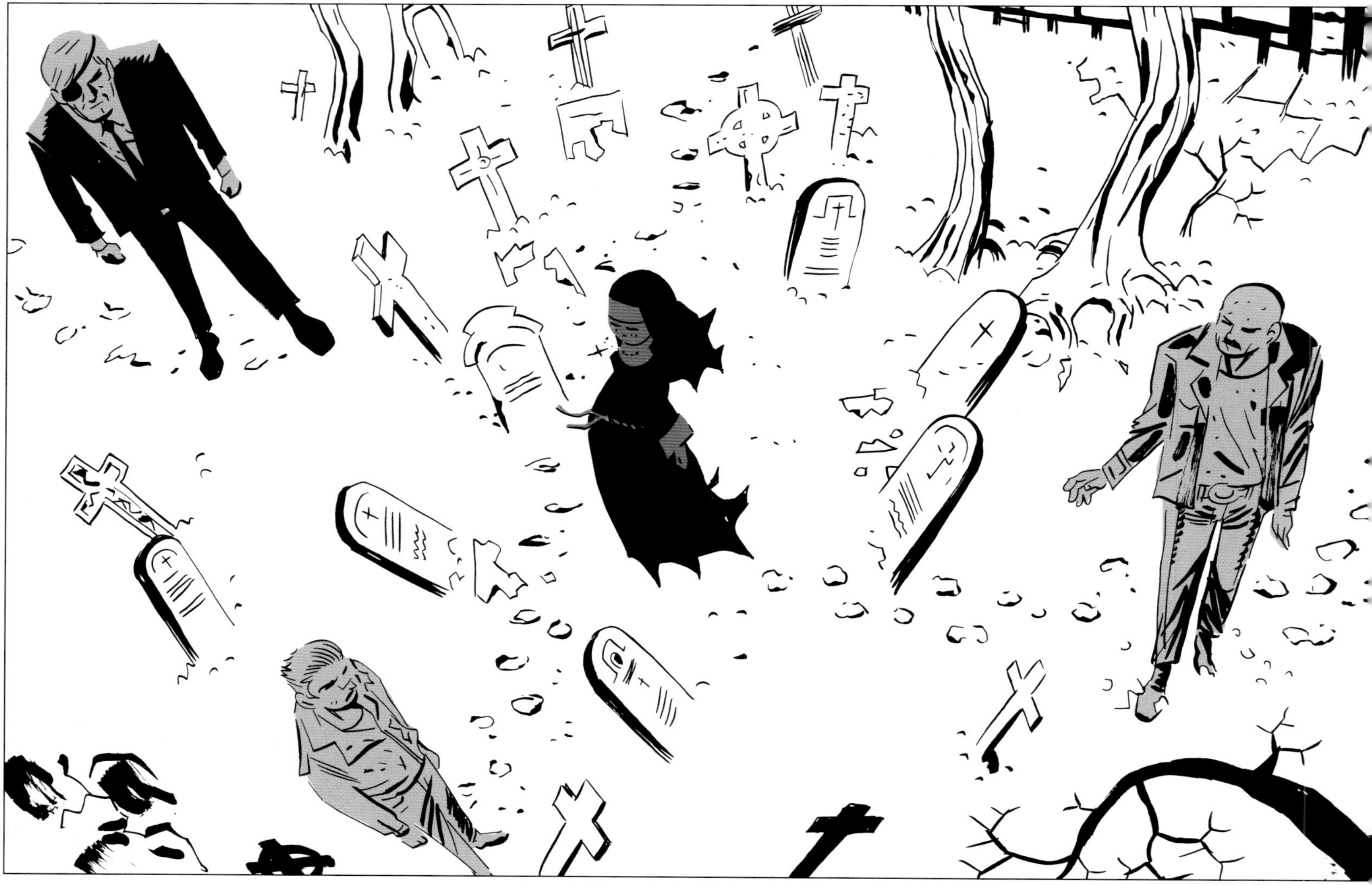

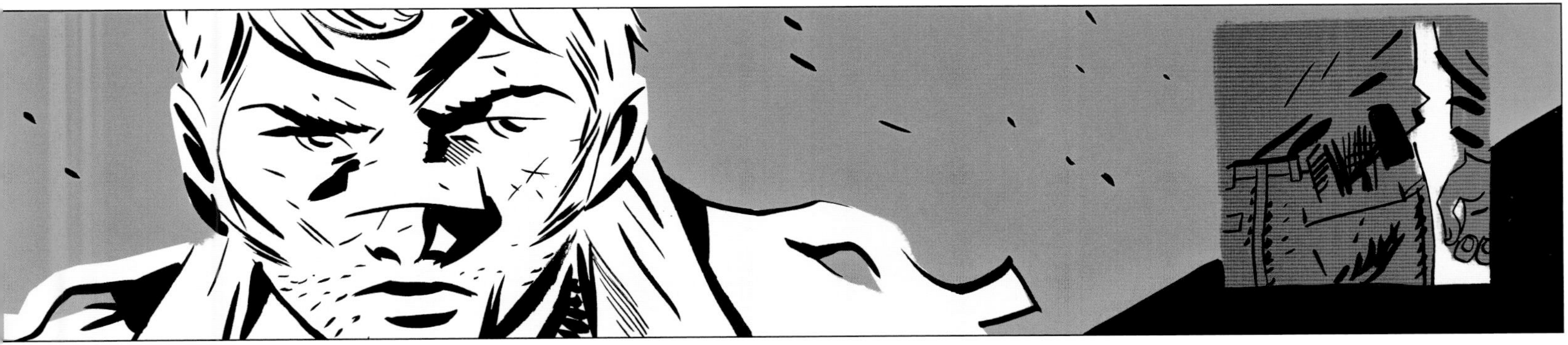
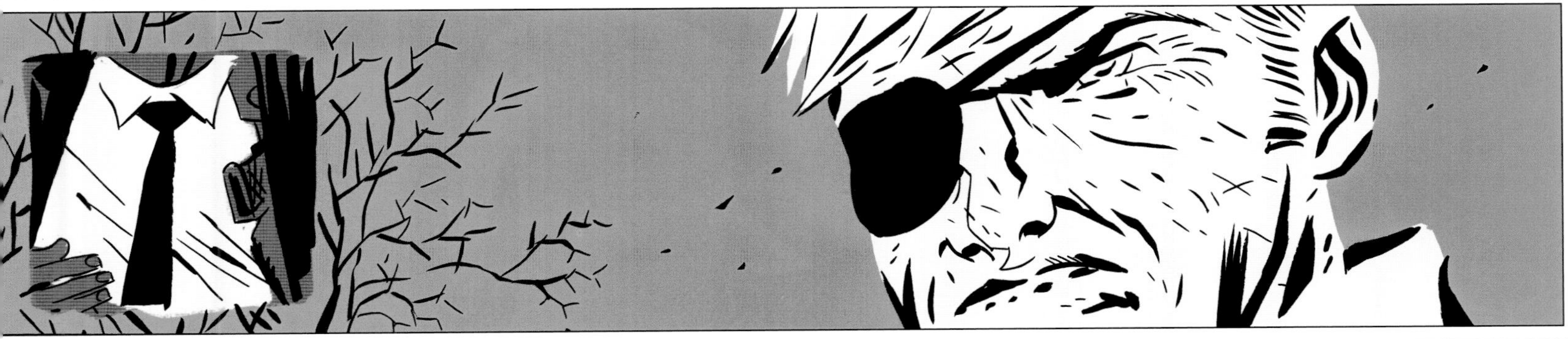
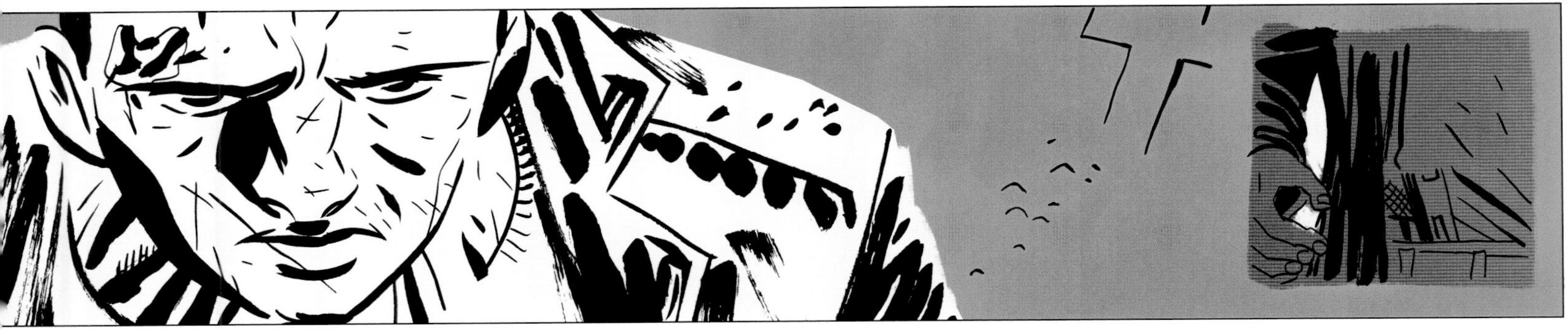

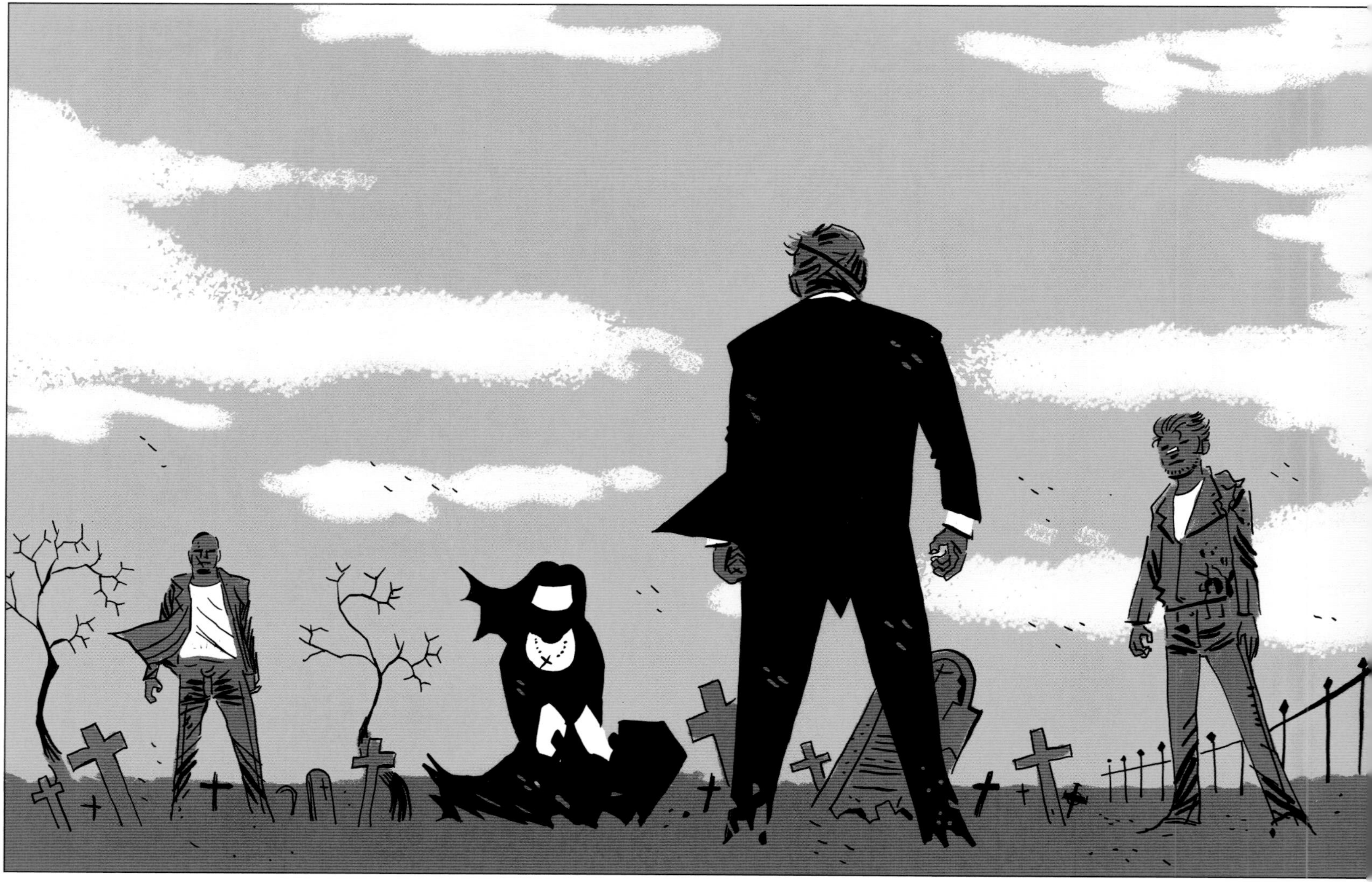

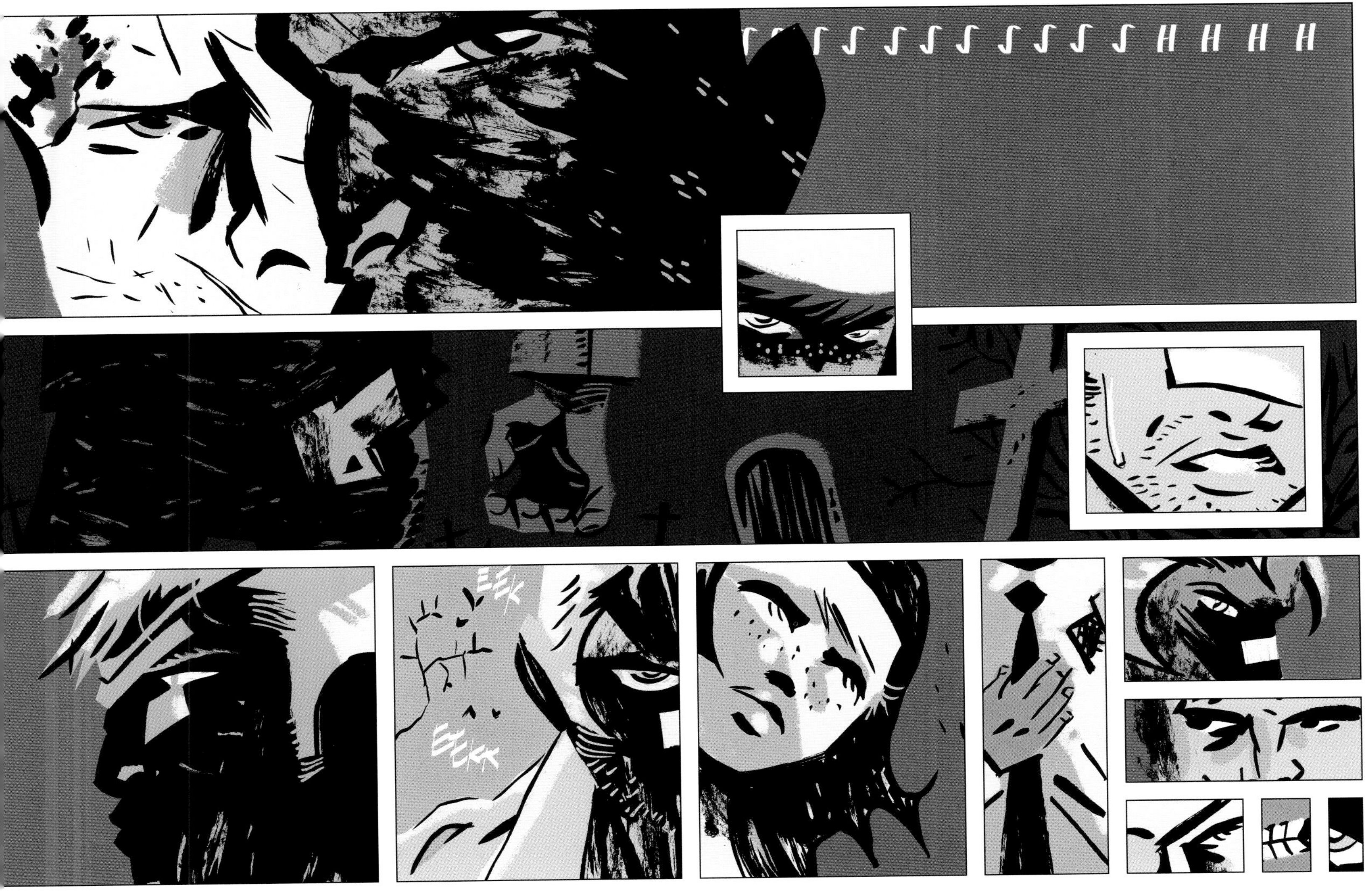
SSSSSSSSSSSHHHH
EEK
EEKK

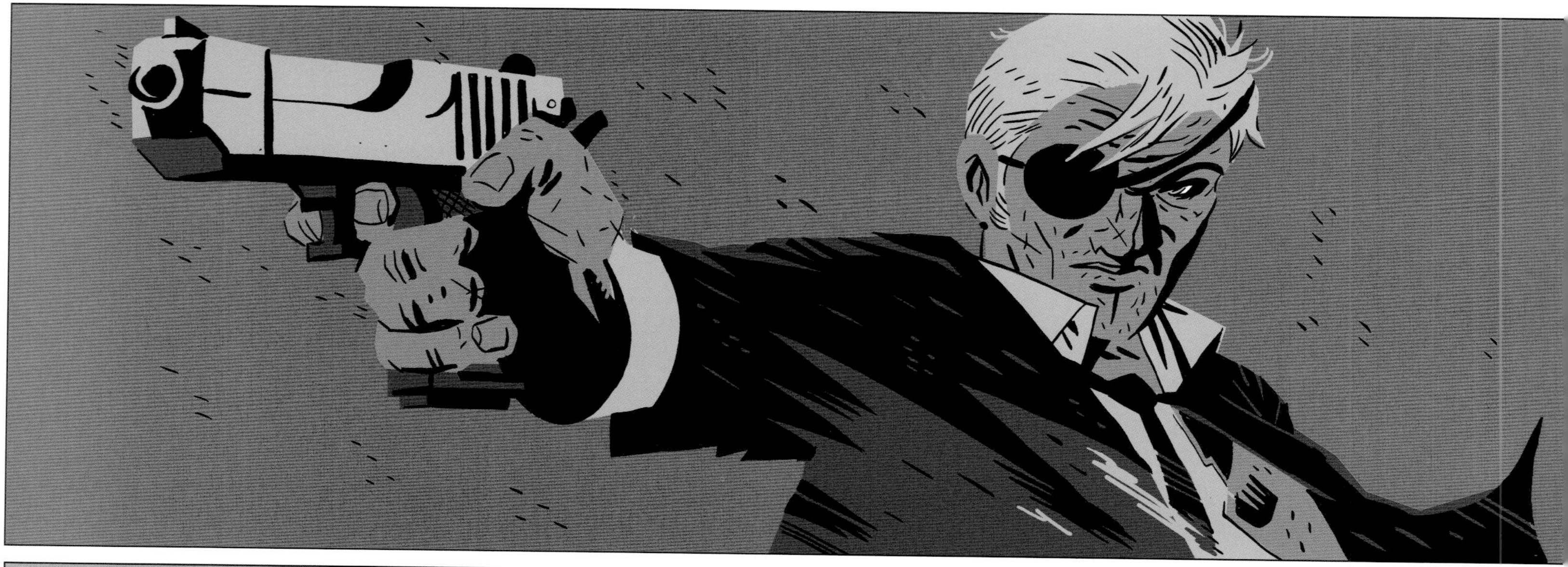

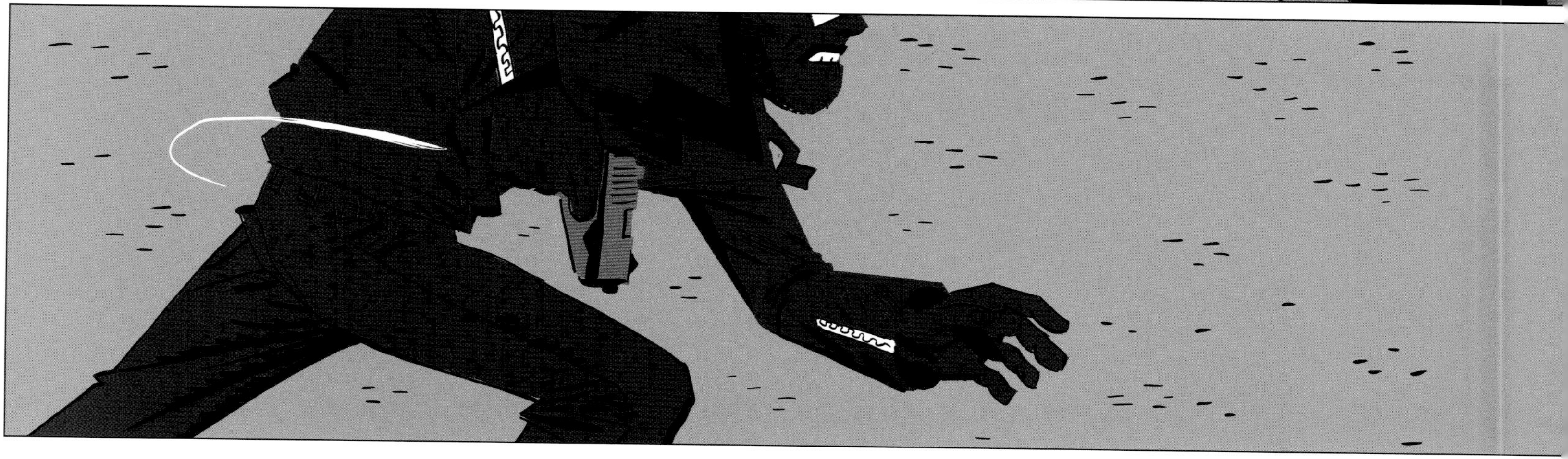

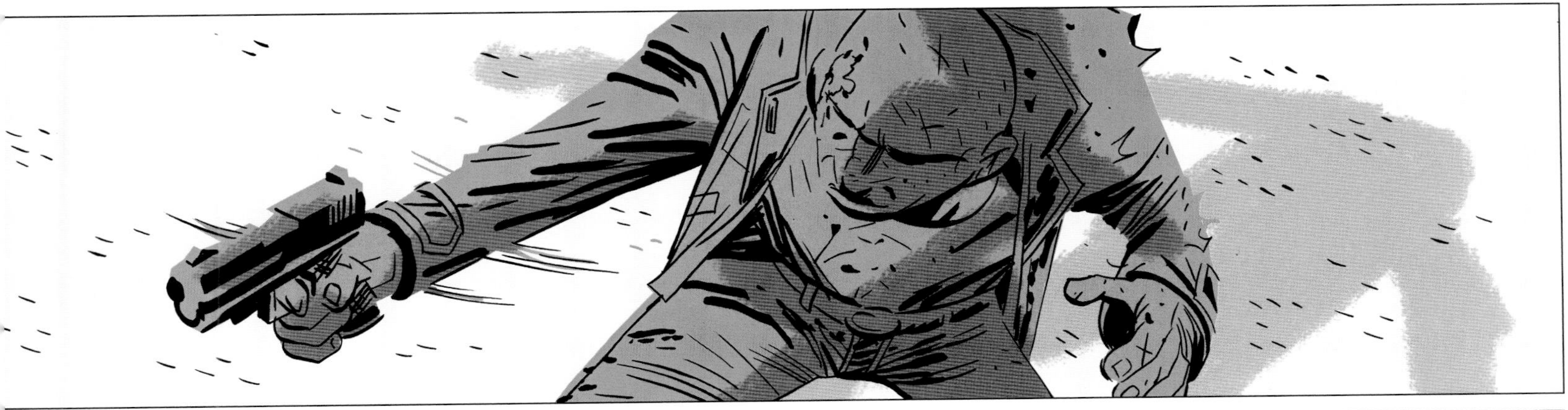

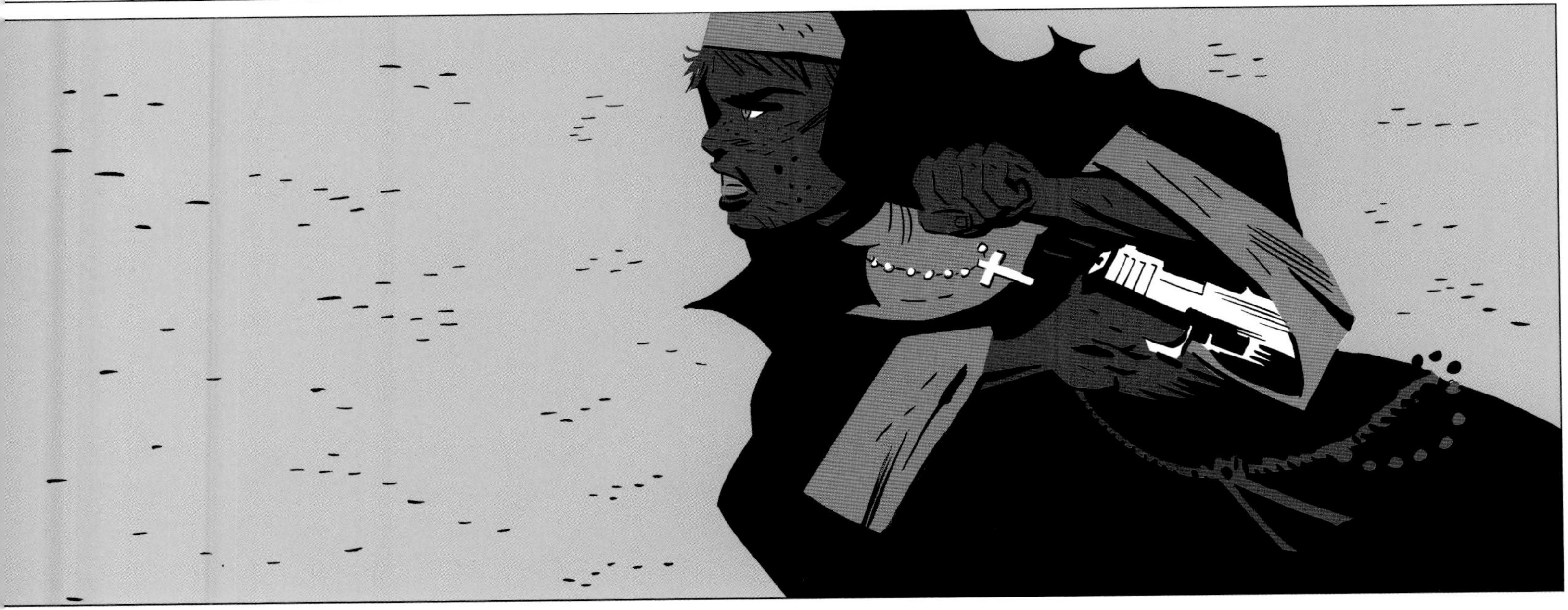

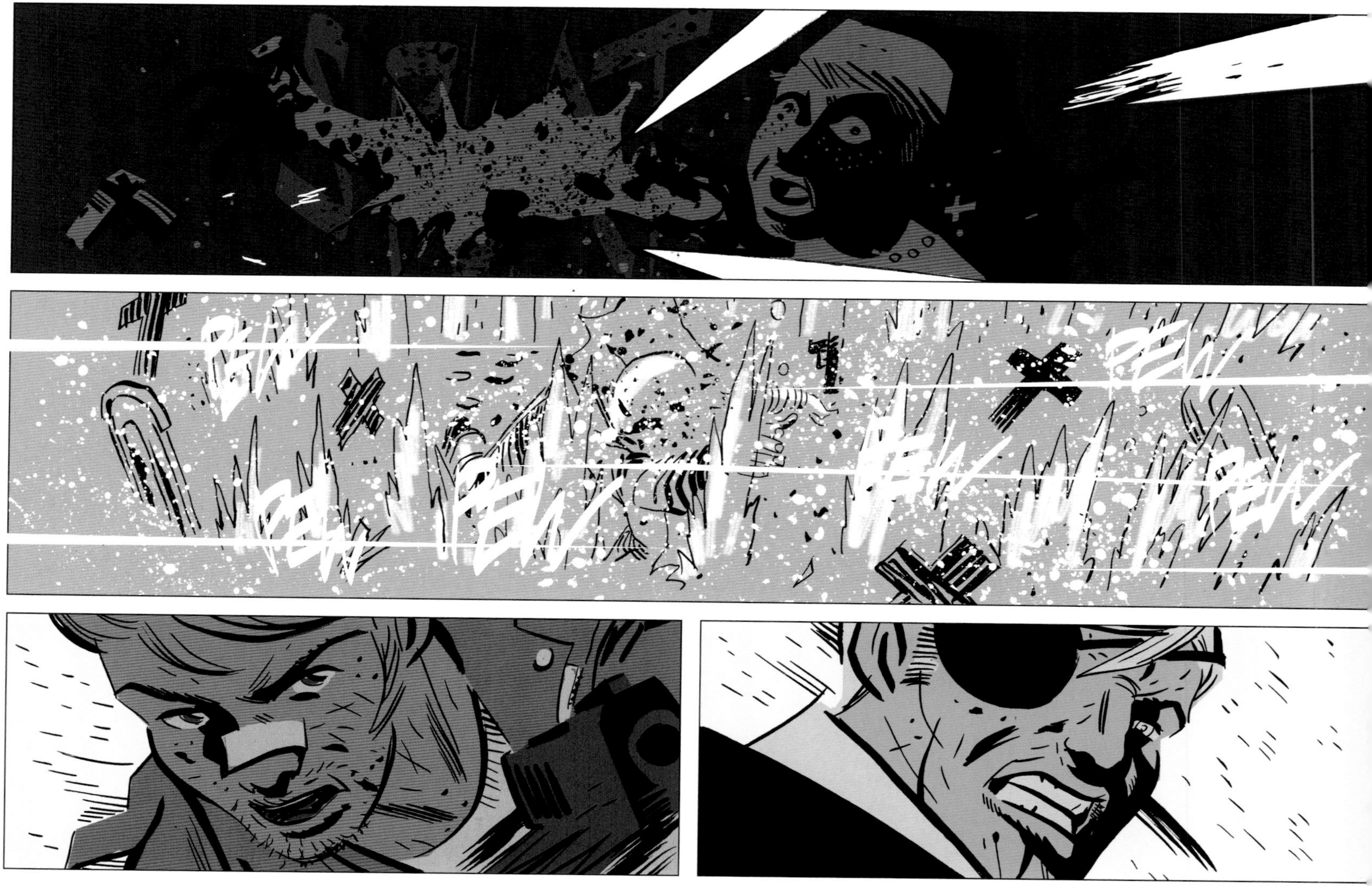
PEW
PEW
PEW
PEW
PEW
PEW

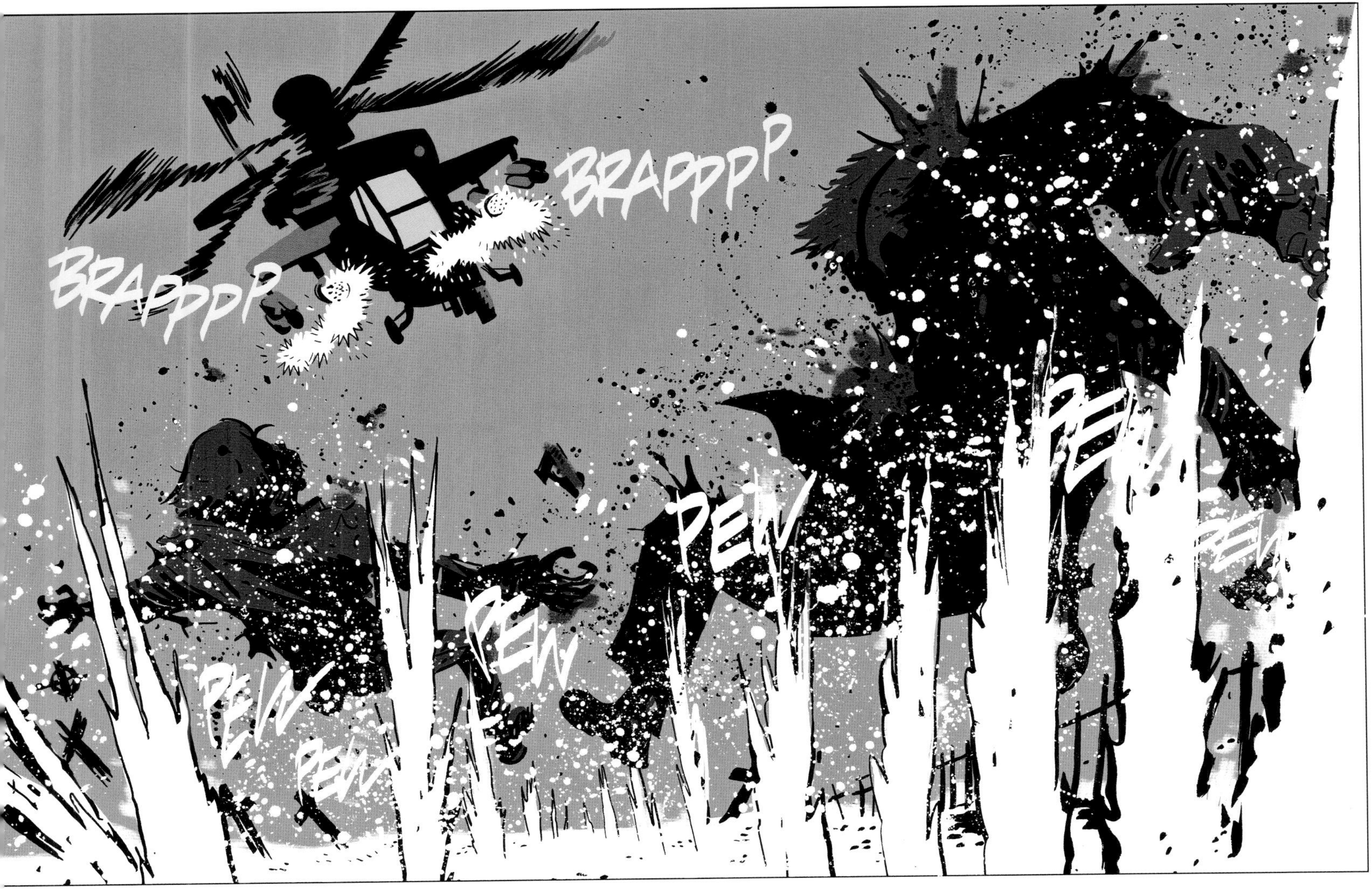
BRAPPPP
BRAPPPP
PEW
PEW
PEW
PEW
PEW
PEW

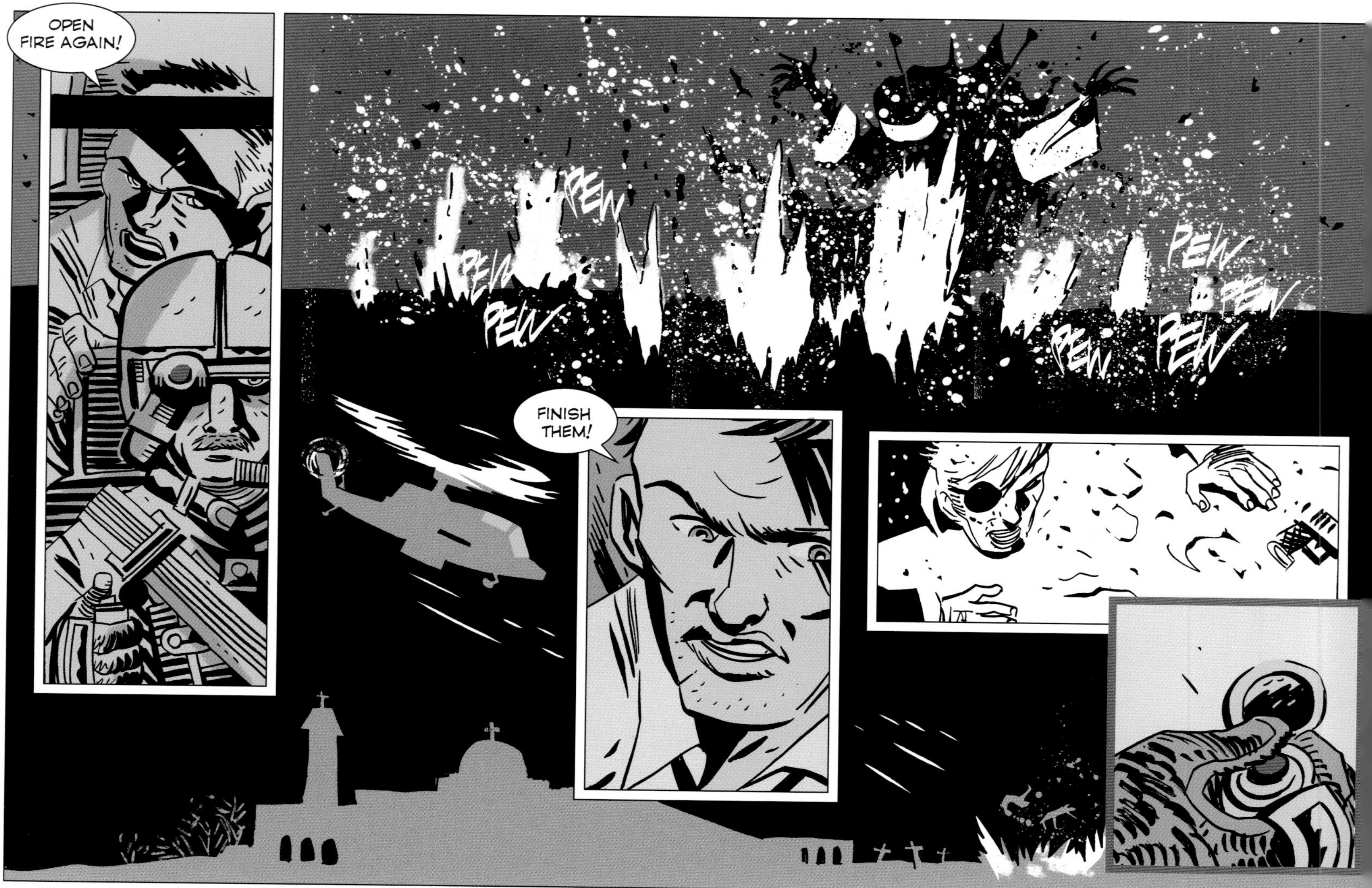
OPEN FIRE AGAIN!
PEW
PEW
PEW
PEW
PEW
PEW
PEW
FINISH THEM!

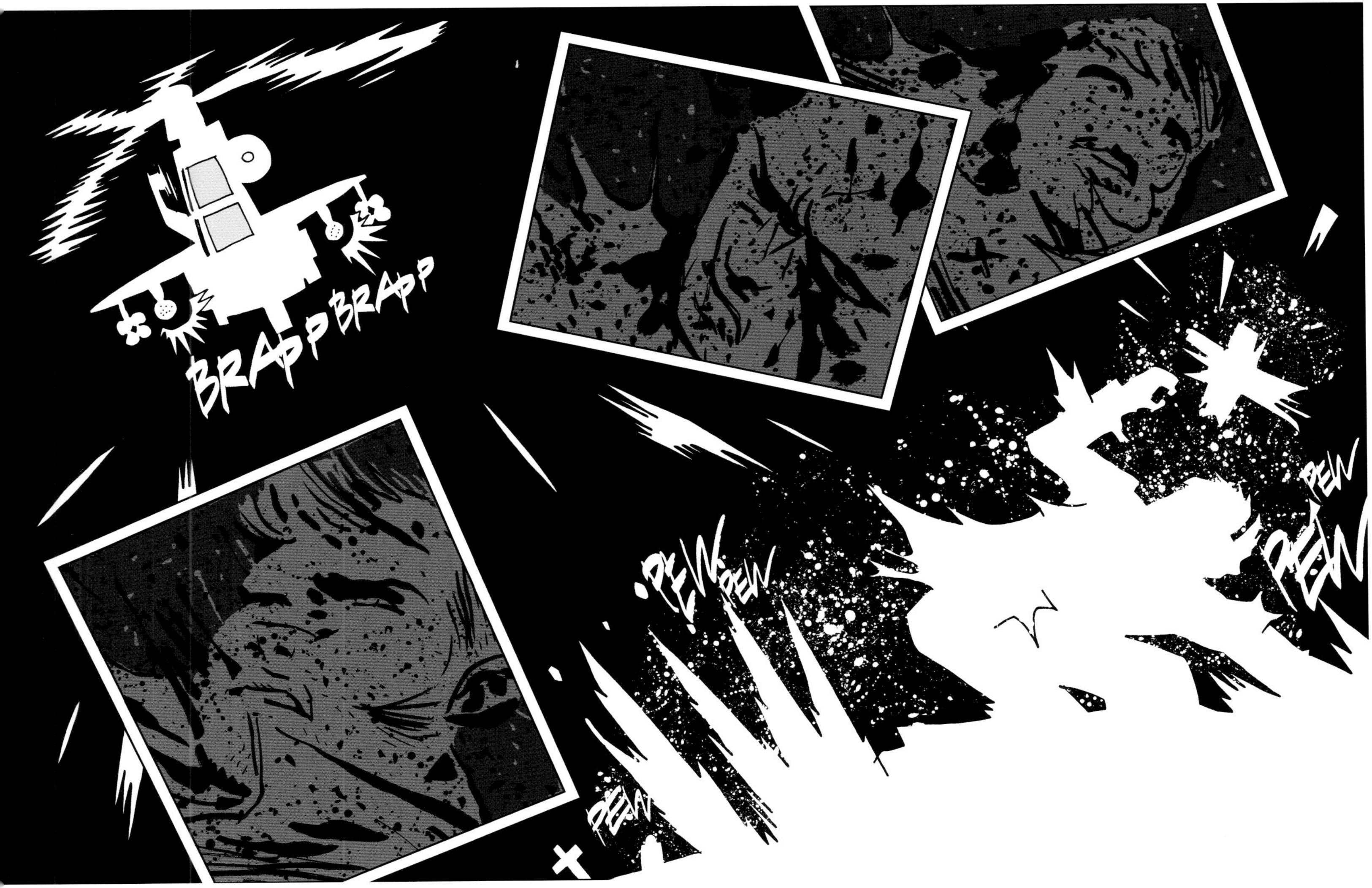
BRAPP BRAPP
PEW PEW
PEW PEW
PEW

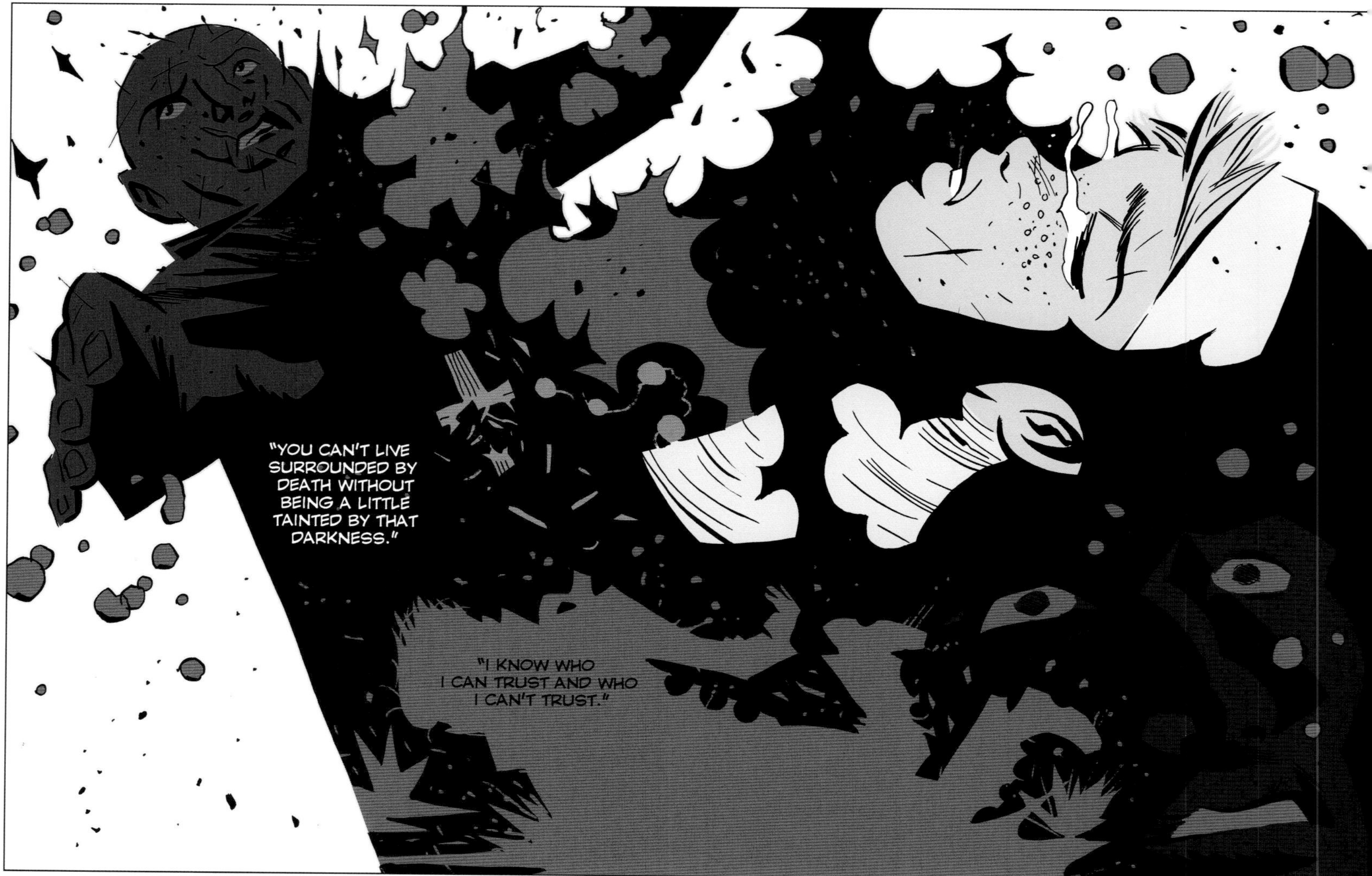
"YOU CAN'T LIVE SURROUNDED BY DEATH WITHOUT BEING A LITTLE TAINTED BY THAT DARKNESS."
"I KNOW WHO I CAN TRUST AND WHO I CAN'T TRUST."

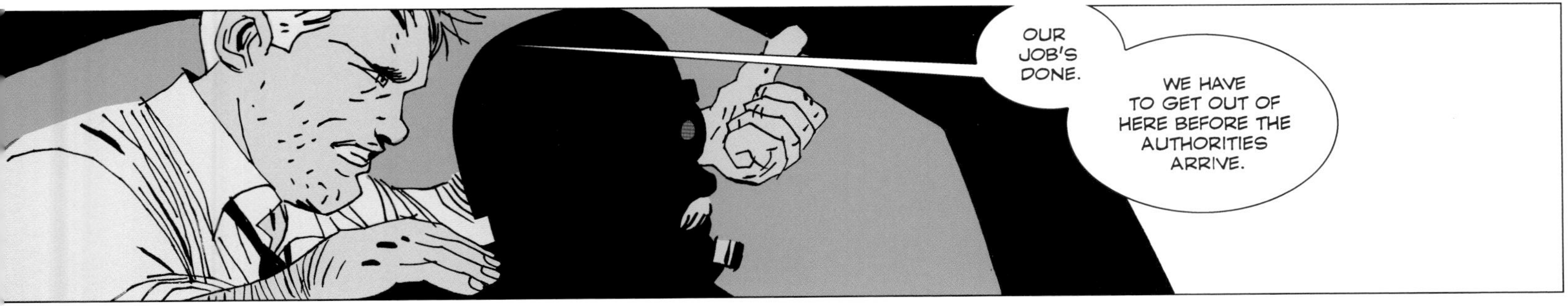
OUR JOB'S DONE.
WE HAVE TO GET OUT OF HERE BEFORE THE AUTHORITIES ARRIVE.

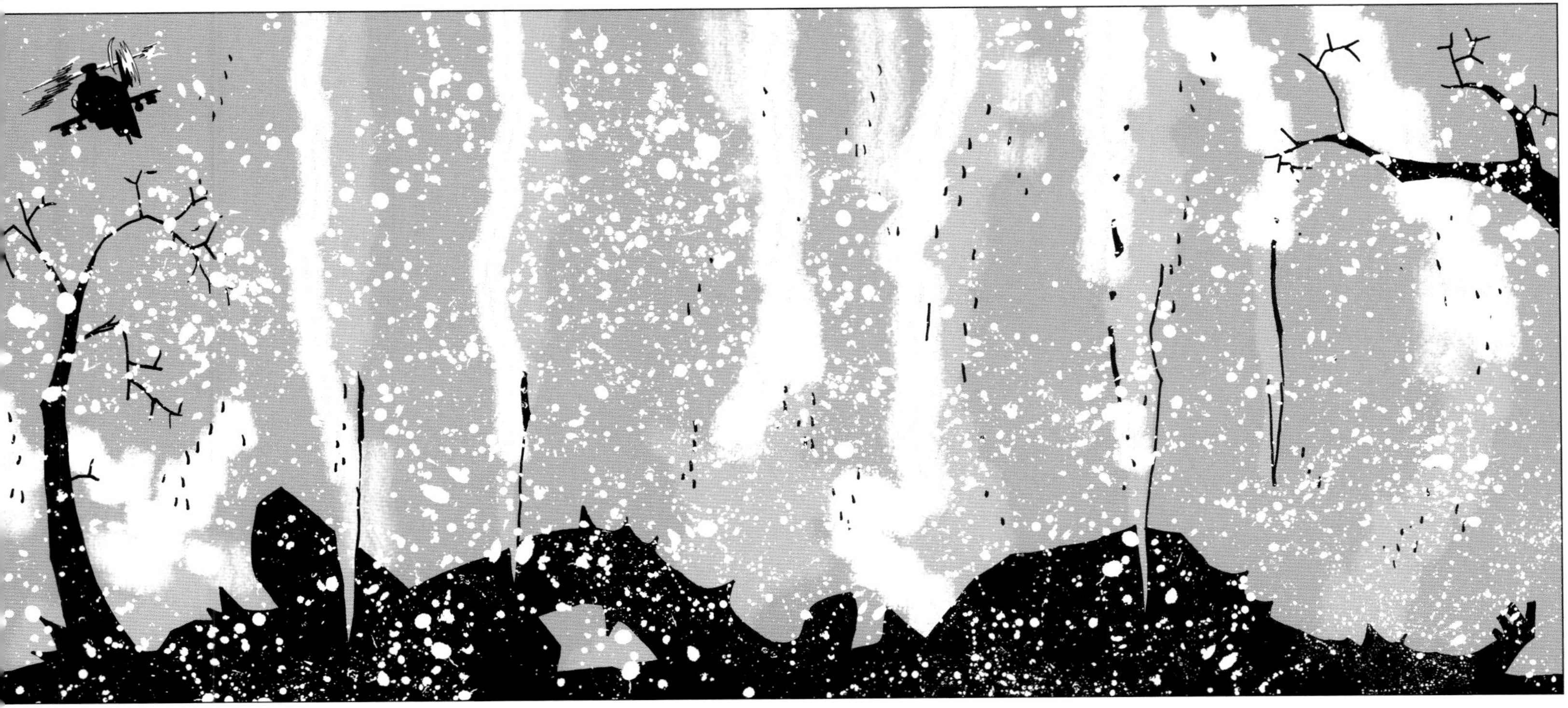

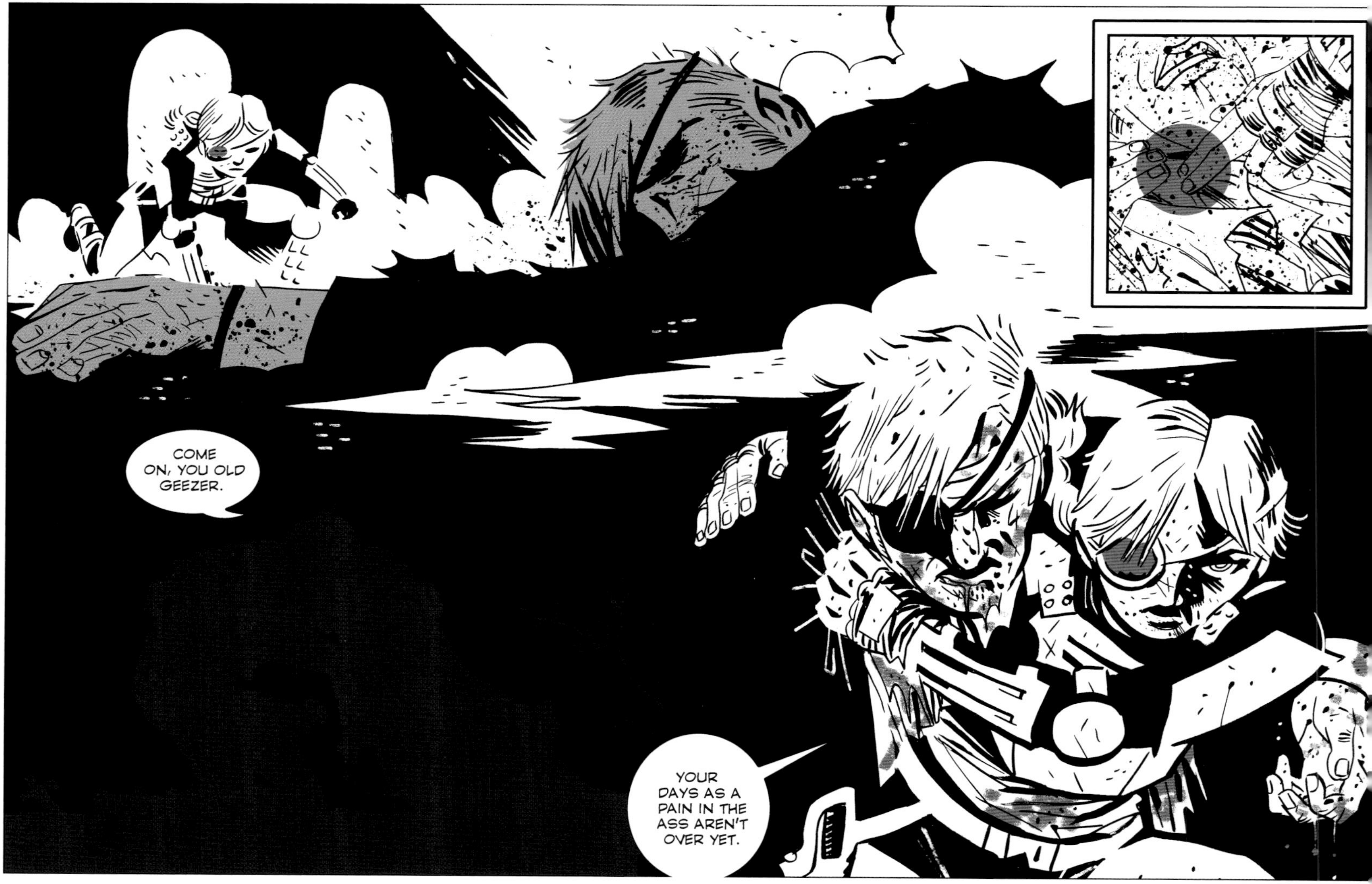
COME ON, YOU OLD GEEZER.
YOUR DAYS AS A PAIN IN THE ASS AREN'T OVER YET.

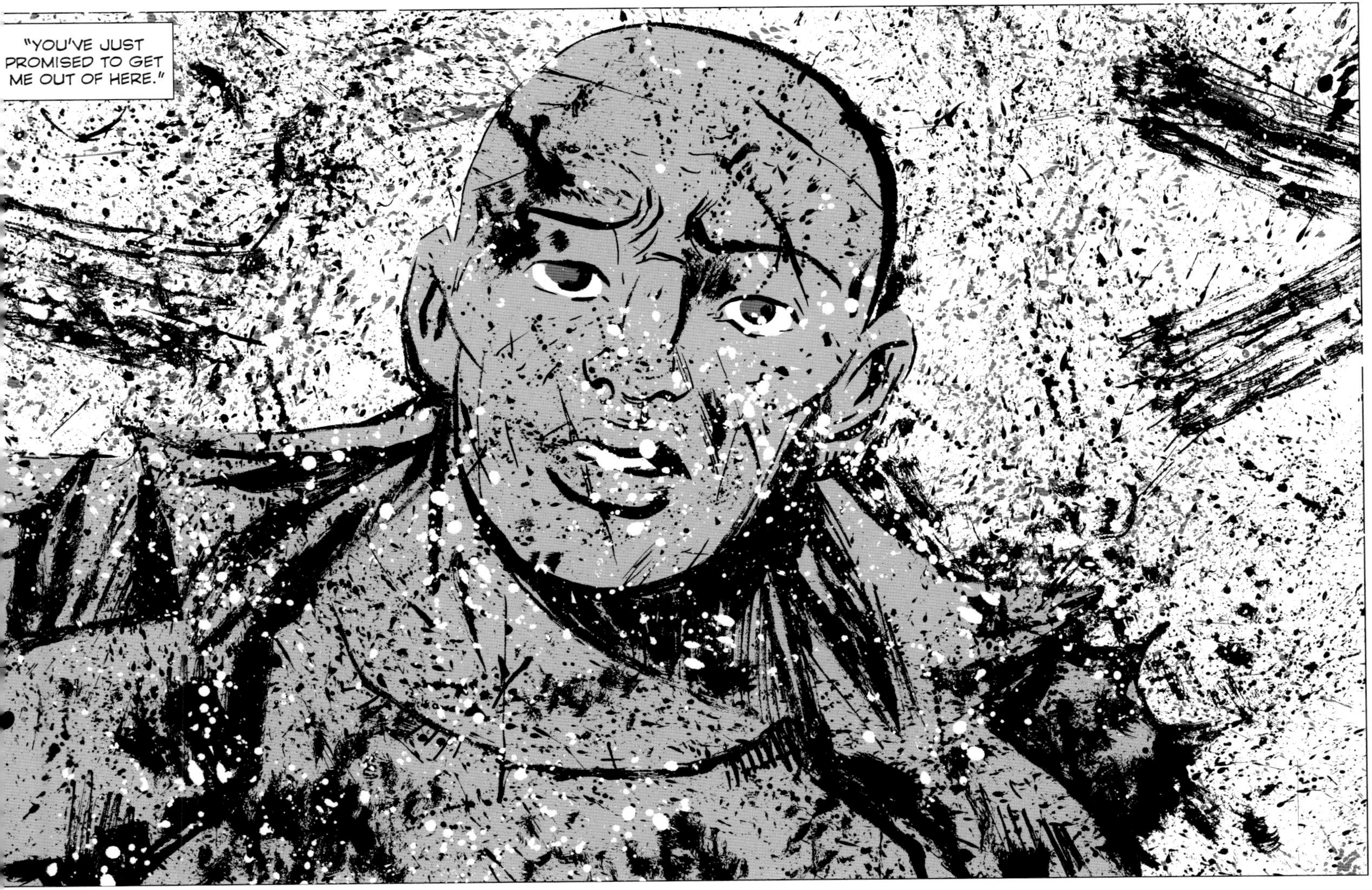
"YOU'VE JUST PROMISED TO GET ME OUT OF HERE."

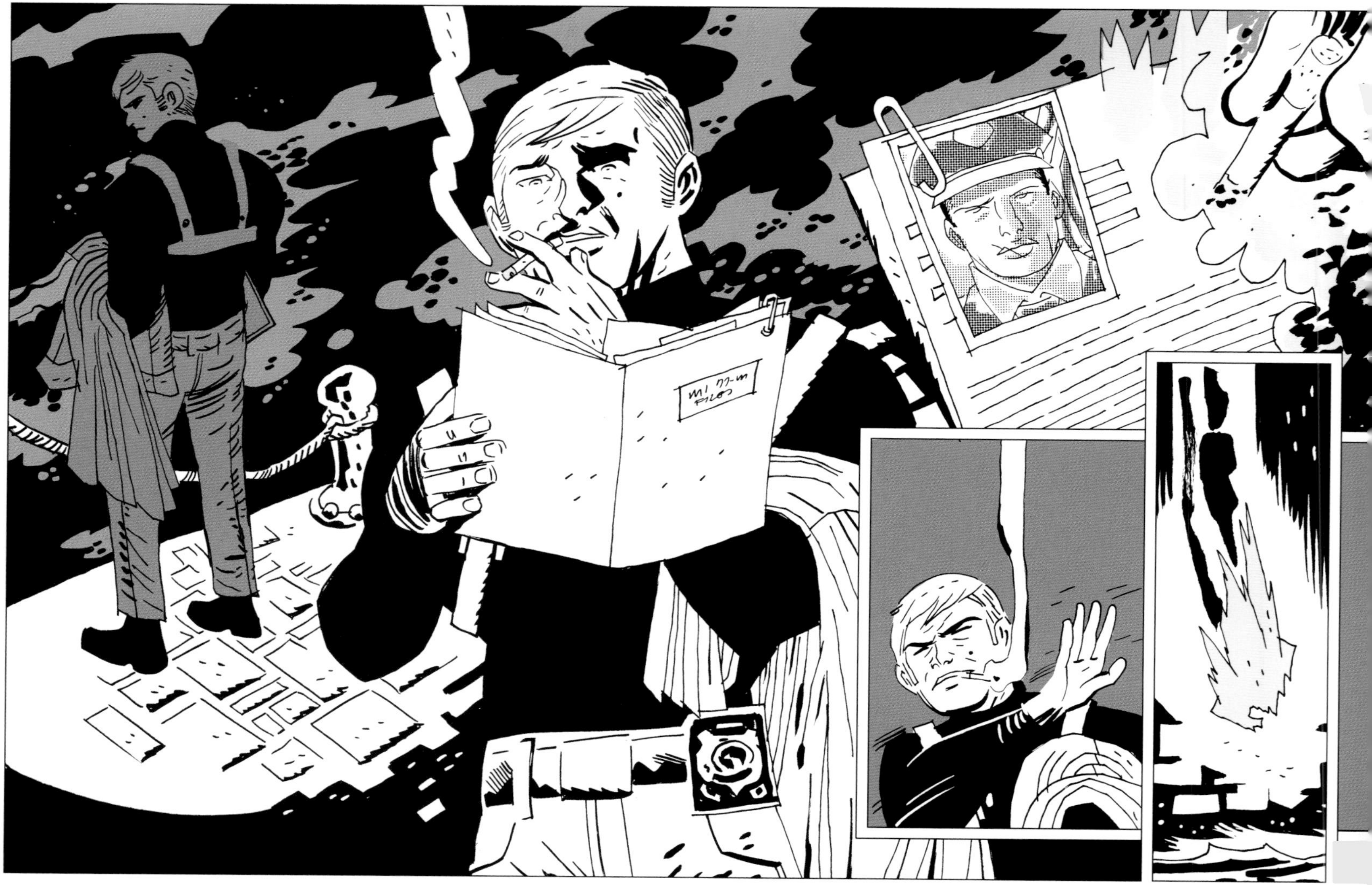

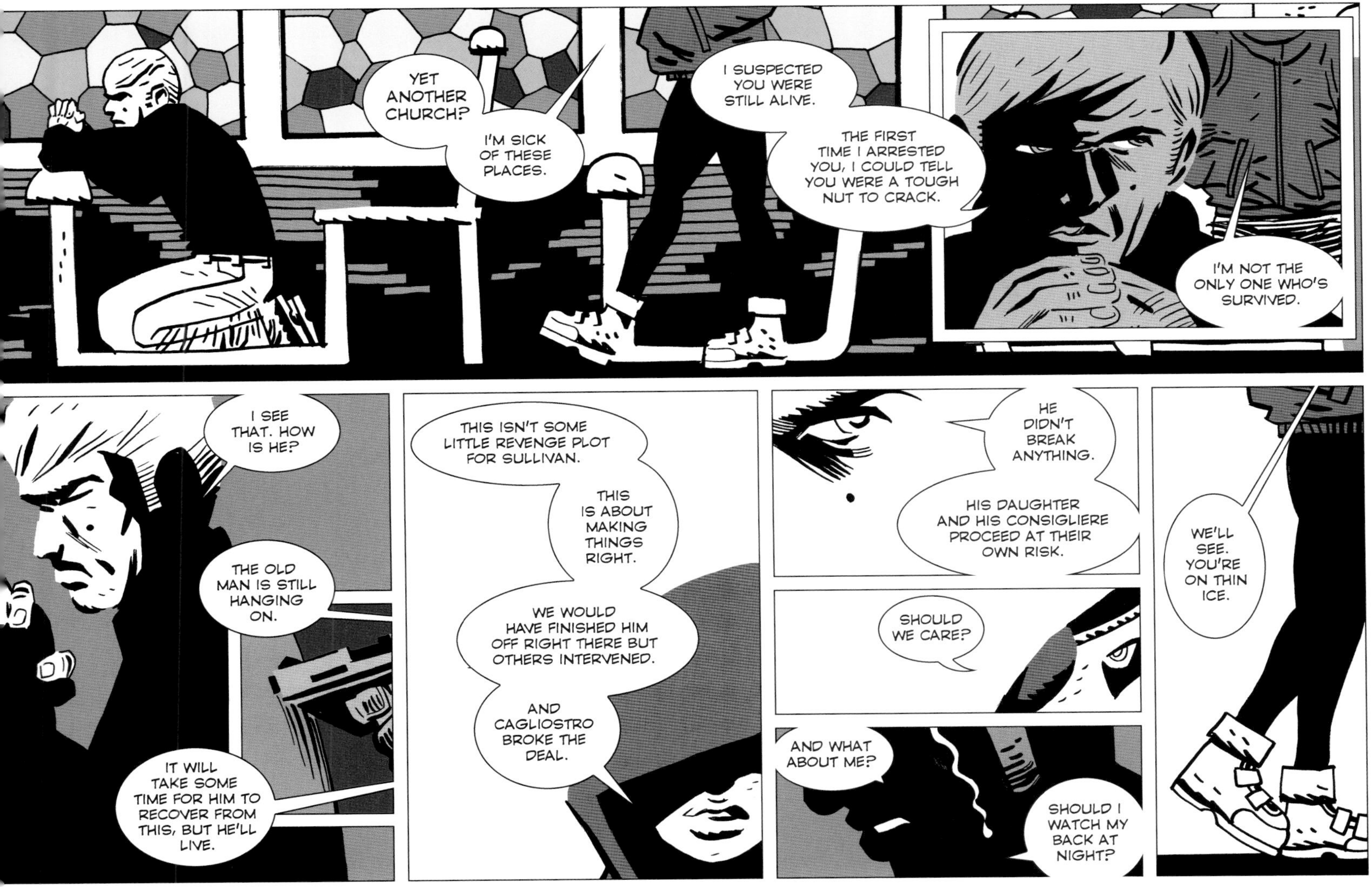
YET ANOTHER CHURCH?
I'M SICK OF THESE PLACES.
I SUSPECTED YOU WERE STILL ALIVE.
THE FIRST TIME I ARRESTED YOU, I COULD TELL YOU WERE A TOUGH NUT TO CRACK.
I'M NOT THE ONLY ONE WHO'S SURVIVED.
I SEE THAT. HOW IS HE?
THE OLD MAN IS STILL HANGING ON.
IT WILL TAKE SOME TIME FOR HIM TO RECOVER FROM THIS, BUT HE'LL LIVE.
THIS ISN'T SOME LITTLE REVENGE PLOT FOR SULLIVAN.
THIS IS ABOUT MAKING THINGS RIGHT.
WE WOULD HAVE FINISHED HIM OFF RIGHT THERE BUT OTHERS INTERVENED.
AND CAGLIOSTRO BROKE THE DEAL.
HE DIDN'T BREAK ANYTHING.
HIS DAUGHTER AND HIS CONSIGLIERE PROCEED AT THEIR OWN RISK.
SHOULD WE CARE?
AND WHAT ABOUT ME?
SHOULD I WATCH MY BACK AT NIGHT?
WE'LL SEE. YOU'RE ON THIN ICE.

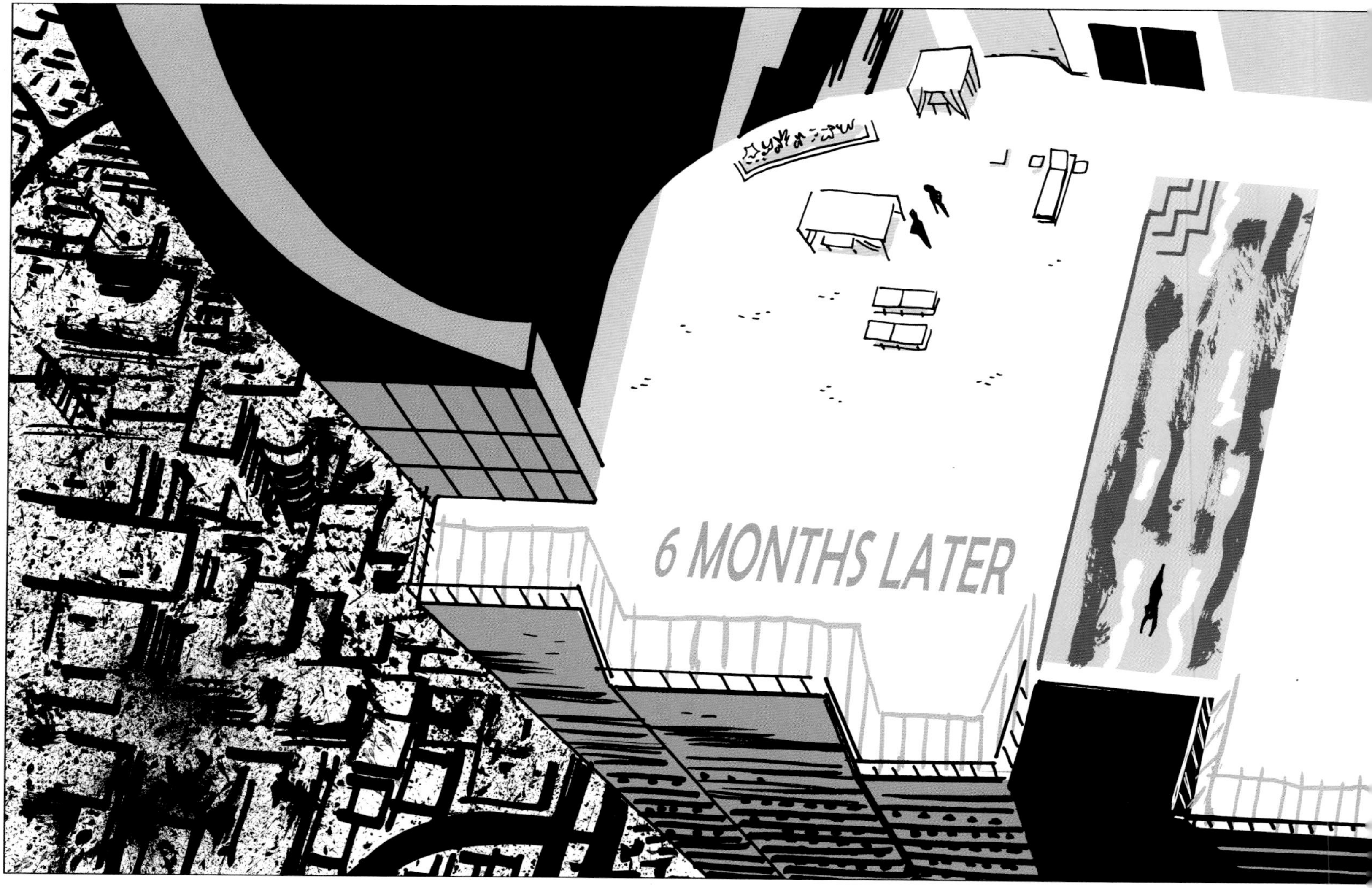
6 MONTHS LATER

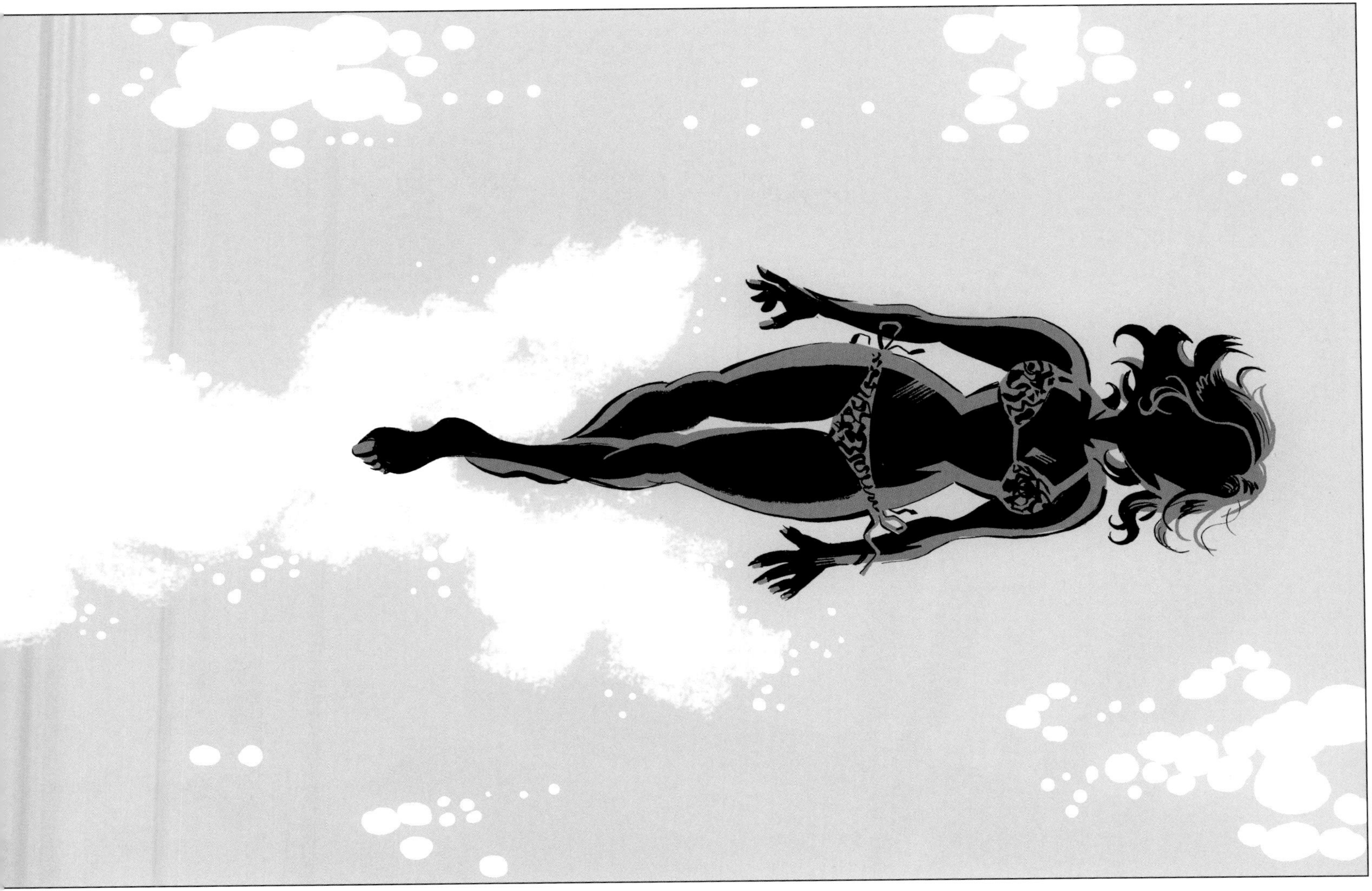

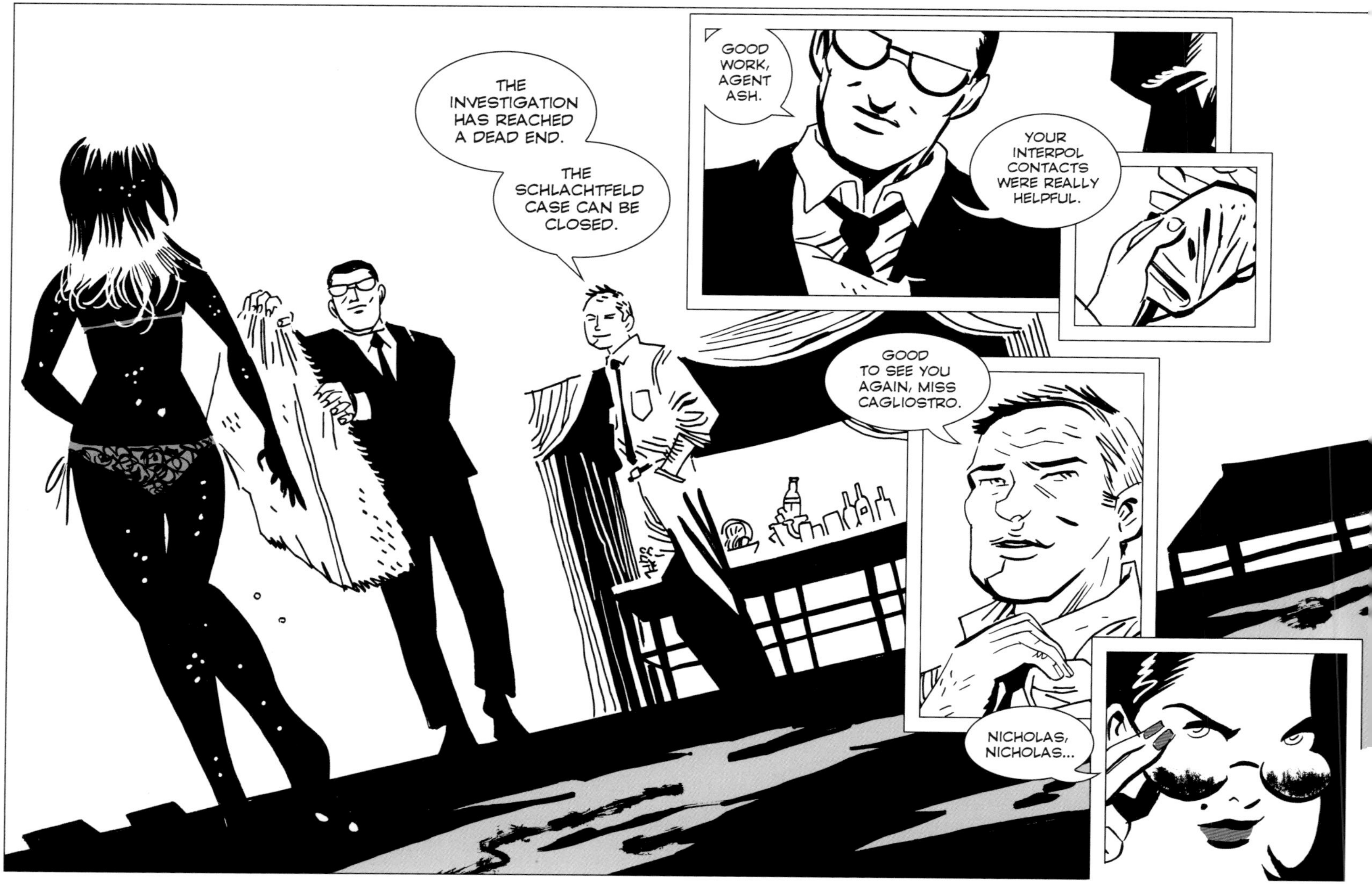
THE INVESTIGATION HAS REACHED A DEAD END.
THE SCHLACHTFELD CASE CAN BE CLOSED.
GOOD WORK, AGENT ASH.
YOUR INTERPOL CONTACTS WERE REALLY HELPFUL.
GOOD TO SEE YOU AGAIN, MISS CAGLIOSTRO.
NICHOLAS, NICHOLAS...

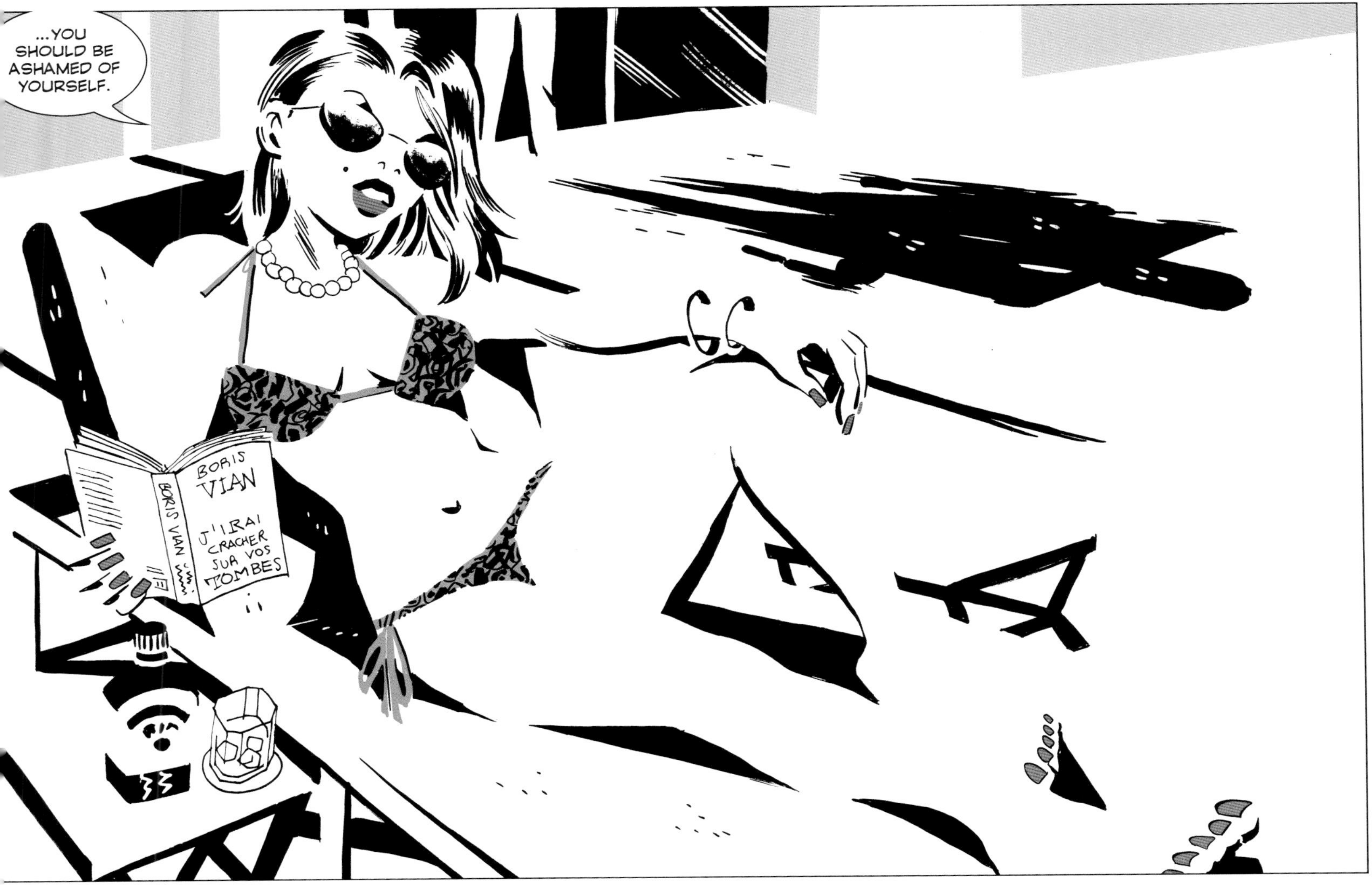
...YOU SHOULD BE ASHAMED OF YOURSELF.
BORIS VIAN
BORIS VIAN
J'IRAI CRACHER SUR VOS TOMBES

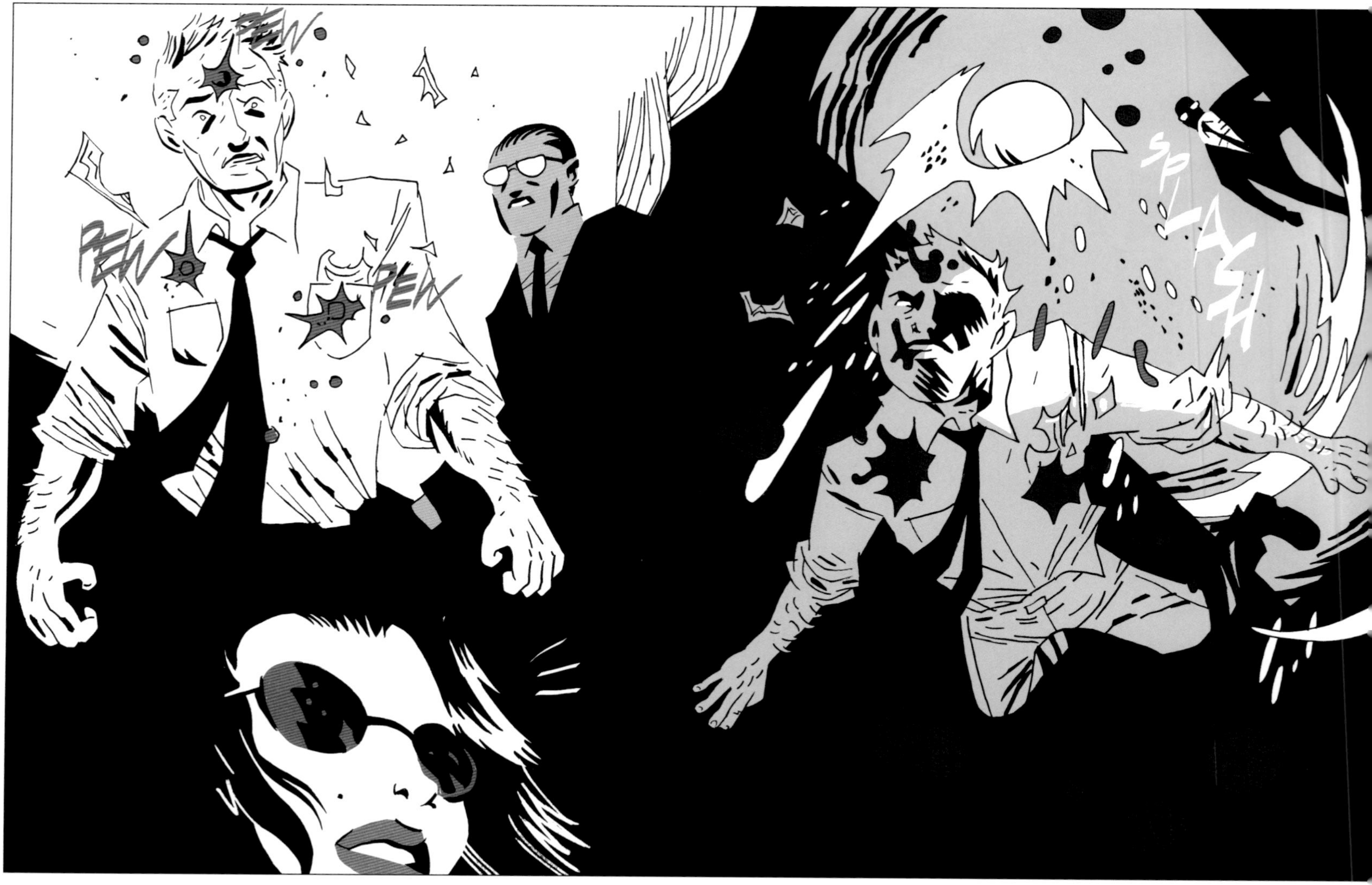
PEW
PEW
PEW
SPLASH

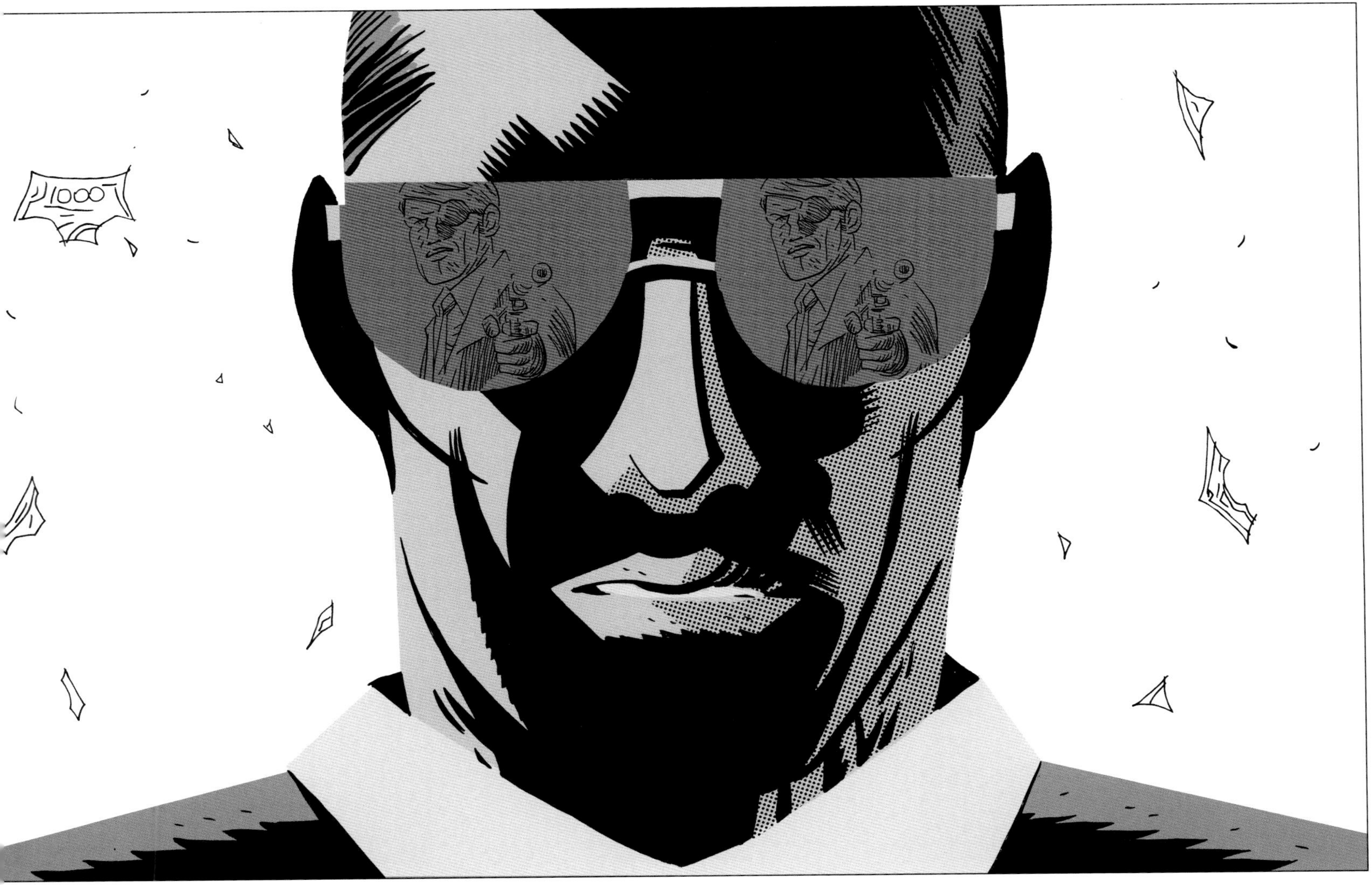
1000

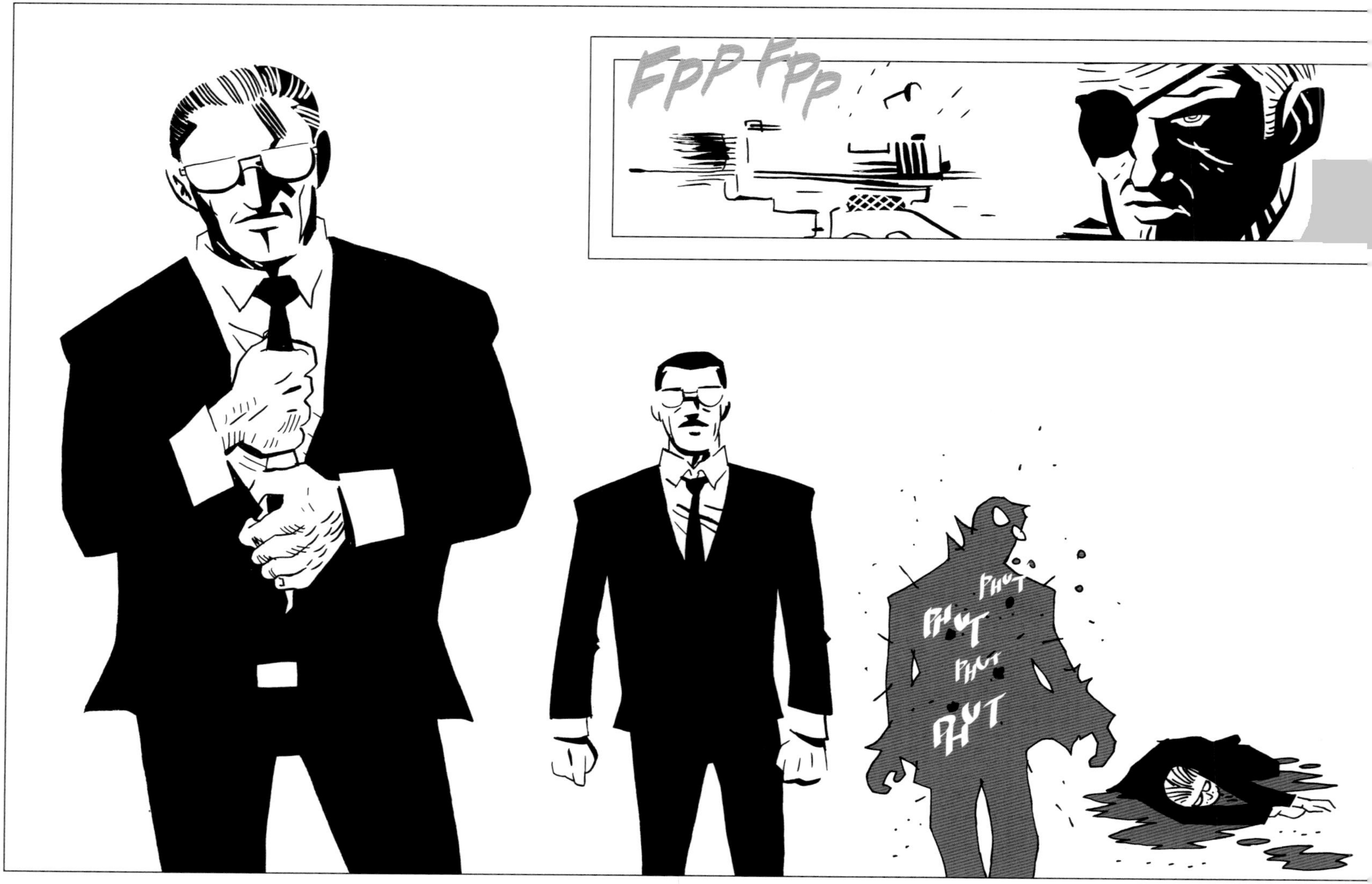
FPP FPP
PHUT
PHUT
PHUT
PHUT

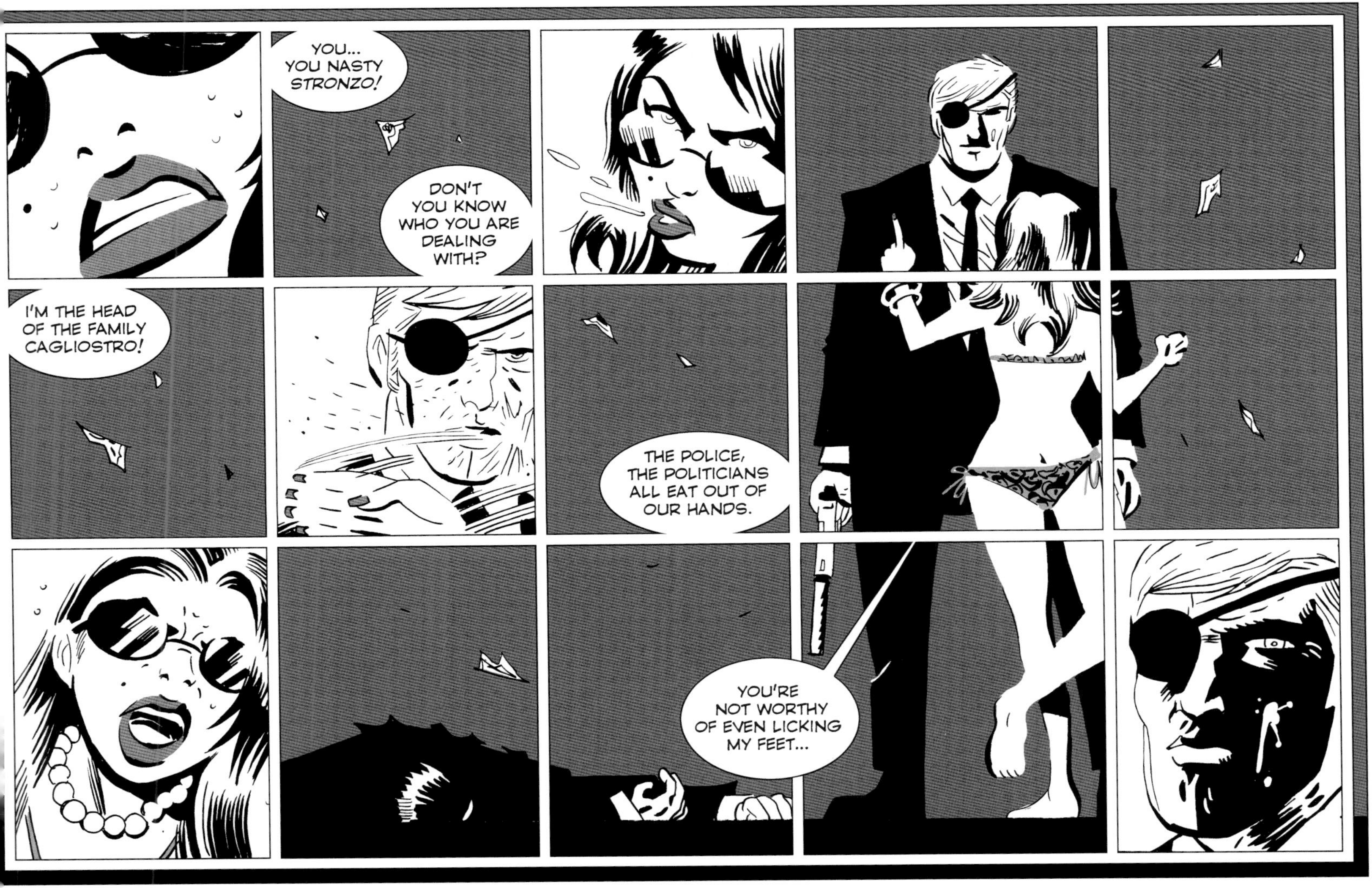
YOU...
YOU NASTY
STRONZO!
DON'T
YOU KNOW
WHO YOU ARE
DEALING
WITH?
I'M THE HEAD
OF THE FAMILY
CAGLIOSTRO!
THE POLICE,
THE POLITICIANS
ALL EAT OUT OF
OUR HANDS.
YOU'RE
NOT WORTHY
OF EVEN LICKING
MY FEET...

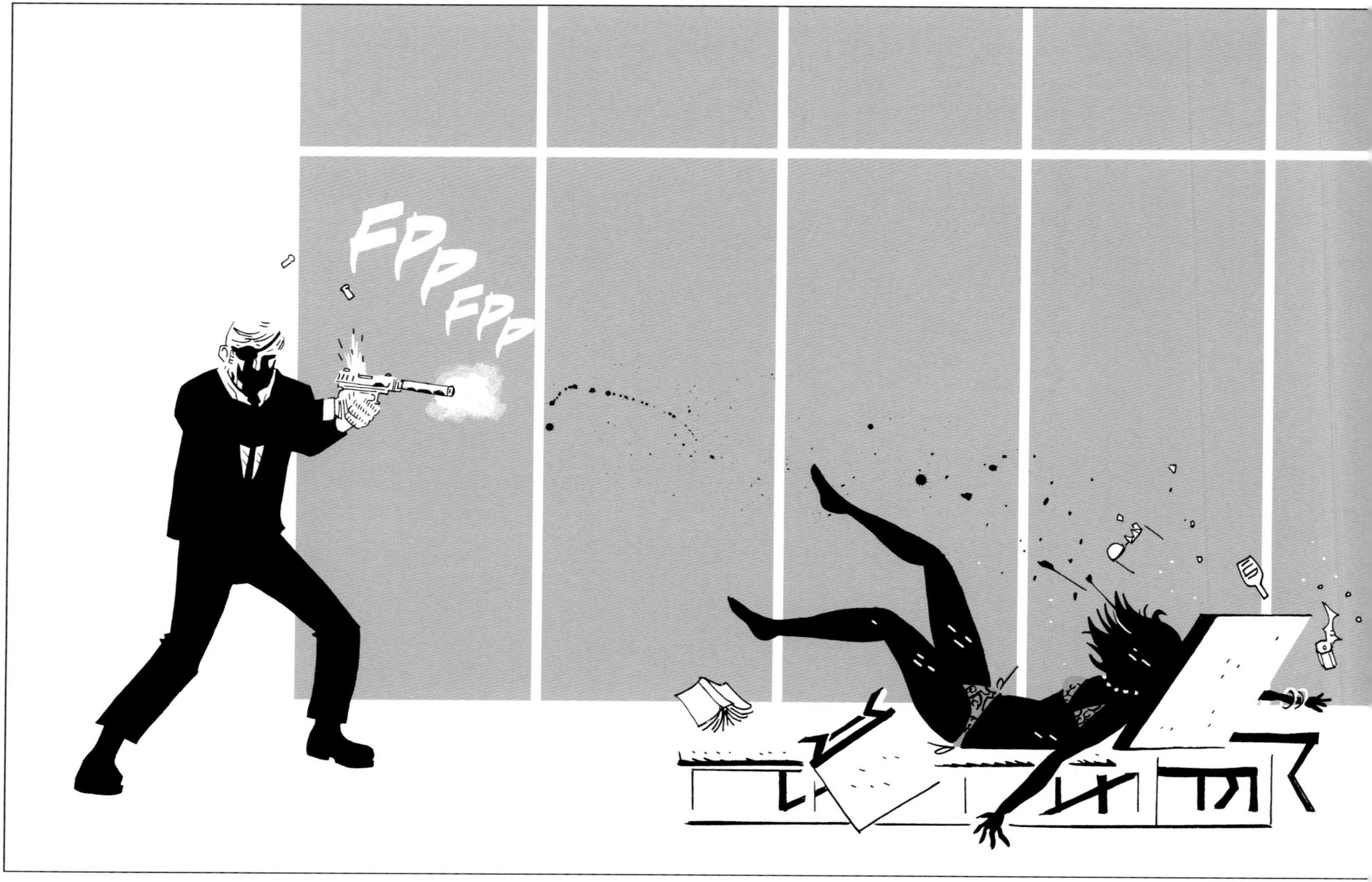
FPP FPP

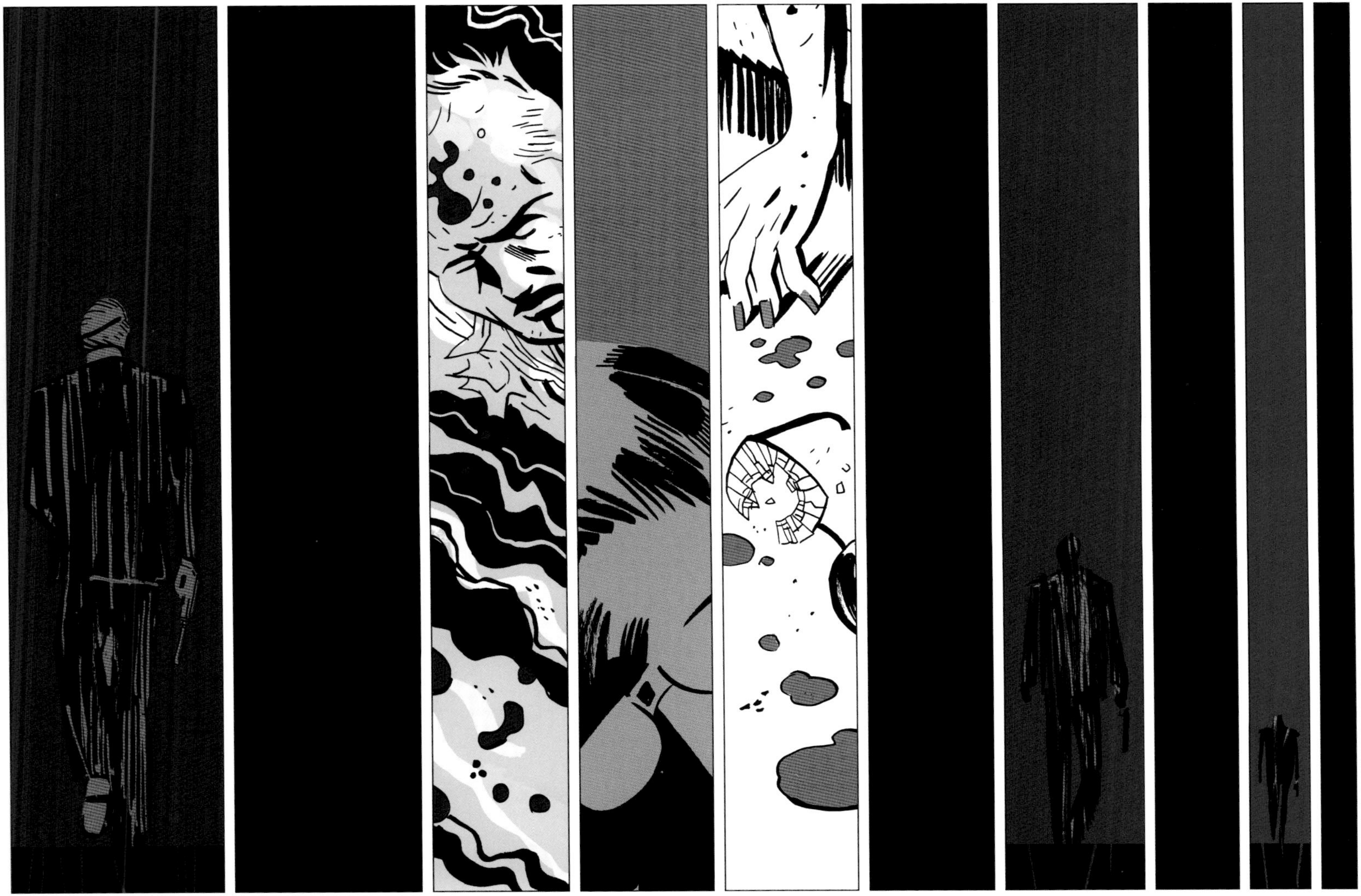

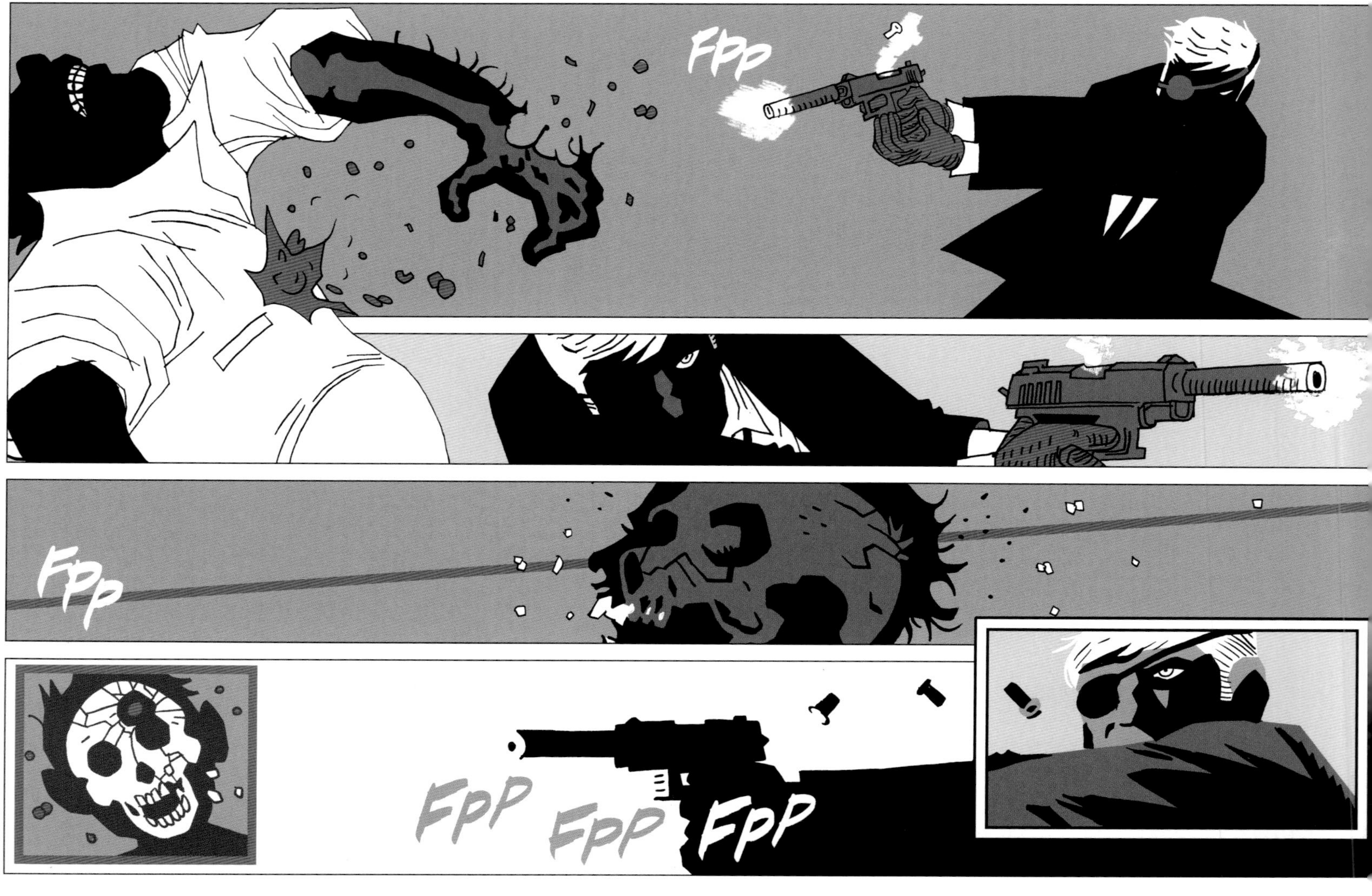
FPP
FPP
FPP
FPP
FPP

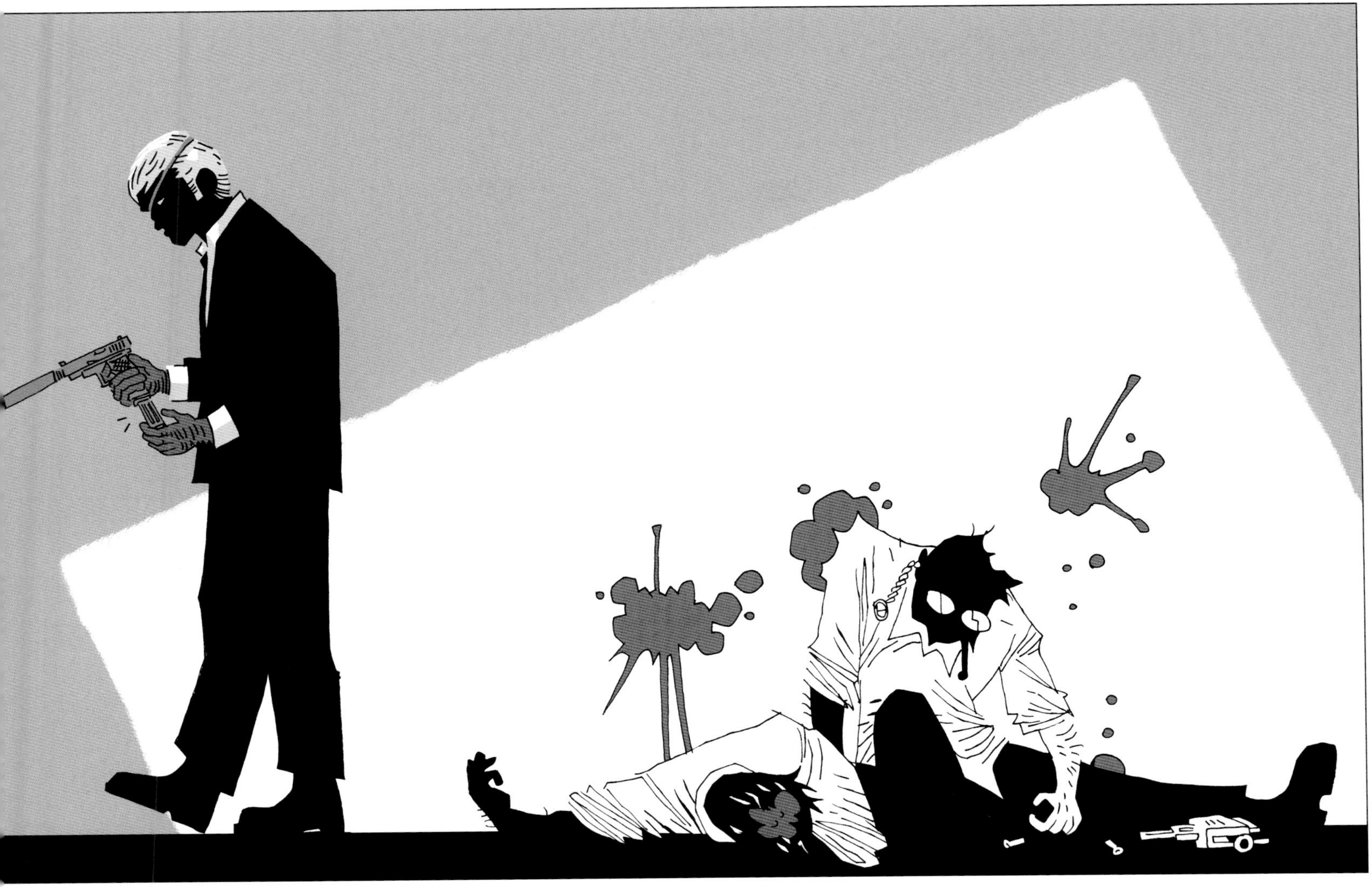

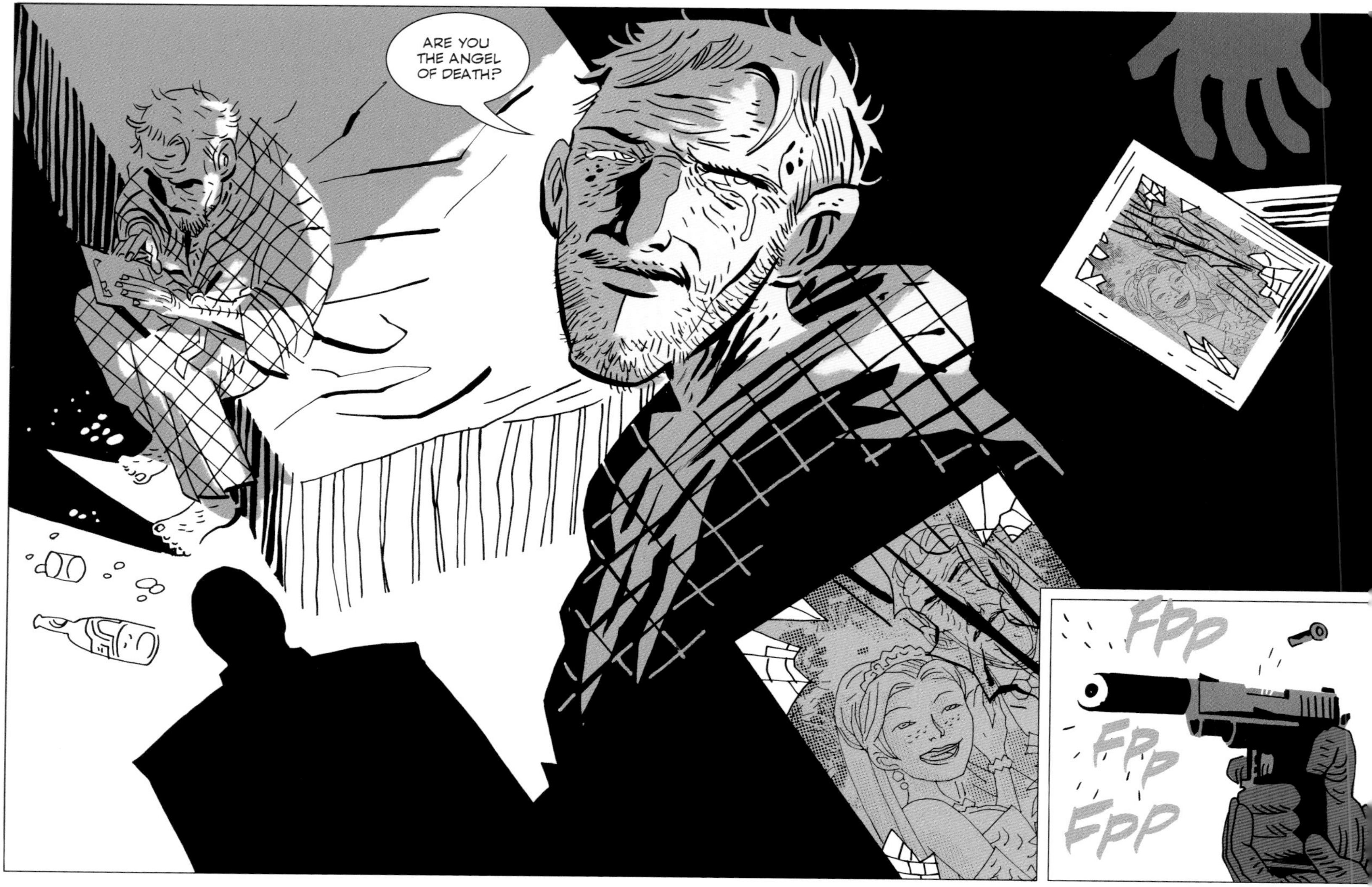
ARE YOU THE ANGEL OF DEATH?
FPP
FPP
FPP

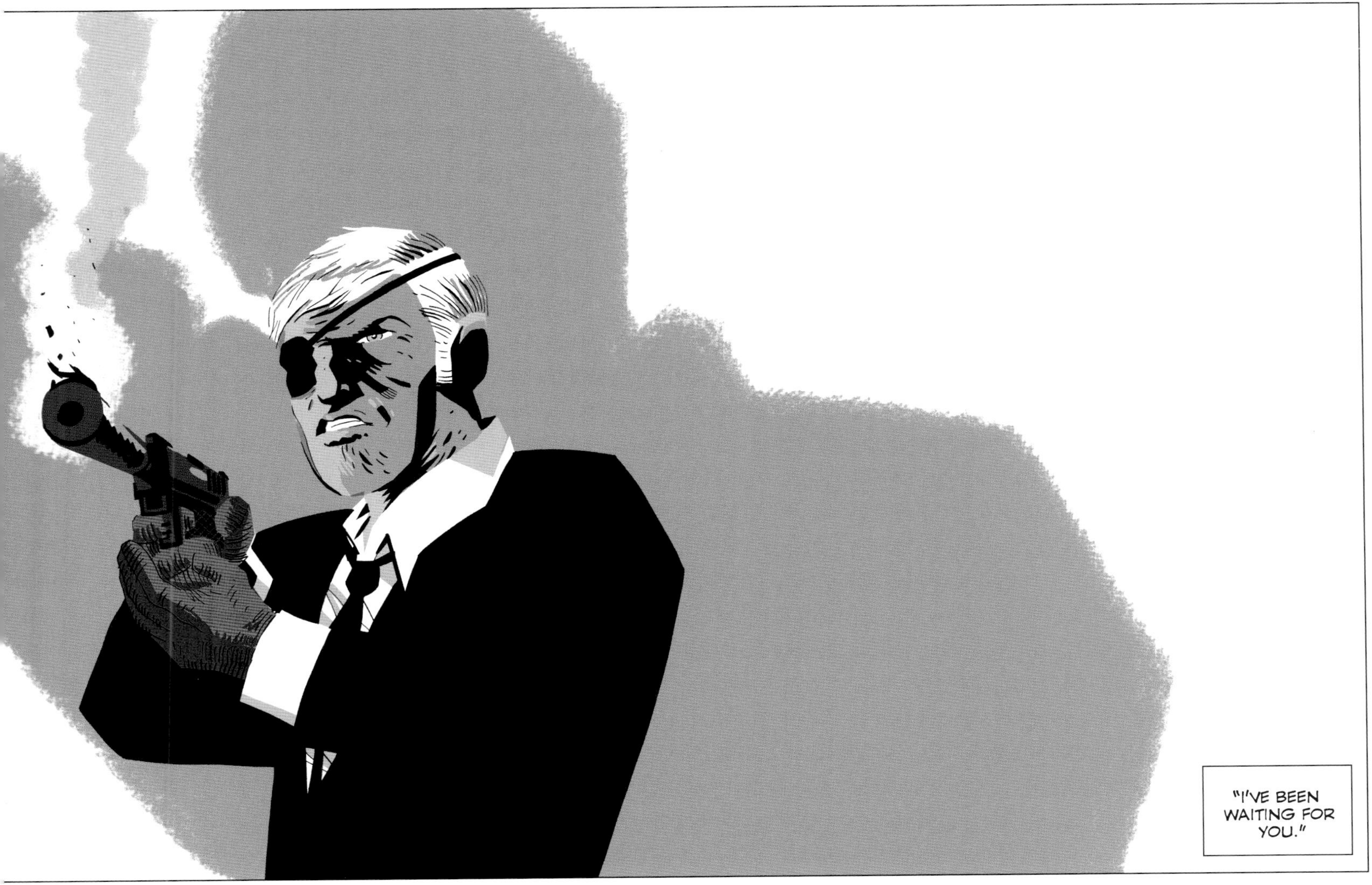
"I'VE BEEN WAITING FOR YOU."

NO MERCY FOR
SISTER MARIA SKETCHBOOK

ADDITIONAL ILLUSTRATIONS AND SKETCHES
BY VICTOR SANTOS

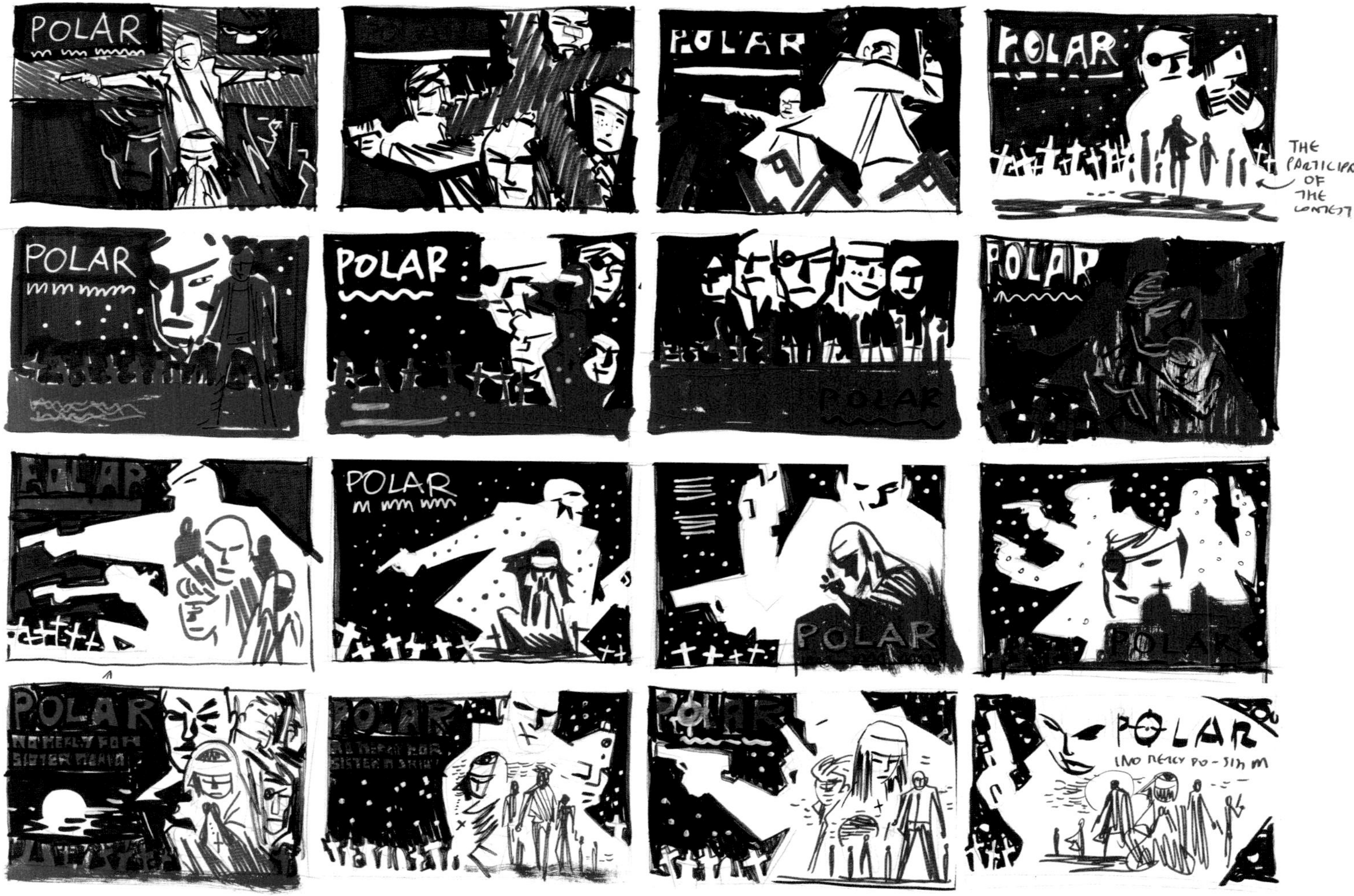
POLAR
THE PARTICIPANTS OF THE CONTEST

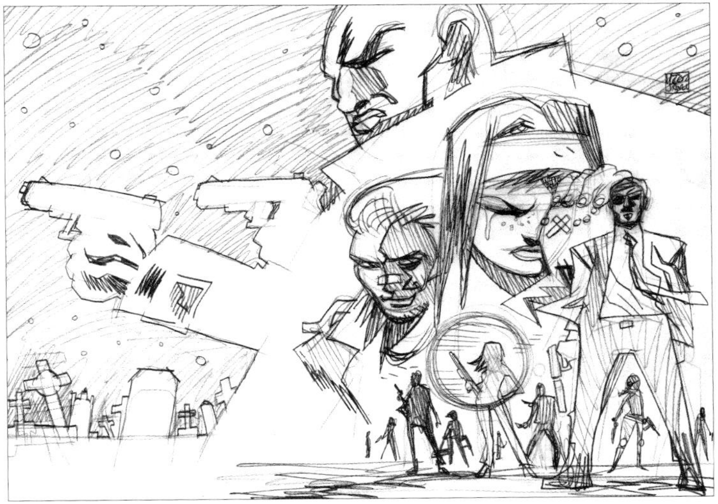

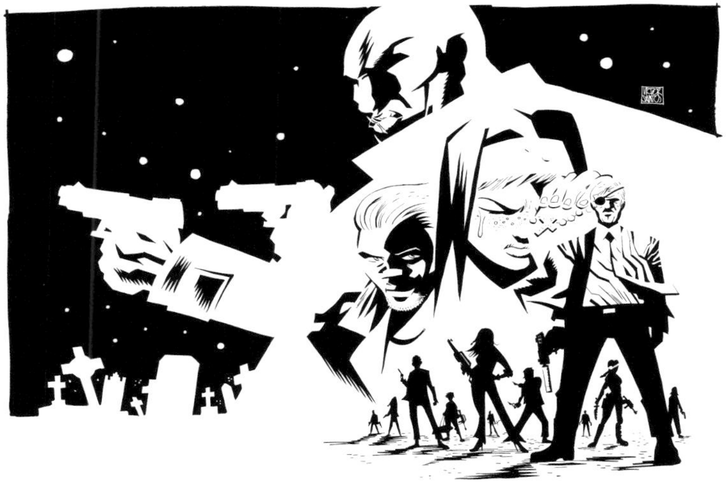

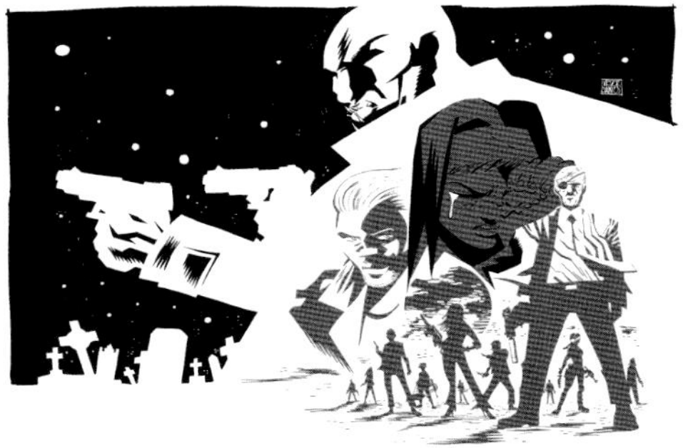

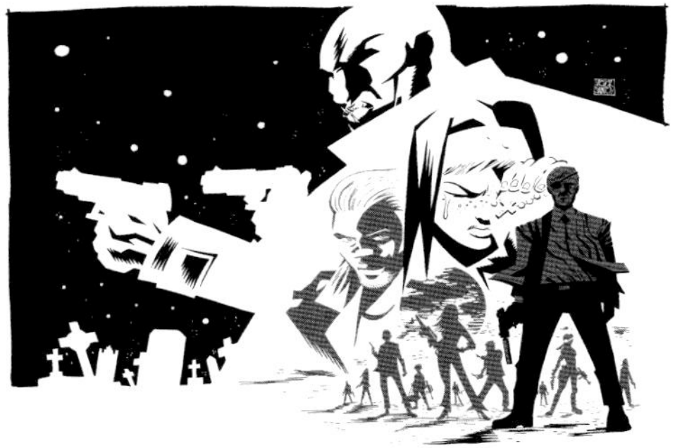

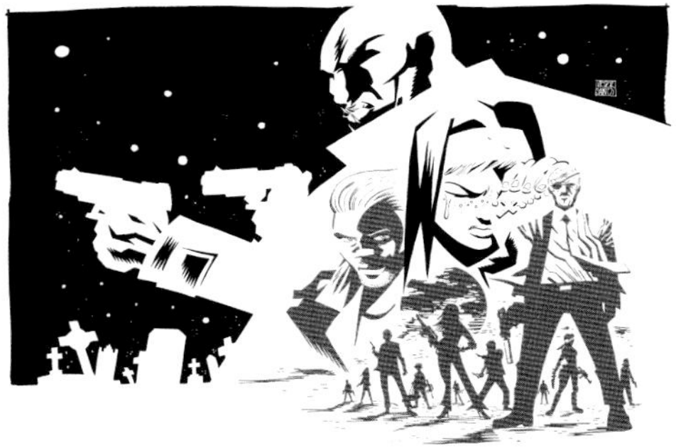

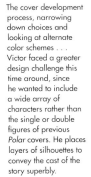

The cover development process, narrowing down choices and looking at alternate color schemes . . . Victor faced a greater design challenge this time around, since he wanted to include a wide array of characters rather than the single or double figures of previous *Polar* covers. He places layers of silhouettes to convey the cast of the story superbly.

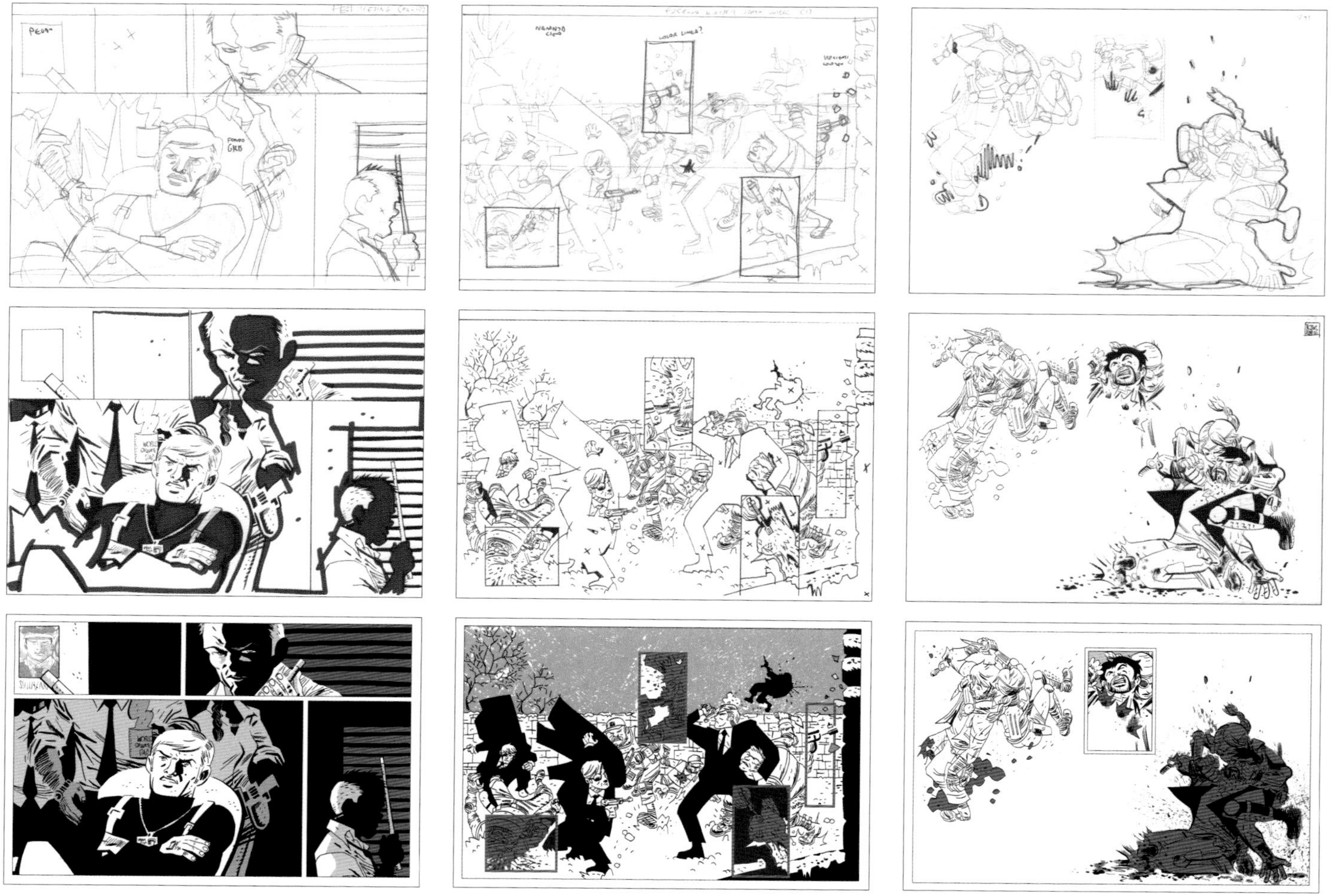

These layouts reveal the creation of double-page spreads in relation to one another . . . Victor created these panels for both the online click and the page turn to work with equal effectiveness.

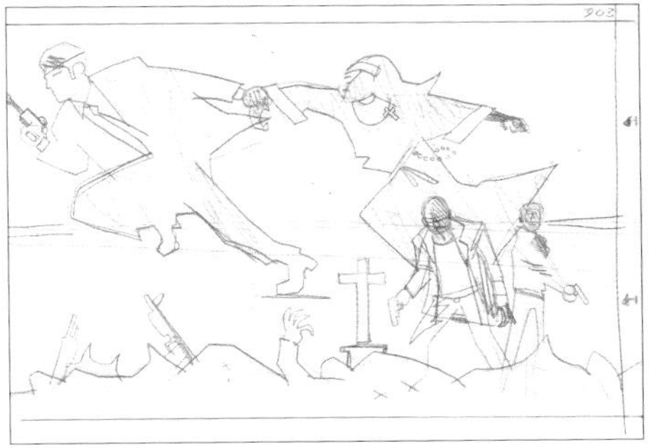
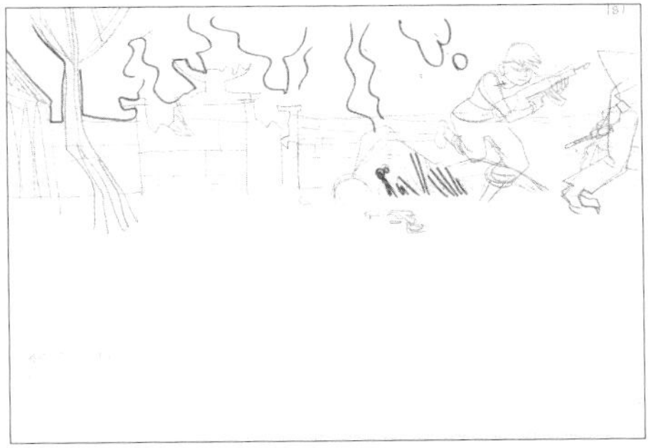
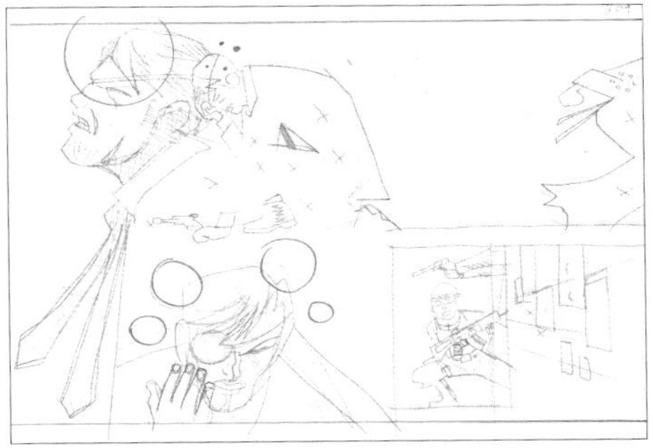
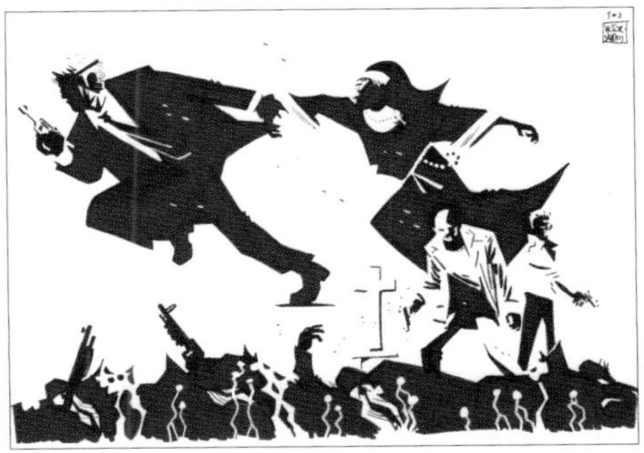
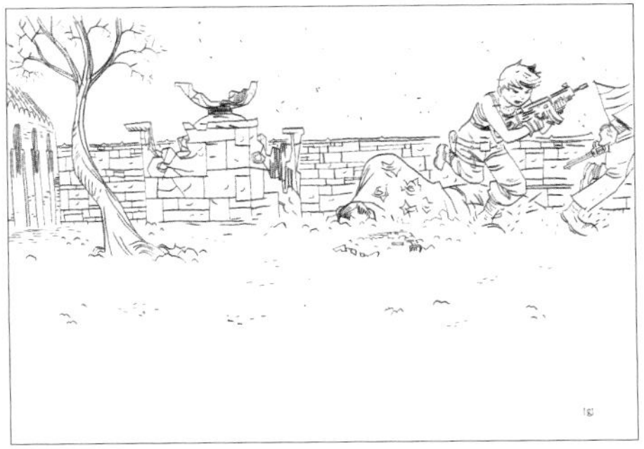
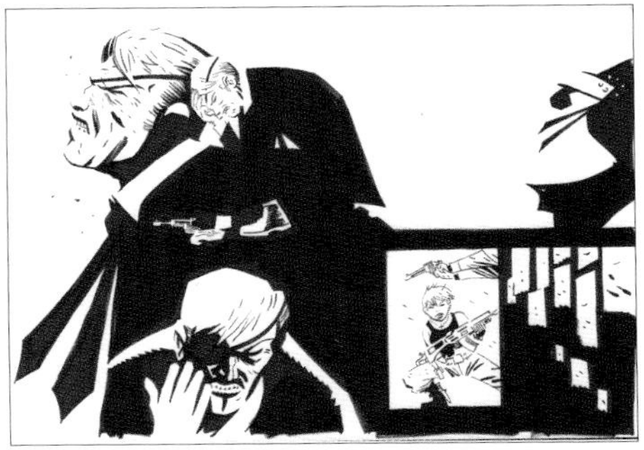
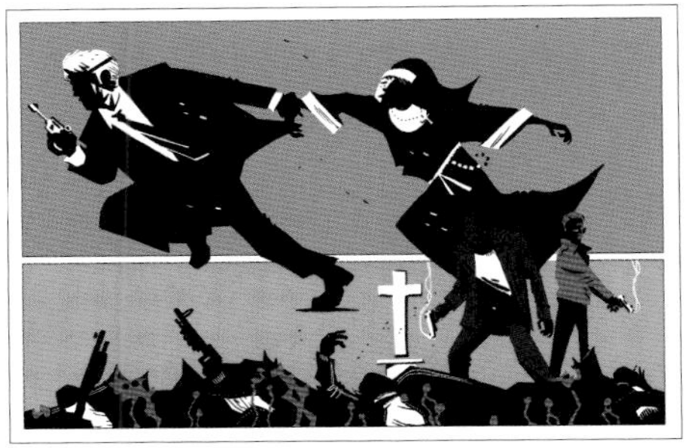
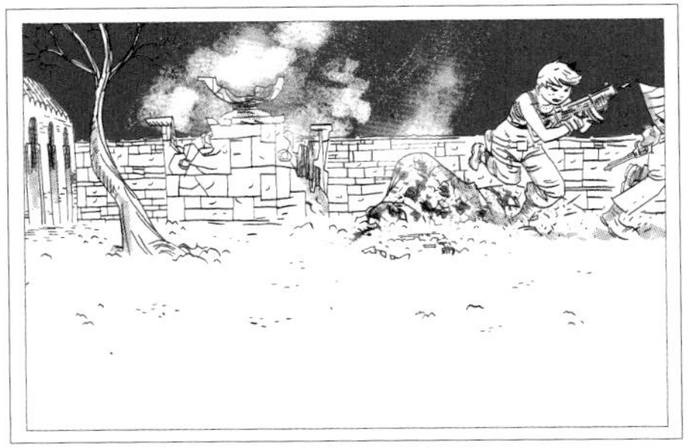
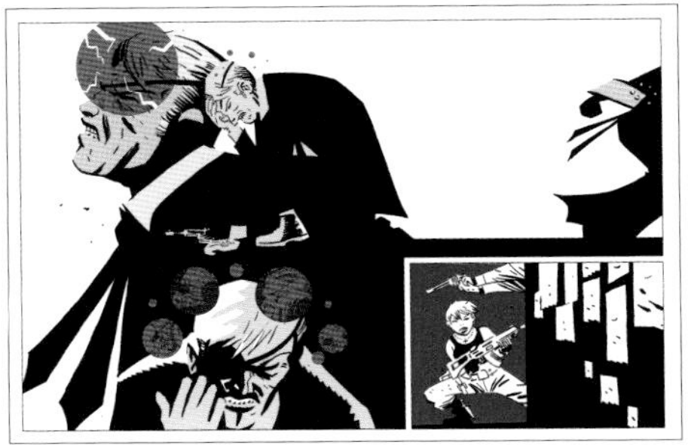

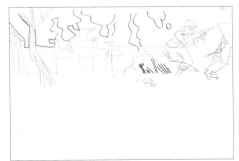

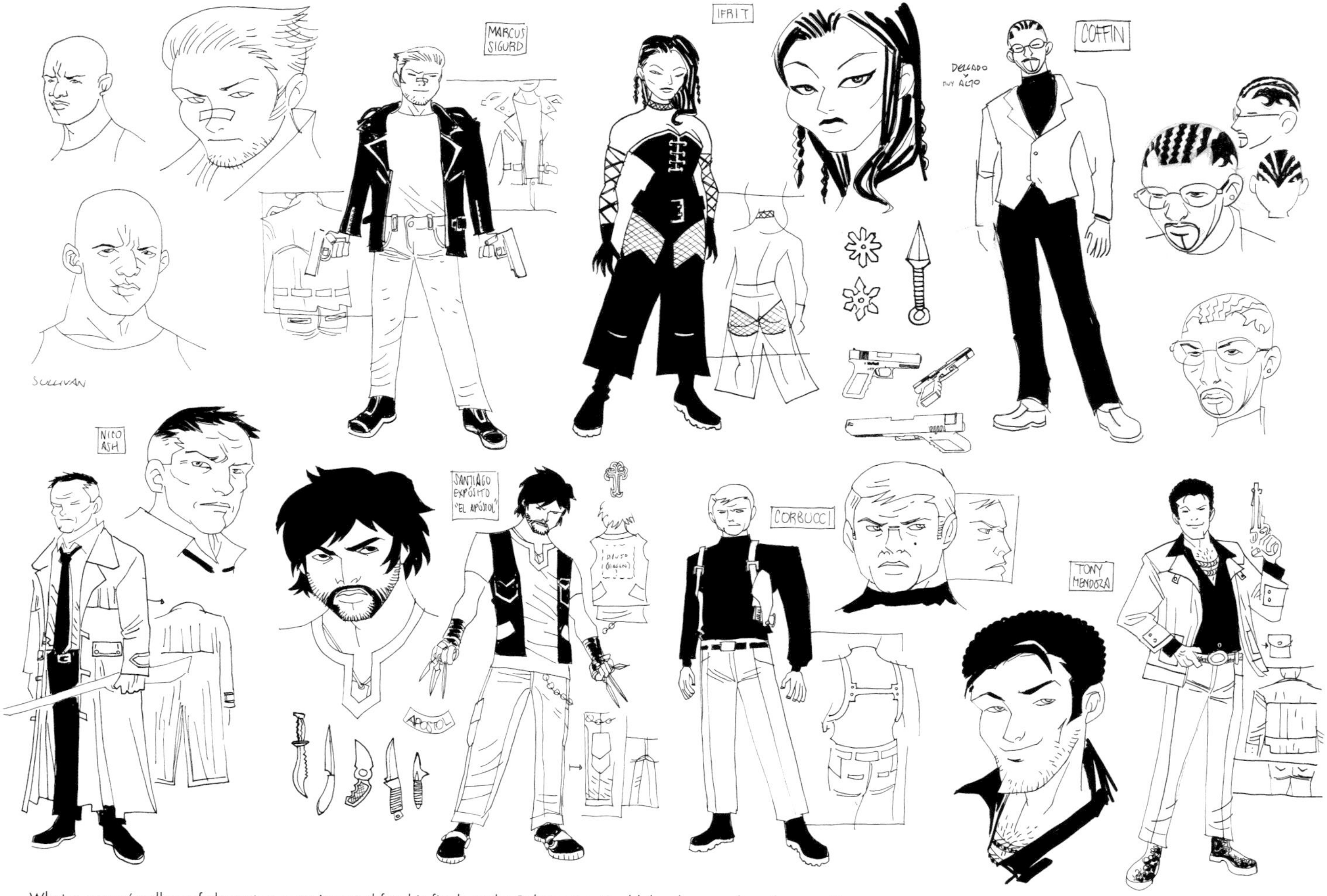
MARCUS SIGURD
IFRIT
COFFIN
SULLIVAN
NICO ASH
SANTIAGO EXPÓSITO "EL APÓSTOL"
APÓSTOL
CORBUCCI
TONY MENDOZA

What a rogues' gallery of characters were invented for this finale to the *Polar* series. Could they be more heavily armed?

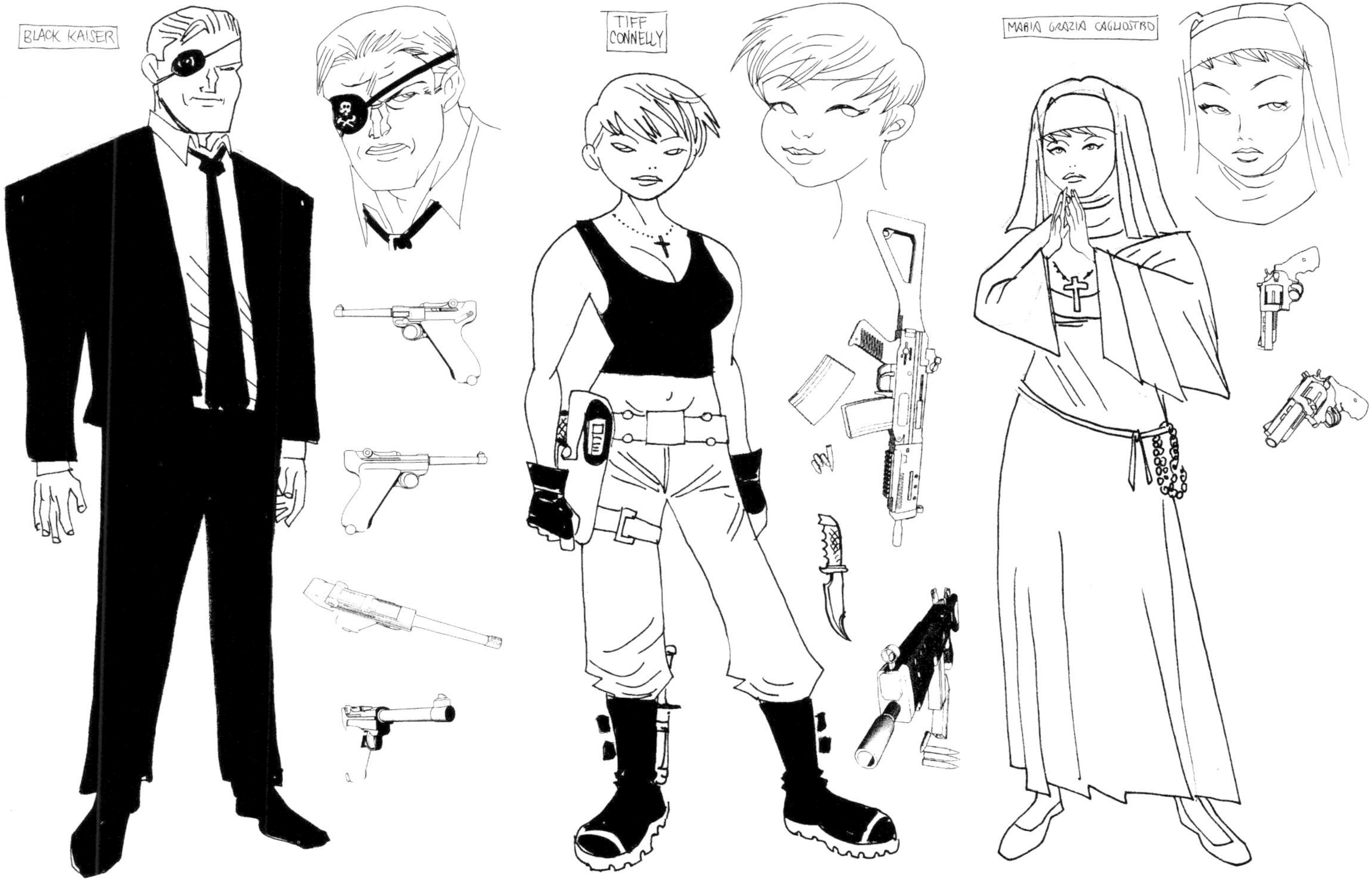
BLACK KAISER
TIFF CONNELLY
MARIA GRAZIA CAGLIOSTRO

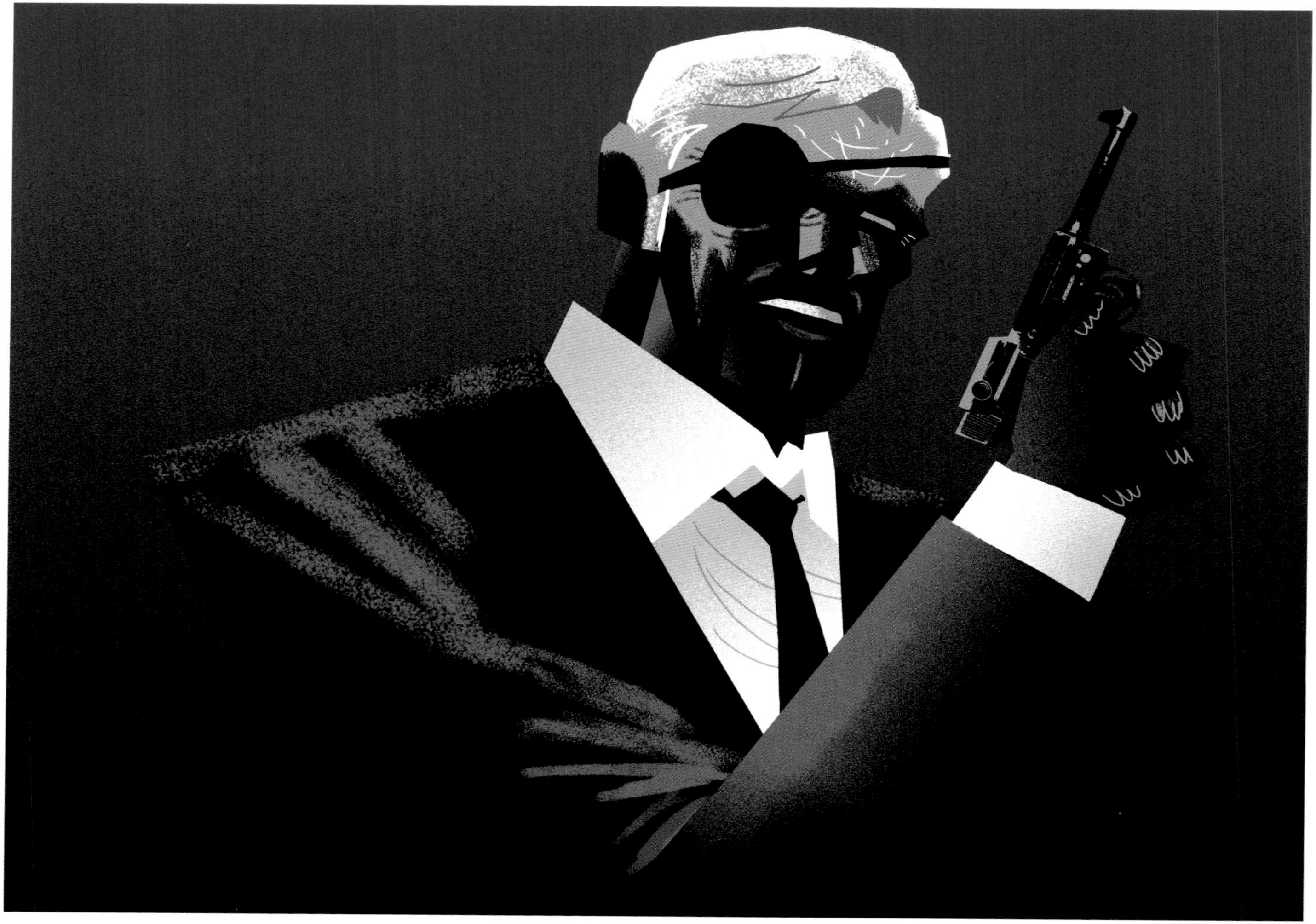

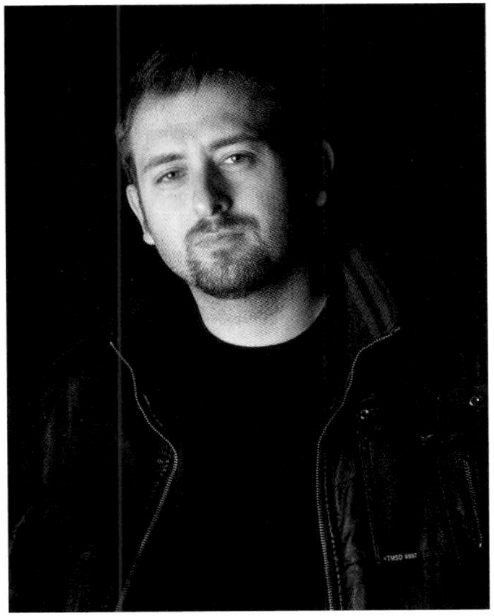

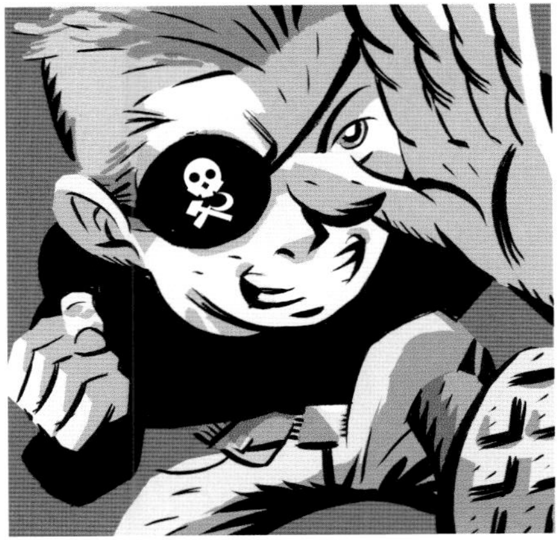

ABOUT THE AUTHOR

Born in Valencia in 1977, Victor Santos has written and illustrated a variety of comics published in Spain and France, including *Los reyes elfos* (The elf kings), *Pulp Heroes*, *Young Ronins*, *Lone in Heaven*, and *Black Kaiser*.

Santos has illustrated numerous comics in the United States, including *Demon Cleaner* and *Zombee*, written by Miles Gunter, and Brian Azzarello's *New York Times* best-selling *Filthy Rich*, one of the first titles of DC Comics' Vertigo Crime line. More recently, Santos has worked on the fantasy epic *The Mice Templar*, written by Bryan J. L. Glass and Michael Avon Oeming, and James Patterson's *New York Times* best-selling *Witch & Wizard* series, written by Dara Naraghi, as well as *Godzilla: Kingdom of Monsters*, written by Eric Powell and Tracy Marsh and published by IDW.

Meanwhile, Santos has continued his career as a writer in Spain with other artists, creating the graphic novels *Silhouette*, *Ragnarök*, and *Ezequiel Himes: Zombie Hunter*. *Polar*, his most personal project to date, is currently in development as a major motion picture with Constantin Film and Dark Horse Entertainment.

Santos has won six awards at the Barcelona international comic convention for his work and three at the Madrid comics convention. He's also won the *Dolmen* magazine critics' award for best artist.

In 2014, Santos completed *Furious*, a superhero series written by Bryan J. L. Glass and published by Dark Horse Comics, and worked with Frank J. Barbiere on Boom Studios' *Black Market* while continuing his work on *The Mice Templar*.

He lives in Bilbao, Spain.

VICTORSANTOSCOMICS.COM   POLARCOMIC.COM

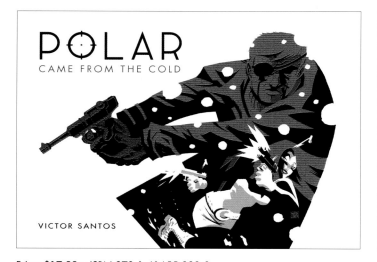

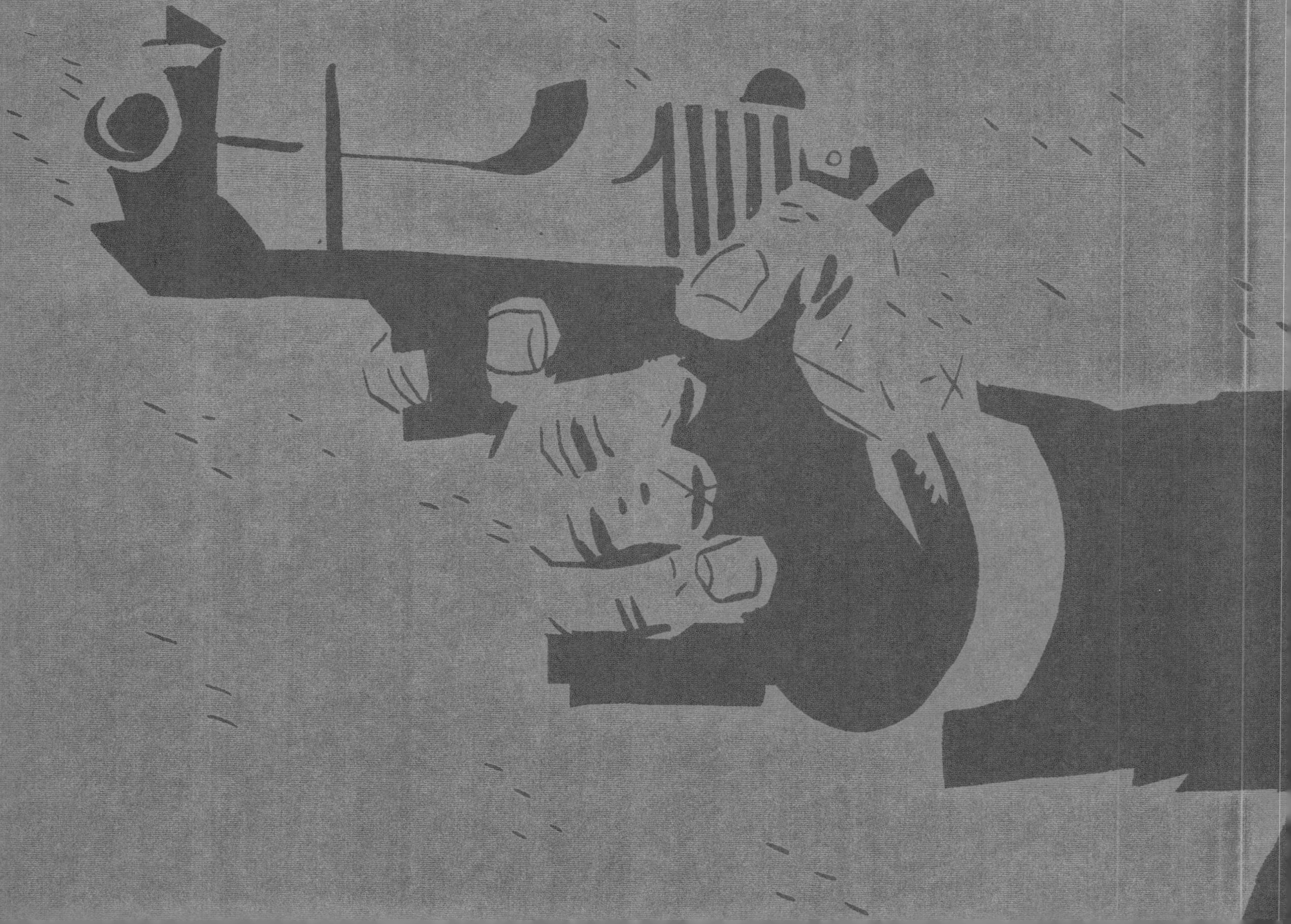